The Films of Carl-Theodor Dreyer

Dreyer in 1968. Photograph by Lilian Bolvinkel

The Films of Carl-Theodor Dreyer

DAVID BORDWELL

University of California Press
Berkeley · Los Angeles · London

University of California Press
Berkeley and Los Angeles, California

University of California Press, Ltd.
London, England

Printed in the United States of America

1 2 3 4 5 6 7 8 9

Library of Congress Cataloging in Publication Data

Bordwell, David.
The films of Carl-Theodor Dreyer.

Bibliography: p. 242
Includes index.
1. Dreyer, Carl Theodor, 1889–1968. I. Title.
PN1998.A3D7 791.43'0233'0924 79-65769
ISBN 0-520-03987-4

To Kristin

"But he's a 'ott krittik,' aint he?"
"Yes, but he's also a 'woodpecker.' "
"Ah-h."

George Herriman, 1939

Contents

Acknowledgments

Since no one writes a book alone, I must thank my collaborators.

Two summer grants from the University of Wisconsin–Madison Graduate School enabled me to research Dreyer's career. I am grateful for this support.

Access to films and written material was provided by several people. Eileen Bowser, Charles Silver, and John Gartenberg at the Museum of Modern Art cooperated beyond the demands of duty. Arnold Jacobs, of the venerable Ajay Films, gave me access to handsome prints of *Gertrud* and *Ordet,* which he distributes in 35mm; Leon Salzman of Bonded Storage courteously let me work on the premises. Gene Walsh and Amy Hustad, then of Contemporary–McGraw-Hill Films, gave me access to 16mm prints of Dreyer's late films. David Allen, Badia Rahman, and Mary Agnes Beach made it possible for me to make frame enlargements an integral part of this book. Teresa de Lauretis kindly translated an Italian article for me, while Trilby Gustafson did the same for several Danish sources. Stephen Heath helped me obtain material from the Bibliothèque Nationale. I am especially grateful to Grethe Jakobson, who translated Danish material, helped me get books, labored patiently over the songs and poems in *Gertrud,* and answered questions about Danish culture.

I must thank the late Jorgen Nielsen and his son Tage Nielsen, Frank Lund, and Svend Holm, all of Copenhagen, for permitting me to reproduce frames from *Day of Wrath, Ordet,* and *Gertrud,* for which Palladium Films is the production and distribution source. The same thanks go to Ove Sevel of Nordisk Films. An afternoon with Henning Bendtsen provided not only information about Dreyer's working habits but also a delightful trip to a drive-in theatre. Thanks also go to Liliane Bolvinkel and the newspaper *Politiken* for permission to reproduce photographs of Dreyer.

I owe a deep debt to the staff of the Danish Film Archive. Karen Jones kindly guided me through the library; Ib Monty gave valuable advice; Arne Krogh's reminiscences suggested research hypotheses; Janus Barfour and Luise Roos helped me find photographs and clippings; Aase Malmkjær calmly adjusted her schedule to my vagaries; and Thor Prydsøe surrendered his Steenbeck viewing machine for weeks on end.

An earlier version of this book was vigorously supported, criticized, and endured by Barbara Bordwell. I thank Arthur Lennig for suggesting the project to me a decade ago. At the same time, Fred Silva saved me from selling encyclopedias and helped me get started on this research. More recently, I have benefited from the advice of several colleagues. J. Douglas Gomery took time to discuss the economic context of Dreyer's career and suggested several fruitful hypotheses. Serafina Bathrick, Maureen Turim, and Diane Waldman gave helpful criticism of the chapter on *Day of Wrath.* Brian Rose's essay on *Ordet* shaped my thinking in several ways. Barbara Pace's work on the same film, her help in obtaining scarce articles, and her comments on my manuscript have substantially improved this book. My gratitude to Edward Branigan, for many discussions of Dreyer and of cinema in general, is profound; this volume will not be in his hands a week before I receive an amiable, devastating critique. My editor, Ernest Callenbach, gave wise counsel, and the manuscript was treated to superb copy editing by the happily named Peter Dreyer. To my parents and sisters, I apologize for a project that kept me from them so often. Finally, I must thank Kristin Thompson. She gave me aid and comfort; she pulled me out of terrible tangles; many of the best ideas in this book came from her.

David Bordwell
February 1979

A Note on Versions of Dreyer's Films

No filmmaker's work has been more mutilated for English-language audiences. Titles have been changed, intertitles rewritten, shots reshuffled. *La Passion de Jeanne d'Arc* circulates in several different versions, the most objectionable being the notorious version prepared by Lo Duca in 1952. I believe that no complete print of the film has yet been found. The American print of *Vampyr* is distributed by Raymond Rohauer; this pastiche (scavenged from French, German, and English prints) lacks several crucial shots and scenes. *Day of Wrath* is known abroad in a British version made for the film's initial foreign release; in this version, the Danish text of the Dies Irae scroll has been replaced by an English translation of the familiar Latin poem; unfortunately, the original Danish text was completely different from the Latin poem. The writer and reader of a book on Dreyer's films are at an unusual disadvantage; what prints are available may be incomplete or inaccurate.

As much as possible, this book returns to the original texts. First, I refer to films by English translation of their original titles. Thus *Du Skal Ære din Hustru* becomes not "The Master of the House" but *Thou Shalt Honor Thy Wife; Die Gezeichneten* is not "Love One Another" but *The Stigmatized Ones.* I have kept only *Ordet* in its original Danish, since it is better known by that title than as "The Word." Second, the prints preserved at the Danish Film Archive permit us to rest our analyses upon authentic versions of most of Dreyer's films. All my quotations and shot citations are based upon these archive prints, with one exception. The Danish Film Archive print of *La Passion de Jeanne d'Arc* has been assembled from many different prints; while it contains shots missing from any other version, it is still not complete. My analysis of *Jeanne d'Arc* is thus based on my own written reconstruction of the entire film.

Finally, there are the illustrations. Most books on cinema do not distinguish production stills (photographs taken during filming) from frame enlargements derived from the finished film. Virtually all the photographs in this book are uncropped frame enlargements made from 35mm prints of the films. When frame enlargements could not be obtained (e.g., from *Once upon a Time,* which survives only in fragments), or when the quality of the original print prevented the taking of frame enlargements, production stills have been used.

Dreyer's Interest

What interest does the study of a director's films hold for us today?

It is evident that film criticism can no longer content itself with itemizing a career's thematic preoccupations or with tracing a director's professional biography. At its present stage, film study is rightly concerned with larger issues. We want to scrutinize the film medium in its specificity. We want to know how films may be productively analyzed. We want to examine how cinema can function historically. From the standpoint of this book, the interest of Carl-Theodor Dreyer's films lies neither in their thematic unity nor in their testimony to a unique personal vision. Dreyer's work claims our attention today because it poses important problems for the study of cinema as art, industry, and historical process. How may we analyze Dreyer's films as narrative and stylistic systems? How do the films relate to dominant conceptions of what cinema is and does? What implications do the films have for contemporary filmmaking? This book seeks to specify and answer these questions. As the object of study, Dreyer's work counts for a lot in what follows, but I hope that the reader will join me in seeing that work as opening onto a broader analysis of cinematic discourse and film history.

THE CHALLENGE OF DREYER'S WORK

If we believe that critical study interacts with filmmaking, we ought to expect that certain films will challenge the ways we usually comprehend cinema. Such films refuse ready categories and confront us, blankly, with the limits of our ordinary thinking. *Avant-garde, experimental:* these are the tags which make us more comfortable with the unfamiliar. We may not, however, be ready to see the disturbing side of films we can't easily label. I suggest that certain works of the modern cinema (among them films of Ozu, Mizoguchi, Bresson, and Tati), while apparently not experimental in any usual sense, work, and work on us, in drastically challenging ways. If we want to examine such films, we must be prepared to discard certain habitual ways of thinking and construct new concepts adequate to the questions the films ask. I shall try to show that Dreyer's filmmaking lays down just such a challenge and that we need some fresh ways of meeting it.

Critical writing has generally ignored the problems posed by Dreyer's work. The legend of a career stigmatized by self-restraint, even self-destruction, has created the myth of Dreyer the dour Dane, ascetic and implacable. The legend has, however, blocked our understanding of the conflicting pressures—personal, industrial, aesthetic—that operated in that career. Similarly, discussions of the films before *La Passion de Jeanne d'Arc* (1928) have treated them as apprentice works, or prefigurations of the greatness to come. We have not examined the films for their relation to film practice of the silent era. Most obviously, we have fallen back on orthodox interpretations of the five major late films—*Jeanne d'Arc, Vampyr, Day of Wrath, Ordet,* and *Gertrud.* Since it is on these films that critical study of Dreyer rests, it is worth examining why three typical interpretive positions do not come to grips with the challenges the films pose.

There is, for one instance, a broadly religious reading of the late films, most extensivly set out by Amédée Ayfre. For Ayfre, the films commit themselves to a single project: the revelation of the spiritual. Working within a medium bound to space and time, Dreyer seeks to make visible, even palpable, dimensions beyond sense experience. Ayfre presents the style and structure of the late films as unified by metaphysical concerns. Why are the spaces within these films so bounded, so confined? "It is a closed area which is, however, traversed by invisible forces, magnetic currents which oppose or flow into one another. This space is porous, like a sponge which, according to the moment absorbs or squeezes out a mysterious fluid. . . . Hence the space has been clarified and simplified only to make its magnetic forces more apparent. It seems that space has undergone an enlargement, in order finally to reveal, like a molecule under an electron microscope, the strange struggles situated within it."[1] What of the temporal rhythm of these films? It is not "that active and utilitarian [rhythm] of everyday life. The minutes which pass are not those of the chronometer or the telephone time-clock. It is a time of the soul, which also seems to have undergone a great enlargement."[2] Cinematic space and time, the films' subjects, themes of good and evil—all cohere to present a spiritual vision: "What the body is to the soul, what the sacraments are to grace, what the word is to thought, the films of Dreyer are to a mysterious world which normally escapes us. They exist only to reveal to us unperceived presences beyond the limits of our everyday world."[3] Criticism more ethereal than this is hard to find, but what is important is the way in which the religious frame of reference permits Ayfre to treat the five late films as unified spiritual statements.

If the religious position stresses the soul over the body, there is a humanist reading of Dreyer which takes its slogan from the last scene in *Ordet,* when Mikkel answers platitudes about Inger's departed soul: "But I loved her body as well!" For many critics Dreyer is a realist in search of the secrets of human nature. The humanist position, probably the one which Dreyer himself would share, nevertheless still sees the late films as unified, usually by a central theme: "honor and duty versus nature and love";[4] "the death-instinct of the male and the life-affirmation of the female";[5] "a fatal demonism of the human individual, a tragic recognition of self-realization."[6] For Tom Milne, Dreyer's work embodies primitive attitudes toward women in love: "As the natural source of all bliss, the Dreyer heroine is adored; as a temptress who sins and causes to sin against the man-made laws of puritanism, she is made to suffer; and in either case, she unconsciously wields a power that is inbred, incalculable, purely supernatural."[7]

Milne's final phrase shows how the humanist reading can easily slide into the religious one. Barthélémy Amengual celebrates Dreyer the realist, but adds that his is "a realism without frontiers . . . which opens itself to the world as to a haunted domain."[8] Jean Sémolué, after suggesting the human consequences of the characters' sufferings, adds: "The condemnation of a will turned from a sense of creation . . . finds its redemption in the exaltation of human will associated with God."[9] Although proponents of the humanist position have devoted relatively little concern to analyzing the films precisely, Philippe Parrain's minute study of Dreyer's style sustains the humanist view through an allegorical reading (e.g., exteriors = nature, interiors = culture; movement leftward is negative, movement rightward is positive, movement in depth is evasive).[10]

There is, finally, the position which stresses Dreyer the aesthete. Although Surrealists accused *La Passion de Jeanne d'Arc* of preciosity, the most thoroughgoing charge of this sort has been leveled by Robin Wood. For Wood, Dreyer's religiosity suffocates and his humanism is bloodless. "In Dreyer, free expression is progressively stifled and development, in the true sense, becomes impossible. . . . Dreyer's God is a god of 'Thou shalt not,' and his cinema, for all its extraordinary distinction, is essentially death-oriented."[11] In the late films, Wood declares, human vitality dries up, suppressed by the "perverse will" that refuses all "sensual expression."[12] Style and narrative exhibit empty academicism. For the sake of a narrowly manageable art, Dreyer has surrendered both vitality and profundity.

Each of these interpretations seems to me inadequate to the stubborn difficulties of the films. Each position is based on the assumption of coherence and internal unity—religious, humanistic, aesthetic. Each ignores or explains away the downright *strangeness* of Dreyer's work. Let us admit from the start that the films pose extraordinary narrative problems. What actually happens in *Vampyr?* How does the supernatural operate in *Day of Wrath?* What justifies Inger's resurrection in *Ordet?* There are also the problems of style—maniacally precise camerawork, decor that exceeds its narrative functions, hieratic acting, curious editing patterns. The metaphysical reading of Dreyer's work lumps these facts indiscriminately together as indices of a transcendent vision, a tactic which discourages us from analyzing them precisely. The aestheticist interpretation recognizes the formal oddity of the films, but sees this as mere decoration. The humanist reading can try to justify such irregularities on grounds of characterization or symbolism, but this leads only to sophistries. Do the camera movements in *Vampyr* or *Ordet* yield psychological insights? Does the lighting on Gertrud tell us anything about her? Can we explain the canted and upside-down framings in *Jeanne d'Arc* psychologically and symbolically? If we are determined to find psychological realism, we can squeeze anything into the character-revelation mold. The camera movements in *Vampyr* would then suggest the "labyrinth of David Gray's mind"; the white decor of *Jeanne d' Arc* might "symbolize the mystical purity of the martyr's vision."[13] In sum, the predominant interpretations simply explain too much and discriminate too little. By using the commonplaces of film criticism, we have comfortably domesticated Dreyer's films.

What we must recognize is the cost of ransacking form and style for such imprecise and banal meanings. As Jonathan Culler points out, our demand for coherence in a text must not prematurely cancel the ways in which the text defines its uniqueness: "We can try to avoid premature foreclosure, to allow the text to differentiate itself from ordinary language, to grant maximum scope to the play of formal features and semantic uncertainties."[14] If we read the films as "about" some slippery religious or psychological states, we ought to realize that this infinitely elastic principle of interpretation pays the price of insipidity. I shall try to show that the films' primary importance is not thematic but *formal* and *perceptual*. If we pay attention, Dreyer's late films work upon us by their recalcitrant refusal to jell in conventional ways. Analysis reveals that the camera movements in *Vampyr* invoke psychological motivation only to reject it; that one function of the framings in *Jeanne d'Arc* is to decrease, not increase realism; that *Day of Wrath*'s slowness of tempo is not motivated by mood, person, or milieu; and that *Ordet*'s and *Gertrud*'s construction of space and time often stands abstemiously apart from narrative or thematic demands. Instead of arguing about which interpretive position is right, we can gain more knowledge by moving to a more abstract level, by seeing the unity assumed by all three positions as itself only a consequence of a larger process. Instead of assuming order and then clamping down a certain interpretive apparatus, we might look at these films as presenting *problems* of order and *problems* of interpretation. We might posit them as dynamic totalities in which several formal systems operate—sometimes harmoniously, sometimes dissonantly. These films cannot be easily tamed. Only by recognizing the power of art to outrun our familiar explanations can we acknowledge that films *can* change the ways we look at them, think about them, talk about them. Dreyer's work makes us do criticism differently.

In an extensive attack on the "self-indulgence" of *La Chinoise*, John Simon cites a moment in the film which was incomprehensible and pauses parenthetically to make a significant complaint: "The dishonest critics who write about this and other films by Godard as if they were perfectly lucid never mention such scenes."[15] We should, I think, generalize Simon's grievance. A critic will often write about the most disturbing films—be they by Godard, Bresson, Ozu, Tati, or Snow—as if they were self-evidently clear and coherent. Equating aesthetic order with a comfortable tidiness, criticism seldom takes as its starting point the difficulties and strangeness of a film. To do so involves honesty, as Simon suggests, but is also involves a willingness to let the disturbing, disorienting features of a film work upon us. Given the inexplicable, the critic can confront it directly, not to explain it away as the manifestation of a secret unity, not to interpret it as if it were an utterance in an esoteric tongue, but rather to demonstrate, display, and situate that strangeness. This book suggests that we can analyze the challenging strangeness of Dreyer's films by drawing on the insights of Russian Formalist poetics and later work in that tradition.[16] The value of this approach can emerge only in the course of specific analyses, but here it may be worthwhile to sketch out some reasons why Formalism will be useful in understanding cinema in general and Dreyer in particular.

It may seem odd that an analysis of cinema should draw upon concepts from literary theory. The fact is, however, that while Formalist theory was at first applied to literary texts, it rests upon general aesthetic principles. The fundamental assumption is that art is an affair of perception, and as such it presents the perceiver with problems of unity and disunity. The unity springs, of course, partly from patterns within the work, such as composition in a painting, sonata form in music, or narrative in cinema. Unity also emerges from the art work's relation to the history of the medium. Thus conventions and the art work's use of other works lead us to expect unity. Yet the Formalists also stressed the importance of disunity in aesthetic experience. The force of art arises from shocks and disturbances which it gives to our perception. Viktor Shklovsky called this *ostranenie*, "estrangement," "defamiliarization," "making-strange."[17] One of the most fecund hypotheses of Formalist theory is that art's drive toward a unified experience is constantly interrupted by swerves, detours, and dislocations. While we find patterns within a painting or a sonata or a film, we also find drastic violations of those patterns. Our attention focuses on the patch of paint of a different texture, on the compelling dissonance, on the scenes that don't quite fit. As Shklovsky notes: "There is 'order' in art, yet not a single column of a Greek temple stands exactly in its proper order; poetic rhythm is similarly disordered rhythm."[18] Disunity is also perceived in the art work's relation to other works. The text defines its strangeness not by imitating tradition but by violating it—by breaking conventions, reordering tried elements, shattering our expectations. In all, Formalism's conception of art as a struggle between a stable unity and a dynamic estrangement has a usefulness that transcends any particular medium.

A general goal of this book, then, is to show how the basic aesthetic principles of the Formalist tradition can help us study cinema. We have an excellent opportunity to test these principles because film is par excellence a medium that relies upon perception. (The very illusion of movement in cinema rests upon perceptual processes.) Film study has too long labored under the sway of literary interpretation; we know how to do "readings" of films, but we have seldom examined how film as a medium creates a unique mode of aesthetic experience. Interpretation's search for overriding unities can ignore the disunities, snarls, and gaps of a work. Formalism sees that the unity prized by thematic readings is part of a larger process of aesthetic perception. Thus interpretation gives way to a mode of criticism that seeks to bring out the nature and consequences of the film's overall dynamic.

More specifically, Formalism will help us with Dreyer's work because the salient problems which that work poses involve us perceptually. By insisting on the interplay of unity and disunity, the shifting relations of pattern to materials, and the relation of the art work to historical norms, Formalism avoids the narrowness of thematic readings and offers a way to study how Dreyer's films challenge us. My purpose, then, is not to offer a fourth or fifth reading of Dreyer but to examine the aesthetic issues his work raises.

SOME CRITICAL CONCEPTS

With the help of a Formalist frame of reference, then, we can identify some ways that Dreyer's films are of interest to us today. If we are to avoid a simple conception of Dreyer as solitary visionary, we need to use the concept of *authorship* in a fresh way. We should also situate the films historically; this will require a notion of *historical background set.* If we are to analyze the films as complex aesthetic systems, we need concepts of *form* and of *representation.* Since this book tries to indicate Dreyer's value for current film study, I should explain at the outset how I intend to construct and use these concepts.

Author. Contemporary "auteur" criticism has sought to replace the author as person by the "author" as a group of films. The minimal conditions for this category are a verifiable signature on the text ("directed by John Ford") and some common traits of theme, form, and/or style. To some extent, this book assumes a coherence of textural features clustering around Dreyer's signature. Yet I shall not treat "Dreyer" solely as a class of films. Part of the interest of Dreyer's work lies in its relation to film history, and the ordinary notion of "authorship" does not help us situate his films in that history. Boris Tomashevsky suggests that the authorial personality be considered a construct, created not only by the art works themselves but also by other historical forces.[19] What is important for art history is not Byron but his biographical legend, the Byronic; not Shaw but Shavianism; not Wagner's house but the Bayreuth mystique. Dreyer, too, has his biographical legend, created from his production practices and his pronouncements on film aesthetics. If we consider authorial personality in this sense, we can link the films to history in fresh ways. We can ask, for instance, what historical functions were fulfilled by Dreyer's declared opposition to mass-production studio filmmaking. The author, then, is not only a group of films but also, and differently, an ideal figure; Dreyer's historical status involves not only the films but the *Dreyerian.*

Historical background set. Crucial to this book is the assumption that Dreyer's work presents certain unique and salient features. But how to identify them? How, even, do we mark salience? This has been a recurrent problem in discussions of Dreyer, most of which have relied upon terms like *transcendental* or *purified* style. Such terms are, however, plainly relational and comparative. It makes no sense to speak of transcendental or purified style unless one understands what is transcended or purified. If such a comparative method is chosen, what is needed is a background set against which we can define Dreyer's difference.

This book examines Dreyer's work as a set of deviations from some historically defined norm within the same medium. If films frequently jostle our aesthetic perception, the disturbance often arises from a clash between the film and dominant practice. That is, our background set can be some other film style. Although several choices are possible here, I shall pick a background set which I shall call "the classical Hollywood cinema."

Why this construct? Historically, it is at once proximate and pertinent, central to a knowledge of the development of cinematic forms. If there is an "ordinary cinematic usage" for the fifty years of Dreyer's career, it is the narrative and stylistic principles of the American cinema. This book attempts to show the value of situating a filmmaker in relation to a model of typical traits of narrative feature films between 1920 and 1960.

One caution suggests itself. My account of the "classical cinema" will be a model, not a collection of inductive generalizations. Every actual film submits the model to certain pressures; no film succeeds in *becoming* the model. But this does not make the paradigm sheer fantasy either. The conception of a "Hollywood film" has a historical existence, registered not only in films but also in the testimony of screenwriters and other studio personnel. (Hence my references to manuals and recipe books which state certain assumptions quite bluntly.) The model of a classical narrative system proposed in chapter three and that of a classical spatial style in chapter four are meant to have the same explanatory status as the concepts of classicism or baroque in the history of painting or music: they are useful for establishing the norms and conventions of dominant stylistic practices of a period.

The model of a classical film will help us mark off salient structures of Dreyer's work; it will also suggest that one of the chief interests of that work lies precisely in its relation *to* the background set. In fact, clear references to the classical norms are embedded in Dreyer's late films. The citations of eyeline continuity in *La Passion de Jeanne d'Arc,* the camera movement across the engraving in *Vampyr,* the analytical editing of the resurrection in *Ordet* and of the banquet in *Gertrud*—all glance at the "normal" way of shooting a scene. In this way, the form of each of these films is born of a struggle with the implanted norm. The norm is not wholly external; it is cited, if only to be contested.

Form. Obviously, though, simply noting deviations from norms is insufficient; we need to grasp the positive moment as well as the negative one, the construction of a new work against the background. For instance, both Yasujiro Ozu and Jacques Tati systematically violate the "180° rule" of editing, but their film styles differ drastically. We need, in short, a concept of film form.

As I have mentioned, Formalist aesthetic theory encourages us to see form as the dynamic relation of unity to disunity in the spectator's perception. This means that we cannot split form from "content" (everything in a film has a formal function) and that we require a concept of aesthetic *systems* working within the films. To grasp the dynamic of Dreyer's work, we must analyze how the films press toward patterned stability, and then how other forces disturb this stability.

In watching Dreyer's films we have, on the one hand, the impression of massive unity; but how is this unity achieved? In this book, my analyses will concentrate on the unity created by three sets of formal principles.

1. *Logical principles of organizations.* Most films are structured by some logic: taxonomic (e.g., a film tabulating species of butterflies), rhetorical (e.g., a polemic adducing arguments in favor of voting for a certain candidate), or causal (e.g., a narrative film). Almost all of Dreyer's films, being narratives, are ruled by a cause-effect logic. We can specify further, though. What kinds of causal agents are significant? (Character? Society? A prime mover—e.g., God?) What degrees of causality are present? (Does one cause motivate one effect? Several effects?) Are there repetitions, variations, contrasts, expansions or cause-effect patterns throughout the narrative? Are there subplots or narratives-within-narratives which parallel or transform the principle narrative? Such questions may be asked of any narrative in any medium; since we are dealing with cinema, we must also ask how the specifically cinematic means of camerawork, *mise-en-scène,* editing, and sound are used to create logical patterns. We shall find that in Dreyer's films, narrative logic situates characters within an impersonal causal scheme (ruled by Nature, Law, and God). Narrative parallels downplay individual psychology, and establish a pattern of abstract oppositions and replacements.
2. *Temporal principles of organization.* Here it is necessary to draw upon the Russian Formalists' distinction between *fabula* and *sujet,* or what has usually been translated as "story" and "plot." The "story" of a narrative consists of events connected by causality and in time. The "plot" is the way these events are actually presented in the telling.[20] Most plots, for example, begin *in medias res* and gradually supply information about earlier story events. Flashbacks, repeated scenes, ellipses, abrupt omissions, limited points of view, chatty narrators—all these are ways that the plot manipulates the presentation of story events. A detective tale plays on the plot/story distinction by withholding certain story events

such as the planning of the crime; not until the end of the plot are the crucial early story events revealed. A more complex example would be *Citizen Kane,* whose plot summarizes much of the film's story in the newsreel and then retells key story events more expansively through the recollections of Kane's associates.

It is important to note two things. First, the story is not the narrative in some primitive form, as perhaps the artist might first have envisioned it. The perceiver constructs the story as he or she goes along; it is a background against which the twists and turns of plot must be read. Secondly, in cinematic narrative, all the devices of film technique may be brought to bear upon the story. Editing, camerawork, *mise-en-scène,* and sound may all participate in constructing the plot.

The story/plot distinction helps us study how a film creates narrative time. The possibilities, as Gérard Genette has pointed out, include *order, duration,* and *frequency.*[21] Events in story order run 1–2–3, but the plot may present these events in any sequence (by flashbacks, flashforwards, etc.). The duration of story events may be ellided by the plot (e.g., two years presented in two hours), expanded by the plot (e.g., two minutes stretched to twenty), or kept continuous (e.g., where two minutes in the story equals two minutes in the plot). And the frequency of events in the story may be variously indicated: a story event occurring once may be shown once or shown several times. In *Citizen Kane,* for example, most of the story events which occur once are shown once in the plot (the norm of narrative cinema as we know it), but some story events which occur only once in the story are shown several times (e.g., Susan's opera premiere). The variables of order, duration, and frequency help us to distinguish different temporal principles organizing the narrative. Such categories permit us to consider how Dreyer's films characteristically structure time. We shall see how the films generate a temporal determinism that rules both story and plot and (in the later films) how the variables of story/plot duration can create a "minimal cinema" which slows down the spectator's viewing rate.

3. *Spatial principles of organization.* Finally, we can consider how a narrative film constructs space and spatial relations. I shall be discussing these organizing principles in some detail, since a film's spatial system depends upon the use of such film techniques as *mise-en-scène* (lighting, costume, setting, behavior and placements of the figures), camerawork (distance, angle, stasis/mobility), editing, and sound. Our analysis of Dreyer's films will lead us to consider, at one point or another, the depth cues at work in the classical cinema's *mise-en-scène,* conventional uses of the mobile camera, the principles of continuity editing, and the functions of lighting and decor in constructing or confusing spatial relations. Since Formalism stresses the perceptual force of the art work, this theory lets us specify how the material qualities of cinematic space affect our experience.

Important as unity is, Dreyer's work compels the critic to formulate strategies of aesthetic disunity. Much of the challenge of his films comes from the ways that the various sorts of organization do not neatly mesh. In particular, a gap opens up between the logical structure of the narrative action and the organization of time and space. While the classical cinema allows space and time to be organized only to transmit narrative information, Dreyer's cinema often radically severs narrative from cinematic space and time. We are watching the story unfold, and suddenly we are not watching it any more; the style flings us into spatial and temporal processes that engage our perception for their own sakes. The clash of systems within the work produces difficulties, and we need to identify the viewing problems we encounter.

In this way, concepts of background set and form let our analysis specify certain logical conditions for the spectator's role. The Formalist approach assumes both conformity with the background set and deviations from it, both internal coherence and internal conflict; it also assumes that aesthetic perception oscillates between organization and disorganization. We are familiar with the notion that our experience of art works must rest upon some unifying principles. Yet unity can be conceived as a movement. Jan Mukařovský suggests: "Unity should not be understood as something static, as complete harmony, but as dynamic, as a problem with which the work confronts the viewer."[22] If disorientation and disturbance, what Shklovsky calls "roughened perception," characterize the spectator's aesthetic experience, the critic can disclose the text's perceptual cues. For instance, pointing out the historical background set permits us to go straight to what a viewer versed in the conventions of the classical cinema will find problematic, difficult, even "ungrammatical" in Dreyer's films. Or again, the concept of form as a dynamic interaction of systems helps us specify where a film creates intelligibility, and where a film starts to foreground its disunities. The critic, I believe, should not seek to resolve these problems or wish them away; I shall try simply to indicate how they are created, and what they imply for Dreyer's interest to us now.

Representational system. A stress upon perception might be thought to militate against meaning. Yet the crucial assumption is that in art, meaning depends upon perception. The art work does not exist simply to transmit a message; if it did, there would be no difference between art and ordinary informational discourse. Art is primarily an engagement of ourselves with materials and forms. We shall see how the art work utilizes representation but also sensitizes us to its limits. "The language of poetry," Shklovsky reminds us, "is . . . a semi-comprehensible one."[23]

Representation is important for us because a film does seek to "say something." But that phrase already implies an entity—an idea, an object, a state of affairs—which antedates the art work and which the work "re-presents." The Latin root of *representation* means both "to show" and "to bring back," which indicates the difficulty: representation is at once a display, a spectacle for a spectator, and a recovery, the return of an absent entity. Representation is least problematic when we pass from displayed token to absent meaning. Representation becomes troublesome when that passage is blocked (the meaning is opaque) or when the passage seems endless (the process becomes circular, with one token's meaning becoming only a place held by another token). Traditions within painting, theatre, literature, and cinema constitute representational systems: coherent ways of establishing spectatorial positions (e.g., various point-of-view devices) and of signifying absent entities (truth, reality).

On the one hand, Dreyer's films are representational: they offer images, tell stories. Since we associate avant-garde work with a refusal of representation altogether, we may be reluctant to admit that Dreyer's films can challenge us very much. One could point out how the religious subject matter of several films partly anchors them in very conventional meanings. Or one could show, as we shall later, that Dreyer's films use written language to ratify the impersonal causation that rules the narrative; a written text interprets the narrative world in relation to timeless and authoritative meanings. But if art works violate tradition as often as they transmit it, we ought to expect that a film may both accept and negate traditional representational strategies. Dreyer's later films do this, intermittently but systematically posing problems for representation.

First, the tendency of these films to pull cinematic time and space away from causal structure makes cinema visible as a *specific* representational system. In *Ordet* and *Gertrud,* in fact, an "anthological" strategy surveys the devices of the classical style, and at the same time defines that style as only one of cinema's representational options. In addition, *La Passion de Jeanne d'Arc, Day of Wrath,* and *Ordet* bring to light certain difficulties in religious representational schemes: the interferences across systems (the word versus the image), the opaqueness and arbitrariness of meaning (the book), the potential infinity of representation. Even when religious discourse is not central, the films' formal dynamics continue to explore such problems: *Vampyr* constructs its narrative as a gloss, in images, upon the preexistent word (omniscient narrator, book), while *Gertrud* offers itself as a veritable repertory of representational systems—theatre, music, painting, science, literature—all of which constantly displace each other. Finally, the last films (*Gertrud* in particular) raise a particular problem, that of the meaningless representation. By splitting cinematic form from narrative function, by setting representational systems in tension with one another, and by broaching the issue of the empty text, the late films throw up obstacles to conventional readings of representations.

This means that our analyses will examine the *functions* of representation in Dreyer's films. Instead of simply reading the films, we must consider the very terms of readability which they propose. At times we shall have to pause over explicit meanings—the narratively significant, the obviously symbolic—in order to ask what creates the significance and the obviousness. At other moments we shall have to pick out ambiguities, not to resolve them but to ask what aesthetic purposes they serve. At still other moments, we shall simply have to point to moments of transgression, conflict, omission, inconsistency, and loss—moments when representation falters and the film jolts us.

None of the critical categories mentioned so far can finally be isolated from cinema's relation to social practice. Yet one of the most persistent criticisms of Formalist theory has been that it divorces art from social ideology. The stress on perception, it is claimed, treats the viewer as the isolated individual, locked in rapt apprehension of the art work. How, then, can Formalist theory situtate an art work socially?

The most common form of ideological analysis concentrates on subject matter, theme, or narrative action in a general sense. The result is a cheerleading criticism that can praise *Day of Wrath* as being "in favor of" feminism, or denounce *Ordet* as a piece of "mystification." Dreyer's films are barely touched by such reductive readings; as one writer in the Marxist journal *Cinéthique* puts it: "Of course there are some idealist films which are also great films (Bresson's and Dreyer's for example)."[24]

The domain of investigation which Formalism has opened up can relate cinema to society in two precise ways. First, Marxist aesthetic theory points out that ideology is often transformed through the "relatively autonomous" processes of art. Art is related to ideology but cannot be reduced to it, and an account of the relation must include the particular aesthetic dynamics of the work. Here Formalism can be of use. The stress on the medium, on the perceptual activity of art, on systems in harmony or collision, on the different functions of structure and style within historical conventions—such theoretical concepts help us locate specific ways in which art mediates social ideology.

Secondly, by showing the systematic and material underpinnings of the spectator's experience, the Formalist approach can suggest some social implications of the cinematic institution. How we perceive a film affects how we consume cinema. An analysis of Dreyer as "author," the relations of the films to contemporary norms, the films' formal dynamics, and their work on representation can help us grasp how they can challenge and change our socially shaped habits of film viewing. It is in the realm of aesthetic perception, not ideological theme, that such "idealist" films as Dreyer's have provided models for avowedly materialist filmmakers like Jean-Luc Godard and Jean-Marie Straub.

Author, background set, form, representation, social functions—these concepts also plot the division of this book's critical labor. The next chapter will situate Dreyer's biographical legend within European film history. Chapters three and four will consider the characteristic formal strategies of the films made before 1927. In chapter five, I will introduce the problems of form and representation posed by the five major late films.[25] A separate chapter is devoted to each of these films. A final chapter proposes some ways to understand the uses of Dreyer's films. Throughout, I shall examine those problems of structure and comprehension that make Dreyer's work of central importance for us today.

An Author and His Legend

Even before we study the films, Dreyer invites an unusual interest. For one thing, his career spans the mature development of the cinema from 1912 to 1968, from (to put it melodramatically) *Musketeers of Pig Alley* to *La Chinoise.* Moreover, although Dreyer's career was long, it was hardly continuous. By the time he died, he was the director who was interesting partly because of what he did *not* do. During the last thirty-five years of his life, he made only four feature-length films and a handful of short documentaries; his unfinished projects *(Mary Stuart, Medea, Jesus)* are more famous than many directors' completed films. After his second film, Dreyer lacked the security of a stable national industry, and worked in Germany, Scandinavia, and France. His isolation is even more remarkable when you consider how many of his European contemporaries eventually came to Hollywood: Murnau, Lang, Christensen, Sjöström, Stiller, Ophuls, even Renoir and Buñuel. If only for his remarkable solitude, Dreyer becomes historically significant.

Our first fact—the span of his career—provides the precondition for our inquiry. The second fact needs analyzing. Can we attribute Dreyer's isolation to vagaries of personality? In the standard biography, Ebbe Neergaard depicts a boy stifled by a strict foster family and a young man who balked at regimen. Neergaard's account of how Dreyer left his post at the Great Northern Telegraph Company has become famous:

> *One day he had to accompany the old accountant down into the fireproof vaults. When they had passed the steel door and were standing in the great cellar with its air of mustiness, the old man suddenly stood still, pondering. Then he pointed quietly at the long row of huge grey, canvas-backed files, dating back several decades, and he said with a certain naive mixture of pride and wonder: 'There you see my whole life.' But the young clerk with the serious expression on his round childish face said nothing; he was overcome by a feeling of horror. He could not rid himself of the thought that he might one day stand there and say to a man fifty years younger than himself: 'There you see my life.' He resigned his post next morning without any idea of what he would do next.*

Is it surprising that such a young man would seek independence, first in the comparative freedom of journalism and then in the still relatively undisciplined film business? In this account, the gaps in Dreyer's career were wilfully opened up by a man of stubborn certainty and infinitesimal patience.

For our purposes, however, the standard career accounts will not suffice. Understanding cinematic form in history should not rest upon biography—intimate, unauthorized, or otherwise. Instead, the most fruitful conception of authorship will be the "biographical legend." Boris Tomashevsky writes: "The biography that is useful to the literary historian is not the author's curriculum vitæ or the investigator's account of his life. What the literary historian really needs is the biographical legend created by the author himself. Only such a legend is a *literary fact.*"[2] Similarly, we can situate a filmmaker's work in film history by studying the persona created by the artist in his public pronouncements, in his writings, and in his dealings with the film industry. Orson Welles constructed one persona, Howard Hawks a very different one. However subjective, even self-centered, such a legend may appear, that legend has an objective function in a historical situation. The biographical legend may justify production decisions and even create a spontaneous theory of the artist's practice. More important, the biographical legend is a way in which authorship significantly shapes our perception of the work. Created by the filmmaker and other forces (the press, cinephiles), the biographical legend can determine how we "should" read the films and the career. We do not come innocent to the films, and Dreyer's legend can shape how we regard them.

By now, the outline of that legend is clear enough: Dreyer as the one incorruptible director; the man whose commitment was to art, not business; the director who, after *Jeanne d'Arc,* would make only films he wanted to make, even if that meant he lacked support for the films he wanted most to make. Such a legend asks us to see Dreyer's films, especially the later ones, as purely expressive objects, works of the filmmaker who would not compromise his personal vision. Our task is not to puncture this legend, as if we could replace it with an easy truth, but rather to analyze the legend's historical and aesthetic functions.

We need to pose three sorts of questions. First, we need to specify the situation to which the biographical legend responded. What concrete circumstances confronted the filmmaker when he entered the realm of film production? We need not go as far as Shklovsky's claim that "the creator is simply the geometrical point of intersection of forces operating outside of him"[3] in order to propose that Dreyer entered an objectively constituted situation in which economic, social, and aesthetic forces operated. Secondly, we can ask what difficulties the artist identifies in his or her historical situation. What are the stale materials, the outworn habits, the clichés which the artist seizes upon? We are not asking whether the artist's view of the situation is correct in some absolute sense, only whether that view coheres with the biographical legend. Thirdly, we can see that legend as a struggle with contemporary norms. How does the filmmaker see his or her work as altering the historical situation, transforming standardized materials? We should not expect a simple transmission of influences but a dynamic action *upon* contemporary practice by the artist's work. As Yuri Tynianov suggests of literature:

> *When people talk about "literary tradition" or "succession" . . . they usually imagine a kind of straight line joining a younger representative of a given branch with an older one. As it happens, though, things are much more complex than that. It is not a matter of continuing on a straight line, but rather one of setting out and pushing off from a given point—a struggle. . . . Each instance of literary succession is first and foremost a struggle involving a destruction of the old unity and a new construction out of the old elements.*[4]

Dreyer's biographical legend seeks to clear a space for itself, and in so doing it must dislodge, rearrange, and contest certain dominant models.

The chief problem which Dreyer identified hinged upon film's status as an art. For Lumière, Méliès, even Feuillade, this problem did not exist. But for those men and women who entered film directing in the second decade of the century, the issue was serious, with implications for both production practice and aesthetic theory. How could a medium so obviously mass-produced, so dependent upon a mass audience, and so ruled by commerce offer the individual a chance to express an artistic vision? How could a medium so tied to pulp literature and melodrama ever become one of the "high arts"?

That Dreyer saw the problem in this light is shown by his reiterated attack upon mass-production filmmaking. One particularly strident passage stands out. In 1931, as the Hollywood production system was completing its economic standardization, Dreyer claimed that the increased specialization of the American cinema made it impossible for a film to be one man's work. Individual creativity was channeled into a bureaucracy of departments, "a complicated and totally impersonal 'administration.' " Production demanded adherence to a factory schedule: "To make a bad film is a very slight crime as compared to exceeding by one hour the work plan of the holy 'Organization.' "[5] The terms of this critique appear banal now; we are no longer shocked to learn that standard monopoly-capital techniques such as division of labor and intensification of the working day were soon applied to the cinema industry. But for many directors who began work around 1910, and who sought to make the cinema an art, the conflict between film as art work and as commodity presented a fresh, difficult problem. Perhaps a Dane would sense the difficulty with a special keenness: large-scale industrialization came very late to Denmark (some historians argue for as late a date as 1890), and the remains of a craft tradition would have been apparent to a young man of Dreyer's age.[6] In any event, Dreyer's biographical legend sought to solve the problem of art in mass production at two levels: that of production practice and that of aesthetic pronouncements. Neither solution is reducible to a simple or direct cause for the films, but both must be specified if we are to understand the historical dynamic of Dreyer's career.

CRAFTSMAN AND ARTIST (1919–1927)

Between 1910 and 1930, production offered several possible work situations to the filmmaker.

1. Within the industry, the director could be under contract to a firm. This was the most common solution.
2. In a significant variant of the first option, the director

could contract him or herself to an "artistic" wing of a firm. For complex reasons, after World War I both France and Germany developed avowedly "advanced" cadres within the industry. Examples would be the German filmmakers who worked in the Decla-Bioskop unit of Ufa or the French Impressionist filmmakers in their work for Pathé and Gaumont.

3. The director could work independently by forming a production company, financing the film by whatever means possible and hiring facilities or players from major firms. Examples would be the films made by L'Herbier and Epstein in the late 1920s.
4. The director could join a group making films outside the industry for specific artistic or political ends. This solution was chosen by the groups who made Surrealist films like *Les Mystères de Château du Dé* or leftist films like *Kuhle Wampe.*

Dreyer's career constitutes a varied series of solutions with respect to these possibilities. Never wealthy himself, he could drum up private financing for only one film *(Vampyr).* He refused the position of avant-garde artist or political filmmaker. In his early career, Dreyer took the first option and simply worked under contract with an industry. When that solution was no longer tenable, he sought other production possibilities. Although he tested the possibility of working within an "artistic" segment of a major firm, by the end of the silent era he had settled on a fifth solution to the problem of the artist in relation to industrial filmmaking.

Paradoxically, the director who condemned commercial film production began by working for the second most prolific studio of his day, Ole Olsen's Nordisk Films Kompagni. It might seem that a country the size of Denmark could not sustain a huge film enterprise, but in its golden age Nordisk commanded an enormous market. By owning theatres, making films quickly and cheaply, and exploiting popular subjects and genres, Olsen's firm became the center of the domestic film trade. At its peak (around 1913) Nordisk retained fourteen hundred full-time workers. The company either absorbed its chief competitors or drove them out of business by luring away their personnel. In 1911 Nordisk produced 77 of the 99 films made in Denmark; in 1912 it made 103 out of 160.[7] The company's greatest strength, however, lay in its flourishing export business. Olsen's films were widely distributed in Germany (where the company owned a circuit of theatres), France, England, and the United States. With control of domestic resources and an expanding international market, Nordisk was able in 1913 to garner profits of 1,200,000 kroner, its all-time high.[8]

In large part, the firm owed its success to its willingness to appeal to a mass public. Since film was now primarily an entertainment business, it became evident that cinema could profitably exploit narrative. In 1910, after Fotorama's successful *White Slave Trade* ran forty minutes in length, Nordisk began turning out much longer films, which virtually assured the dominance of narrative cinema over other modes. Thereafter, Nordisk developed several popular genres—the crime film, the romantic melodrama, and the chase farce—while also copying the American Western and the historical epic. The company's specialty genres were the so-called nobility film, which dealt with the peccadillos of the upper class, and the "Bohemian" film, laced with the exoticism of apaches, artists, and circus performers. The formulaic nature of the Nordisk genres may be gauged by the firm's widely publicized "rules for screenwriters," one of which commands: "The plot shall take place in the present and deal with 'elevated society.' Pieces which deal with the lower classes and with farmers will not be accepted."[9]

The Danish cinema also relied upon adaptations. Nordisk adapted works by Dumas, Dickens, Shakespeare, and other writers of international popularity, as much out of the need to retain a worldwide market as out of respect for literary values. This strategy, a contemporary account tells us, "is supported by the cultivated strata of society and the press. A film made from a famous work is certain to receive an attentive acceptance, even from those who ordinarily consider themselves opposed to film."[10] The remark suggests that adaptations sought to restrain censorship and draw the upper and middle classes to cinema. In parallel fashion, Nordisk also assured itself of a certain cultural esteem by hiring celebrated stage actors to perform in its adaptations.[11]

This industry's demand for narrative material brought in Carl-Theodor Dreyer. A journalist specializing in aviation pieces, courtroom reports, and witty sketches of celebrities, he composed three scripts for a small firm in the years 1912–13. He then went over to Nordisk Films as a part-time worker in 1913. What problems did he define in these circumstances? Guided by his later aversion to

Actors taking a break in the courtyard of the Nordisk studio, circa 1913.

mass-production filmmaking, we ought to pay attention to how Nordisk divided production labor.

Dreyer entered studio film production at an early phase of rationalization: the planning stage (scripting) and the execution stage (filming) had been separated, but the division of labor was not as precise as it would become. So his duties overlapped somewhat.[12] One task was that of writing intertitles. Since a film's "script" might be only a synopsis jotted down in pencil, the director would freely improvise while shooting the scene. Only after the filming were dialogue or expository titles composed and inserted. Dreyer's second duty, related to title writing, was film cutting. Again, this job was hardly what it is now. Since most scenes were filmed in a single shot, cutting came to little more than weeding out bad takes, assembling the footage in an intelligible order, and inserting the titles. Dreyer's third and most important function was that of literary consultant. Nordisk had nothing on the scale of the story department which Hollywood would develop a few years later; someone had to supervise scriptwriting. Working with other authors in a discarded gypsy wagon on the Nordisk lot, Dreyer sifted through submitted manuscripts, wrote original scripts, obtained film rights to current literary material, and adapted novels and plays to film. Dreyer's name appears in the credits of twenty Nordisk films between 1913 and 1919, but doubtless he worked uncredited on many more. In such circumstances, the beginning of Dreyer's career defined his labor within a literary, narrative conception of cinema.

"A marvelous school," Dreyer later called these five years of literary work.[13] Apparently, the pupil's lessons were acceptable to his superiors. Although only two of his scripted films survive, each one is a characteristic Nordisk product. *Pavillonens Hemmelighed (The Pavilion Mystery;* Karl Mantzius, 1914) is a thriller full of what Danes called "sensations"—robberies, abductions, trapdoors, secret laboratories—culminating in an explosion. Of no interest with respect to Dreyer's own films, this work shows that he was able to accept the confines of the Nordisk *policière* genre. *Ned Med Vaabnene (Surrender Arms;* Holger Madsen, 1914) is altogether different, made from a "literary classic." Almost immediately after he was hired, Dreyer obtained the rights to Berthe von Suttner's moralizing pacificist novel. The film trades on the literary status of the source by beginning with von Suttner at her desk starting to write the story we shall see. Carefully designed for neutrality (the soldiers wear unidentifiable uniforms), *Ned Med Vaabnene* was an international success, even though it was released after the beginning of World War I. It is likely that the film spawned the many didactic antiwar films through which Nordisk hoped to regain its crumbling international market. The value which the firm placed on Dreyer's specialized literary abilities may be gauged by the fact that in 1915, he began full-time work for Nordisk at 4,200 kroner per year plus commissions, when the average wage for a Danish workman was 1,400 kroner per year.[14]

However harmonious Dreyer's working situation might have been in many respects, we must be alert for the particular difficulties which an artist identifies. True, by 1912 the Danish film firms had not been thoroughly rationalized. The overlapping nature of Dreyer's Nordisk duties probably introduced him to several phases of the production process, and surviving memos from one project (*Glædens Dag,* 1916) suggest a relatively collaborative work situation. Nevertheless, Dreyer's powers were circumscribed. As a scriptwriter, he worked under genre and censorship limitations, and he would have seen his work altered or scrapped at later phases of production. As a titler, he would have learned how footage could be replaced by an all-inclusive intertitle. He saw how cutting could become thoroughly routine; he later recalled that for an 800-meter film a director would shoot only 850 meters.[15] He would have seen how each reel had to be cut to end on a thrilling note, so that the audience would be held during reel changes.[16] In all, Dreyer's job would have shown him how Nordisk ran according to factory-management principles.

Indeed, during Dreyer's years there, Nordisk became much more economically rationalized. World War I put an end to what was called at the time the "golden age" of Danish film.[17] Though 1913 had been a record year for Nordisk, succeeding years saw the company plunged into a steady decline. Despite Denmark's neutrality, the war wiped out many of the foreign markets on which Nordisk depended. Russia and France banned Danish films as pro-Germanic.[18] In 1916 Nordisk was forced to close its American office. In 1917 the new firm of Ufa bought up Nordisk's German theatre chain.[19] Lavishly produced "big films"—beginning with *Atlantis* (1913), and including *Pax*

A production still from August Blom's *Atlantis* (1913).

Æterna (1917) and *The Sky Ship* (1918)—failed to recapture an international public now more interested in American films. Nordisk production plummetted: 123 films in 1916, 61 films in 1917, 44 films in 1918, 39 in 1919, and 8 in 1920.[20] The result was a severe tightening of production spending. On the way to locations, actors had to ride in third-class compartments; tardy actors were fined two kroner or more.[21] The Danish film school was in the awkward position of preparing its graduates for foreign employment; "abroad, students can earn twenty to thirty marks per day, but Nordisk will pay only five kroner per day."[22] Thus began an exodus of talent that all but emptied Nordisk. Asta Nielsen and her director-husband Urban Gad had left before the war, and between 1914 and 1920 some of the firm's biggest stars went elsewhere. August Blom, in a 1917 letter to Olsen, traced the firm's decline to economic causes: the business necessitated a certain number of films, but most of them shouldn't have been made; the end came with "the beginning of the factory-manufacture of films."[23]

So at Nordisk Dreyer could not have been unaware of the demands of commercial film production. Given these demands, could one create art works as traditionally conceived? It was clear to him that only the director's role yielded enough control over the production process to make a film a work of art. Obviously in Denmark the director was still somewhat constrained. At Nordisk the director had to answer to two men: the producer, Harald Frost, and the studio manager, Wilhelm Stæhr, who made budgetary

August Blom directs in shirtsleeves at Nordisk, circa 1912.

decisions. Of course, shooting had to be as cheap and fast as possible. The director might explain the scene to the cast in advance, but he would probably not hold rehearsals. During filming, the director would coach the actors ("Shut the door! Turn left!") and since the actors probably did not know the lines they were to speak, the director would feed them the dialogue. When the scene was finished, the crew would run in and pull down the sets, carpenters would slide the new sets into place, and actors would breathlessly change costume.[24]

Impromptu as it seems, the director's job remained incompletely defined; because production tasks had not been as strictly assigned as they would later be, certain areas of artistic control remained open. Since the script was often little more than a précis, dialogue could be prepared by the director. Sets were furnished from warehouses, antique stores, and studio prop rooms, and the director could take as much hand in this as he cared to. In addition, he usually had authority to cast the film. He could supervise the cameraman's lighting scheme. Even the rough-and-ready shooting style could be turned to the director's benefit in the control it offered over acting style and tempo. Such latitude in this role led Urban Gad to conclude that despite the intervention of many workers, "none is more decisive in relation to the value of the work than the director is. . . . The director's spirit still permeates what is done."[25]

"The saying goes," wrote Dreyer to Frost in October 1917, "that when a man has been in one post for five years, one must either advance him or get rid of him. I wonder if my five years are not over?"[26] Dreyer chose an opportune moment, since directors had been leaving Nordisk as quickly as had actors. By 1919, August Blom and A. W. Sandberg were the only major directors still working for the company; the others had gone to Germany or to other Danish firms. By the spring of 1918, Dreyer had been promoted to the rank of director.

Dreyer's first film, *The President*, enabled him to expand and exploit some regions of freedom within the director's role. He was able to select the source and write his own script, since he had bought the rights to Emil Franzos's novel when he was a literary consultant. The script adhered to Nordisk's genre of the upper-class melodrama. (Studio manager Stæhr is reported to have praised *The President* as "a good old-fashioned nobility film.")[27] Although Dreyer selected the performers, acting took a back seat: "I let the actors do what they liked—I was more interested in the composition of the image."[28] With an assistant, he planned the sets in detail. Instead of letting a subordinate routinely order decor from a warehouse, he searched for the furnishings himself.[29] In sum, Dreyer sought an unusual degree of control over the *mise-en-scène*. When *The President* was finished in 1918, he refused to attend the screening scheduled for Nordisk producers: "My work is too dear to me and too seriously meant for me to be bothered by listening to two different and unimportant opinions."[30] The salaried literary consultant now disdains the opinions of his employers, forfeits the role of assembly-line worker, and claims the film as his own.

The production of *Leaves from Satan's Book* permitted Dreyer to define the extreme edge of the problem of making a work of art in the film industry. Although executives viewed the project as an attempt to regain Nordisk's former glory,[31] Dreyer expected opposition: "Manager Stæhr, in his unremitting hatred for everything youthful and new . . . will doubtless blindly persecute [A. W.] Sandberg and me."[32] After Stæhr accepted his budget of 120,000 kroner, Dreyer immersed himself in preparations for the film. He looked forward to searching out furnishings and designing the sets: "There will be a lot of work in finding drawings and photographs in the libraries (a matter I will take care of myself)."[33] But after three months of rewriting the script (over the original scenarist's protests), selecting the cast and crew, and researching the film, Dreyer declared that he would have to raise his budget to 240,000 kroner. Nordisk responded that it could provide only 150,000. Dreyer wrote to Stæhr that for that amount he could not make a film "in strictest regard to art" and he cast doubt on the producers' ability to judge the situation. In his preparations, Dreyer saw himself as seeking to control the entire production process:

> *I daresay that I can argue that never has such preparatory work been done in this country, and probably never before has a director been as prepared for directing as I am now. Is all this not enough to convince the General Manager? Did you tell him that the black pigs, the guinea fowl, and the monkeys which I shall use sometime in July had already been reserved in January? Have you told the General Manager that I have searched all over town in order to find original Southern Europeans as extras in my Spanish story and that I have gotten everybody moving to find Finns for my Finnish story? . . . Have you told the General Manager how I have been sitting in the library for*

> *months seeking out every detail of my sets? I have left nothing to others; I have taken care of everything myself. Doesn't all this demonstrate that my goal is higher than that of making a* film-product?[34]

If Dreyer and Nordisk should part, he warned, the reason would be that "Nordisk Films Kompagni wants to make a *film-product* (which in my eyes is the same as a *bad* film) while my goal is the *film which sets standards.*"[35]

Nordisk's response, which came from Ole Olsen himself, exemplifies the problem which Dreyer confronted. "As the company's economic leader, [I] cannot take the responsibility for making the company run such a financial risk and allot so much to a single film. I also daresay that I am in a better position than you to judge how far we can extend ourselves in that regard. . . . You have obligated yourself to comply with our economic regulations."[36] Olsen would offer no more than 150,000 kroner. On 25 March 1919, Dreyer gave in. "Circumstances of course do not allow me to expose myself to a suit involving 70,000 to 100,000 kroner. I accede, therefore, to the will of the General Manager and agree to make the film just as you wanted. But at the same time," he added, "I solemnly deny any responsibility for the finished film."[37] The next day Olsen notified Dreyer that he would be withdrawn from *Leaves.* Dreyer wrote back to assert that he had not resigned from the film and, now realizing that he must give up any idea of *his* film, he accepted a budget of 150,000 kroner. Olsen urged Dreyer to start shooting.[38]

Even after *Leaves* was completed, Dreyer's conception of art continued to clash with mass-production methods. He learned that for the premiere in Oslo the theatre staff had cut and accelerated the film so that its original running time of two hours was reduced to ninety minutes. Attaching letters from a friend and an Oslo projectionist attesting to the "scandalous" screening, Dreyer wrote Frost a letter mixing pleas with indignation:

> *It is, I think, quite humiliating for Nordisk Films and quite depressing for those of us who have sacrificed six months or a year to produce a worthy work for our firm to find that that same firm does not have the power and the ability to* protect *our work and, yes, apparently lacks even any interest in doing so. My request to you, Mr. Frost, is that you do your part to see that the film here at home will come out in a respectable form and that no important changes will be made in it unless I am consulted.*[39]

We may surmise that it seemed extraordinary, and extraordinarily fruitless, for a Nordisk filmmaker to seek to control how his film was projected in another country.

Leaves from Satan's Book was Dreyer's last film for Nordisk. Several factors doubtless led to his leaving: Neergaard has suggested that *Leaves* deviated too much from Nordisk policy; Dreyer claimed that when Olsen quit (in 1923), the firm was dying; the Danish film industry as a whole was not prospering; more generally, Denmark was suffering monetary instability, price fluctuations, and steeply rising unemployment.[40] But the most pertinent artistic reason is that Dreyer was unable to solve the problem which he had defined: how to make an art work in the context of mass production.

Dreyer's career in the 1920s added a fifth alternative to the list which I proposed earlier. Directors did not need to pledge themselves permanently to a single firm, not even to an "artistic wing" of that firm; but neither did they have to be independently financed. A director might operate on a film-by-film basis, working on a single project for a single company on whatever terms might be acceptable. The filmmaker could then move to another firm, perhaps even in another country. Although this solution is common now, it was rare in the early days of monopoly film production. This alternative made Dreyer an international traveler. Between 1920 and 1926, he made seven films in five countries, and no two films for the same firm—a situation which could hardly have made him feel financially secure. But in return the artist was independent.

He seized upon precedents for that independence. There was Griffith, the paradigm of the autonomous director. There was Sjöström, who "was perhaps the first in Scandinavia to realize that one cannot *manufacture* films if they are to have at least some cultural value."[41] Above all there was another Dane, Benjamin Christensen, ten years Dreyer's senior. In 1913, at the peak of Nordisk's success, Christensen had taken over the tiny firm Dansk Biografkompagni, where he directed and starred in two striking films: *The Mysterious X* (1913) and *Night of Revenge* (1915). In early 1920, fresh from the battle over *Leaves from Satan's Book,* Dreyer saw Christensen as a man fighting to work independently of commercial constraints. "In Denmark, films have always been *manufactured.* It created a positive sensation when a man appeared—Benjamin Christensen—who did not manufacture his films but worked them out with care and affection for every little detail."[42] To seek influences amid all these figures would miss the point. What Dreyer read in the careers of Griffith, Sjöström, and Christensen was a craft heritage opposed to the routinized labor of "manufacturing film-products." Such a vision of artistic autonomy was already nostalgic in 1920. Nevertheless, Dreyer declared his faith in the film artisan, the creator who made one film from top to bottom, seeing it through every phase of the production process.

The conception of the director as artisan shaped production habits which would remain constant throughout Dreyer's career. Every film rested upon a mountain of preparatory research. He would accumulate files of notes, clippings, and photographs. Pictures of costumes, furniture, settings, paintings, and statues would later be used to show the staff and cast the sort of images he wanted. Preben Thomsen recalls that for *Medea* Dreyer collected material "as if in preparation for a thesis."[43] To avoid a mechanical split between scripting and shooting phases, Dreyer's scenarios never mentioned camera positions and set details: he would make these choices during filming. He worried over minutiae that most directors would leave to the crew. "Every night I prepare my work for the next day. It is very important to do this, because it is only then that you know your actors and you know the settings exactly and how they are placed and where the armchair is, etc."[44] Later in this chapter we shall see how Dreyer's work with actors determined the regimen of shooting; at this point, it is enough to note that after *Leaves from Satan's Book,* part of his biographical legend included work methods which rejected the ordinary division of production labor.

Dreyer's view of the director as artisan also explains the bewildering variety of his film work during the 1920s. Although there was some continuity of cast and crew (he tended to use the same set designer, Jens G. Lind, and favored Johannes Meyer and Mathilde Nielsen as players), he was on the whole isolated, hopscotching from country to country, working free-lance. Economic conditions favored traveling. The silent cinema gave directors relative freedom to work in foreign countries. More important, the European film industry had been shaken by the postwar invasion of American films. Such unsettled conditions gave birth to hopeful small firms, and set large firms searching for something which would compete with the Hollywood product. During the 1920s, Dreyer was able to synchronize his urges for independence with the goals of the European cinema.

In some circumstances he was able to avoid monopoly filmmaking altogether. There were many small firms on the fringes of the big companies. In 1921 he made *The Stigmatized Ones* for the tiny Primusfilm of Berlin, using a cast composed primarily of Russian emigré actors. The firm seems never to have made another film. The following spring found Dreyer back in Denmark, where the theatre owner Sophus Madsen had formed a company to produce a new version of *Once upon a Time,* which Dreyer shot that summer. For Victoria-Film of Oslo Dreyer made *The Bride of Glomdal* in the summer of 1925, but the Norwegian film industry was marginal, turning out only two or three films a year. Even the Danish firm Palladium, which by 1925 had surpassed Nordisk, was hardly a major force: its product consisted almost wholly of a popular comedy series, and it employed only one director permanently. So it was unusual for Palladium to sponsor Dreyer's *Thou Shalt Honor Thy Wife* in 1925. During these productions, he was able to follow some of his most characteristic habits, especially the collection and scrutiny of pictures pertaining to the given film's milieu, and the construction of ambitious sets (a Russian village for *The Stigmatized Ones,* an apartment complete with functioning plumbing, lighting, and heating for *Thou Shalt Honor Thy Wife).* At times, it seems, Dreyer sought out firms which could not have hired him on a regular basis.

On two occasions, Dreyer did work for large-scale film companies. In 1919 Svensk Filmindustri launched an attempt to compete with American production. As part of its international campaign, it bought studio facilities in Hellerup, the filmmaking suburb of Copenhagen, and engaged Benjamin Christensen and Dreyer. During 1920 Christensen worked in Hellerup on *Häxan (The Witch,* also known as *Witchcraft through the Ages)* while Dreyer went to Sweden to film *The Parson's Widow.* In an essay titled "Swedish Film," Dreyer records a hope that Sweden, having overtaken Denmark, would also surpass Hollywood: "Sweden has for the time being every chance of keeping, for a long time to come, the leading position it has won."[45] Given Svensk Filmindustri's ambitions, the firm might well have retained Christensen and Dreyer, along with Sjöström and Stiller. But it seems likely that Dreyer, or Svensk, or both, were unwilling to continue their alliance in the face of a declining market.

More like the *Leaves from Satan's Book* tangle were Dreyer's relations with a second big firm. In 1924 Dreyer

A production still from Benjamin Christensen's *Witchcraft through the Ages* (1920).

completed *Michael* for the mighty Ufa of Berlin. Like Nordisk and Svensk, Ufa held a near-monopoly in domestic film commerce but still watched the American advance nervously. Engaging Dreyer seems to have been part of a strategy to internationalize Ufa's directorial personnel. (The firm had already hired Christensen a year before.) Under Erich Pommer's supervision, Dreyer shot *Michael* for Decla-Bioskop, the "artistic" wing of Ufa that also produced Lang's *Mabuse* and *Niebelungen* films, and Murnau's *Schloss Vogelöd.* Dreyer thereby found a good deal of the autonomy which he had sought:

> *For the conscientious film director, Pommer was the ideal producer. Once a decision was made on major problems, such as script, casting, sets, etc., he would not interfere with the director's work. Now and then he would come to the set and if everything was all right he smiled brightly. In artistic questions, he easily yielded to sound arguments.*[46]

During the shooting of *Michael,* there was the prospect that Dreyer might make another film for Pommer. But after *Michael* was completed, a dispute arose when Pommer changed the film's ending without Dreyer's approval.[47] Although the evidence is sketchy, it seems likely that the controversy led to Dreyer's leaving Ufa.

The pattern is evident. Dreyer either avoided working for monopoly firms or worked for such firms only when he could get considerable directorial control over the project. The eclecticism of these films—open-air comedies and romances in the Sjöström tradition, *kammerspielfilms* ("chamberplay films"), adaptations of popular plays—constitute an attempt to turn to artistic advantage the different working situations offered by different cultures. By 1927 Dreyer had found a project commensurate with his demands. The success of *Thou Shalt Honor Thy Wife* in Paris prompted the Société Générale de Films to contract with him to film *Jeanne d'Arc,* for which he was given a large budget and a free hand. He had avoided the pitfall of Hollywood, where (as the fates of Sjöström and Christensen showed) one couldn't do anything really personal. He had succeeded in becoming the craftsman with control of the production process and the artist who was *creating* films instead of manufacturing them.

ON THE MARGINS OF FILM PRODUCTION (1928–1968)

At the end of the 1920s, Dreyer's independence was well synchronized with opportunities in the industry. *La Passion de Jeanne d'Arc,* financed by a consortium, and *Vampyr,* financed by an individual, concluded the first twelve years of his directorial career. Subsequent decades would reveal some problems inherent in the role of free-lance director.

La Passion de Jeanne d'Arc was backed by forces larger than any mere film company. In an attempt to check the spread of American films through the European market, there were many attempts to create international production firms. One such consortium was "Westi," founded by the German industrialists Vladimir Wengeroff and Hugo Stinnes. Wengeroff explained Westi's purpose:

> *In each European country, there should appear every year one or two perfectly directed films, whose subjects will be found in celebrated literary masterpieces or composed specially by one of the great national writers; the best artists must offer in this work the best of their talents, and every possible artistic care must surround the creation of such a film. . . . The costs of one of these films will be between $150,000 and $200,000.*[48]

Westi was the principal backer of the Société Générale de Films, a firm founded by the Duke d'Ayen. Although Westi eventually dissolved, the Société Générale was able to continue. Apparently still adhering to the Westi plan of producing prestigious films, the Société Générale financed *Napoléon vu par Abel Gance,* Epstein's *Finis Terrae,* Maurice Tourneur's *L'Équipage,* and *La Passion de Jeanne d'Arc.* In making the film, Dreyer was given what he later called "a free hand. . . . I did absolutely what I wanted."[49]

But the financial failure of *La Passion de Jeanne d'Arc* cut short Dreyer's cosmopolitan freedom. Although he had been commissioned to make another film for the Société Générale, the firm—now hurt by the losses of Gance's *Napoléon* as well—broke its contract. Dreyer was thrown back on his own resources. At this time in France, patronage filmmaking was not unusual: the Vicomte de Noailles financed *Blood of a Poet* and *L'Age d'Or.* Here, for the only time in his life, Dreyer made a film financed by an individual, the young Baron Nicolas de Gunzburg. Shot in a rundown chateau with many nonactors, *Vampyr* was a model of independent production. It could not, however, guarantee Dreyer steady work. By 1932, after ten films, he was confronted with the difficulty of maintaining his freedom in a changing European film industry.

The "holy organization" against which Dreyer had railed in 1931 now dominated filmmaking in virtually every country. After the coming of sound, monopoly control of filmmaking sharply increased. Sound patents and technological priorities forced small firms out of business and increased consolidations. In the silent cinema, a polylingual filmmaker could move from country to country, but sound encouraged the hardening of national boundaries. Dreyer's problematic position at this time is dramatized by the necessity of making three versions of *Vampyr* (French, German, and English). With a reputation for being a financial risk and a tenacious commitment to directorial control, Dreyer became not only independent but also unemployable. After *Vampyr,* he did not complete a film for ten years.

For the rest of his career, from 1932 to 1968, Dreyer was marginal to world film production. He was able to make films only in unusual economic circumstances. In 1936 he began *Mudundu* with Italian and French backing, but after months in Somalia, he quit the project, blaming the producers for hiring an inappropriate actress to play the heroine. The complaint starts to sound familiar: "The men who sat in Paris supervising things from a distance made it impossible for me to finish the film on which I had done all the important preparation."[50] By now the biographical legend is mature.

After *Mudundu,* Dreyer faced several alternative sources of financing. One possibility was government subsidy, and during the 1940s, he made several short documentaries under Danish government sponsorship. But in general, work was available only when a national film industry decided to invest in what was called in the 1930s a "prestige picture" and what later became known as the "art film."

Day of Wrath provides a typical example. When the German invasion of Denmark in 1940 cut off the importation of American and French films, the Danish film industry had to produce more films for domestic consumption. Dreyer still had thoughts of working outside Denmark, but in the absence of any foreign offers, he seems to have sensed an opportunity: "Now with all the waterways closed and all the borders blocked, I wondered how I could get involved in film again."[51] After making a short government documentary to show that he could still direct, Dreyer submitted a script to Nordisk. Nordisk hesitated, but Palladium accepted, and Dreyer was given a free hand in production. He devoted himself entirely to the project. He moved to Hellerup to be near the studio and worked well into the night after each day's shooting. The terms have not changed since *Leaves:* "I always concentrate completely on the work. . . . I have been involved in every single detail."[52]

Yet after *Day of Wrath,* no contract was forthcoming. During a visit to Copenhagen, the Swedish producer C. A. Dymling offered Dreyer the opportunity to make a film in Stockholm. Dymling bought a play which Dreyer wanted to film, but the result, *Two People* (1945), was so embarrassing that it played only two days in Sweden. Even this project has been grist for the biographical legend. Dreyer blamed Dymling for assigning him actors he did not want, and to the end of his life he disavowed *Two People.* Once, when asked about it, he answered curtly: "That film doesn't exist."[53] Dreyer's veto has succeeded: *Two People* has slipped out of sight, and we think of *Ordet* as the film following *Day of Wrath.* As a result, Dreyer's legend spaces his output into forbidding ten-year intervals, a practice which recalls what Robert Craft has written of Webern: "He limited himself to ultimate consequences and to composing the silence not only within a work but between one work and the next."[54]

After the war, prosperity in another national cinema offered Dreyer a fresh opportunity. During the years 1946–48, the English cinema was healthy: record numbers of films were being made and attendance was never higher. The government called for more domestic production, raised quotas, imposed stiff tariffs on imported films, and established a national financing corporation. Accompanying this was a trend toward historical films and adaptations from English literature *(Henry V, Hamlet, Great Expectations, Oliver Twist).* Arthur Elton, who was supervising the "Social Denmark" series, seems to have encouraged Dreyer to submit a proposal for *Mary Stuart* to Film Traders Ltd. With his usual thoroughness, Dreyer had researched the period, and he and his son had written the script in English. After a visit to London in 1946, he returned to Denmark hopeful, but prospects faded.[55] By 1948 the boom in the British film industry was over.

Dreyer saw yet another possibility open up with his plans for a film of the story of Jesus. It seemed for a time that he could get financing, with the help of the American theatre producer Blevins Davis. Throughout the early 1950s, Dreyer struggled to make the film. The timing might have seemed right, given the success of Biblical epics at the same period, but financing did not come through.[56] In the meantime he continued to write and direct government documentaries, and in 1951 he was assured of a steady income through the award of a theatre managership.[57]

The early 1950s were somewhat hopeful times for the Danish film industry. There had been a steady increase in gross ticket receipts during the preceding decade, and the growing art-house audience abroad made it possible to export more Scandinavian films than at any time since 1925. *Sunset of a Clown, Smiles of a Summer Night,* and *Miss Julie* were yielding Bergman and Sjöberg international reputations. Furthermore, Danish production habits were congenial to Dreyer's methods. Crews were small, with a fairly loose division of labor. The producer's role was minimal; as long as the director was on schedule and under budget, he was generally let alone. The director governed the editing of the film. Danish production also favored shooting in continuity as much as possible.[58] In short, when the chance to make a film did come along, Dreyer could operate very much as an artisan.

In such circumstances, *Ordet* became possible. The government paid Dreyer to prepare the script, and Danish Cultural Film proposed the idea to Tage Neilsen of Palladium, who agreed to finance the project.[59] Dreyer hinted that the subject was not the one he would have chosen; nevertheless, he regarded the project as preparation for the Christ film.[60] *Ordet* won acclaim for the Danish industry, receiving immediate international distribution and an award at the Venice Film Festival. The independent director of the silent era had become an art-film director.

Gertrud ended Dreyer's career on a cadence stressing his marginal relations with production. Again financed by Palladium and shot and edited quickly, the film had some chance of being well-received in foreign art houses. But wherever it appeared, *Gertrud* was immediately denounced as tired and feeble—a response that hurt Dreyer financially no less than personally. He was by now seventy-five and in poor health; prospective backers of the Christ film worried that he would not be able to complete such a huge project. Financial support (a characteristic mixture of cartel finance and Danish government subsidy) finally came through only a few days before he died.

Dreyer's biographical legend, then, placed him in a peripheral position with respect to the industry. He became an independent director, working without a long-term contract, seeking money for this or that project from individuals or governments, and being supported by large firms or monopoly capital only when a moment of desperation or affluence guaranteed him a certain autonomy. Doubtless, being anchored in Scandinavia limited his choices, since independently financed production was never as strongly established there as in, say, France. Dreyer was also, in a sense, twenty years ahead of his time. In 1930 his free-lance status was rare and thus precarious; not until 1950, with the generation of Bresson, Tati, Fellini, and Antonioni, could independent filmmakers survive by appealing to international audiences.

AN AESTHETIC OF EXPRESSIVITY

Dreyer's biographical legend encompasses not only production practices but also a body of verbal discourse. From almost the beginning of his career, he published essays setting forth his views on cinema. When his career lagged in the 1930s, he took up film reviewing. The specialized press interviewed him repeatedly during his career. What all these words constructed was not a full-blown theory of cinema. Rather, this literary man—ex-journalist, scenarist—created a body of discourse that sought to define his artistic practice. Most generally, Dreyer attempted to solve the problems that every artist confronts—the outworn forms, the pertinent traditions, the ways of distinguishing one's own work. More specifically, his discourse addresses the problem of the art work in mass-production filmmaking. As a result, his pronouncements set his films in a particular perspective. Dreyer's aesthetic precepts are of little theoretical interest, but they have shaped attitudes toward his work. To understand the historical function of the biographical legend, we must understand the aesthetic precepts which he defended.

By 1920, in his view, Danish film production as a whole had become cliché. He cited in particular the Nordisk nobility films and criticized their reliance upon such melodramatic devices as "revolvers, jumps from the fifth floor, and similar sensationalisms."[61] He accused the film industry of pandering to the masses and frightening away the intelligentsia. For Dreyer, melodramatic plots of physical action constituted outworn forms which had to be negated by an application of "taste and culture."

This conception of art was conservative by standards of advanced twentieth-century thinking. Like the French Impressionists and Griffith, Dreyer held to a view which was not truly contemporary with the work of Braque or Picasso, Schoenberg or Berg, Kafka or Apollinaire. Instead of looking to the avant-garde in other arts, progressive filmmakers skipped a generation back to Romantic and Symbolist conceptions of art. Yuri Tynianov remarks, "In the struggle with the father, the grandson turns out to resemble his grandfather."[62]

Strictly speaking, Dreyer was not even contemporary with his contemporaries, for his thinking set him apart from the main tradition of silent film theory. How much did the cinema owe to literature and theatre? Almost nothing, contemporary theorists would have responded. Cinema was either a synthesis of all arts or an autonomous and pure art close to music. Either way, cinema's distinctness from theatre and literature was axiomatic. But for Dreyer, cinema was only an extension of these arts. Disputes about the essence of cinema dealt merely with technique; his aesthetic proposed a return to basic human truths. Cinema would be narrative and, specifically, psychological. The filmmaker could counter the melodramatic excesses of the commercial product by depicting profound and subtle psychological experiences. "Art shall represent the inner, and not the outer life."[63] If film seeks

A production still from an unidentified Nordisk "sensation-film" of the 'teens.

depth, it must draw upon the psychological arts par excellence—literature and theatre. Dreyer once defined a film as "a merging of novel and drama in the form of pictures."[64] He urged poets and novelists to try their hands at cinema, and he believed that the spirit of Stanislavsky's theatre work should be transferred to the screen. Sjöström was a significant director because "he began to search among the most outstanding works of literature."[65] The man who wrote scripts and intertitles for Nordisk saw cinema as explicitly literary and theatrical.

With the coming of sound, Dreyer's views bound the cinema even more closely to the theatre. Although his aesthetic of psychological realism rejected the exaggeration of theatre conventions (artificial sets, exaggerated acting), he identified cinema as dependent upon stage texts. "Since I define the real sound film as a film capable of fascinating by its psychological content, its story, and its remarks alone, without help from exaggerated sound effects, musical accompaniment, and inserted musical numbers, the psychological play is probably to be considered the most suitable material."[66]

In this insistence upon a theatrical cinema, two tendencies stand out. One is generic. To what theatrical mode will the genuine sound film correspond? Late in his career, with his biographical legend firmly established, Dreyer's answer was invariable: "If something links *Jeanne d'Arc, Vampyr, Day of Wrath,* and *Gertrud,* it is the fact that little by little, I am coming closer and closer to tragedy."[67] He wrote of how *Jeanne d'Arc* and *Day of Wrath* met Aristotle's requirements for tragic unity, and expressed the belief that someday a filmmaker would find "the form and style appropriate to tragedy."[68] Nearly all his favorite ideas for projects came from tragic literature *(Orestes, Light in August, Medea, Mourning Becomes Electra, Desire under the Elms, Winterset).*[69] Dreyer's esteem for the tragic genre is related to a second tendency in his aesthetic. He asserted that theatrical adaptation would raise the quality of films: "The films shall therefore—without losing their filmic individuality—be lifted to the same artistic level as the most understanding theatre performances."[70] It was the *good* theatre that theatrical cinema in the tragic mode should imitate.[71] What artistic role would this theatrical cinema assign to the filmmaker? It is no accident that the zone of directorial labor which escaped Nordisk's rationalization was seen by Dreyer as the privileged area of creativity. For him, the film artist governed chiefly the staging, lighting, design, and performance of the narrative action—in short, the *mise-en-scène.* And just as Dreyer refused to define a painting's style apart from its use of figures, so cinematic style, in pursuit of human truth, would attend primarily to the person.[72] If cinema's mission is to be narrative and psychological, at the center of the medium stands the actor.

From Dreyer's writings, his recorded comments, and his day-to-day directorial practice, the actor emerges as the biographical legend's most explicit answer to the problem of artistic values within commodity production. What Walter Benjamin saw as characteristic of filmmaking—the fact that the actor plays to a machine, and that his or her role is built out of many small bits rather than out of a continuous performance—Dreyer seeks to overcome with a conception of the actor as consummately human.[73] In this conception, a film studio could not rationalize casting, since the director must intuit the actor's essence: "The *inner* similarity is the decisive issue—namely similarity in regard to mentality, character, and temperament."[74] Once chosen, the actor must "express"—literally, press out, make manifest—the inner qualities which the director has perceived. The director avoids the routine of mass-production labor by refusing to formalize performance tasks: Dreyer compared the director to a midwife, standing by while the actor creates the performance from within, "out of his own artistic strength."[75] All the famous Dreyer tactics—setting up screens around Falconetti, living with cast and crew while filming *Vampyr,* shooting *Jeanne d'Arc* in chronological order, abjuring the use of a megaphone in the silent era, barring bystanders from the set, refusing to break down a script into shots, even developing the long-take shooting style of his later years—can be seen as specific attempts to create an intimacy, pressure, and concentration during the act of filming that would counter the routines and schedules of studio filmmaking.[76] Dreyer believed that through an almost mystical rapport with his players the director could transcend the mechanical constraints of mass production.

The sign of that transcendence, the site of human expressivity, would be the face. Compare these remarks:

1920: With the coming of the facial close-up the days of the grimace were over. Film had found its way to human representation.[77]

1926: Everything human is expressed in the face. . . . The face is the mirror of the soul: this must become the slogan of the silent era.[78]

1943: Gesture endows the face with soul, and facial expression is an extra-important plus to the spoken word. . . . Mime is the original means of expression of inner experience.[79]

1955: There is nothing in the world that can be compared to the human face. It is a land one never becomes tired of exploring.[80]

1964: What I seek in my films, what I want to obtain, is a penetration to my actors' profound thoughts by means of their most subtle expressions. For these are the expressions that reveal the character of the person, his unconscious feeling, the secrets that live in the depth of his soul. This is what interests me above all, not the technique of the cinema.[81]

For Dreyer, the purity of facial expression makes genuine artistry possible in a mass-produced art. Once filmed, the representation of the soul rises above the contingency of cinema as commodity.

Cinematic style must then be put at the service of the actor. For one thing, the close-up offers the director a way to magnify facial expression and "record inner dramas."[82] For another, decor can support and intensify the revelation of personality. Correct settings can put the actor into the proper mood: the sets of *Jeanne d'Arc* and the four-walled rooms of *Gertrud* were designed to make the actors feel as if they were living the drama. Dreyer spoke of simplifying a set so as "to leave only the things that contribute to characterizing the people."[83] Judiciously executed, decor can "draw the spectator's eyes toward what is essential in every single shot—usually, the acting."[84] No wonder that Dreyer's scripts contain almost no shot breakdowns or notes as to camera positions. Henning Bendtsen, cinematographer for *Ordet* and *Gertrud,* recalls that only after having adjusted the sets and rehearsed the actors would Dreyer start to plan how the scene would be lit, shot, and cut.[85] The primacy of the actor recruits other film techniques in the cause of human expressivity.

Under this aesthetic there lies a necessary enigma. What does the director coax from his script and players? It can only be the glimpse of a realm beyond ordinary experience. "It is not the things in reality that the director should be interested in but rather the spirit in and behind things."[86] Why must the calm whiteness of the decor be broken by so few objects? "These things are there for symbolic reasons. Even if the symbols cannot be readily understood, I believe that the dominant mood of the development of the action on this purified background will be able to be sensed immediately."[87] Stylization and abstraction of lighting, decor, and performance can express what words and ratiocination cannot. The mystical quality of Dreyer's aesthetic is perfectly functional, solving a specific problem. The ineffable cannot be mass-produced.

Dreyer's aesthetic can also be seen as justifying his independence after leaving Nordisk Films. For an independent director, making films in a variety of economic and cultural situations, an aesthetic predicated upon an ahistorical, suprasocial human essence serves a useful purpose. Danish operetta, Swedish pseudo-folktale, Norwegian romance novel, the transcript of a trial in medieval France, English horror story, Scandinavian plays—all exemplify the fundamental expressiveness of the human soul. The transcendental aesthetic paints Dreyer as an author beyond national differences, a visionary artist revealing timeless truths. How well this biographical legend was accepted may be judged by a remark made by a French critic in 1927, which could as accurately have been written forty years later:

> *Of Danish nationality and upbringing but of Swedish descent, Carl Dreyer no more follows the cinematic style of one country than of another; instead, he belongs to a class of directors who create a more generally human cinema, international in its accessibility to all people, of whatever race, of whatever country, class, or condition.*[88]

Within Western film production, Dreyer constructed his artistic personality around a single problem: that of art in mass production. To this problem, specific production practices and theoretical precepts would constitute a solution. The ideas informing those practices and precepts challenged contemporary norms by applying a Romantic conception of visionary creation and transcendent value to a twentieth-century art form. All of which is not reducible to saying that Dreyer's aesthetic views simply reflected his production circumstances, or that as a young man he blueprinted an aesthetic project and set out to live it. Historically, Dreyer the *auteur* was defined by the man's experiences, certain aesthetic assumptions current in his milieu, and the evolution of the European film industries. That all these forces did not neatly mesh is perhaps best indicated by the several difficulties within the biographical legend.

One inconsistency arises if we consider how Dreyer hoped to create a cinema of literary value. It is true that every one of his feature films was an adaptation of fiction or drama, yet no artist's material is pure or raw; it already carries a certain historical weight. The sources for Dreyer's films were surprisingly homogeneous. He was drawn to turn-of-the-century fiction and drama, generally in the Scandinavian realist tradition. There is the rural pastoral: Kristofer Janson's story which became *The Parson's Widow* (c. 1900), Jacob B. Bull's novel *The Bride of Glomdal* (1908). There is the melodramatic novel: Karl-Emil Franzos's *The President* (1883), Aage Madelung's *Love One Another* (1912). There is also the *fin-de-siècle* decadence of Hermann Bang's *Michael* (1904) and of Hjalmar Soderberg's *Gertrud* (1906). Popularized realism in the theatre yielded Svend Rindom's comedy *The Fall of a Tyrant* (1919, filmed as *Thou Shalt Honor Thy Wife*) and Hans Wiers-Jensen's Ibsenesque *Anne Pedersdotter* (1908, filmed as *Day of Wrath*). Even the non-Scandinavian sources tend to be of the late nineteenth century: Marie Corelli's *Sorrows of Satan* (1896), the putative source for *Leaves from Satan's Book;* and Sheridan Le Fanu's *In a Glass Darkly* (1872), filmed as *Vampyr.* Nor did the material which Dreyer adapted have great literary stature. Nearly all of his sources were popular in their time, but they are today considered minor genre work or kitsch. Even the most respected original sources—Holger

Drachmann's nationalistic fairy tale *Once upon a Time* (1885), Kaj Munk's *Ordet* (1932), and Bang's *Michael*—enjoy fame only within Scandinavia. Dreyer's aesthetic of universal human essences does not square with the narrow range of his sources, nor does his concern for what he had called, in Sjöström's case, "the most outstanding works of literature" exhibit itself in the selection of such mediocre works.

In a similar way, the idea of the theatre to which Dreyer appealed after the coming of sound was hardly that of the advanced currents of his day. It must be remembered that during the nineteenth century the Danish theatre had been a stronghold of the Naturalist style. Even the Norwegian Ibsen and the Swede Strindberg premiered several of their most important plays *(The Pillars of Society, A Doll's House, An Enemy of the People, The Father, Miss Julie)* in Copenhagen. Danish directors and performers provided definitive productions of such works, and Strindberg established his "Scandinavian Experimental Theatre" in Copenhagen. But when French and German productions were exploring new ground, a diluted Naturalism continued to dominate the Danish theatre until at least 1920. Dreyer's emphasis on the actor and on "inner truth," echoing the precepts of Strindberg's and Brandes's Naturalist manifestos, reached back to a conception of psychological realism that was already clichéd on the stage.

But Dreyer's biographical legend must be judged functionally as well. Most simply, it works to give us a particular attitude to the films. Negatively, the legend defines the work by virtue of Dreyer's refusals—his aversion to mass-production filmmaking, his distaste for popular genres, his stiff rejection of the audience. ("Consciously, I don't do anything to 'please' the public. I only think of working my way to a solution that satisfies my own artistic conscience.")[89] Positively, the legend constitutes the films as unified, autonomous works. Any flaws—the compromises of *Leaves,* the ending of *Michael,* the failure of *Two People*—are attributed to meddlesome producers. Ideally, the films spring from a consistent artistic vision and seek to transcend the constraints of the film industry. It is no wonder that humanist and religious readings find Dreyer's work so massively unified, since the biographical legend encourages us to approach the films looking for a coherent personal vision untouched by the vagaries of the film industry.

In ways that we shall examine, certain forces in Dreyer's work do square with the protocols of the biographical legend. In particular, the films move toward a heavily determined overall unity. But drawing on the legend uncritically answers too neatly to its very purpose. When we set the films against the styles and forms which dominated international filmmaking during Dreyer's career, his work becomes troubling in ways that cannot be explained by the author's persona. The films' difficulties tally only partly with the aesthetic principles which Dreyer articulated. The aesthetic autonomy which the legend seeks is compromised by the problems that the films pose. Early in his career, working within classical premises, Dreyer nonetheless tests contemporary conceptions of narrative and cinema. With *Jeanne d'Arc* Dreyer's own view of his work begins to come unstuck. No matter how faithfully he believed that he was obeying an aesthetic of modest realism, *Jeanne d'Arc* and the major films that follow challenge dominant norms of film structure and style in complex and fundamental ways.

There is thus no simple congruence between legend and films. Working with a conservative aesthetic and a production practice modeled on a Romantic conception of the artist, Dreyer created some of the most radically modern films of his period. Not the least interesting aspect of Dreyer for us today hangs upon the ways the films *contradict* the biographical legend.

Early Films: Narrative Form

This and the next chapter cannot minutely analyze Dreyer's early works. If I treat the early films as a group, it is not because I think them unworthy of individual examination: indeed, some such examination of each of them has been a necessary preparation for the generalizations I shall make. My task here is to disengage some common principles of narrative functioning.

The stress falls upon common *principles,* not common *themes.* This means that we cannot reduce the films to those schematic dualities which critics have traditionally located in Dreyer's work: faith versus dogma, freedom versus confinement, female versus male, duty versus love. Such dualities have several drawbacks. They are uncomfortably abstract and static. They deal only with the films' "stories," not their plots; these pairings cannot tell us how causal patterning, story time, and point of view function in Dreyer's work. In other words, such dualities are based upon sheerly thematic categories and cannot explicate the films' formal features. By what principles, we want to know, do Dreyer's early films tell their stories? What systems of narrative logic and time dominate these films, and how do those systems interact?

CLASSICAL HOLLYWOOD NARRATIVE

To answer such questions, we must recall that Dreyer's early career corresponds almost exactly with the maturity of the silent cinema as an art form. The year that he joined Nordisk as a part-time literary aide was also the year of Griffith's *Musketeers of Pig Alley* and *The New York Hat,* Ince's *The Deserter,* Méliès' *A la conquête du pole,* and the first works of Sjöström and Stiller. When Dreyer made his first film in 1918, the silent cinema had already produced the Italian epics, the early Griffith features, the Feuillade serials, the Chaplin and Linder shorts, Benjamin Christensen's *Mysterious X* and *Night of Revenge,* and DeMille's *The Cheat.* Dreyer's 1920s work coincided with the golden age of European national styles and the international supremacy of the Hollywood cinema. By 1926 Hollywood's conception of a film dominated most of the world. Other conceptions were minority options, perceived and judged in relation to American practice. If we construct a model of narrative structure in classical Hollywood filmmaking, salient aspects of Dreyer's early work stand out sharply.

The fundamental premise of the classical model is that the narrative must cohere. All questions asked in the course of the narrative must be answered by the end; all events must take their course; nothing may be introduced that will not contribute to the narrative's denouement. "The perfect photoplay leaves no doubts, offers no explanations, starts nothing it cannot finish."[1] Closure is thus not only the aim but also the measure of a unified narrative. The story depends upon being read as a continuous chain of causes and effects; the last effect of an initial cause defines the end.

What sorts of causes propel the story? Principally, the psychological traits of the characters. One rule book asserts bluntly: "In the motion-picture plot, every situation, every crisis, every progressing step, must arise from some definitely understood motive on the part of the character controlling that particular situation, crisis, or advancing step."[2] The principle of psychological causality subordinates impersonal or apersonal causes (nature, acts of God, the supernatural) to personal causes—characters' feelings, wants, and thoughts. This means that the narrative will have a protagonist and that the narrative will consist of the protagonist's desiring some state of affairs, confronting obstacles to that desire, and, usually, overcoming them. If the protagonist is active, strong, and goal-oriented, then the unity of a causal chain—the satisfaction of desire—will yield the closure of the narrative.

It is essential to note that this model of narrative structure subordinates time and space to the chain of cause and effect. The next chapter will examine how classical cinematic space is constructed; here we can simply note how narrative time acquiesces to the continuity of cause and effect. Causality determines temporal continuity by assuring that the order of events in the plot (the narration we encounter) conforms to the order of events in the story (the presumed sequence of events). "Always make certain," notes one recipe book, "that the following scene is the scene that follows. Perfect continuity insures perfect illusion."[3] As for duration, events of no causal moment will be absent or abbreviated; intervals will be freely skipped in order to stress the critical causal relations. Time is frequently controlled by means of the device of a deadline, whereby duration fuses intelligibly with the chain of cause and effect. The "race for life" or last-minute rescue perfectly exemplifies how causal intelligibility determines duration, as do the endings of films as different as *Seven Chances* and *America.*

Dreyer's proximity to the classical model is easily established. During and after World War I, American films based upon these premises saturated Europe and Scandinavia. In fact, similar principles were already informing European filmmaking, as Urban Gad's book *Filmen* (published in Denmark in 1919) demonstrates. Gad offers virtually a synopsis of the rules for screenplay construction in Hollywood practice. A film consists of "an understandable series of causes and effects" which must cohere and close: "The plot should be as self-contained as a circle."[4] Closure must be achieved not by nature, chance, or fate but by characters' decisions and actions, springing from their "instincts, interests, and goals."[5] The flow of time must be harnessed to the narrative action, and flashbacks must be minimized. As a scriptwriter, Dreyer would have worked, however intuitively, with the protocols dominant in his day. That his own work conforms to the model is, then, hardly startling. But the very fact that by the end of the decade Gad could so easily formulate the principles suggests that already they were becoming canonized. What is interesting, then, is how Dreyer's films inflect and extend the dominant practice.

THE IMPERSONAL CAUSE

Narrative logic demands formal unity. The narrative must cohere. Dreyer's early films, like their Hollywood contemporaries, will not admit the arbitrariness of their unifying operations. Instead, they motivate their pressures toward unity by appeal to conventional signs of closure.

Some of these systems differ in no way from those used in the classical model. Like most narrative films, Dreyer's works utilize not just one closural device but several, thus "overdetermining" their conclusions. For one thing, Dreyer habitually draws upon certain events which traditionally embody *the end*—death, marriage, reunion, silence, night, the closing of a door, the shutting of eyes, etc. *The Stigmatized Ones* ends with the image of the characters sitting in grim silence. *The Bride of Glomdal* closes with a wedding; *Michael, Leaves from Satan's Book,* and *The Parson's Widow* end with the death of a main character. In *The Parson's Widow, The Stigmatized Ones, The Bride of Glomdal,* and *Thou Shalt Honor Thy Wife,* the reunion of a pair of lovers constitutes the conclusion. *The President* includes a reunion, a wedding, and a death in its final minutes. In addition, the ending of the narrative proper may be strengthened by the ending of a frame story, as when the book shuts in *The President* and when Satan finally receives his reward in *Leaves from Satan's Book.* Events in the ending may also explicitly cite the beginning. The final suicide in *The President* occurs in the same locale as the film's first death. The first shot of *The Parson's Widow* irises in from the two lovers gamboling in a natural setting; the last shot repeats the setting, but the lovers are now strained and serious, and we iris *out* on them. The first words of *Michael* are "In the House of the Master"; at the end of the film, the journalist Switt shouts up to Michael's apartment: "Your master is dead!"

In another respect, however, Dreyer's films are quite unusual. In the classical model, impersonal causes (war, famine, social pressures, natural catastrophe) provide a circumstantial background, while *personal* causes—especially character psychology—propel the narrative. In Dreyer's films, *impersonal* causal systems prevail. Not that characters' psychology is absent. Michael betrays Zoret because of infatuation with the princess; in *The Stigmatized Ones,* Sachka rushes to save Hannaliebe because he loves her; and so on. Characters still reflect, decide, and act. But Dreyer inserts psychological causality into a wider frame of causal reference, one that predetermines the characters' actions to an unusual degree. This wider pattern may be internal to the world of the narration. In *The Parson's Widow,* we learn that old Dame Margaret and her first husband reacted to the old parson's widow exactly as Sofren and Mari react to her; in this way, the narrative creates a rhythm over and beyond the characters' individual desires. Or the larger causal force may exist in some narrative

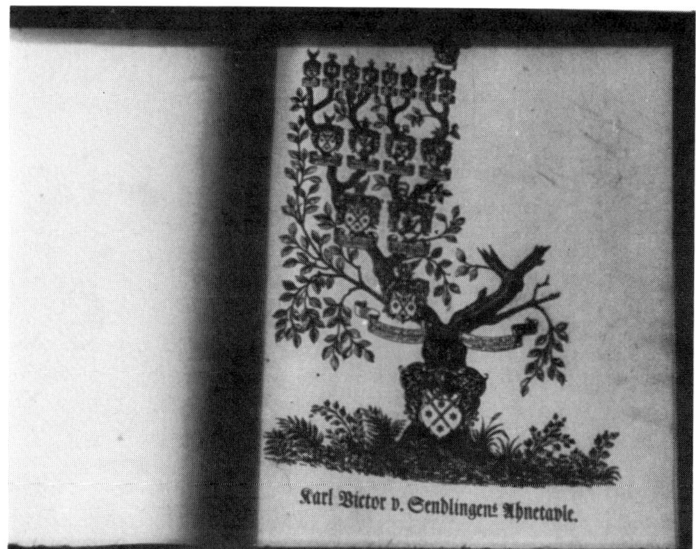

1. *The President.*

frame, as in *The President,* which begins with the image of Viktor's family tree (fig. 1), thus diagramming the force that makes each generation repeat the same mistakes. The film's causal principle may even be identified with a *previous* narrative; *Leaves from Satan's Book* presents four stories, three of which reenact the causal patterns of the first, in a theme-and-variations manner. What exactly is the nature of this wider causal force?

There are, for one thing, impersonal systems identified as primarily social: the law and the family. Dreyer's early films usually represent the social as what constrains and punishes. In *The President,* the law enters quite literally: the protagonist is a judge, forced to try the case of his illegitimate daughter's murder of *her* illegitimate baby. *Leaves from Satan's Book* identifies the law not only with the state but also with the established church. Similarly, in *The Stigmatized Ones,* the socially determined status of the Russian Jews becomes the precondition for the characters' behavior. In a comic variation, *The Parson's Widow* shows community customs forcing the young Sofren to marry old Dame Margaret.

Family ties also provide a social cause to motivate narrative closure. In *Thou Shalt Honor Thy Wife,* Ida's mother and an aunt intervene to make Ida leave the tyrannical Viktor. In three episodes of *Leaves from Satan's Book,* family concern motivates the heroines' decision to accept death. *The President* baldly uses the advice of Karl-Viktor's father ("Never marry a commoner") to determine the son's decisions. In *The Bride of Glomdal,* the chief obstacle to the marriage of Tore and Berit is her father's refusal. Within the world of these narratives, then, both law and family shape a causal force larger than the protagonists' personal wills. Seldom questioned, these causal constraints are assumed to be customary, to be struggled against but not fundamentally changed.

Two other systems join with the forces of law and family to fortify narrative unity in these films. One is nature. Most literally, by simply depicting natural settings, the films anchor the narrative in a culturally stereotyped conception of harmony. Dreyer's early films identify country settings with romance: all three seduction scenes in *The President,* the romance of Sachka and Hannaliebe in *The Stigmatized Ones,* even the one rural shot in *Michael.* The most elaborate instance, *The Bride of Glomdal,* presents Tore's love for Berit as profoundly "natural": Tore, planting and plowing, is associated with the earth, while Berit, often viewed against bright grass or birches, is associated with growing things. When the couple stretch out on the ground or ride through the countryside, Dreyer cuts to long shots that harmonize them with the landscape. Less overtly, Dreyer's early films represent nature as a principle of narrative ordering, an a priori system whereby authority and submission are predetermined and roles are assigned to old and young. Dreyer's early films resemble Ozu's late films in implicitly appealing to a supernature which guides individual destinies into a coherent pattern.

Another pervasive, impersonal cause operates in these narratives, one which I must label Christianity. Like "the rhythm of nature," Christianity offers powerful motivation for narrative closure. Some of these films avow a thoroughgoing dependence upon Christian religiosity; the most obvious instance is *Leaves from Satan's Book,* in which the Jesus story becomes the pattern for subsequent episodes. But more interestingly and more symptomatically, most of the films typically rush Christianity in at only one or two strategic moments. Again and again, the films feel the need to cite Christianity at the *end,* to certify the film's conclusion. Into a purely secular narrative like *Michael,* concerned only with the vaporous world of *fin-de-siècle* artists, Dreyer suddenly inserts religious iconography: de Monthieu dies slumped over a cross, and in the final scene at Zoret's deathbed, the decor's *chinoiserie* is replaced by a crucifix. The close of *The Bride of Glomdal,* a tale in which religion softens the heart of a selfish father, announces that God wants the lovers united. *The Parson's Widow* ends with a cross-shaped iris isolating Sofren and Mari. Although religion is not personified in *Thou Shalt Honor Thy Wife,* the scriptural title locks in, from the outside as it were, a pattern for the film's action and particularly for its ending. Perhaps most astonishing is the end of *The President,* which has relied wholly on causal patterns of social and "natural" sorts. Abruptly, as Karl-Viktor is about to kill himself, Dreyer cuts to a prison guard singing a hymn pleading for Jesus to give us "a blessed death," and the film concludes with the last page of the book proclaiming, "Glory to God in the highest." Nothing could better demonstrate the excessive degree of closure of these early films than their urge to summon up banal religious cues to reinforce an ending already determined by other causal factors.

The presentation of several impersonal causal orders—social, natural, religious—stacked one atop the other and guiding the characters' behavior yields a cinema which pushes classical premises of closure to an extreme. The classical film strives to be unified, but unnoticeably so; by creating an abstract scheme of impersonal causes, the Dreyer film creates a noticeably rigid and inexorable unity. How strong that unity is can be reckoned from the effect of impersonal causality upon the use of narrative parallels, of the protagonist, of story and plot time, and of verbal language in the films.

The viewer infers abstract orders of narrative causality partly because the films put such emphasis on parallel situations. This tactic is a response to a problem that confronted filmmakers during the late 'teens: how does one stretch a narrative to the length of a feature film? Griffith had provided two models: the novelistic tale which crams contrasting characters and subplots into a single epoch *(The Birth of a Nation),* and the film of episodes, built on the comparison of different historical epochs. The feature films of Ince and DeMille conform to the novelistic mode, whereas Tourneur's *Woman,* Christensen's *Häxan,* and Lang's *Der Müde Tod* exemplify the film of episodes. The crucial point is that both modes knit short narratives together by means of explicit parallels in character or situation.

Like his contemporaries, Dreyer relies upon parallelism to solve the problem of filling out a feature-length film. *The President*'s parallel flashbacks motivate the frame story, and shifts among several points of view give *The Stigmatized Ones* and *Michael* a novelistic breadth. Like *Intolerance, Leaves from Satan's Book*—one of the longest silent films made in Denmark—strings together four historical periods on the basis of distinct comparisons. Even the more compressed films, like *The Parson's Widow* and *Thou Shalt Honor Thy Wife,* depend upon parallel construction, in ways that we shall see.

In his early work, Dreyer uses parallel construction in two distinct ways. Often a character or situation will be compared to another, and the film will alternate between one and the other to draw the parallel to our notice. This is often a fairly local effect, as in the welter of motifs that accompany most narrative situations in these early films. In *Thou Shalt Honor Thy Wife,* Ida is compared to her caged bird; in *The Stigmatized Ones,* Hanna is compared to her sister, while the idealistic Sachka is contrasted to the brutish Fejda; in *Michael,* the characters' situations are constantly represented in the art works that surround them. An elaborate use of such static parallels comes in *The Bride of Glomdal,* wherein geography serves to stress the parallels between Tore's and Berit's families. Crossing and recrossing the river between the families' farms becomes a ritualized gesture, like a pause in a line of poetry balancing the two sides of an antithesis; the film's general lack of forward momentum stems largely from its insistence on rigorously matching each situation at Tore's farm with another at Berit's.

More dynamic is a second sort of parallel construction we can call replacement. Here the abstract pattern of a situation is mapped out in one part of the film, and the parallel situations develop sequentially, as a series of variations on the initial action. Instead of shuttling to and fro to compare characters, the film now forces the characters, like figures in a dance, to move from one narrative position to another, filling roles vacated by other characters. Such cyclical replacement constitutes Dreyer's version of the contemporary film of episodes. *The President* initiates this kind of construction. Karl-Viktor's father seduces a working-class woman and has to marry her, to his father's annoyance; Karl-Viktor himself seduces a lower-class woman, but abandons her and disowns their child; the daughter, Victorine, is seduced and cast off by an upper-class man, and she kills their child. The parallels could almost be generated mathematically from the variables (marry/not marry, son/daughter, etc.). At the close, the unhappy wedding of Karl-Viktor's father is superseded by the happy wedding of Victorine. Karl-Viktor's father wrote his will before dying; Karl-Victor composes a farewell note and commits suicide. Such patterns of replacement compel us to infer an overall causal scheme larger than any individual character.

A similar pattern of replacement rules the other early films. In *Once upon a Time,* the finale is built upon deceiving the princess into believing that there is another princess coming to marry another prince; of course, she and the Danish prince are slotted for the marriage roles. *Michael* presents Michael's takeover of Zoret's artistic position in a scene we shall examine in the next chapter. In three other films, the patterns of replacement determine virtually the entire narrative structure, and these need to be examined in a little more detail.

For sheer intricacy, none of the films surpasses the density of parallelisms at work in *Leaves from Satan's Book.* The motivation for the parallelism lies in Satan's power to move across different epochs. God charges Satan with tempting mankind; for every person who does not succumb, a thousand years will be lifted from Satan's sentence. Each of the film's four episodes parallels the others, so that narrative patterns of betrayal are reenacted as variations on a theme. The kernel of the action consists of six phases: (1) Satan disguises himself as a figure of authority; (2) A character emerges as a potential traitor; (3) Satan tempts the character; (4) Some action forces the character to decide; (5) The character decides; (6) The results of the decision stand revealed.

In the first episode, Satan as Pharisee successfully tempts Judas to betray Jesus. The Spanish episode begins to vary the theme. Now we find *two* acts of betrayal, one brief, the other prolonged. First the majordomo informs the Inquisition that Don Gomez has committed heresy. Then Satan, posing as the Grand Inquisitor, persuades the monk Don Fernandez to betray Don Gomez. The monk passes through the six phases of the pattern, and he finally succumbs, raping Isabella before realizing his crimes.

The third episode rings still more changes on the basic action. The six phases are presented when Satan impells the servant Joseph to betray his mistress, Genevieve. After her death, however, Joseph is struck by remorse and tries to save Marie Antoinette's life—in the process *replaying* the stages of temptation, decision, and consequences. In the Finnish segment, two figures are again cast as potential betrayers—the lustful neighbor Rautaniemi, easily swayed by Satan, and the housewife Siri, who stabs herself rather than betray her husband or her country. Significantly, the first woman to occupy the position of potential traitor negates the pattern of betrayal; nevertheless, the overall pattern places her act within a wider frame of reference than sheer character psychology could.

As if this were not enough, within some episodes of *Leaves* there are parallel subplots as well (e.g., in the Finnish episode, the vengeance of Naimi is interlaced with the Siri main plot). Such a dense weave of parallel lines of action enables the viewer to extract an overall pattern of causation in which each character, regardless of epoch, participates.

Cyclical replacement is treated with more variety in two other early films. In *The Parson's Widow,* the basic comparison—the parallel of Dame Margaret (Sofren's legal wife) with Mari (Sofren's betrothed)—is subjected to rich comic variations. Drunk, Sofren sees Dame Margaret as a beautiful young woman (figs. 2–3). Once married and in Dame Margaret's house, Sofren plots to replace Dame Margaret with Mari, but Margaret's old maidservant Gunvor constantly acts as a stalking horse. Sofren sneaks up on Mari at the loom but Gunvor takes her place; Sofren plans to visit Mari that night, but at the last minute Margaret orders Gunvor and Mari to switch beds. The permutations take a somber turn when Sofren, thinking Margaret is in the loft, shifts the ladder to make her fall; it is, of course Mari who falls. When Margaret realizes their love and wills herself to die, the pattern of replacement is completed as Mari, in the very last shot, duplicates Dame Margaret (figs. 4–5).

Thou Shalt Honor Thy Wife is simpler, more stringent. The film compresses the action into two days, separated by a month, and organizes its parallels into two columns: Before and After. The replacements pivot around the changed attitudes of Viktor. Early in the film, Ida goes about her morning chores while Viktor sleeps; later the humbled Viktor does the same chores. When Viktor finds the parlor festooned with dripping laundry hung up to dry, he is enraged; later he does the laundry himself. Before: he orders that the wet baby be taken out; after: he fumblingly changes the baby's diapers. At first he blows smoke at Ida's birds; eventually he waters and feeds them. At one point he strikes his daughter, but later he chases her in a spirit of fun. And near the beginning of the film he orders his son to stand in the corner; but at the end, to get Ida

2. *The Parson's Widow.*

3. *The Parson's Widow.*

4. *The Parson's Widow.*

5. *The President.*

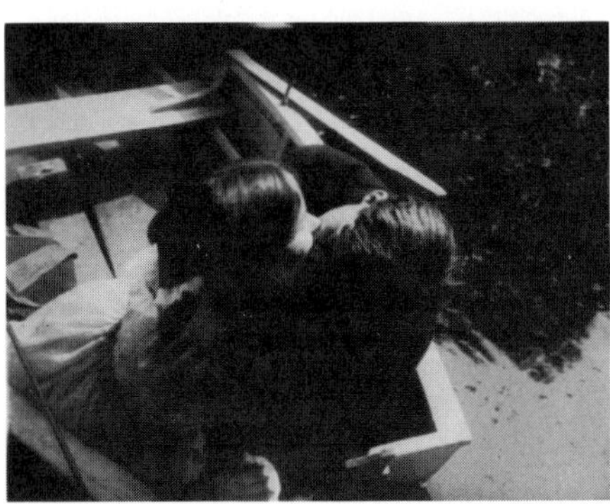
6. *The President.*

7. *The Parson's Widow.*

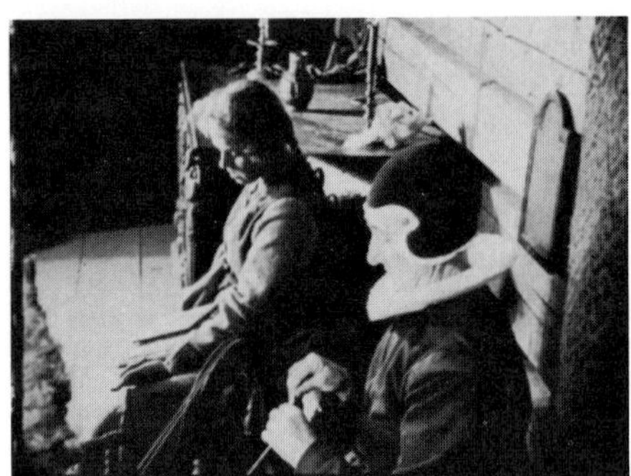
8. *The Parson's Widow.*

back, Viktor must stand in the corner himself. Thus Viktor's transformation is expressed purely through the nuances of parallel situations.

Such narrative parallels claim our attention all the more powerfully because Dreyer has staged, shot, and cut the film with an eye to stressing them. In *The President,* it is not enough that both Karl-Viktor's father and Karl-Viktor himself seduce women; both scenes must take place by a stream and be filmed from angles which stress the water motif (figs. 6–7). Similarly, in *The Parson's Widow,* Mari and Dame Margaret must be constantly likened through name, shot composition, and costume (fig. 8). It is not enough that there be a wedding at the beginning and the ending of *The President;* shot for shot, *mise-en-scène* and editing insist that we compare each scene's interplay among priest, bride, groom, and father (figs. 9–21).

Most important, narrative parallels motivate a stylistic procedure which will rule virtually all of Dreyer's career: alternation. If, in order to exhibit the pervasiveness of an abstract, impersonal causal order, the film must present parallel situations, then it must also find a way to bring these explicitly to our attention. At that particular moment in film history, the most effective means for doing so was crosscutting. Perhaps what Dreyer learned from *The Birth of a Nation* and *Intolerance* was how to use alternating crosscutting not simply as a suspenseful effect but as a

9 10 11 12 13 14 15 16 17

fundamental tool of narrative meaning, a way of foregrounding parallel situations. In *The President*, crosscutting functions to parallel motifs (an old man and young children, a prisoner's escape and a lawyers' banquet). The start of *The Parson's Widow* contrasts Sofren's still-childish impulses (shots of Sofren wandering across a landscape) and the demands of the position he seeks (the tolling churchbell). Throughout the films, the doublings and cyclical replacements are represented through crosscutting. *Michael* constantly juxtaposes shots of the old artist Zoret in his studio with shots of Michael elsewhere, and the film's finale rests upon a powerful crosscutting between Zo-

18

19

20

21

ret's death chamber and Michael lying in the princess's arms. Even in as claustrophobic a film as *Thou Shalt Honor Thy Wife,* Dreyer cannot refrain from cutting away from Ida's chores to Viktor's nervous wanderings through town. In this context, traditional crosscutting for suspense becomes not simply an isolated effect but rather the culmination of the entire film's system of alternations. The penultimate mob slaughter of *The Stigmatized Ones,* the rapids sequence of *The Bride of Glomdal,* and the final "race for life" of *Leaves from Satan's Book* become logical consequences of each film's overall alternating construction. Indeed, with the constant to-and-fro shifts of *The Bride of Glomdal,* we may say that Dreyer masters the technique of extending the principle of parallelism to the editing of almost every sequence. It is a mastery that will profoundly inform the late films.

Impersonal causal systems and pervasive narrative parallels change the status of the protagonist. The goal-orientation of the Hollywood hero springs from a desire to remake circumstances, and the development of this desire, the move toward the goal, constitutes the primary line of action. But since Dreyer's characters are enclosed within larger causal systems, the protagonists become more passive. Things happen to them; they register effects more than they create causes. The persecuted martyrs in *Leaves from Satan's Book,* Hannaliebe and her family in *The Stigmatized Ones,* and the old artist Zoret in *Michael* are defined primarily as victims. In *Once upon a Time,* after the princess flees with the prince to the forest, she must suffer passively in her new role, just as Ida undergoes Viktor's petty torments in *Thou Shalt Honor Thy Wife.* Sofren and Siri, in *The Parson's Widow,* must first submit to social law, then to natural law, and finally to a vaguely Christian law. Sometimes a character will struggle against the causal system in which he/she is enmeshed, as when Viktor and Victorine in *The President* try to break free of social and hereditary forces, but even in their rebellion the characters find themselves replaying fixed patterns. The protagonist's most common actions thus often amount to evasions, concealments, and flight. In such a determined world, the most decisive action is to refuse to define oneself as passive and to choose to die. Hence Dreyer's protagonists may commit suicide (Viktor in *The President,* Siri in *Leaves*), accept martyrdom (Jesus, Marie-Antoinette in *Leaves*), or waste away (Zoret in *Michael*)—all these terminations providing, incidentally, yet another cue for narrative closure. We can, if we like, interpret Dreyer's predilection for martyrs as expressing some personal vision or world-view, but our inquiry leads us to expect that no world-view preexists the films. In shaping his narratives, the formal demands of Dreyer's chosen mode of unity necessitated a specific sort of protagonist.

In *The Parson's Widow,* the characters' passivity is most explicit: it is unnatural for young Sofren to marry elderly Dame Margaret, and so she surrenders her will to live, clearing the way for Sofren's union with Mari. It might be argued that Sofren is goal-oriented—he wants to wed Mari—and that his desire motivates the basic moves of the narrative (circumventing or killing Dame Margaret). It is important, however, that Sofren achieves his goal considerably before the film's end, when Margaret discovers the lovers' plot and blesses their union. The rest of the film —Margaret's death and funeral, the couple's marriage —corrects the earlier portion, situating Sofren's goal-orientation within the larger framework of "naturally necessary" continuity. And at the film's close, Sofren realizes that this larger force has determined even his earlier rebellion. Although goal-oriented protagonists may sometimes appear in these films, then, their behavior remains located within a preordained causal framework.

The demotion of the protagonist as causal agent is only one consequence of Dreyer's overdetermined narrative form. Impersonal causality and narrative parallelism also affect narrative time. Here, as elsewhere, the premises of the dominant classical paradigm are accepted but pushed toward greater visibility. For one thing, Dreyer accepts the notion that plot time should bring out significant causal chains in the story. But the presence of abstract causal orders and the profusion of narrative parallels mold time into particular shapes. Most obviously, the order in which story events are presented can stress parallels. Here Dreyer often deviates from strict adherence to chronological order by providing flashbacks to point out parallels. In *The Stigmatized Ones* and *Michael,* interpolated flashbacks motivate the action in orthodox causal ways. But at least one film, *The President,* creates a symmetrical disposition of flashbacks to compare the three generations of Karl-Viktor's family:

1. Karl-Viktor's father confesses his youthful errors to his son.
    2. Flashback: Karl-Viktor's father and mother meet and marry.
3. Karl-Viktor's father dies.
4. Thirty years later: Karl-Viktor confesses his youthful follies.
    5. Flashback: Karl-Viktor meets and abandons woman.
6. Karl-Viktor concludes story.
7. Court: Victorine reveals her reason for killing her child.
    8. Flashback: a man meets and abandons Victorine.
9. Court: Victorine is bound over for trial.

Bracketed, each flashback stands parallel to the others and impells us to compare them as repetitions of the same abstract causal pattern.

If flashbacks can unify the narrative, so can glimpses of events to come. While strict flashforwards are absent from Dreyer's films, he does signal upcoming information. Within the story action, these clues usually take the form of prophecies, predictions, and foreshadowing motifs. "I will paint Caesar as he was murdered by his foster son Brutus," claims Zoret in *Michael,* thus predicting his protégé's treachery. In *Leaves from Satan's Book,* Don Gomez's dablings in astrology permit him to foretell his own death. In *Thou Shalt Honor Thy Wife,* Mads warns Viktor: "You'll be put in the corner yourself, rely on that." In *Once upon a Time,* the prince looks into an old gnome's magic teakettle and sees a hazy future image of himself and the princess making pottery.

More characteristically, the forecast of things to come issues from outside the world of the story, from a source as impersonal as that of the narrative's causality. Intertitles create an omniscient narrator who can move from present to past ("Now as a thousand years ago the waterfall sings by the old Norwegian village. If we listen closely, it tells a lot about the days gone by"—*The Parson's Widow*) but also from present to future ("Satan's work must still continue"). The book that opens *The President* displays a family tree schematically representing future generations. At the start of *Michael,* an unclaimed voice speaks the film's motto: "At last I can die, for I have known a great love"—the words uttered by the dying Zoret at the film's end. In sum, either through characters' prophecies or through the predictions of an overriding narrative intelligence, the plot's ordering of story events sharpens our awareness of a predetermined causal scheme and its rigorous parallels.

What of the plot's treatment of the duration of story events? The early films pursue two tendencies. Across the film as a whole, the action may stretch over several weeks *(Michael, Thou Shalt Honor Thy Wife, The Bride of Glomdal),* months *(The Parson's Widow, Once upon a Time),* years *(The Stigmatized Ones),* decades *(The President),* or centuries *(Leaves from Satan's Book).* Such extensive timespans permit Dreyer to demonstrate the pervasiveness of the narratives' large-scale causal orders and cyclical replacements. Yet within these considerable durations, Dreyer works upon an opposed principle, that of concentration. Though the overall film may cover a long period of time, it characteristically skips a great deal, so that long intervals separate scenes which occur in a relatively short span. *The President,* for instance, jumps a gap of thirty years between its first and second parts; to preserve the disparity and still retain concentration, the second part also flashes back, this time to scenes which could have been inserted into that gap. Similarly, although *Leaves from Satan's Book* sprawls across centuries, the first episode (Jerusalem) consumes less than a day, and the last episode (Finland) only a few hours. In general, the early Dreyer film prefers to concentrate its scenes within short spans, even if that means omitting long stretches between scenes.

In the light of the temporal concentration in Dreyer's earliest films, we ought to be cautious about measuring his debt to the German *kammerspielfilm.* In the next chapter, we will pursue the spatial implications of *kammerspiel;* for now it is important to consider it as a dramaturgical device. In stage terminology, the *kammerspiel* originally referred to the design of the physical theatre. Max Reinhardt's Little Theatre (opened 1902) and Kammerspiel House (opened 1906) and August Strindberg's Intimate Theatre (opened 1907) were constructed to create a new relationship between audience and stage. "We looked," explains Strindberg, "for a *small* house, because we wanted the voices to be heard in every corner without forcing the actors to shout."[6] In the early 1920s, however, when Carl Mayer sought to create a *kammerspielfilm,* he had in mind not the physical layout of the theatre but features of narrative structure and *mise-en-scène*. Georges Sadoul has pointed out several features of the style—focus on lower-class life, suppression of intertitles, confinement to a very few settings, and a concentration of the action into a short time span.[7] The major *kammerspielfilms* were made at Ufa between 1921 and 1925, and it was during his stay there that Dreyer made *Michael,* considered by many to be a *kammerspielfilm.*[8] Though *Michael* does squeeze its action into somewhat narrower bounds of locale than was typical of Dreyer's previous work, the film violates most of the *kammerspiel* conventions. (It takes place among the rich, the story occupies several weeks, and the film contains many intertitles.) Dreyer's next film, *Thou Shalt Honor Thy Wife,* does stick almost entirely to one apartment and to middle-class life, but it abounds in intertitles and its story action takes a month. It seems, then, that the *kammerspielfilm*'s insistence on the rigid unities of time and place confirmed certain of Dreyer's already existing tendencies to composing a film as a set of compressed scenes; but those scenes could still be separated by considerable time spans.

There is one more way that causal patterns and parallels alter the film's treatment of time. The classical model seeks to map narrative logic onto duration, and a common solution to the problem is to create deadlines. Except for portions of *Leaves from Satan's Book* and *The Stigmatized Ones,* Dreyer has little recourse to precisely defined deadlines. The reason is evident: if the alternating construction is to stress parallels, then those parallels must not be outweighed by the localized causal emphasis created by a deadline. Instead, Dreyer tends to represent time as a duration synchronized with the larger causal structures that rule the film. Three films find arresting images for this impersonal time. *The President* begins with Karl-Viktor's father writing and glancing at a nearby hourglass. At the film's end, after Karl-Viktor has killed himself, Dreyer cuts back to the hourglass, the sands stopped—as if the sands had been sifting for the decades the story consumes. In *Leaves from Satan's Book,* the death of Siri is juxtaposed to the ticking of a clock with a heart-shaped pendulum. The same clock and pendulum start up at the conclusion of *Thou Shalt Honor Thy Wife* to tick out the very title of the film. In all cases, duration is measured as a "closed" rhythm, congruent with that impersonal causal rhythm that rules the entire narrative.

THE BOOK

The classical norms which we have examined imply a mimetic assumption about cinema. As representation—re-presentation, a surrogate taking the place of what is necessarily absent—classical narrative seeks to suggest that it relays events of a noncinematic order. The narration which we see is the retelling of a series of events completed elsewhere than on the screen (in life, in imagination) and the screen is simply the necessary place-holder for the absent events. In his early films, Dreyer accepts this assumption, but he pushes it to the point where it becomes visible *as* an assumption, by means of a device which often dominates his narrative procedures. That device is written language, as word, and particularly as book.

It would be remarkable, of course, if the films had no recourse to language, since the silent cinema habitually made use of both dialogue and expository intertitles. It is worth noticing, however, how well the extra-diegetic voice of the ordinary expository title works within Dreyer's impersonal causal scheme. The sourceless narrator who introduces us to the characters at the beginning of every early Dreyer film helps position them within an overarching intelligibility. Such sourceless intertitles can even anticipate the narrative action, as does that which begins *Michael:* "At last I can die happy, for I have known a great love"; the epigraph hovers over the entire narrative before it is finally spoken by Zoret. In *Jeanne d'Arc* and *Vampyr,* the problem of the source of such utterances comes forward; in the early films, however, the intertitles represent a realm of absent events which become visible only through the written word.

More unusual and more powerful is the use of the symbol of the book to signify the authority behind narrative representation. For centuries the book has stood as an emblem of already completed actions, temporal continuity, logical coherence, and even godly wisdom. "The idea of the book," writes Jacques Derrida, "is the idea of a totality, finite or infinite, of the signifier; this totality of the signifier can only be a totality if a constituted totality of the signified preexists it, watches over its inscriptions and its signs, is independent of it in an ideality."[9] Derived from a founding and preexistent unity, the book constitutes a model of the adequacy of token to truth. Such a tradition affords Dreyer a perfect device for narrative representation.

The book guarantees a teleology of closure, what Barthes calls "a flow of words in the service of an event or idea which 'makes its way' toward its denouement or conclusion."[10] We need look no further than the first shot of Dreyer's first film (fig. 22): hands open a book entitled *"The President,"* and ensuing pages itemize the credits for the film. Not by accident do we call the first portion of a text the "opening." Since it is at this point that our entry is solicited, the opening becomes the most "open" part of the text, the threshold of greatest uncertainty and play. *The President* immediately reduces such play by making the metaphor literal; the book, once opened, must eventually *close.* At the film's end, the book indeed returns. The "closing" of a text—the moment when it shuts us out, when we shut it—is traditionally the moment of finitude, and the narrative action of *The President,* as we have seen, determines its conclusion in causal, parallel, and temporal terms. But the reappearance of the book "overdetermines" the ending, adding a surplus of certainty, sealing our reading as completed. The book is not *in* the film; in effect, it *is* the film, securing for our reading a comprehensive teleology. We shall see the same tendency reiterated in Dreyer's major late films, especially *Vampyr* and *Day of Wrath.*

The device of the book embodies the very principle of impersonal causality that guides Dreyer's narratives. The episodes that we see become only "leaves from Satan's book." A story illustrates a book's precept: "Thou shalt honor thy wife." *Once upon a Time* is both a title and the (stereotyped) beginning of a text. Sometimes the principle of writing will itself be dramatized within the film —the courtroom reporters in *The President,* the scribes in *Leaves*—but these are images of a social book, not to be confused with the transcendent word that encloses the narrative action. (The opposition of the two types of writing will be made most explicit in *Day of Wrath.*)

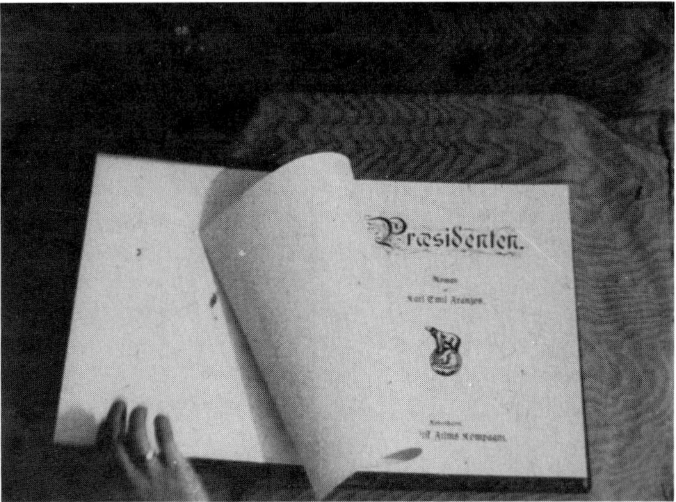

22

That the notion of the omniscient book is a fundamentally Judeo-Christian one is confirmed by that long tradition whereby the founding intelligibility behind the book becomes God, whom monks named the *dictator* ("He who dictates the text"), whom artists in the Christian tradition represented as carrying a book. "In the beginning was the word, and the word was with God." It is to this tradition that we shall look, in the last chapter, for an instance of how ideology informs Dreyer's films. For now it is enough to notice how religion as a causal agent meshes with the use of an overarching written text to define the films' narratives. The abstract causality of Dreyer's early films is absorbed into a sourceless master-text which at once explains the action to us and postpones any rationale for the explanation.

The reliance of a film upon the authority of the word expresses symptomatically the problem of cinema art which we have already seen Dreyer facing. If cinema was to escape its mass-production origins and become true art, he believed, it must base itself upon literature. Dreyer, Nordisk's former literary consultant, turns to the literary text to authorize cinematic unity. We recall his script for *Surrender Arms,* which opens with Berthe von Suttner writing the novel we are about to see on film. The unity of the book, as representation and as high art, helps solve the problem of aesthetic value in a commercial industry.

It is obvious, though, that written language cannot be factored into the cinema without remainder. Film may absorb the word but it necessarily transforms it. Yet the transformation works in favor of Dreyer's narratives, for filming the book permits an impersonal authority to control not only causality but time. The book is written to be temporally linear, but it does offer a margin of play. Michel Butor reminds us that the overall simultaneity of the book (the entire text is in hand "all at once") does yield a certain freedom (to linger, skip, go back, read in reverse, etc.).[11] But filming the book renders it relentlessly successive and thus programs our reading time. Dreyer's filming of the book thus yields an even greater narrative linearity and unity than the book itself could. Paradoxically, through cinematic transformation of the book as representation, certain of Dreyer's early films seek to efface cinema, to see it as a mere vehicle for a rigidly predetermined word.

We can, then, see another way in which Dreyer's early films parade their closure principles. The films' abstract causal patterns raise the issue of a force larger than personal psychology only to settle the question by fiat, by citing a tradition whereby the word is only a shadow and a sourceless author determines what we see. Features of narrative closure are explained by reference to an ahistorical order which we must simply accept. The representational system of language as book situates the viewer as *reader,* a subject unified by the process of following a text. In the early films, the role of written language is thus fairly simple; it provides an authority for the impersonal causality, parallelisms, and temporality informing the narrative. The later films, however, will trouble the device by making the narrative as a whole revolve around a search for the *right* word, the correct reading, the concealed text.

Narrative logic and temporal relations—two major systems operative in cinema—have already helped us to characterize Dreyer's early work, to mark its differences from the norms of the period. We have gone beyond the simple sorts of thematic oppositions mentioned at the outset of this chapter by identifying a principle—the impersonal cause—which oversees the narrative's production—the creation of parallels, of the protagonist, of time, and of written language. All of these structures could, of course, be thematized. The real need, though, is to see them as in process, a set of systems in dynamic interaction.

But one other system claims our attention. What strikes us most upon seeing the early films is their plastic beauty. Shot for shot, the films prior to *Jeanne d'Arc* constitute remarkable explorations of how cinematic space may be constructed, and it is to those explorations that we must now turn.

Early Films: The Construction of Space

Just as the films before *La Passion de Jeanne d'Arc* do not question the premises of narrative and temporal unity, so they do not attack dominant conceptions of the relation of narrative to cinematic space. But just as the early films make visible their own tendencies toward closure, so some qualities of Dreyer's spaces test certain aspects of classical practice. To understand how Dreyer's style works, we need to examine how the classical cinema treats space.

NARRATIVE AND SPACE IN THE CLASSICAL CINEMA

What does it mean to claim that space is motivated by narrative structure? In general, we can assume that in artistic form not all components are equal, that as Yuri Tynianov phrases it, "one factor may be put forward at the expense of the others."[1] The dominant structure motivates, or justifies, other structures. For example, a poetic tradition may require rhyme, and this motivates the poem's choice of words. Boris Tomashevsky has pointed out that a device may be motivated "realistically" (i.e., as verisimilitude), "compositionally" (as functioning in the text's overall construction), or "artistically" (as a device calling attention to itself).[2]

The concept of motivation is indispensible to an examination of Dreyer's early films, since they bear a complex relation to contemporary principles of film form. It is apparent that by 1918 there had arisen a dominant conception of cinematic style as a unified system. In the previous chapter, we saw the problem as that of telling a story, but that is only part of the matter. The most pressing problem became that of telling a story *on film*, mapping a narrative pattern onto cinematic material—the moving image in space and time. The solution to the problem was to define narrative logic as the dominant force, the one which would control filmic time and space. After Ince, the very practice of studio film production tended to treat the story as the preexistent given which was to be transcribed onto film. Cinematic space became a means of manifesting and sustaining narrative.

In this way, the classical narrative cinema can be seen as using realistic and compositional motivation to construct a coherent, homogeneous representation of space. Space is closed and unambiguous, defined by written material (titles) or establishing shots. Space is continuous, even across shot changes, through applications of the "axis of action" or 180° rule, the shot/reverse-shot, the eyeline match, and the match on action. Space is balanced: the *mise-en-scène* centers the single character and arranges groups symmetrically. Since space is chiefly a container for action, it must not be motivated "artistically," as a device calling attention to itself; space must not come forward to distract from the narrative. Decor, for example, is motivated realistically (a bank contains desks and a safe) and compositionally (props are used in the action). Focus and lighting blur and dim backgrounds in medium and close shots of characters; just enough background remains to anchor the figures in space, but the background cannot claim attention in its own right.[3] Filmic space becomes the scene of narrative action, which in the silent cinema means chiefly figure movement. The serial, the slapstick comedy, the Western, the adventure film, the historical epic, even the comedy of manners, all utilize narrative space as a site for moving humans, animals, vehicles, or natural forces. Stasis serves merely to punctuate bodily action. Finally, the space of the classical cinema is anthropomorphic. The human body becomes the measure of all space, and the character funishes a narrative meaning for the displayed body. Thus narrative space relies not only on dynamic physical action but also on the human face, what Pascal Bonitzer has called "the symbol and standard of the unity of the body . . . the summit of a scenographic pyramid."[4] Expressivity of torso and face charges narrative space with human presence. In such ways, camerawork, editing, and *mise-en-scène* work to motivate the subordination of space to narrative logic.

This is not to say that the system always succeeds, for there is always the possibility of inadequate motivation. Cinematic space may struggle to pull away from narrative demands. From the perceiver's point of view, there is not only the story but also flickering snippets of space. Film images rush at us, teeming with perceptual and cognitive ambiguities. The images must be constantly watched over, held in check. To account for such phenomena, Tynianov saw motivation in art as a negative force, tending to smooth out the struggle among factors.[5] In the cinema, Stephen Heath has pointed out that this struggle between containment and dispersion arises from "the relative unspecification of film and the consequent need for a work of specification, for *specification procedures* (modes of signaling actions, of marking them for functional integration) in order as it were to raise the recording of actions to the level of notation from which, in language, the novel begins."[6] The system is torn by a struggle: narrative logic as the dominant element seeks to subordinate space, while space will not always lie peacefully back.[7]

The foregoing outline remains, of course, only a sketch; we shall need to amplify it later. For now, the central point is that Dreyer enters film history just when the classical spatial system is concluding its development. Because of this, that system affords a necessary background for the stylistic work of his early films. I shall not try to exhaust these films' stylistic operations, nor shall I discuss the many ways in which the early films are quite ordinary for their day. I shall indicate only those areas which differ markedly and interestingly from this paradigm. Not that the difference is drastic: in Dreyer's early films, the goal of a unified, narratively comprehensible space is hardly in question. What we find instead is an adherence to general premises coupled with idiosyncratic deviations from specific conventions. Still, the deviations are not simply haphazard: they constitute a unified spatial style. They result from problems of motivation created for the canonized system. Let us take a concrete example.

The story of *The Parson's Widow* is this: In order to get a post in a village church, Sofren has had to marry the previous parson's wife, Dame Margaret. Sofren has smuggled his mistress Mari into the parsonage as his sister, and the young couple have sought to devise ways to circumvent Margaret while they wait for her to die. One day while both Margaret and Mari are in the loft, Sofren boldly shifts the ladder, hoping to hasten the old woman's end. But it is Mari who falls. Our specimen sequence shows Sofren carrying Mari to the house (figs. 1, 2, 4), Dame Margaret following (figs. 3, 5, 6), and Sofren collapsing in grief (figs. 7–15). Stylistically, this passage is highly characteristic of Dreyer's early films.

In its editing, the sequence relies upon narrative motivation. Each cut serves the ongoing action. At the outset of the sequence, crosscutting directly compares Sofren's movements to Dame Margaret's. Apart from the implied temporal simultaneity (while Sofren carries Mari, Margaret follows), there is also the rigorous "rhyming" of locales:

inside the barn (1. Sofren;— 3. Margaret)
outside the house (2. Sofren;— 5. Margaret)
inside the house (4. Sofren;— 6. Margaret)

The rhymes culminate in shot 7, when Sofren and Margaret meet at Mari's bed. Later the image of Sofren in the next room (10) is inserted between images of Margaret beside Mari (9, 11). Here the shot of Sofren's face appears at the moment of maximum tension. When Margaret goes to the doorway (shot 12) she establishes an axis of action between herself and Sofren. Cutting to a reverse angle (on the other side of the doorway), Dreyer gives us a bit of classical shot/reverse-shot, eyeline-match editing (13/14). The eyeline cutting furthers the exchange of glances that leads to the final composition (shot 15), thus maintaining the role of editing in orchestrating the development of the drama.

The *mise-en-scène* of the segment, though, shows a more striking individuality. Where another director would have used several close-ups, Dreyer uses several long shots. Virtually every long shot exhibits what I shall call a *tableau* composition. Like the classical long shot, the tableau moves toward balance and symmetry, but achieves it within a shallower, sparser, more static visual field. In Dreyer's tableau, the background plane tends to stand at a 90° angle to the camera. Characters move left and right or (less often) forward and back, but almost never diagonally. Often a vertical axis bisects the frame (see shots 2, 4, 5, 7, 9). Architecture determines the figures' behavior: most of the compositions are framed by some regular geometrical shape (rectangle or triangle) and room is left around each character, reserved as it were for each one's movements. (The chair awaits Sofren in shot 6, two shots before he will sit in it). The drive toward compositional symmetry in fact overrides the sequence's one deviation from the classical

1 2 3 4 5 6 7 8 9

rules (the reversals of screen direction from shot 5 to shot 6). Details of setting are organized with regard to shape and frame placement, and often attract attention in their own right. (Note the decentered framing which includes jug and plates in shot 4). The characters' costumes are spare—black dress or suit, ruff or tabbed collar—and function as quasi-abstract shapes in the compositions (e.g., shots 7, 13, 14). Lighting, at moments quite flat, is used principally to define the edges of the characters' figures and pick them out slightly from background planes,

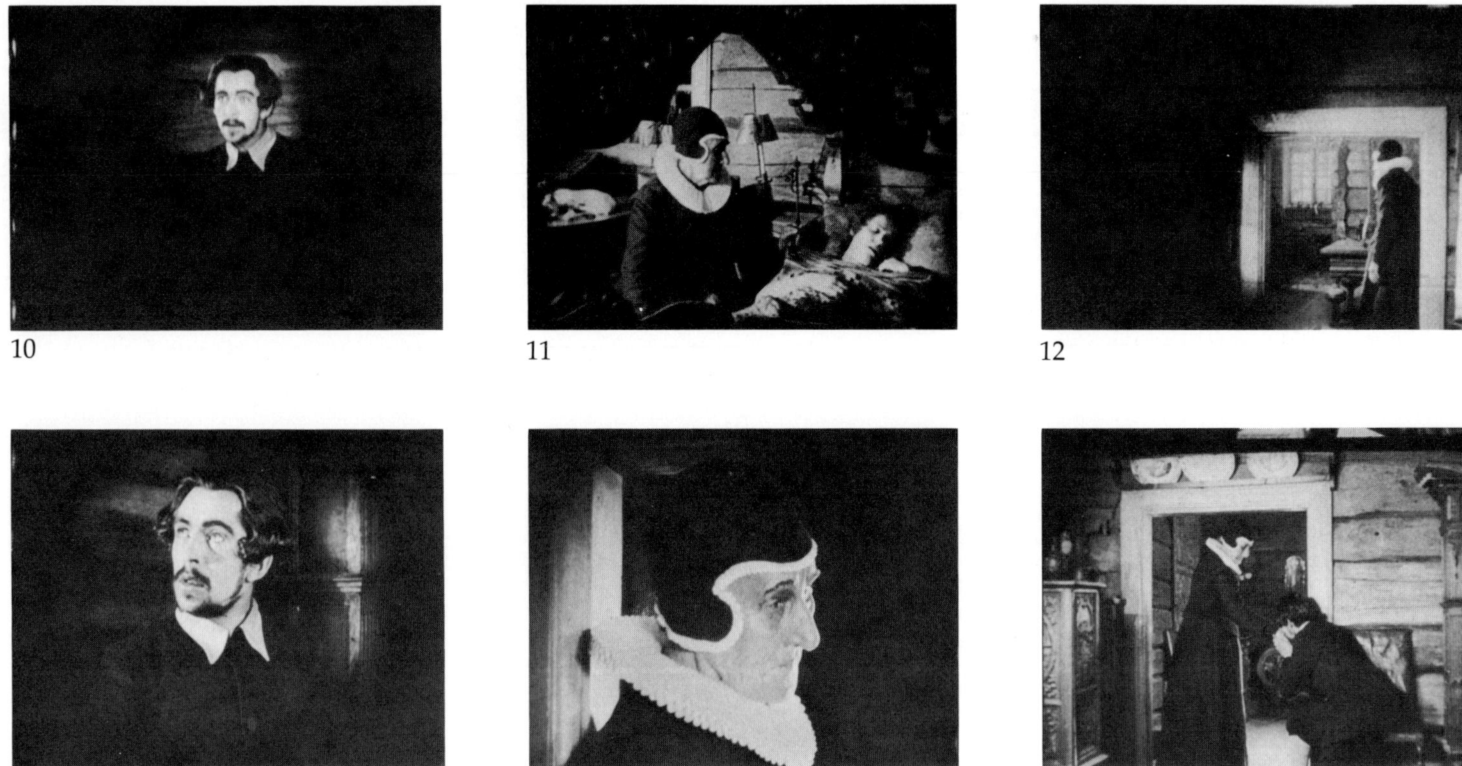

10 11 12

13 14 15

as in the subtle silvering around Dame Margaret (6–8). Throughout the characters' movements are slow and deliberate, their gestures restricted to turning the head, extending a hand, kneeling.

The rigorous tableau quality of the long shots is balanced by the expressivity of the faces. Just as doorway and bedstead frame the bodies, irises frame the heads. In the tenth shot, the abrupt isolation of Sofren's face signals a drastic shift from the tableau space. The climactic moment of the scene, when Dame Margaret reassures him that Mari will live, is underlined by two medium close-ups of the pair (13 and 14). Moreover, the prominent backgrounds now virtually vanish from the facial shots, and lighting functions to render nuances of expression, as in the delicate play on Margaret's features (14).

The interplay of tableau and face does not constitute a merely localized effect, for part of the force of the duality stems from its subtle recurrence throughout the film. We have already seen how *The Parson's Widow* is built largely out of parallelisms; we can now see that our earlier analysis (pp. 29–30) also illustrates the *mise-en-scène* structures of tableau and face. Indeed, one clear-cut parallelism emerges from the sequence just examined. Near the end of the film, Margaret bids farewell to her farm and goes into her house to die. Mari and Sofren follow her inside. Several shots in the sequence stand parallel to ones we have just considered. Compare, say, figures 16–17 with shots 6, 8, and 12, or figure 18 with shot 7: quite exactly, Mari replaces Margaret as housewife and Margaret replaces Mari as victim. In such ways, tableaux and facial expressions may subtly echo each other across a film.

While this sequence from *The Parson's Widow* has great interest of its own, the dialectic of tableau and face exemplifies the spatial dynamics of Dreyer's early films. The motivated relationship of space to narrative has been slightly displaced; the films shift the center of gravity of the classical system. Dreyer accepts the classical premise of closed symmetry within the frame but pushes it even further by an emphasis on the tableau: a long shot which exhibits quite shallow spatial relations, geometrical decor,

16

17

18

and slow figure movement. Thus in Dreyer's hands the *un*noticeable balance of the classical shot becomes *noticeably* rigid, "painterly." The long shot coordinates architecture and figures, the space flattens, and the spare decor stands out in its own right. At the other pole stands the tight facial shot. Just as the tableau derives from the classically symmetrical shot, so the face extends the anthropocentric concerns of the dominant spatial system, but with two differences. First, the face is often radically split from the surrounding tableau space. Second, the relative stasis of the tableau is counterbalanced by situating intense narrative activity in the human face. The drama takes place in and through glances and expressions. By constructing space around these two poles, Dreyer's films modify orthodox filmmaking practice.

THE TABLEAU AND THE FACE

In various ways, Dreyer insisted upon himself as an artist working with chamber space. He prided himself on having designed many of the sets of his early films. In *Thou Shalt Honor Thy Wife*, "For the first time we shot in four-walled sets."[8] His goal for the sound film was "the impression that a film photographer, equipped with camera and microphone, had sneaked unseen into one of the homes in the town just as some kind of drama is taking place within the family. . . . Film must go inside *houses*, inside *homes*."[9] He claimed (incorrectly) the *Michael* was the first *kammerspielfilm*. Anyone who goes through Dreyer's voluminous preparatory notes and clippings is astonished at the man's obsession for details of room decor, from upholstery patterns to the carvings on bannisters. And our segment from *The Parson's Widow* exemplifies how, throughout Dreyer's films, the architecture of the interior dominates.

Dreyer's chambers are not offices, factories, or public meeting halls. In his early films, the social chamber may be a theatre *(Michael)*, a courtroom *(The President)*, a prison *(The President, Leaves from Satan's Book)*, an inn *(The Parson's Widow, Leaves)*, or, most often, a church. The church interior is the site of most social ceremonies, the space within which individuals confront each other through marriages, funerals, and worship. But the most common interior space remains that of the home. All of Dreyer's films are dominated by domestic interiors, from the ghetto apartments of *The Stigmatized Ones*, the palaces and cottages of *Once upon a Time*, and Dame Margaret's house in *The Parson's Widow* to the farmhouses in *The Bride of Glomdal* and the upper-class interiors of *The President*. *Leaves from Satan's Book* pointedly contrasts interiors across four epochs. And of course *Michael* and *Thou Shalt Honor Thy Wife* take place almost completely in domestic space. The latter film's opening titles could stand as an emblem of the *kammerspiel* bent of Dreyer's early work: "In the many streets of the big city, house stands by house. And in the houses, people live in layers, like wild birds who make their nests in the cliff . . . nest over nest. . . . Each morning the thousands of homes in the city wake up, and every single home is a world unto itself. . . ."

In these interiors we find the source of the tableau in Dreyer's early films. As image and structural principle, the tableau is firmly tied to a tradition of what we might call chamber art. Historically, the stylistic premises of this tradition are the perspective discoveries of quattrocento painting and theatre, whereby space is conceived as a cube to be filled by human figures. With the increasing secularization of subject matter in northern baroque painting, chambers housing the Virgin or various saints were replaced by everyday interiors, the bedrooms, parlors, and kitchens of bourgeois homes. Of this chamber tradition the master is undoubtedly Vermeer, who in his short career specialized in depicting middle-class habits and habitats, burghers and ladies at peace among their carpets, lutes, oil paintings, harpsichords, bowls of fruit, jewelry—all bathed in the radiance from an adjacent windowpane.[10]

The bourgeois interior reappears in two modified forms that relate directly to Dreyer's work. In the theatre of the late nineteenth century, the plays of Ibsen and Strindberg initiated a tradition of chamber drama which, although sometimes repugnant to the middle class, finally became accepted as the norm of intimate psychological theatre. This naturalistic theatre, with its conventions of domestic tragedy, dominated the Danish stage of Dreyer's youth until well after World War I. Less well known but even more important for an understanding of Dreyer's film style is the painting style cultivated by the Dane Vilhelm Hammershøi (1864–1916). Indeed, Hammershøi's career might be regarded as the reductio ad absurdum of the entire chamber tradition. Confined indoors nearly all his later life, he spent years painting pictures of chairs, bookcases, sofas, blank windows, open doors, figures quietly reading or discreetly turned from the viewer, even completely empty corridors and parlors. "Room in 25 Bredgade": he applied the same title to several pictures. Although he may seem a minor imitator of Vermeer, his work stands in a more illuminating relation to Dreyer's than does the work of any master. There was a Hammershøi revival in the Danish art world of 1914–18, the years during which Dreyer was learning film craft; Dreyer claimed to admire the painter's work[11]; and one need only glance at Hammershøi's pictures to notice a Dreyerian insistence upon bare white walls, soft-angled lighting, severe surfaces, and the subordination of figure to architecture and decor (fig. 19). There are other pertinent sources, too, such as the stylized stage designs of Max Reinhardt and the tendency of Danish cinema as a whole toward plastic experimentation (fig. 20, from Blom's *Atlantis*).

Yet to frame the problem as one of sources is partly to take the films on their own terms, since Dreyer very probably saw the painterliness of the frame as one way of distinguishing his films from the "film-product" of commercial manufacture. His citation of painting traditions became a habit: Breughel and medieval miniatures in *La Passion de Jeanne d'Arc,* Böchlin in *Vampyr,* the Flemish masters of genre paintings and anatomy lessons in *Day of Wrath,*

19. Vilhelm Hammershøi. *Room in 30 Strandgade* (1901).

Hammershøi and Whistler again in *Ordet* and *Gertrud*. To stop with sources is to accept the films' aspirations to high art without considering how the tableau operates in cinema. Our primary question, framed by the Russian Formalists, is not "Where from?" but "What for?"[12] Hammershøi, *Atlantis,* and the rest are significant because by inserting certain features of the chamber-art tradition into another medium, Dreyer created a specifically cinematic phenomenon, the tableau.

For the tableau image in painting functions very differently in film. Cinema, especially in the 1920s, seems unwilling to tolerate the stillness and fixity of such a composed totality. More than one theorist at the time identified movement as the very essence of the film medium; stasis became "uncinematic." Later Ernest Lindgren writes: "What has the filmmaker to correspond to the color and

20. *Atlantis* (1913). Production still.

visual design of the painter, the solid masses of the sculptor, the musical sounds of the composer? . . . Undoubtedly the answer to that question is movement."[13] The tableau in Dreyer's films puts a certain pressure on such assumptions. When an alien stylistic element (e.g., the tableau) is introduced into a homogeneous system (e.g., narrative logic's control of cinematic space), the consequences are not peaceful. The alien element, if stressed, can deform others. The result for Dreyer's early films has been accurately, if disapprovingly, defined by a writer describing *The President's* "slow, academic, and tedious tempo, its need to dwell upon 'beautiful images' at the expense of movement and psychological ambiguity."[14] More positively, the features which we have observed in the scene from *The Parson's Widow* recur in Dreyer's other films, and an analysis of those recurrences will let us see how the tableau in cinema obeys certain norms but alters others.

The tableau harmonizes the entire frame space as a composed field. Viewed as a long shot, usually from a straight-on angle, the tableau presents a unified, closed organization. There are none of the sinuous interlacings of a von Sternberg composition, nor of the crisscrossed diagonals of an Eisenstein shot. Here horizontals and verticals dominate, curves tend to be regular and symmetrical, and stability of framing prevails. Objects and figures tend to interact across one plane rather than recessionally: the characters in figure 21 are grouped as if in a frieze. Even though the depth is more pronounced in figure 22, it is provided by regularly receding distinct planes, and the depth remains subordinate to the overall symmetry of the architecture.

Within this stable frame space, the figures tend to be caught in carefully poised gestures. "Still lifes with human beings": E. H. Gombrich's description of Vermeer's paintings applies as well to Dreyer's tableaux.[15] Some of Dreyer's early films contain sequences bustling with activity, but the most characteristic scenes have comparatively little physical action. It is remarkable that only twenty-five years after the invention of "the art of movement," a director began systematically to challenge the primacy of motion in that art. When movement does occur within the tableau, it tends to be slight and slow. The figures' displacement is ruled by the economy of the tableau space, as when the characters in *The Bride of Glomdal* slowly cross their rooms or as when the king and princess in *Once upon a Time* move within the geometrical ambit of the court. In the specimen example from *The Parson's Widow,* Sofren's movements are situated within the circumscribed space of the house. Indeed, movement often occurs less for its own sake than as a passage from one tableau to another. In *Leaves from Satan's Book* (fig. 23), Jesus, in pausing in the crook of a tree, becomes part of a pair of curves gently balancing him against the sleeping, statuesque disciples. The empty passage of a barn rests in calm recessional perspective (fig. 24); Dame Margaret enters, and her head balances the heap of clothes on frame right. Most important, as all these instances suggest, the figures are subordinated to the overall design of the shot. The reframings of Hollywood cinema, in their terse acquiescence to the actors' behavior, have no place in Dreyer's work. The tableau remains an architectonic principle, whereby the human figure is defined within a rigorously stable environment.

It may seem, though, that the stable tableau is not a shallow one, for Dreyer's early films often make use of depth cues to mark out several distinct planes. Does this mean, as André Bazin would have it, that we must discard Dreyer the "pictorialist" in favor of Dreyer the "realist" of deep space? No. In the early films, depth paradoxically functions to reaffirm the tableau composition. The fixity and stability of the tableau can be perfectly well supported by deep space as long as the depth generates a closed, harmonious totality and not a more open frame in which the viewer's eye is constantly pulled between various

21. *Leaves from Satan's Book.*

22. *The Parson's Widow.*

23. *Leaves from Satan's Book.*

24. *The Parson's Widow.*

planes. Dreyer seldom relates foreground to background in dynamic ways. Either the movement in the shot is too fleeting, and the composition in depth is unsustained, or there is little movement at all, and the composition in depth freezes into a tableau. In either event, the complexity of dynamic deep space, as found in Renoir or Mizoguchi, is cancelled. Even in *The Stigmatized Ones,* Dreyer's most ambitious attempt at deep space, we can discover a dramatic interaction of characters in depth only if we yank one frame out of context; when the film is projected, the effect is hardly noticeable. Conversely, a depth shot may be held for some time, but only when the movement has died down. While the couple in the distance of figure 25 chat quietly, the nearer figures simply sit, as if decorating the doorway. Renoir's busy foregrounds and Mizoguchi's constantly shifting diagonal axes remain irretrievably different from such compositions as these. Even Dreyer's contemporary Lang, another stylist of an architectural turn, maps his tableaulike shots in more pronounced depth (usually produced by recessional groupings and a riot of busy patterns in costume and decor). In Dreyer's films, the stillness of the tableau demands static planes.

Indeed, a deep-space shot can actively serve the tableau principle. In Dreyer's early films, depth yields middleground shapes which can frame the tableau. Regular, solid shapes, such as doors and arches, become privileged. A doorway may frame a dinner, a father's greeting, or a funeral (figs. 26–28), just as they frame Sofren's and Margaret's movements in *The Parson's Widow* (figs. 4, 6, 8). Similarly, arches may endow the tableau with a massive monumentality (figs. 29–30) or lend a gentler supporting shape (figs. 31, 32, 11). In such ways, depth provides the closed geometrical patterns and groupings which the abstract decor yields in shallower compositions. Again, it is

25. *The Stigmatized Ones.*

26. *Michael.* Production still.

27. *The President.*

28. *The Parson's Widow.*

29. *Once upon a Time.* Production still.

a matter of the subordination of the playing space to the total frame space: the abstracting qualities of the decor no longer spread themselves out alongside the figures but interpose themselves between the viewer and the figures.

Most often, of course, the space is not very deep at all. The tableau seldom frames the chamber obliquely; walls and furniture vary only slightly from a perpendicular axis. Furnishings and other projections from the rear plane are minimized. Actors tend to play close to the wall and interact parallel to it. All the pictorial cues for flatness of space—comparable familiar size of objects, uniformly clear edges and smooth textures, horizontal rather than diagonal lines—operate in Dreyer's tableaux. Another director would have shot a sleeping man (fig. 33) from a three-quarters or head-on view; not only does Dreyer shoot Jakov in profile, but the area which the man inhabits is so shallow that his body projects scarcely further from the wall than the thin shelf behind him. (Compare fig. 34.) In figure 35, virtually the only cue positioning the crockery behind Joseph and Genevieve is the ancient rule that the higher an element is in the composition, the further away it is assumed to be. At times the shallowness of the scenographic space is positively oppressive, as when the kitchen in *The President* becomes a chamber utterly empty at its center, a room with all its furniture shoved up against the rear wall (fig. 36). When Karl-Viktor and his servant go to a wall, he turns and literally opens it (fig. 37), momentarily pushing the shot into depth before the composition again recovers flatness (fig. 38). Here Dreyer bares the device of the tableau as dependent upon a flat space. In such shots as these, the painterly tradition of chamber art shoulders its way into cinema and deforms, by the flatness of *mise-en-scène* and framing, the way interior spaces are normally portrayed.

The implications of the tableau are most strikingly sensed in the functions of decor. As we have already seen, Dreyer tended to view the prominence of decor in his films as an index of psychological realism, whereby rooms conveyed "the occupant's personality."[16] This idea is common in the chamber-art tradition, which is predicated upon the assumption that the home offers a secure site for the construction of the individual as private citizen.[17] No wonder, then, that Dreyer was able to conceive of his domestic settings as psychologically revelatory; chamber art celebrates the domestic interior partly because this space defines the individuality of the inhabitant through decor selected and arranged *by* the inhabitant.

30. *Leaves from Satan's Book.*

31. *The Bride of Glomdal.*

32. *The Parson's Widow.*

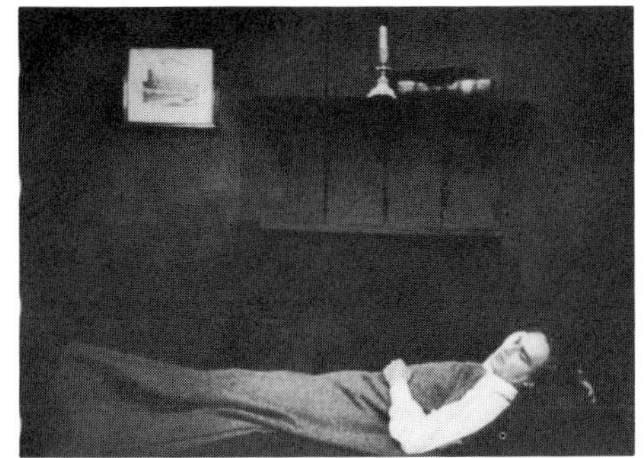
33. *The Stigmatized Ones.*

34. *The Bride of Glomdal.*

35. *Leaves from Satan's Book.*

36. *The President.*

37. *The President.*

38. *The President.*

39. *The Parson's Widow.*

40. *The President.*

41. *The President.*

42. *The Stigmatized Ones.*

43. *The Bride of Glomdal.*

44. *The President.*

45. *The President.*

Yet the settings pose more complex problems than Dreyer seems to have realized. The decor is not obviously "Expressionist," nor even merely expressive; most of the objects do not become props interacting with the performers. How to explain the fact that the settings just *sit* there? At one level, these meticulously familiar objects simply work toward verisimilitude, a touch of reality. At another level, however, the objects' realism cannot justify the emphasis which the frame places upon them. Sofren pauses in the doorway (fig. 39), but the shot gives considerable weight to shelves, clothes on a line, and a bench. The narrative interest of the scene in figure 35 is the relation between Joseph and Genevieve, yet the unusual prominence of the upper area of the shot and the tidily balanced composition stresses how the crockery ranges along each side of a vertical axis. The presiding judge Karl-Viktor (fig. 40) is hardly more important than the still life at his desk. Objects may be sprinkled around the characters, as if floating in a vacuum (fig. 41). Whereas the classical cinema strives to align the space of the action with the total frame space, Dreyer's tableau tends to make the arena of the action only a part—and sometimes the lesser part—of the architectural space of the entire frame. Our attention swerves to objects and furnishings; details of these chambers become as clearly articulated as the figures.

Our attention is not seized capriciously; set design and lighting point out the objects and furnishings of these

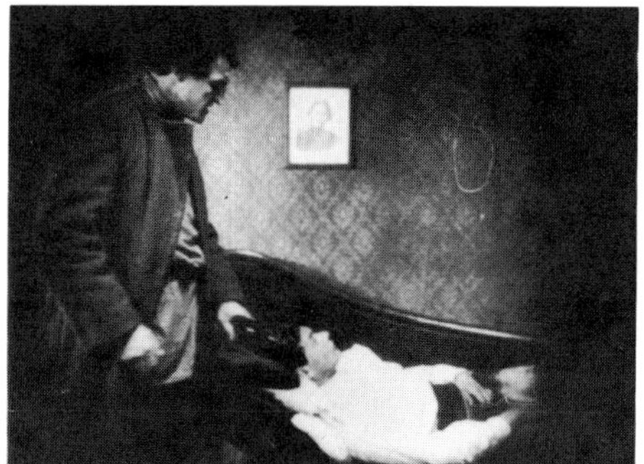
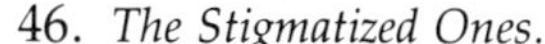
46. *The Stigmatized Ones.*

47. *The Parson's Widow.*

48. *Leaves from Satan's Book.*

chambers. For Josef von Sternberg, as Rudolf Arnheim has put it, "space was most visible when crowded with objects."[18] For Dreyer, as for Vermeer and Hammershøi, space is most visible when empty. Neutral white or black walls, stripped bare, act as the ground for patterns that verge on the starkly geometrical. Outlines may be painted or carved into the wall itself, as in the palmleaf wallpaper in figure 40, the zigzag streak (fig. 42), or the scalloped arch (fig. 43). Or the pattern may emerge from the arrangement of objects upon a neutral wall, an arrangement that will be geometrical either in an elaborately detailed rhythm—e.g., the canopy-shaped sweep of cameos in figure 44—or in simple, severe blocks (fig. 45). In either case, the neutralization and patterning of decor seals the figures within an architecture that fans out on either side of them, perpendicular to our gaze. Dreyer's set design generates a stable ground against which every figure and item of decor stands out.

Moreover, in the tableau shot the lighting is crisp and clear. No patches of Impressionist *flou* blur the volumes and edges of the objects. Speaking of a "linear" style in painting, Heinrich Wölfflin writes: "Seeing by volumes and outlines isolates objects. . . . Interest lies more in the perception of individual material objects as solid, tangible bodies."[19] Dreyer's flattish frontal lighting, supplemented by a slight edge lighting, refuses to privilege figure over settings, so that the surrounding objects stand out through line and tonality. Backgrounds come forward. Even when there are areas of darkness and light, the overall *Gestalt* of the decor is never lost. Lighting can become another abstracting element, either accenting the shallowness of the frame space (fig. 46) or projecting strong geometrical patterns (fig. 47). Even sidelighting will not diffuse the defined shapes: in figure 48, the lines of the arch, the hanging weight, the brazier, and the rack all remain articulated. Dreyer's lighting gives the objects what Wölfflin calls "distinctness plastically felt."[20]

What, then, are the functions of such aggressive decor, settings that so quickly outrun verisimilitude and psychological expressivity? Isolated, patterned to claim our attention, these plates and cameos and lamps and picture frames challenge, quietly and subtly, the primacy of the narrative action. The evocative quality of Dreyer's early films stems in part from the way that decors become narratively peripheral but visually prominent. In one sense, what Yasujiro Ozu does by cutting from narrative action to details of setting, Dreyer does through the arrangement and lighting of decor: the shallow, linearly composed tableaux consistently lure our eye toward apparently significant but ultimately inscrutable objects; we do not grasp their meanings, only their spatial qualities; the objects exist chiefly as shape, sheen, and pattern. Freud pointed out that the German term for the "uncanny" was *unheimlich*, "what does not belong to the *home*."[21] In a comparable way, Dreyer's interiors literally *defamiliarize* domestic space. His use of the chamber-art tradition distorts the norms of classical cinema by abstracting interior space to such a degree that decor is sometimes pulled out of gear with the demands of narrative logic; setting becomes a spectacle in its own right.

Only sometimes, however. Even these decors are not so radical that the tableau refuses the premises of the classical cinema. Instead, the idiosyncratic features of Dreyer's style spring from a play within those premises, and the tableau is one term of that play. The tableau extends features of the dominant style, even defamiliarizing our view of the normal way in which human movement and interior space are represented; at its most radical limit, the tableau emphasizes decor to a point exceeding its narrative functionality. By itself, however, the tableau does not fundamentally question classical principles. It does not repudiate its ultimate dependency upon that chamber art tradition which, in its historical dimension, reaffirms a unified and comfortable conception of the person *at home* in a private space.

The commitment of the tableau to a stable and consistent space is evident from the control of camera movements and editing. Dreyer's early films rely little on camera movement. (Our segment from *The Parson's Widow* is typical in this respect.) When the camera does move, it follows, expectably, a lateral path. A track in or out would destroy the shallow space and burst open the tableau into depth. Instead, Dreyer's commonest camera movements seek to minimize depth cues. The favored movement is the pan shot across fairly static subjects. In *Leaves from Satan's Book,* after a long shot of the Last Supper, Dreyer cuts to a medium shot of disciples at the right of the table and pans slowly left; every man is framed in a balanced tableau composition. In *The President,* pan shots not only fix the tableau but also symmetrically "bookend" one segment. The courtroom scene begins with a pan left from the jurors past the judges to end on Victorine's arrival in court; the scene ends with a pan right from the departing Victorine past the judges to end on an almost vacant jury box.

In addition, the tracking shot has the potential to create tableaux. The most famous camera movement in Dreyer's early work is the symmetrical tracking shot which follows Marie Antoinette to her cell in *Leaves from Satan's Book.* At the beginning of the shot, we have Marie Antoinette and her guards framed in the characteristic doorway. When they turn a sharp 90° and continue their walk parallel to the wall, the camera starts to track laterally with them, still sustaining balanced and fairly shallow compositions. Marie Antoinette enters her cell, again framed, while her jailer stands posed outside: this last composition ends the shot. Moving laterally and at a constant speed, Dreyer's camera will have none of the sudden flights of German or French Impressionist camera movement of the period. Later, in *Vampyr,* Gertrud would begin to use arcing pan and track movements which turn the figures into pieces of sculpture, but the early films simply insist on preserving the flat tableau.

Similarly, Dreyer's editing never systematically violates the conventions of the currently emerging classical style. As our segment from *The Parson's Widow* illustrates, the ordinary methods of crosscutting are perfectly suited to the films' dependence upon narrative parallelisms. In *Leaves from Satan's Book,* every one of the four episodes relies upon crosscutting to signify not only temporal simultaneity but also narrative similarity or contrast. For instance, in the French Revolution episode, while Joseph rises to power among the Jacobins, scenes of Marie Antoinette's life in prison compare her suffering with the harsh revolutionary regime. *The Stigmatized Ones* uses crosscutting to parallel the various strands of action in the climactic pogrom. In *The Bride of Glomdal,* crosscutting matches Berit's father's farm with the farm belonging to Tore's family, and what emerges is the contrast of a barren, selfish life and a fertile, loving one. More importantly, such crosscutting offers no threat to the tableau *mise-en-scène;* when spatially disparate compositions are juxtaposed, the thematic parallels depend in part upon the posed stability of each tableau.

Cutting *into* the scene creates more difficulties. Since the tableau depends upon a large-scale spatial balance, a cut may seem an interruption, a breakdown in the tableau's unity. In his career as a whole, Dreyer found two solutions to the problem. The later solution was that of the long take, which permits the sustaining of the tableau—better, the gradual development of the shot through several tableaux. In chapter five we shall see the consequences of this. Dreyer's earlier solution to the problem was to cut within the scene. The rupture of the tableau demands something of equal value and narrative importance to replace it. The lack implicit in the cut could be a significant moment of disruption, surpassing the tableau and questioning certain premises of the classical paradigm; but instead Dreyer turns to the answer codified by classical cinema: the human face.

We have long known that the faces in Dreyer's films have a special quality. In writings and conversations he was explicit—"Everything human is expressed in the face. . . . The face is the mirror of the soul"—and he asserted his admiration for the lifelikeness of the faces in Griffith's films.[22] For Jean Sémolué, Dreyer resembles Rembrandt in his dedication to facial expressions: "The spiritual quest and the aesthetic quest which constitute the films of Dreyer meet in the human face."[23] For others,

Dreyer's faces offer the actor an occasion for virtuosity, as one reviewer of *Leaves from Satan's Book* suggested when he wrote that Clara Pontopiddan "in a close-up cried out in dumb anguish all her suffering and pain."[24] Yet these remarks leave the real problems untouched, for in one sense there is nothing unusual about Dreyer's faces. Almost every director of narrative films privileges the face over other parts of the body. (Only Eisenstein and the early Ozu seem fascinated by palms, knees, ankles, elbows, shoulders, and buttocks.) We again strike the classical groundings of Dreyer's early work: just as his chamber tableaux extend rather than contradict dominant principles of spatial construction, so his use of faces extends the anthropocentric concerns of the classical style. So wherein lies the particularity of Dreyer's method?

The answer, as usual, lies in function. What do these faces *do* within the spatial systems of the early films? First, the faces gain an unusual salience through their opposition to the tableau. Close-up or medium close-up, these shots shift us into another realm. Whereas in the tableau, the figure is subordinated to architecture, light, and decor, in the facial shots the human countenance triumphs over the surroundings. If the tableau continues the tradition of chamber art, the facial shot returns to the tradition of portraiture. As a genre, the portrait becomes prominent with the secularization of the late Renaissance, and developed into the sort of painting which sought to represent the uniqueness of the individual, to express definitively a singular personality.[25] In the northern countries especially, middle-class aspirations and self-definitions find their representation in portraiture. Dreyer's aesthetic, as we have seen, explicitly appeals to the portrait tradition in its psychological conception of acting and the close-up. Thus the significance which we intuitively assign to Dreyer's close-ups has its source in a systematic principle whereby tableau and face constitute dialectical poles informed by two artistic traditions.

Apart from the systematic quality of Dreyer's reliance on the face, a second function stands out. The tableau seldom permits the dynamic representation of emotional qualities; its abstraction creates an ascetic geometry. As a result, Dreyer's actors restrict their bodily movements and postures to a few simple types: sitting, standing, kneeling, hesitating in a doorway, trudging down a road or street. Yet Dreyer's aesthetic demanded the projection of the most intimate human qualities, the "soul." In order not to relinquish the tableau, Dreyer turns the face into a theatre. The face reveals what the tableau cannot. For dynamic movement in long shot is substituted dynamic movement in close-up; an acrobatic range of bodily behavior (such as we find in Keaton or Eisenstein) is replaced by a subtly nuanced range of facial behavior.

Whereas backgrounds and surroundings stand out in the tableau, the facial shot minimizes or eliminates them. Sometimes a geometrical pattern or decor will be retained in order to accompany the facial expression, as when steps behind Judas form a simple alternation of dark and light bars (fig. 49) or when the student is framed alongside severe verticals (fig. 50). Or geometrical patterns in the surroundings may be superimposed upon the face, emphasizing decor within the scene but not minimizing the facial expression (as in figs. 51 and 52). Most often, though, Dreyer clips the face free of its surroundings and creates a physiognomic space distinct from the tableau. In the early films, this operation is performed by costumes (often neutral) and by yet another geometrical device, the iris. The face will be picked out as a circle of brightness in a darkened frame; in some films, every face is isolated in an iris. Thus the close-up has the same harmonious frame balance as the tableau. As a result of the iris, surroundings fall back (fig. 53) or vanish altogether (fig. 54). In *Michael* and *Thou Shalt Honor Thy Wife,* the iris is used to cut the face drastically free of surrounding space; entire scenes will be played with characters' specific locations remaining somewhat indeterminate. Thus lighting helps not only by sculpting the contours and textures of the face (figs. 55–56) but also by consigning backgrounds to a flat grey or black. We are left with what Béla Balázs calls "microphysiognomy." Dreyer's use of faces constitutes an extreme application of that strategy which Balázs saw as characteristic of silent cinema as a whole:

> *Facing an isolated face takes us out of space, our consciousness of space is cut out and we find ourselves in another dimension: that of physiognomy. . . . The facial expression on a face* [sic] *is complete and comprehensible in itself and therefore we need not think of it as existing in space and time.*[26]

Such spiritualization of the human expression through "despatialization" lies at the root of Dreyer's reduction or elimination of decor in the facial close-up.

The use of facial close-ups is by no means fixed throughout the course of a film; indeed, one of their virtues

49. *Leaves from Satan's Book.*

50. *The Parson's Widow.*

51. *The Parson's Widow.*

52. *Leaves from Satan's Book.*

53. *The Stigmatized Ones.*

54. *Thou Shalt Honor Thy Wife.*

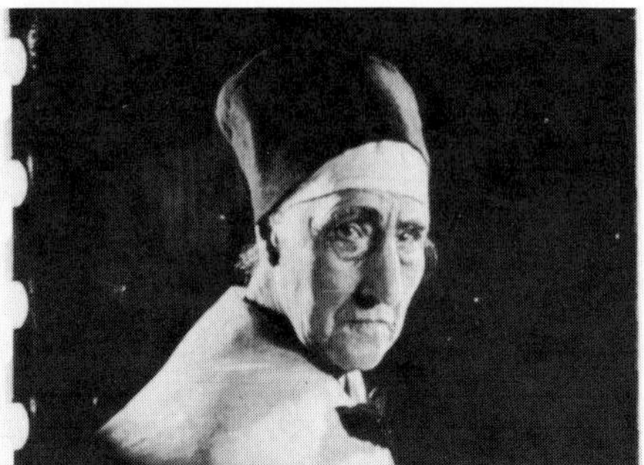

55. *The Parson's Widow.*

56. *Leaves from Satan's Book.*

is that they permit subtly varied shifts. Such a shift takes place in the most famous example of facial expression in Dreyer's early films: the death of Siri in *Leaves from Satan's Book.* Jean Sémolué points out that Siri's death scene "announces *La Passion de Jeanne d'Arc* less because of the theme of sacrifice and renunciation than because of the pitiless and striking way in which the advance of death across the heroine's face is filmed."[27] Much of the force of Siri's death emerges from the minute stripping-down of her close-ups. At an earlier point in the scene, the closest shot of Siri has shown her framed in the characteristic iris, but the geometrical pattern of the blanket remains as a trace of background decor (fig. 57). The decor is all but gone later when she prays, and again an iris isolates her face and hands (fig. 58). At the final moment, when she stabs herself, Siri's face hovers, tightly framed in an iris; the sur-

57. *Leaves from Satan's Book.*

58. *Leaves from Satan's Book.*

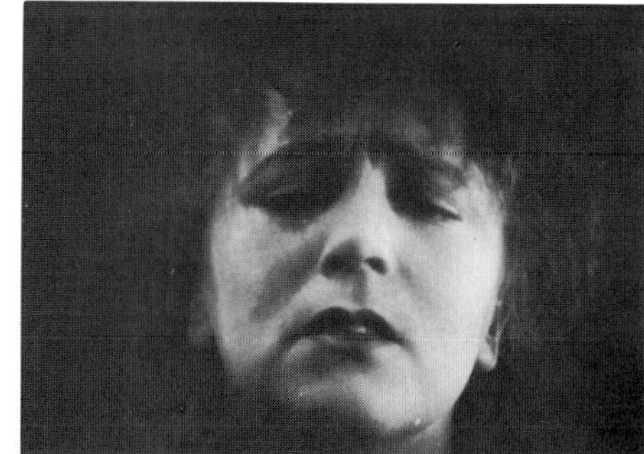
59. *Leaves from Satan's Book.*

60. *Leaves from Satan's Book.*

61. *Leaves from Satan's Book.*

62. *The President.*

63. *The President.*

64. *The Stigmatized Ones.*

65. *The Stigmatized Ones.*

rounding space has sunk out of sight (fig. 59). As Balázs says of *Jeanne d'Arc,* "We move in the spiritual dimension of facial expression alone."[28]

The goal of heightening the face modifies other film techniques. Dreyer's editing within a locale, as we have already seen, conforms to the classical paradigm. The exchange of glances favored by eyeline-match cutting is used in Dreyer's early films as a way of channeling expressive energies from face to face. In our segment from *The Parson's Widow* we have already seen how the eyeline-matched close-ups isolate Sofren's and Dame Margaret's emotional states. But Dreyer again extends the classical Hollywood paradigm: when the expressive qualities of each face become so stressed, the juxtaposition of faces in an eyeline match becomes a way of savoring the sheer material differences among faces. For example, in *Leaves from Satan's*

Book, eyeline matches link Jesus' disciples to the Roman soldiers (figs. 60–61). The narrative point—that the disciples await the soldiers' assault—is accompanied by the sharp facial contrasts between the bearded Jews and the fierce Romans. In *The President,* the style's attention to faces is overtly bared when the protagonist is honored at a banquet. A plaque of his profile is unveiled, and the scene's editing contrasts the inscribed face (fig. 62) with the faces of the onlookers (fig. 63).

In *The Stigmatized Ones,* there is a beautiful example of the spatial linkage and facial contrasts afforded by Dreyer's eyeline cutting. Jakov, the lawyer who has converted from Judaism to Christianity, invites a prostitute into his private clubroom. As he bends over her, she looks up (fig. 64). Her face is isolated by the shot scale, the dimming of background, and the iris framing. And although Jakov is bending to touch her, his face is isolated in a similar close-up (fig. 65). The stringent elimination of all but facial detail foregrounds a new element: the cross dangling from a chain round Jakov's neck, reminding us of his conversion to Christianity. The cut simultaneously presents the couple's intimacy and the contrast between the woman's apprehensiveness and Jakov's desire. In such ways, Dreyer is able to utilize eyeline cutting not only to convey narrative relations but also to compare faces as faces.

Eyeline-match editing remains, of course, a localized effect, lasting for no more than a few shots. Sooner or later the scene must return to the tableau. (Only in *La Passion de Jeanne d'Arc* will Dreyer seek to build almost an entire film out of images of faces unmediated by any reminders of scenographic space.) In the early films, the control of tableaux through crosscutting and continuity matching alternates with moments of intensified action in facial close-ups. As the segment from *The Parson's Widow* shows, the spatial development of the scene follows its narrative trajectory. Tableaux: Sofren brings Mari into the house, and Dame Margaret follows. Facial shots: Sofren and Dame Margaret exchange glances. Tableau: Sofren kneels before the old woman. The tableaux/close-ups/tableau pattern of space maps itself snugly onto the crisis/climax/resolution pattern of the classical narrative scene. (For another example, the reader is invited to turn back to chapter three to examine the parallel wedding scenes in *The President,* wherein fixed tableaux bookend a culminating series of facial shots.)

Despite the importance of the tableau, however, these examples make it clear the Dreyer aims finally to reveal the face. The tableau leads us toward that revelation, situating the face but not absolutely confining it. Then it modulates out, reestablishing the total scenography. The climax of the scene turns upon the face. In explaining his disregard of historical accuracy in the Finnish decors in *Leaves from Satan's Book,* Dreyer writes: "If, when you saw the film, you did not feel most touched by the soulful and heart-gripping acting of Clara Wieth . . . then you were first and foremost too preoccupied with the external setting, which is so unimportant for the artistic point of the story."[29] Severed from the torso, squeezed free of architectural space, the face becomes the final sign of the human.

If we recall Dreyer's dislike of the melodramatic cinema of his day, his style makes sense as a solution to the problem he had defined. The pictorial rigor of the tableau and the intimacy of the face break from a cinema of melodramatic "sensations." Dynamic movement, absent from the long shot, surfaces as facial movement in close-up; a locale that is architectural, shallow, and sparse is contrasted with an intimate, full physiognomic space. At one pole, the tradition of chamber art deforms the normal means of representing place in the cinema; at the other pole, the tradition of portraiture deforms cinematic conventions of bodily space. And just as decor sometimes deflects our attention from narrative causality, so does the concentration upon the nuances of facial expression often propel the face into the realm of the pure sign. But the decor remains diegetic, the face remains a *narrative* sign. On the whole, the spatial system balances, and the polarity does not pull representation apart. By a basic adherence to narrative intelligibility, Dreyer's early style, however unique, remains an extension of the spatial principles of the classical cinema.

MICHAEL

If one were to choose a single one of Dreyer's early works to exemplify the tableau/face principles, the film would have to be *Michael,* for it lays bare the formal dialectic of the early films. *Michael* takes as its subject the world of artists, and its milieu creates a new level of interplay between tableaux and faces.

Michael is the protégé of the artist Zoret. When Michael meets Princess Zamikow, they are attracted to each other and eventually become lovers. Michael moves into his own studio and, to support himself in splendor, sells gifts from Zoret and even starts stealing from him. Paralleling Zoret's increasing misery is a subplot tracing Herr Adelsskjold's reaction to his wife's affair with the Duc de Monthieu. After the public acclaims his last painting, Zoret wastes away and dies while Michael lolls in Princess Zamikow's arms.

It is evident that *Michael* displays the parallelisms, replacements, and prophecies that are characteristic of Dreyer's narrative structure. A dinner-table conversation about a death's head causes Zoret to declare that he will paint Caesar, and that Michael will model for Brutus. In the same way, the customary replacement of age by youth is presented here as the flagging of Zoret's artistic inspiration: he stops abruptly while painting the princess's portrait, the iris framing him moves right to frame Michael, and Michael feverishly completes the portrait. Subsequently, Michael begins to ape Zoret's tastes in clothes and wine, sets himself up in an apartment furnished from Zoret's studio, and proceeds to court the princess in terms precisely parallel to the way his master had treated her.

The world of artists, would-be artists, dealers, models, and critics not only furnishes the subject of the narrative but also complicates narrative logic and visual representation. Most generally, the milieu motivates the comparison of people to *objets d'art* and projects the characters' erotic drives onto their aesthetic tastes. Characters meet or seduce or possess one another through art works. The homosexual relation between Michael and Zoret is initiated by Michael's seeking the master's opinion of his sketches. The subplot involving Alice Adelsskjold, her husband, and her lover de Monthieu manifests itself in a similar way: presented with a statuette of a woman's torso, both Alice and de Monthieu handle it tensely before he sets it down and caresses it (fig. 66). In a series of doublings, the three major characters are reflected in different art works: Zoret paints a portrait of the princess, depicts Michael as *The Seeker,* and portrays himself as an abandoned old man. Again, as Zoret is showing the princess his work, he points out a painting of embracing lovers; the princess and Michael exchange glances. After the princess has left, Zoret pledges his devotion to Michael by giving him *The Seeker.* In the early sections of the film, then, the art works represent a network of erotic relationships.

Yet all relations are eventually subsumed by religion. The subplot replaces the erotic instance by a religious one when Alice's lover dies beside a cross. Similarly, once

66

Michael rejects Zoret, the film uses art objects to transform Zoret's doomed passion for his protégé into a spiritual state. Worldly wealth no longer matters to Zoret: he pays for Michael's prodigality, he allows the boy to rob him of the English glasses and the Algerian sketches. After Michael refuses to model for him, Zoret is seen for the first time framed alongside a blank canvas, a statue of a youth, and a crucifix on the wall. As Michael steals more and more from Zoret to furnish his own studio, the culmination of this spirituality is the Job-like image Zoret paints of himself: a bent old man on an island rock. A visitor declares: "That is a man who has lost everything!" In a counterbalancing movement, the transfer of art works shifts Zoret's sheerly carnal qualities onto the Michael–Princess Zamikow affair (its chief emblems being the painting of a naked Michael and the portrait of the princess). Thus the shot of Zoret alone beside the figure of the old man clinches the replacement of erotic passion by a pure, holy suffering. The art works operate to sustain the spiritualization of Zoret's love.

Visual representation is also affected by making *Michael*'s milieu that of life among the artists. Expectably, the tableau/face dialectic is present, now exaggerated by the use of middle-ground lighting and the ubiquitous iris. The facilities of Ufa are put to use in the film's construction of tableau compositions. Low lighting and extreme long shots render Zoret's atelier ("the house of the master") as a *fin-de-siècle* museum. The iris not only adds its abstracting qualities to Dreyer's *mise-en-scène* but also eliminates the overall lines of the building itself: whereas Lang would emphasize the structure of the architecture, Dreyer stresses the enclosure of art objects within the huge rooms.

The chiaroscuro lighting and the iris have a different effect on the faces in the film. Disembodied heads swim starkly out of the enveloping darkness. The usual tendency of the Dreyer facial shot to sever expression from tableau is exacerbated here by the iris and the lighting: entire scenes are played in close-ups. For example, when the art dealer calls on Zoret, iris and lighting isolate each man's face, shorn of body and background. Later, the princess asks Michael for money, and although they are inches apart, they might as well be on different planets, so absolutely do the shots make each face free-floating (figs. 67–68). In such *mise-en-scène,* we glimpse the face beginning to override the tableau—a tendency of which *La Passion de Jeanne d'Arc* marks the culmination.

Specific to this film, though, is the way in which the art-world milieu pushes the tableau/face dialect to complex extremes. The setting realistically motivates the presence of art objects, but specific aspects bare the device of the tableau/face dialectic. The Russian Formalist term "baring the device" has been explained by Kristin Thompson as "a specific type of artistic motivation which foregrounds the artistic structure to which the device belongs. . . . The moment of foregrounding calls attention to related elements that form a structure in other parts of the film."[30] In *Michael,* the *objets d'art* bare the tableau/face structure. Art works enter the film as *images* of tableaux or *images* of faces, and each can relate in turn to the characters as arranged in a tableau or to the characters' faces. The result is an exhaustive survey of the combinatory possibilities which anticipates the "anthological" systems at work in *Ordet* and *Gertrud*.

1. *Art work as face/characters in tableau.* In Zoret's studio stands an enormous statue of a head (fig. 69). This head, looming above or behind the action in extreme longshot, not only troubles shot scale but also juxtaposes a colossal face to the tableaux formed by the figures.
2. *Art work as tableau/characters in tableau.* Throughout *Michael,* paintings which depict tableau-compositions are juxtaposed with characters themselves participating in the tableau which is the shot. When Zoret shows the princess his collection, one cut makes Michael's posture of holding the lamp mirror the gesture of the seeker in Zoret's painting (figs. 70–71). Later in the film, Michael moves into his own apartment, taking many of Zoret's works with him and mimicking Zoret's style of living. A tableau within a tableau centers Michael silhouetted in the foreground while one of the stolen pictures stands in the distance. In the same apartment, the pettiness of Michael's ambition is rendered by *his* version of Zoret's monumental paintings and classical statu-

67

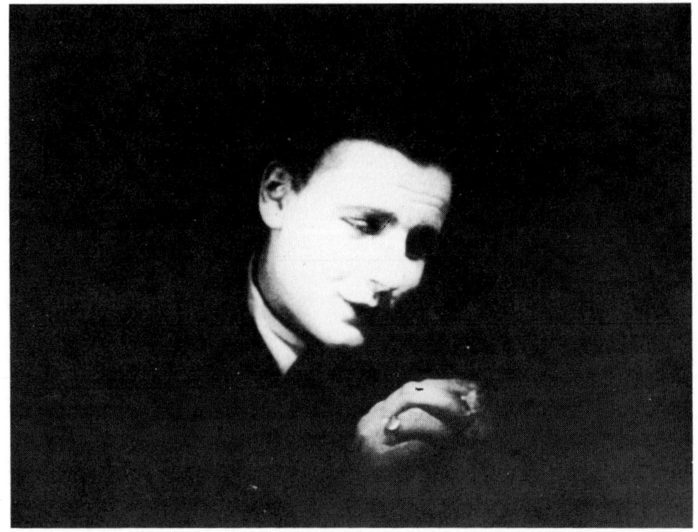

68

69

70

71

72

73

74

75

76

ary: miniatures, statuettes, and dolls. In his loneliness, Zoret begins painting his triptych. We see him at work on the central panel, and the shot compares him and his majordomo to the broken old man in the painting (fig. 72). The doubling of tableaux within the shot asserts itself most subtly when Zoret is showing the princess his collection. Zoret has been asking Michael to shine a lamp this way and that, but for one moment Michael usurps the role of *metteur-en-scène* and constructs his own tableau. Instead of illuminating a picture, Michael swings the lamp onto the princess herself, flashing the light sensuously over her sparkling dress as if she were another *objet d'art* (fig. 73).

3. *Art work as tableau/character's faces.* We have already seen

this juxtaposition at work at the moment when, as Zoret points out the painting of an embracing couple, the princess and Michael exchange looks. Later, at the ballet, the stage performance is constantly juxtaposed with tight framings of the faces of the onlookers. But the most striking relation of a tableau image to a character's face occurs during the public reception of Zoret's triptych. He is proclaimed "the artist of sadness" and is awarded an oakleaf-cluster medallion (reiterating the earlier Caesar allusion). As he stands before the center panel, the crowd offers a toast to him. "Where is Michael?" he asks, and the shot pairs his face with the figure of the abandoned old man (fig. 74).

4. *Art work as face/character's faces.* The ways in which these three combinations lay bare the tableau/face device should suggest the degree to which *Michael* overtly concerns itself with issues of visual representation. One particular scene stands out for its insistence upon the face. While painting a portrait of the princess, Zoret is unable to render the eyes, and he passes the brush to Michael. The camera tracks in to Michael as he looks right. A mask and iris frame the princess's eyes (fig. 75); the camera tracks in to Michael's eyes (fig. 76). After a close-up of the princess, the camera tracks back from Michael as he paints quickly. Zoret approves: "Yes! Now they are her eyes!"

It is not just that the painting's expression becomes the pivot for the erotic rapture of the princess and Michael. The scene also dramatizes the status of facial representation in Dreyer's aesthetic: the problem of manifesting the soul in the face. The princess's beauty appears, unnameable but visible to all, in her face. The artist's task is to copy this expressive essence faithfully. But Zoret's failure indicates that technical skill will not guarantee an accurate copy. The artist must feel the mysterious expressive force; only the infatuated Michael can capture the eyes. Fairly obviously, the scene is a scale model of Dreyer's anthropocentric aesthetic of film: the actor must reveal the soul. Thus the portrait scene posits cinematic representation as unproblematic: the sensitive artist (Michael, Dreyer) can adequately represent unnameable essences in an easy passage from sign to meaning. What the book does for narrative representation—in creating a final authority for the causation of events—the face does for spatial representation: in the face resides a meaning which art can expose but not explain.

77

Michael's final sequence, in recapitulating the narrative parallels, also resolves the tableau/face interplay. Crosscutting intersperses shots of Michael's bedroom with Zoret's death chamber. Michael's cluttered apartment is dominated by *The Seeker,* that effigy of himself, a token of Zoret's love and Michael's narcissicism (fig. 77). Zoret's room, in contrast, stands bare, as if Michael had stripped it to the walls. All that remains are a crucifix and a panel painting of youths—the last *objets d'art* in Zoret's milieu, their juxtaposition continuing to spiritualize Zoret's erotic passion (fig. 78). As Zoret dies, Dreyer matches tableau to tableau, boldly exposing the homosexual/heterosexual parallel: Switt at Zoret's bedside, the princess in bed with Michael; the manservant clasping Zoret's hand under the cross (fig. 79), the princess caressing Michael beneath an erotic painting (fig. 80).

But this deliberate procession of tableaux remains most Dreyerian in the way in which it modulates into climactic facial shots. In close-up, Zoret bequeathes all his possessions to Michael. At daybreak, when Switt shouts up from the courtyard that the master is dead, the princess rushes from the window to the suffocating gloom of the boudoir and rocks Michael like a baby: "Be calm, be quiet, I am with you." The final shot of the film cuts short the spatial dialec-

78. Production still.

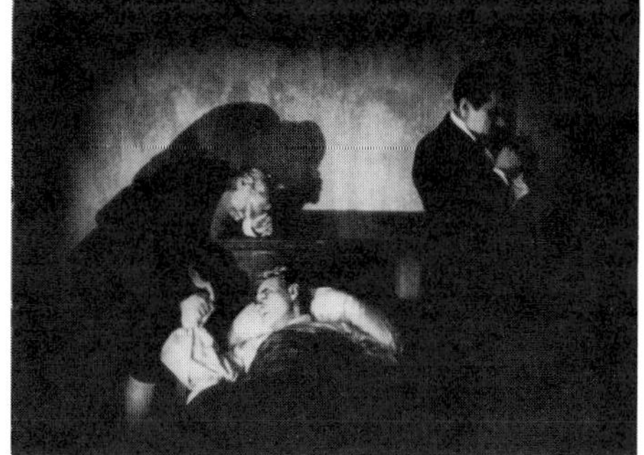

79

80

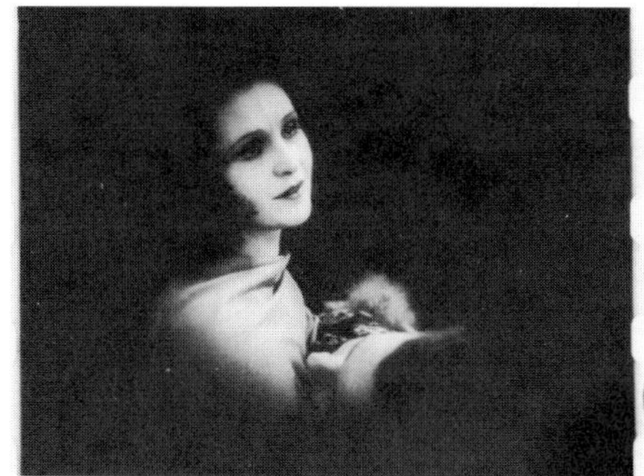

81

tic by prying itself loose from the tableau and closing on the ambiguity of the woman's face shining in the darkness (fig. 81). The image anticipates the perpetual repetition of Jeanne d'Arc's expressions and the facial medium close-ups that conclude *Day of Wrath* and *Ordet*. In *Michael,* as in Dreyer's early work as a whole, the tableau remains secondary to the spatial and narrative authority of the soulfully expressive human face.

Problematic Unities

La Passion de Jeanne d'Arc, Vampyr, Day of Wrath, Ordet, Gertrud. By consensus, these are the major works of Dreyer's career, and each bristles with problems for audience and critic. Our attention is claimed by the bizarre stylistic gymnastics of *Jeanne d'Arc,* the confusions and obscurities of *Vampyr,* the mysteries of motivation in *Day of Wrath,* the miracle of *Ordet,* the stasis of *Gertrud.* The films face us with several choices. We might, as recent critics have, turn away, back to the early films, which are more conventionally attractive: thus, Ebbe Neergaard can find *Thou Shalt Honor Thy Wife* Dreyer's masterpiece, while others have proposed *The Parson's Widow* and *Michael* as equal in interest to *Day of Wrath* and *Jeanne d'Arc.*[1] While I admire the early films, I think that to emphasize them is to postpone the much more formidable problems of aesthetic perception posed by the later films.

Two critics have already suggested that Dreyer's late films might be viewed as problematic in this strong sense. Using a religious frame of reference, Paul Schrader has proposed that there exists a "transcendental" film style which moves from a recording of the "everyday" through "disparity" into stasis. Ozu's films, Schrader explains, posit the banality of the ordinary, then show a discrepancy between the everyday and the eternal, and conclude by surpassing the discrepancy, not resolving it but transcending it.[2] In Schrader's view, Dreyer's films lack unity and balance and thus remain stuck in disparity, never achieving a transcendent stasis.

> *His films, like the Gothic cathedral, are an unstable equilibrium of world-affirming and world-denying impulses. His films are rife with contradictions: in* Day of Wrath *a stylized martyrdom is followed by pastoral scenes of summer romance; in* Ordet *the ultimate invocation of the Holy is followed by a sensuous kiss. Joan of Arc's struggle to both stay alive and "be with God" is a typically Gothic struggle.*[3]

Though Schrader correctly emphasizes internal frictions, he speaks only of disjunctions in tone from scene to scene—not particularly radical or disturbing contradictions. Jean-Louis Comolli points out somewhat more pervasive problems. After enumerating several terms under which Dreyer's films could be comfortably categorized ("classics," "masterworks of senility," "Nordic works," "a cinema of the soul," "modernism"), Comolli notices a split between the old-fashioned subjects and themes of the films and the disturbing formal and stylistic qualities:

> *Is it not precisely in this space (this chasm) which seems to separate everything on the side of subjects, themes, meanings . . . from everything that is on the side of forms and, finally, of cinema—is it not in this* abnormal *gap that the initial problem lies?*[4]

Comolli's formulation seems to me correct. He goes on, however, to propose an ultimate fusion of style and theme, whereby the film's examination of repressive social power is conducted by "a formal mechanism just as repressive and rigorously governed, just as implacable in its functioning, as those of the orders and societies denounced."[5] This is to return to a theory of unity, and an excessively simple one. What we must keep before us is the gap—not in order to resolve it but to specify the conditions of its existence.[6]

The critic can pinpoint an art work's problematic aspects by, first of all, reactivating those problems for the perceiver. Although it defamiliarizes the world, art itself can become excessively familiar. So the critic can usefully *re*-defamiliarize art, as Victor Shklovsky indicates: "The aim of the formalist method is not to explain the work, but to call attention to it, to restore that 'orientation toward form' which is characteristic of a work of art."[7] The critic can also suggest the *functions* of the work's strangeness, the role which that strangeness plays in the overall dynamics of the text. This entails that the critical rummaging for meanings will no longer be rewarded by the triumphant discovery of unity but rather that the critic will be ready to recognize as well the forces of disunity, loss, fault, rupture.

I cannot here detail all the ways in which problems crop up in Dreyer's later work. That is the business of the following chapters. I shall, however, suggest my general argument. The late films present, first of all, important changes in principles of narrative logic. In the early films, an abstract and impersonal causality rules the narrative, and this force frequently manifests itself in a written text. Such a text becomes a guide to the intelligibility of the film; it represents the very *principle* of intelligibility of the film. The process resembles Frederick Jameson's description of Flaubert; Dreyer's films, too, contain "thematizations of the peculiar type of reading demanded by the text . . . allegories of the reading process itself, or in other words figures for the very attempt to interpret and to assign textual meanings."[8] But in the late films, this impersonal causality becomes more uncertain; often the late films proceed without a sense of clear causal relations. The cause is, however, never completely absent; the movement of the film is to locate that cause, to name and master it. In these films, protagonists and viewer search for the correct reading of the narrative action. And some such reading is always provisionally found, thanks to the preeminence of the written text. In the late works, the film posits an absent cause only to install a book, a scroll, a word, a poem as the answer.

Or, rather, the sign of an *unnameable* answer, for our reading is complicated by the way the late films play among various representational systems. Through a circuit of interferences, each discovered text cannot be simply taken as truth, for it is qualified by the representational medium of cinema. The records of Jeanne's trial—her words—remain in the film, visible in the intertitles; but the *images* have an entirely different representational status. In *Vampyr,* the authority of the nondiegetic voice of the intertitles clashes with the perceptual uncertainty of the film's space and time. The scroll that opens *Day of Wrath* posits a representational harmony of word, image, and music that is fractured in the course of the film. In *Ordet,* the problem is that of representing the Holy in a consistent manner: man and child must resolve the narrative through miracle, but neither must be deified. *Gertrud* identifies the absent cause with the very source of representation itself, and we find that there is no transcendent source, only a perpetual shuttling from one representation to another, from word to gesture to picture to film image. In all these films, a final authority for representation is constantly displaced; our ultimate reference point is nothing more (nor less) than the structure of the film itself. Setting speech, writing, music, static images, and moving images against one another in dynamic interaction, each film challenges our ordinary reading of representations.

The lingering problems of narrative logic are no greater than other, insistent difficulties. If we examine the late films against the background of the classical model from 1928–64, we find frictions *among* the various systems of the text. Dreyer's early films constructed time and space generally within the premises of the Hollywood style. But by disrupting the relation of narrative logic to cinematic time and space, the five major late films assault two premises of the classical norms: that movies must move, and that they must move continuously. The research and tinkering that devised the motion picture itself was guided by the purpose of analyzing and synthesizing movement. We have already seen how Dreyer's early tableau style contested, intermittently, this kinetic conception of cinema. The contest appears, sharpened, in the three later films *(Day of Wrath, Ordet,* and *Gertrud).* In *Jeanne d'Arc* and *Vampyr,* however, what is at stake is whether film must move continuously, especially continuously in space. In attacking these two premises, Dreyer's major late films challenge the dominant style. Whatever the narrative problems, the films utilize principles of space and time in ways which open that gap of which Comolli speaks.

In the classical cinema, space must be continuous. If causality is the armature of narrative logic, continuity is the armature of spatial structure. By means of the "continuity system" of editing, the sequentiality of viewing time and the ambiguities of isolated images can be harnessed to a larger principle of coherence. The flow from shot to shot seeks to cancel dispersion and to guide the viewer's perception to salient narrative material. No theme is reiterated more in the recipe books than the marriage of unnoticed continuity cutting and story intelligibility. 1928: To avoid irritating the viewer's eye, "there must be a gradation in the use of camera distances."[9] 1937: "The story should flow smoothly and the various shots should match perfectly. . . . The moment the audience is aware of the various cuts and devices used, the story will suffer."[10] 1953: "The decisive consideration at the juncture of any two shots must be that the transition should be motivated by dramatic necessity. A continuity of shots in which each cut is dramatically useful will often appear smooth even if the mechanical matching is imperfect."[11]

It is within the context of the dominance of the continuity style that we can locate the difficulties of *Jeanne d'Arc* and *Vampyr.* In *Jeanne d'Arc,* Dreyer's unprecedented insistence upon the face cracks open the narrative space of classical cinema. We know that the tableau/face dialectic makes the role of editing problematic; even in our sequence from *The Parson's Widow,* preserving parallel tableaux meant violating screen direction. With *Jeanne d'Arc,* the promotion of the face radically deemphasizes the tableau, thereby deforming spatial relations. The blank decor, the paucity and illegibility of establishing shots, the steeply canted camera angles, the intrusive titles, the camera movements, the mismatched eyelines and shot/reverse shots—all these function positively to foreground the faces, but they also destroy a coherent narrative space. In *Jeanne d'Arc* virtually every contemporary principle of editing and camera movement is assaulted. The result is a contradictory, eccentric space that Dreyer's characteristic narrative principles struggle to contain. Here is why *Jeanne d'Arc* is both the fulfillment of Dreyer's aesthetic and the first major challenge to it. Dreyer reiterated that *Jeanne d'Arc* owed nothing to the avant-garde; he was simply filming the soul as revealed in the face.[12] But in pushing this (rather conservative) aim to its limit, he splintered the homogeneous space of his early films and, in ways which we shall examine in the next chapter, challenged the reigning norms of spatial continuity.

Vampyr, while not as single-minded as *Jeanne d'Arc,* also troubles spatial coherence. The most allusive and enigmatic of Dreyer's films, *Vampyr* depends so heavily upon the device of the absent cause that narrative logic's ability to hold the film together is considerably weakened. In this film, the face is more adjusted to the tableau, but the tableau now presents problems. *Mise-en-scène* and camerawork present an uncertain, perceptually inconsistent space. Along with violations of conventional continuity editing, *Vampyr* initiates an inquiry into how camera movement can produce spatial and temporal discontinuity. While the contemporary American cinema was stressing the power of camera movement to orient the viewer and unify the scenographic space, *Vampyr* exploits the camera's power to disorient and disunify through a rigorous control of offscreen space and a systematic breakdown of subjective point of view. In *Jeanne d'Arc* and *Vampyr,* then, Dreyer's narrative principles seek to hold in check explorations of space which emphasize stylistic contradiction. These two films define a phase of Dreyer's work in which a refusal of the dominant style results in new, disruptive systems.

Returning to the concerns of Dreyer's early films, the last three major works of his career again pose the question of whether movies must move. In *Day of Wrath, Ordet,* and *Gertrud,* the tableau principle returns in force. But *mise-en-scène* and camera movement transform the early works' conception of chamber space, pushing the principle of the early tableaux to a new level. Instead of the missing fourth wall of customary filmmaking, the late films utilize a "circular" *mise-en-scène* that insists on the total enclosure of the interior. The system was already at work in *Thou Shalt Honor Thy Wife,* in which we may see one side of the family parlor or its exact opposite. For example, in one scene Viktor makes a complete circuit of the parlor; he starts out alongside Mads (fig. 1), proceeds to the table (fig. 2), then goes to fetch his pipe (fig. 3), and eventually returns to Mads, whom we now see from the rear (fig. 4). It is also possible to see some of the spatial discontinuities of *Jeanne d'Arc* and *Vampyr* as proceeding from a willingness to film from all vantage points within the chamber.

It is in the later films that the transformation of the tableau's chamber space into a "circular" *mise-en-scène* is most minutely worked out. A room will be divided into various zones, and the characters, with insistent thoroughness, interact at various times in different zones. Meanwhile, the camera shows constantly varied aspects of those zones. Sometimes a camera movement uses up a room in a single sequence (e.g., Laurentius' death chamber in *Day of Wrath,* the banquet lounge in *Gertrud*), but more often the film reveals, scene by scene, fresh areas of a familiar place. In *Day of Wrath,* one side of Absalon's sacristy is shown during his interrogation of Herlofs Marte, the other side only in the film's last sequence. The first sequence of *Ordet* presents one side of Inger's and Mikkel's bedroom, the last scene reveals the other side. In *Gertrud,* we see one aspect of Erland Jansson's apartment when Gertrud comes to sing for him, another aspect when she comes to sleep with him. And at the center of each of these films stands a parlor which, in the course of the narrative,

1

2

3

4

is exposed in its entirety through the shifting of characters from zone to zone: the rectory in *Day of Wrath,* the farmhouse parlor in *Ordet,* the Kannings' sitting room in *Gertrud*—spaces obsessively traversed and worked over, each sequence revealing new facets.

Circular *mise-en-scène* alters the role of the mobile camera. Camera movement (fragmentary and often illegible in *Jeanne d'Arc*) becomes in *Vampyr* a major device, as the tracking camera stakes out its own areas of attention within and against the narrative, forging inconsistent spatial relations. The late films continue to utilize camera movements which answer very well to Dreyer's architectural, four-walled conception of chamber space. As Jean Narboni points out: "Very often a sequence will seem to consist only of lateral movements of the camera; then, recomposing it in memory, we will discover that imperceptibly it made a complete circuit of the decor, the film constituting in a way the horizontal projection of a very large circle."[13] In three later films, characters moving from zone to zone are followed by a camera which creates unusual spatial relations.

One particular application stands out. Henning Bendtsen, Dreyer's cinematographer on *Ordet* and *Gertrud,* has recounted how *Day of Wrath* introduced a new movement effect into Danish cinema. Since Danish studios did not yet possess crab dollies, Dreyer asked that the dolly tracks be laid parallel to the set, but in curves.[14] To this laterally arcing camera trajectory, Dreyer added a panning movement *against* the direction of the tracking movement. The camera thus moves with the figures, but it also arcs and pans around them, revealing new room areas in the background. In this way, camera movements can eventually expose the entire room while keeping the figures relatively constant in angle and aspect. Such arc-and-pan movements occur in *Vampyr,* especially when Gray explores the doctor's lair, but the movements come to prominence in *Day of Wrath. Ordet* uses the arc-and-pan effect in almost every mobile shot, and the device appears frequently in *Gertrud.* Such an unusual camera movement reveals an urge to unfold a complete chamber space, to multiply tableaux by systematically unfurling the entire decor around the figures, squeezing a figure's line of movement into a point of rotation. Thanks to the circular staging of the action and the circular camera movements, one function of the tableau—the stressing of space as a system in its own right—reappears in *Day of Wrath, Ordet,* and *Gertrud.*

The later films' return to a tableau principle is supported by another strategy. What is at stake in these late films is an attenuation of rhythm and a sparseness of cinematic devices achieved through a theatricalization of cinema. Certain obvious habits mark these late films as "stagey." Toward the end of his career, Dreyer's sources for his films shifted decisively: of the eight films before *Jeanne d'Arc,* only two were based on plays, but all four films after *Vampyr* were. Indeed, it is hard to name a director of Dreyer's importance who has relied as heavily upon stage sources. Furthermore, Dreyer sought his casts from the elite of stage actors. Virtually every major actor in these three late films came from either the Royal Theatre or the New Theatre, the two most celebrated troupes in Copenhagen. There is also the *kammerspiel* quality of these later works, which reduce the action to a few plot lines carefully circumscribed in locale and time—what Phillippe Parrain calls the "centripetal" principle of Dreyer's works.[15] There are, though, less apparent reasons for considering these late films as operating within a "theatrical" conception of cinema.

In the silent cinema, as Ben Brewster has pointed out, the issue was not one of narrative versus non-narrative cinema, but of "true cinema" versus "theatrical cinema."[16] Thanks to the polemical work of Soviet, French and German film theorists, theatrical cinema was rejected as "canned theatre." The screenwriter Frances Marion stresses the necessity of drastically altering a stage piece when transferring it to film: "The film version of a stage play . . . usually requires a much greater variety in its setting. The proportions of the action and the dialogue often are the reverse of those required by the screen, and many of the ideas conveyed through lines in the play must be given in new acting scenes in the film version."[17] Ernest Lindgren claims: "In many cases directors who lean considerably on the work of their actors and who realize their need to feel their acting in its entirety seek to help them by avoiding frequent breaks in the action and by shooting whole scenes with very few cuts. This is simply to throw away the characteristic virtues of the film medium and to revive all the demerits of the photographed play."[18] Normal practice dictates that a play must be opened up, transposed into shots which can be cut together, scored in the key of cinema, so to speak. Now we have already seen how, with the coming of sound, Dreyer proposed an aesthetic based in large part upon the theatre. ("The psychological play is probably to be considered the most suitable material."[19]) Although Dreyer foresaw that a play would change in becoming a film, what is remarkable about his late films is how little they concede to cinema as normally understood. Dreyer uses theatrical sources to force a rupture between cinematic style and narrative structure. He refuses to ventilate the play and insists on lengthy dialogue sequences. The play text thus becomes a pretext for the slowing of the film's rhythm and consequently the slowing of the viewer's "reading rate." An old-fashioned reliance upon theatre becomes, in the context of contemporary film practice, a significant archaism, virtually a refusal *to be cinema.* "In order to become perceptible," Boris Tomashevsky observes, "a device must either be very old or very novel."[20] *Jeanne d'Arc* and *Vampyr* choose to be novel; the last three films choose to be antiquated.

In the last period, the long take becomes fundamental to Dreyer's "theatricalized" style. As we saw in chapter four, the problem with constructing scenes around tableaux is that of breaking the tableau by a cut. The long take, allied with lateral and arcking camera movements, permits Dreyer to *maintain* the tableau, to unfold it as a series of gradual transformations. *Vampyr* initiates that stately and deliberate tempo which most viewers associate with the Dreyer shot, and *Day of Wrath* pushes toward shots that are quite lengthy for its day (almost fifteen seconds on the average). But not until *Ordet* (average shot, one minute) and *Gertrud* (average shot, ninety seconds) does Dreyer begin to play entire scenes in one or two lengthy takes. Several consequences follow from prolonging the tableau in this way.

Art "defamiliarizes," but what gets defamiliarized? Ordinary perceptual reality, for one thing. Just as important, though, art works defamiliarize *other* art works. This is most evident in parody, when the parody jolts our perception of the model. In fact, the power of art to defamiliarize other works is responsible for the complex and often negative relation that holds between a work and its sources, traditions, and background sets. What happens in Dreyer's two last films is that the classical style of filmmaking is itself explicitly cited and defamiliarized. Against the background of the *plan-séquence,* figures of orthodox film practice can emerge nakedly, disturbingly. In *Ordet* and *Gertrud,* conventional editing devices (e.g., shot/reverse shots) are employed in a glancing, fragmentary manner. An orthodox camera movement is so rare in these films that when it does appear it has a quoted quality, enveloped as it is within a shot of whose duration we are always acutely and minutely aware. The power of the long take to *cite* certain stylistic figures will be exploited in *Ordet* and *Gertrud* to create vast and systematic compilations of devices of the classical cinematic style.

The theatricality of the late films, their slowing of figure and camera movement, of cutting rate—of cinematic rhythm in general—make time as well as space relatively independent of narrative demands. Dreyer's writings record a concern with a film's rhythm, but he tended to see a slow rhythm as both narratively motivated (suitable for serious, psychological subjects) and visually satisfying ("The eye with pleasure follows gliding camera movements. . . ."[21]). But their particular use of the long take renders his films, however fascinating, narratively difficult. Their assault upon norms of movement and tempo makes them simply resist normal assimilation. For the kinesthetic qualities of the dominant cinema these films substitute stasis or near stasis; conventional notions of *moving* pictures are questioned not through discontinuity but through a continuity so attenuated that the narrative action is stretched thin, punctured by what Reisz and Millar would call "dramatically meaningless intervals."[22] Must the characters in *Day of Wrath* and *Ordet* cross and recross their rooms quite so often, and so slowly? Must *Gertrud* and her men keep changing seats so many times? Dreyer was preternaturally sensitive to the implacable momentum of cinema, the fact that in watching a film you can't stop and go back. "While the spectator in a theatre always has time and place to 'recollect,' i.e., to compare the remarks that are being said with previously mentioned information, the film is flickering away so quickly on the screen that the audience cannot possibly manage to pay attention to lines that don't have present value" (1933).[23] "In theatre, there is always time to reflect, but not so on film" (1954).[24] The very weakness of the comparison (the tempo of a theatre performance obviously need not offer any time for reflection) suggests Dreyer's fear of the inexorable forward drive of cinema. An impulse to slow cinema down is already implicit in the static tableaux of the early films. In the later films, theatricalization resists narrative legibility, and as a result impedes ordinary film consumption. Through style, the later works seek to break the momentum of a film, to freeze it into a series of tableaux, to find within the very art of movement a pervasive stasis, to withhold the smoothly flowing pleasure of film viewing.

Both of the strategies I have sketched out—discontinuity in *Jeanne d'Arc* and *Vampyr*, theatricalization in the later films—are related, in complicated ways, to Dreyer's historical situation. From aesthetic principles of psychological realism and serene classicism, there sprang films which contested those very concepts. Refusing ties to any avant-garde, Dreyer claimed only to be representing universal, even mystical truths. But our analysis will show that within the context defined by dominant film practice, these late films display powerful avant-garde tendencies. These contradictory, illegible films result from a career spent outside major production. In ways that Dreyer's biographical legend did not anticipate, the refusal to "manufacture" films emerges from the very style and structure of these works. Through discontinuity and theatricalization, the films become unconsumable as "film products."

The gesture of negation performed by these five films must not, however, be seen as the only one. Although each film threatens to burst apart, there are always forces struggling to keep it unified. Discontinuity and theatricalization are contained, to various degrees, by the principles of narrative unity consistent throughout Dreyer's career. The overdetermined narrative, basing itself on symmetrical parallels and replacements and on the hidden text, seeks to hold the forces of negation in check.

So it is not just that, as in every work of art, there are formal disparities. In Dreyer's late films, the gap between almost stultifying narrative structures and semi-independent spatio-temporal systems is simply too great. Here is one source of the disparity identified by Comolli—the radical tendencies of the films' style collide with highly traditional forces for order. *Day of Wrath,* the central film in the series, comes closest to balancing unity and rupture; but in *Jeanne d'Arc* and *Vampyr* on the one hand and in *Ordet* and *Gertrud* on the other, stylistic forces are at such odds with narrative structure that the films are always hovering on the brink of unintelligibility or vacuity.

It is this process, the dynamic interaction of narrative structure and cinematic representation—sometimes in harmony, often in friction—that the next five chapters trace. In every instance, the strategy will be to go straight for the *problems* posed by the film, not in an attempt to solve them or dispel them but in order to see them as a result of the film's dynamic activity.

La Passion de Jeanne d'Arc

The need for criticism to recognize disunity and contradiction is nowhere more pressing than in the analysis of *La Passion de Jeanne d'Arc.* The polite respect accorded a classic must not obscure the plain fact of the film's strangeness. It is one of the most bizarre, perceptually difficult films ever made, no less disruptive and challenging than the early films of Eisenstein or Ozu. Moreover, *Jeanne d'Arc* plays upon representational systems—especially images and language—in disturbing ways. Since many critics (including myself in a monograph on the film) have argued that it possesses a splendid unity, it is time to defamiliarize this classic and to notice its gaps and dislocations, its estranging features. With respect to the style of Dreyer's previous films and the norms of the classical cinema, *Jeanne d'Arc* powerfully rejects dominant relationships between narrative logic and cinematic space.

La Passion de Jeanne d'Arc proposes a new treatment of the tableau/face dialectic of Dreyer's early films. We have already seen, particularly in *Michael,* a tendency to push the expressive face beyond its surroundings (by means of the iris and long-held facial shots). In *Jeanne d'Arc,* the face is promoted still further, thus altering the function of the tableau. No longer do tableau compositions establish the dramatic space, regulating the movement from facial shot to facial shot; now, the film's intelligibility hinges upon our connecting one close-up with another. More to the point here, in being demoted, the tableau undergoes a radical recomposition. The flatness always latent in the tableau is pushed to the limit; the straight-on camera angle and balanced framings are contorted and awry; the usual insistence on graphic patterns within the shot turns obsessive; and, more particularly, camera movement and editing destroy the stability of the tableau. Before *Jeanne d'Arc,* Dreyer's tableaux had been chiefly a matter of personal style, quietly contesting the primacy of the human and of movement in the cinema. A new emphasis upon the face and a stylistic interrogation of the tableau work to bring space forward and to break abruptly with the very premises of classical scenography.

To understand this break, we need to qualify chapter four's sketch of the classical Hollywood spatial system a bit. According to this system, the narrative action occurs within a generally homogeneous space. The consistency of the depth cues is reaffirmed by cast shadows, muted lighting for background elements, the correct perspective diminution of distant planes, and even camera movement. The scale of the figures is kept constant with respect both to other figures and to the background. Camera distance and angle work to this end, framing figures and setting so that the two are congruent, and so that scale does not alter drastically from shot to shot. The camera is anchored or maneuvered in such a way as to present a stable and firm "ground" for the scene.

Most important, the construction of space in a scene is based primarily upon the unfolding dramatic action. Editing according to the famous "axis of action" rule, or 180° system, assures that the audience is never confused about the location of characters. By assuming an imaginary axis bisecting the scenographic space and by insuring that only shots taken from the same side of the line are cut together, the 180° system assures consistent backgrounds and screen directions from shot to shot. Other devices support this stability. The match-on-action cut blends two shots by means of the flow of movement. The establishing shot maps out the overall space of the scene, while the reestablishing shot is called in when a new character enters a scene or when spatial relations otherwise significantly shift. The "eyeline match" cuts from a shot of A looking, say, off right, to B, whose direction of glance will indicate whether he or she is returning the look. In such ways does classical continuity editing stitch shots into the smooth fabric of a unified narrative space. Camera movement will also support the coherence of the dramatic action—by following a moving character, surveying a setting, moving into or

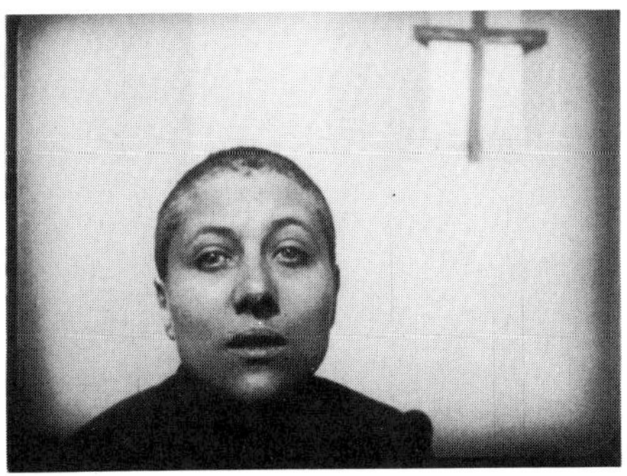
1

2

3

out from a significant object or character.

Even what we might call graphic space cooperates with the construction of a stable story space. The screen presents itself not as a surface but rather as a window opening onto the spectacle. To efface the surface of the screen, not only does the *mise-en-scène* teem with depth cues (overlap, lighting and texture gradients, consistent perspective, movement, relative size, etc.), but the composition of the shot follows some basic rules of thumb. The upper half of the screen, and especially the central area of this half, constitutes a privileged zone of dramatic activity. The shot will be symmetrical, usually along a vertical center axis. Lights and darks will tend to be balanced. And, of course, the principal action will not occur on the very edge of the screen. In sum, space must not "come forward," since it functions to guarantee the homogeneity of the spectacle. Rupture this space, dissolve the mutual dependencies amongst the various devices, and you stress space as a system in its own right, capable of being put into new and disorienting patterns. Such a rupture of the classical norm is the effect of the style of *La Passion de Jeanne d'Arc.*

AN ECCENTRIC SPACE

Consider, as a point of entry, the way in which *Jeanne d'Arc* sets up a play between depth and flatness. Not that the scenic space of the film has no depth, but depth cues are scarce. How far is Jeanne from the wall with the window —inches, feet, or yards (fig. 1)? Uncertainty about depth pervades not only close shots but also medium- and full-figure ones (figs. 2–3). The film refuses to define multiple planes by distinct background features, by lighting, or by linear perspective. The blank settings—either as pure white walls or as empty sky—push all figures to the same plane, making almost everything foreground against neutral background. Since the decor is scraped clean of reference points, objects and figures often float suspended in a luminous vacuum. Similarly, although the lighting of facial contours and textures creates attached shadows, there are seldom any cast shadows to confirm depth.

A sense of depth is further sabotaged by the distortion of linear perspective. Figures 1–3 certainly suggest no systematic diminution of planes around a vanishing point, and the decor often utilizes false perspective. The windows "behind" Cauchon (fig. 4) are skewed, ambiguous shapes that catch us in contradictory cues: according to the optical recession of planes, the right one should seem further back, but according to cues of familiar size and perspective diminution, the left one (being smaller) should seem the more distant. Cauchon's peephole (fig. 5) illustrates the same distortions, though now from foreground to background. Similarly, the recessed area of Jeanne's cell (fig. 6) contains no fewer than three inconsistent cues: the crooked crosspiece of the window, the perspectivally frontal window frame, and the exaggerated leftward slant of the diminishing arch. (Compare how a later shot of the recess [fig. 7] yields a completely different, though equally contradictory, set of depth cues.) Even reckoning Jeanne's body into the calculation, we cannot ascertain the depth of the recess, the height of the arch, or the size of the window. As a result, overlap of edges becomes the primary depth cue in the film, although it, too, can sometimes make the space slip into ambiguity: the principle of overlap demands that the three priests in figure 8 must be on three planes, yet the composition and the neutral decor stack the men like heads on a totem pole. In the absence of firm cer-

4

5

6

7

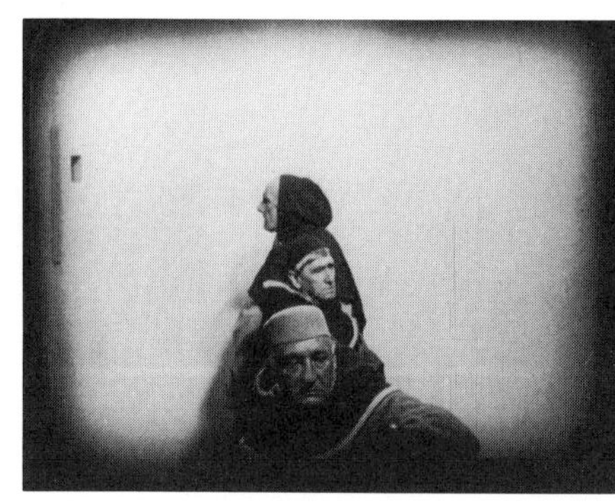

8

9

tainties about planes, even the characters' movements can become ambiguous; we can, for instance, rely only upon change of figure size to determine whether Loyseleur (fig. 9) is moving downward or rearward, or both.

The sense of figures hovering in a gravityless space is exacerbated by manipulations of camera angle which cut figures free of the ground. When the angle is not straight-on, it is almost always low, looking up at the figures (figs. 10–11). Set against neutral wall or sky, the characters fill the shots with distended volumes. Even the crowd of people is typically viewed from below. Moreover, the low angle usually shears off the characters at the waist or chest, so that, swathed in ecclesiastical drapery, the judges seem not to walk but to glide or drift. More spectacularly, the tilted or canted camera angles heave figures and setting to the right (figs. 12–13) or the left (fig. 14). We may even find one figure canted while another is *not* (fig. 15). With no firm ground, characters struggle through these tilted frames: entering a doorway comes to equal climbing uphill (fig. 16). Dreyer even inverts the bodies in order to deform the classical norm's assumption that the gravitational field of narrative must pull the camera into an orderly orbit (fig. 17).

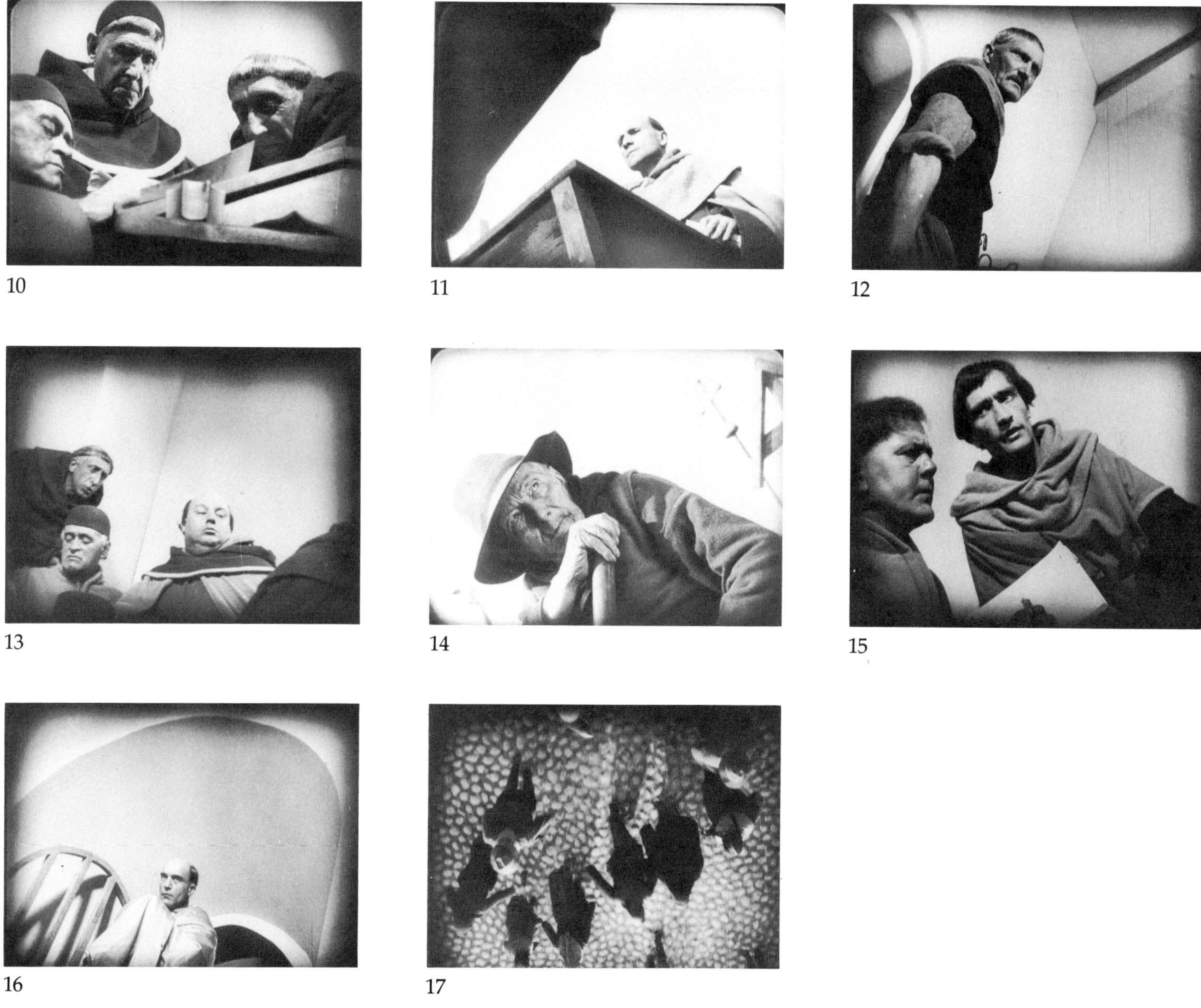

10

11

12

13

14

15

16

17

18

19

20

21

22

23

24

25

In *La Passion de Jeanne d'Arc,* the framings are as eccentric as the camera positions. The principal action will not necessarily coincide with the center of the frame. Compositions swing radically, almost madly, out of balance. Jeanne's face may be found tucked into the lower right corner (fig. 18), poised at the right edge (fig. 19), split by the left side (fig. 20), or sinking down below the frameline (fig. 21). Significant gestures become secreted in crannies of the frame. We find a procession or the guard's mocking grin not in the center but wedged in the upper left (figs. 22–23). A soldier's attack on a bystander occurs almost offscreen, at the bottom edge of the frame (fig. 24). Judges file out of Jeanne's cell via the lower left (fig. 25).

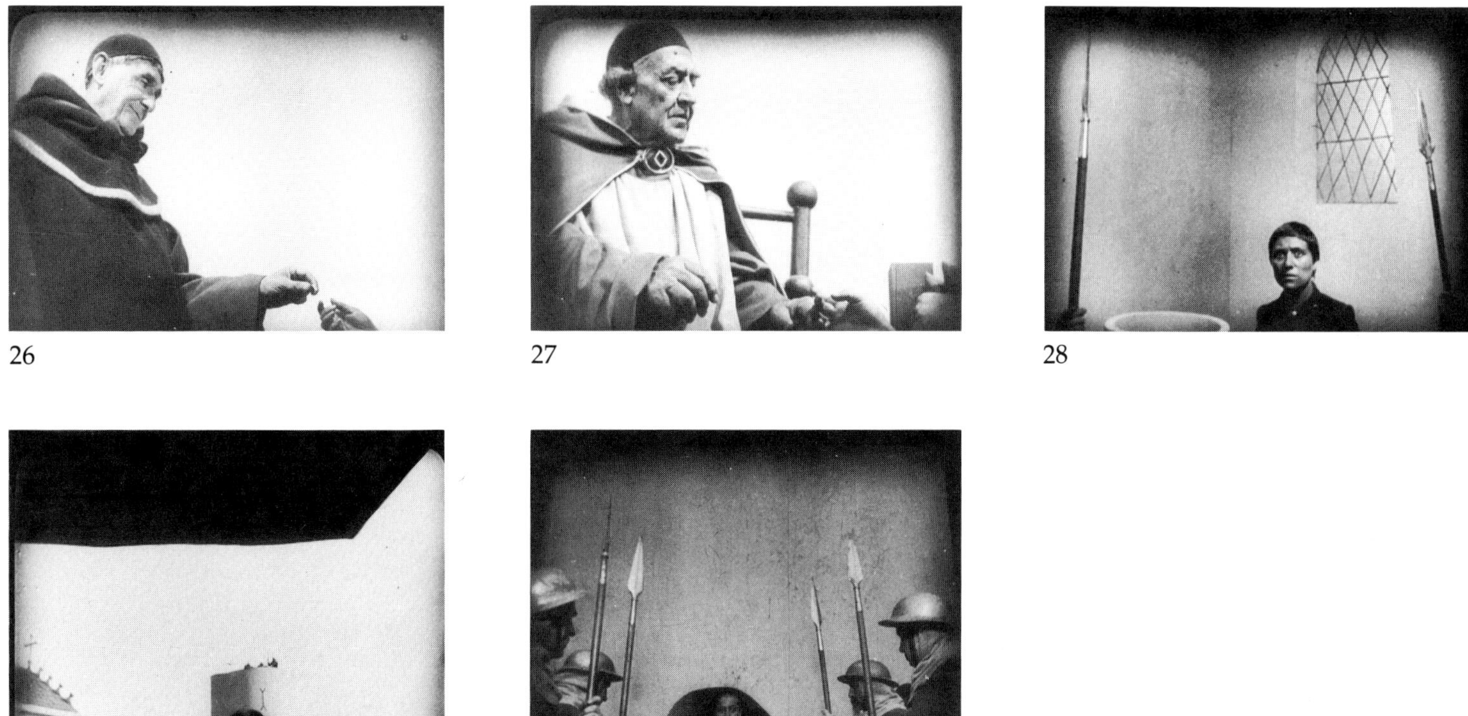

26 27 28

29 30

Once the privileged zone of classical screen space has been emptied out, once the characters have been flung to every corner of the frame as if by centrifugal force, areas and gestures can rhyme across the entire film. Loyseleur's visit to Jeanne is likened to Cauchon's later visit by a compositional echo in which the priest dominates the left half of the frame and Jeanne's hand steals into the lower right corner (figs. 26–27). Our first view of Jeanne situates her along the bottom frame edge, flanked by soldiers' spears (fig. 28). Later, she sits outdoors, again at the lower frameline, facing a tower full of soldiers (fig. 29). In the last scene, she starts toward the stake, surrounded, in a parody of perspective, by the arch, white space, and spears (fig. 30). One of the reasons why we remember the film as one composed wholly of close-ups is that even in long shot, faces are often isolated by such unbalanced framings.

Graphic patterns come forward to fill the vacuum left by the eviction of conventional scenography. Virtually

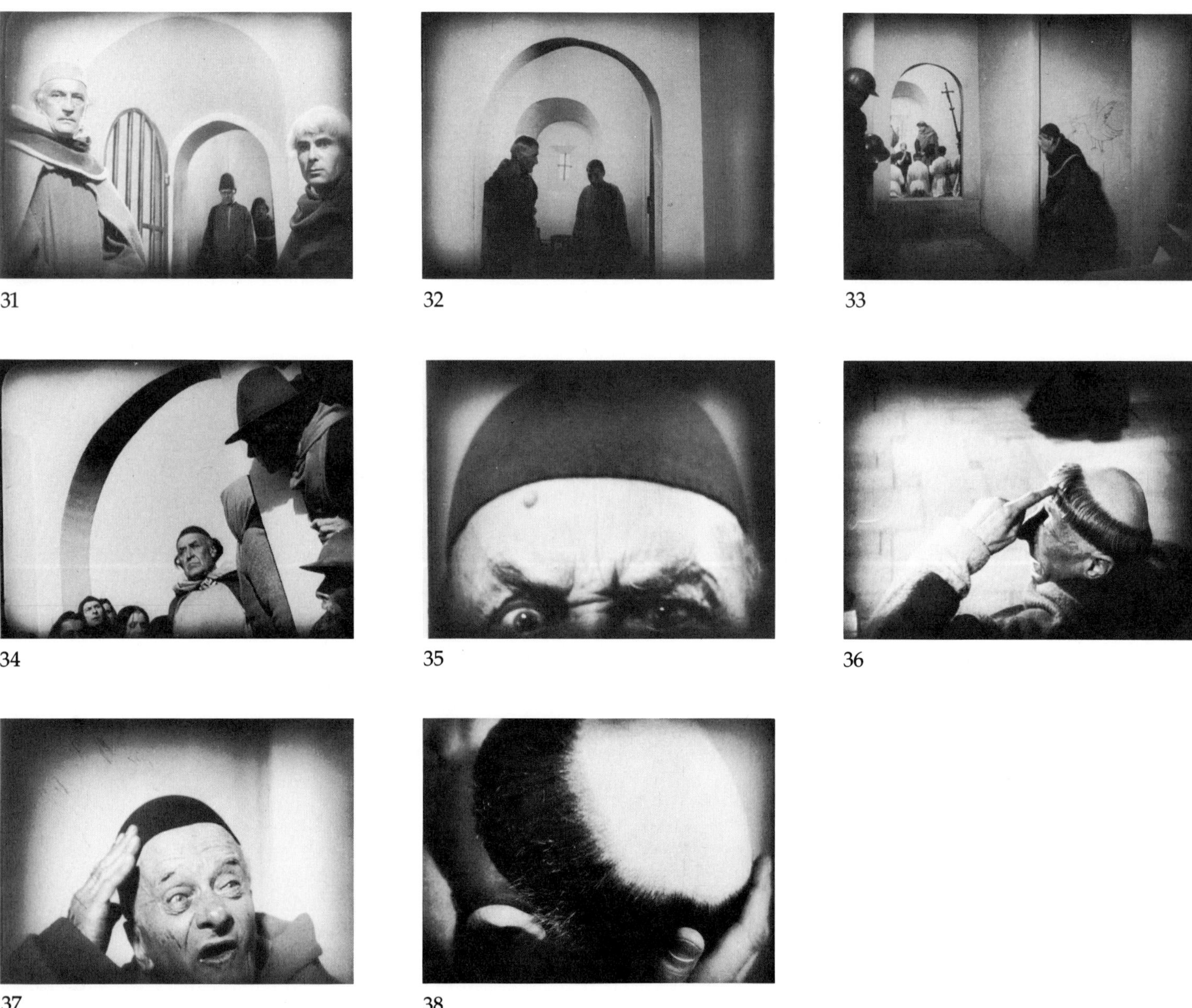

31 32 33 34 35 36 37 38

every shot of *La Passion de Jeanne d'Arc* revives the then anachronistic silent-film convention of vignette framing, so that a purely decorative overlay serrates and stylizes the screen surface. Even more noticeable are the numerous graphic motifs which, although *in* the scenographic space, are raised to extra-narrative prominence. One such motif is that of the arch. Many shots in Jeanne's cell, with the curved ceilings and doorways, are built from echoes of the arch pattern (figs. 31–33). Elsewhere, the first interrogation, the courtyard walls, and the drawbridge (fig. 34) all repeat the arch. One specific variant is, peculiarly, the top of the human head. The *mise-en-scène* in the first sequence forces the motif on our attention by close-ups (fig. 35), priests pointing to their tonsures or skullcaps (figs. 36–37),

39 40 41 42 43 44 45 46 47

and a series of shots associated with de Houppeville's abasement before Jeanne (fig. 38). Thereafter, skull, arch, and even soldier's helmet echo each other (figs. 39–40).

Another graphic motif runs through the film: that of two lines intersecting each other at a sharp angle. The emblem of Rouen castle—a vertical line with a "v" at each end—schematizes the motif (fig. 41). Indeed, arch and angle engage in an interplay closer to pure abstraction than any of Dreyer's tableau shots. Rafters and ceiling corners angle out from characters' heads (figs. 42–43); corners of canopies jut out like shapes in a Malevich composition (fig. 44). A vector gashed in a wall drives downward into the shot (fig. 45), while the human head is nipped between the pincers of dynamic diagonals (figs. 46–47).

48

49

50

51

Similarly, the cross (associated with Jeanne) and the Brueghelian torture wheels (associated with the populace) undergo a series of graphic permutations—cross into shadow of window (fig. 48), torture wheel into juggler's prop (figs. 49–50)—before uniting in the final scene, which identifies the crowd with Jeanne as much by the melding of motifs (fig. 51) as by the narrative action. In another film, such patterns might be ignored, but the sparse *mise-en-scène* of *La Passion de Jeanne d'Arc* foregrounds abstract configurations and refuses to subordinate graphics to the role of invisibly supporting the narrative action.

Effacement of depth, camera angles which balloon the figures upward and cut their ties to the ground, decentered framings which make the characters perch virtually anywhere in the frame, and graphic motifs which play across the screen surface—all these devices yield a cubistic space which sets elements in a tug-of-war with each other. Here a shot is less a slice of a spatial whole than the intersection of a number of forces—geometrical shapes, oddly tilted heads and shoulders—set against a blank surface. It is easy to read figure 52 as simply a collage composed of a contorted shape, an arc, and two faces; it is nearly impossible to read it as a bit of "realistic" space. Warwick sits on a level plane above the crowd, while his men, no more than a heap of helmets, slope behind him; has the castle been built leaning (fig. 53)? While an upper wall cuts in at an impossible angle, two spears thrust diagonally against it, framing the skewed figures of Jeanne and an old woman (fig. 54). A lectern and a canopy become massive rectangles dominating two tiny heads (fig. 55); human size and scale vanish. Three men engaged in prayer are spread weightlessly across the frame, like figures dangling from a mobile (fig. 56). Throughout the film, the frame becomes a suspension system.

What photographs can hardly indicate is how even the moving camera warps the film's space. As I suggested earlier, by perceptual rights the moving camera should orient us more firmly to the dramatic space than static shots do. For one thing, camera movement strongly cues depth through what psychologists call the "kinetic depth effect." Foreground and background planes get picked out by moving at different rates with respect to the camera lens. For another thing, camera movements supplement the sense of a ground, a balanced gravitational field within which the camera can confidently maneuver. Finally, the tracking shot can be used to stitch together the represented space so that respective positions of elements remain consistent.[1] There are corollaries to these demands for spatial and narrative unity: the camera movement must not call attention to itself by being abrupt or too swift; the movement must

52

53

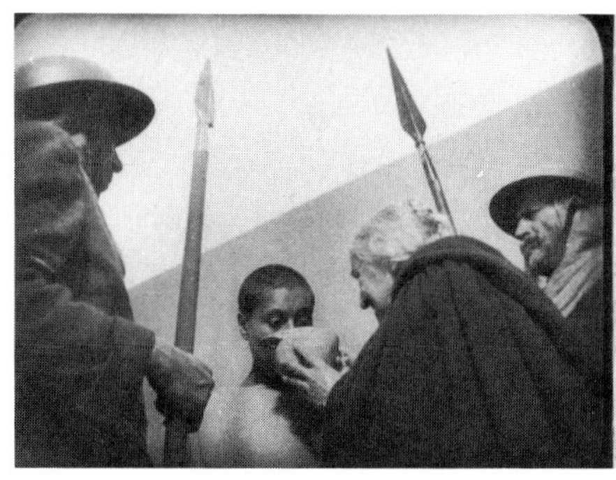
54

55

56

make a definable narrative point; and one must not cut away from a moving shot until the camera has momentarily come to a stop. Through the kinetic depth effect, the reiteration of a stable ground, and the linking of narrative elements into a coherent field, classical camera movement affirms the unity of spatial representation. But *Jeanne d'Arc* (and later *Vampyr*) will show that such unity is not an inevitable consequence of the moving camera.

We can observe, for example, that the ambiguities of frame space are not dispelled but are rather augmented by *Jeanne d'Arc*'s camera movements. When a shot presents only one plane against a neutral background, and when that plane is a face in close-up or medium close-up, camera movement makes a strange thing happen: the viewer cannot be certain whether to attribute the movement to the figure or to the camera. Thus, in the first scene, gliding tracking shots down the judges create an ambiguous effect: the heads roll through the frame as if on a conveyor belt. A priest's face will slide into the frame, and the blank background and absence of bodily movement cues prevent us from determining whether he moved or the camera did. In the torture chamber, sawtooth shapes lunge out at us and funnels drive through the frame, but we can attribute the movement either to the torture machinery or to the camera. The result is that often we cannot be sure if characters are shifting their places within the scene.

Even when perceived movement can be attributed to figure movement, camera mobility can still distort and derealize frame space by means of careful synchronization of camera and subject action. In an ordinary film, if subject movement is recorded by a static camera, the frame space becomes defined by the relative displacement of the figures. What happens here, in contrast, is that the camera often moves to compensate for any figure movement, thus keeping the ambiguous spatial relations constant. The most obvious examples are those shots with neutral white backgrounds and figure movements in close shot. In the first scene, precisely as a skinny judge rises in indignation

57

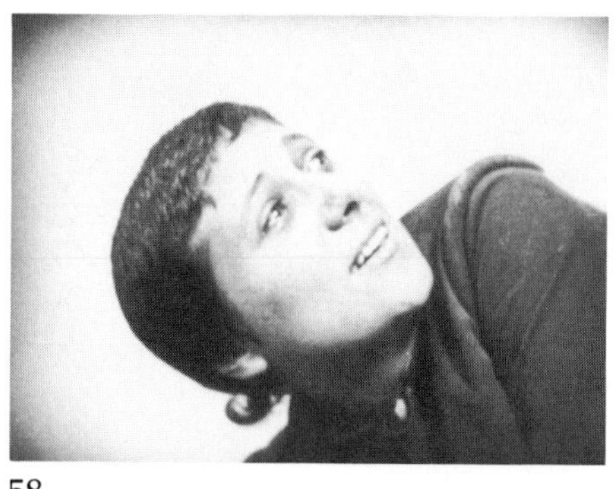
58

59

60

61

62

63

and two judges' heads spring into the frame, the camera tracks abruptly back, reestablishing and fixing the shallow space presented at the start of the shot. Similarly, as the judges pass a whisper down their ranks, the camera movement coordinates itself with their leaning to and fro, thus minimizing the shot's depth cues. In another shot, the camera follows the fat priest lumbering rightward to question Jeanne, but because of the low angle, neutral background, and carefully timed tracking movement, the only cues to his displacement are the conveyor belts of heads sliding past (fig. 57). And when, during the second interrogation in her cell, Jeanne turns from right to left (fig. 58), we cannot say whether it is the camera or Jeanne's body which leans this way and that. In long shots, such rigid coordination of camera and subject movement can at times disorient us spatially, as in certain shots during the final scene of Jeanne's immolation. For example, a rhythmic track in and out shows, from a low angle, maces dropped from a tower to a waiting soldier—an astonishing shot which makes the tower heave and buckle. In such shots, camera movement no longer aims to demarcate planes; instead, the camera cheats the kinetic depth effect and times its movements to coincide with those of the subject, reasserting the ambiguities of frame space.

If *Jeanne d'Arc*'s camera movements forego the kinetic depth effect and often undermine the gravitational stability of a ground, it is no wonder that those movements also often fail to stitch together the film's narrative space in a coherent manner. The movements are hardly subordinate to story action; Dreyer calls our attention to them. First, the movement is frequently gratuitous by the standards of classical narrative. When Loyseleur enters Jeanne's cell, the camera pans upward, revealing less and less of his figure until the frame is quite unbalanced (fig. 59). When Massieu enters, the camera moves left and all but leaves him behind. The camera tracks right from a guard to reveal—nothing.

Secondly, camera movement gains still more autonomy by the fact that a moving shot will unabashedly be interrupted by a static one. There is no attempt to soften the cut by smoothly melting two moving shots together. Instead, we have, as in scene one, a static shot (of Jeanne) cut abruptly to an already moving tracking shot (of the chain-clad book). Throughout the film, camera movements are foregrounded by sudden juxtapositions with shots at rest. Most obviously, this effect climaxes in such scenes as the torture-chamber interrogation, wherein short tracking shots of the spiked wheel quickly alternate with equally short shots of Jeanne's static face. Later, during the second interrogation in Jeanne's cell, high-velocity whip pans are intercut with static close-ups of Jeanne. And the confusion of the final immolation and slaughter is in part a product of the many lateral tracks and pans which are juxtaposed to shots containing no camera movement.

Finally (and most radical of all) are those camera movements which split the dramatic space apart, confusing rather than concretizing relationships. Consider one stunning example, the space-warping pan shot illustrated in figures 60–63. The judges are sitting in a row looking at the seated Jeanne. Now the camera pans left to right down them. What happens? At the beginning of the movement the judge is looking off *left* at Jeanne; at the end of the movement, other judges are looking off *right* at her. This space is simply impossible. Since the camera swivels across the judges, they cannot all be looking at the same point, but the narrative context insists that they are. Jeanne cannot be in two places at once, but the pan shot (assisted by the eye-lines of the priests) asserts just that. Camera movement here freely cleaves open scenographic space.

Gravity is cheated too. *Jeanne d'Arc*'s camera movements cooperate with the framings in eliminating the ground as a founder of stable spatial relations. Bodies are seldom shown below the waist and are often sprinkled variously across the frame. Sometimes camera movement frees itself from any reference point on ground or floor. At other times, the conveyor-belt effect of heads flowing through the frame becomes an escalator effect when the moving camera is tilted or canted. In the first interrogation in Jeanne's cell and in the torture-chamber scene, the judges' faces slide up and down through the shot. In the final communion scene, a close-up of choirboys puts them first at an upper-left-to-lower-right diagonal, and then, the tracking camera shifts its slope so that the boys are now rolling from upper right to lower left. Instead of a camera with its tripod legs firmly on the ground of the scene, we have a camera whose movements at skewed angles conspire with the decor and the framings to break the gravitational pull of the narrative space.

That break is most successful, of course, in the final sequence of the film, when before and after Jeanne's immolation the camera executes its most eccentric movements. While a priest administers communion to Jeanne, the populace rushes into Rouen castle. The unsettling nature of the shot depends upon inverted camera movements. The soldiers are seen walking upside down to open the gate; as we follow them, they slowly become viewed from directly above; as the crowd gathers, it is seen right-side-up (figs. 64–65). The shot calls attention to the bizarre camera operation. Later, another pan shot inverts the crowd as the earlier one had inverted the soldiers. At the end of the scene, two equally disorienting camera movements parallel the earlier pair. Now, as the people frantically flee through the gateway, the camera views them from directly *below* and pans up, against their movement (figs. 66–67).

Unlike the somersaulting movements in Dupont's *Variety* (1925), these shots make no attempt to suggest subjective viewpoints; unlike camera movements in the classical paradigm, these shots deliberately avoid the demand that the camera efface itself before the spectacle. The camera is no longer that "ideally placed *possible* spectator" considered by Ivor Montagu to be the center of film style.[2] The unmotivated inversions of the camera mark the paroxysmic culmination of the film's search for camera movements which dissolve the classical scenographic space and the stability of the viewer's vantage point. With *Jeanne*

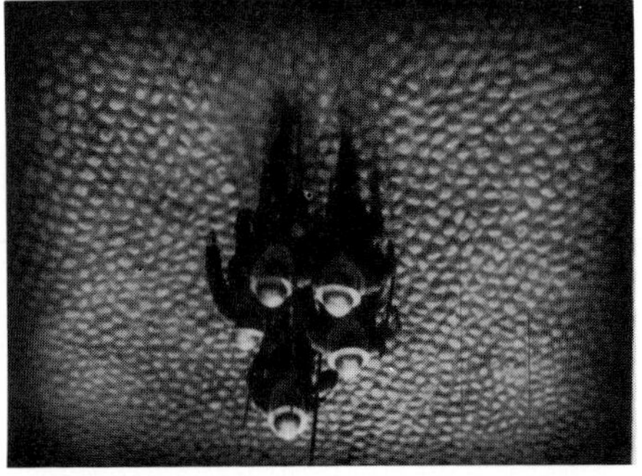
64

65

66

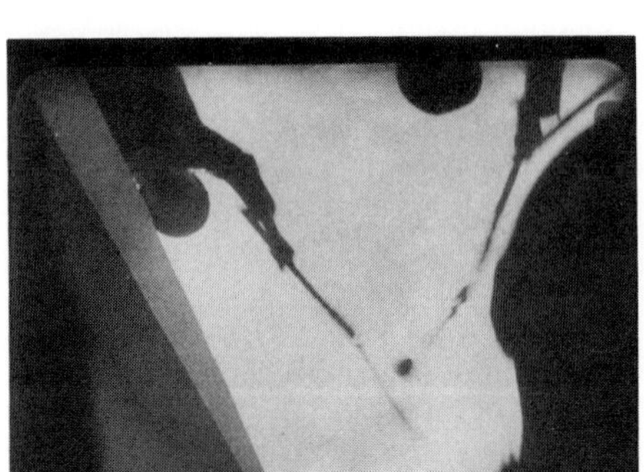
67

d'Arc, camera movement definitively enters Dreyer's style, and in the most disturbing way possible.

All of the film's strategies for dismantling the secure space within the frame might be fruitless if that dismantling did not obstinately persist when one shot is juxtaposed to another. We have seen above that the classical norm stresses continuity from shot to shot, achieved through matches on action, establishing and reestablishing shots, the 180° system, eyeline matches, and a general consistency of *mise-en-scène.* All this seeks to secure smooth flow, effortless intelligibility. But the editing of *La Passion de Jeanne d'Arc* bristles with obstacles, discontinuous spaces, problematic reading.

At once a surprising violation confronts us. Of the film's over fifteen hundred cuts, fewer than thirty carry a figure or object over from one shot to another; and fewer than fifteen cuts constitute genuine matches on action. Within the narrative cinema, this tactic constitutes a virtually unprecedented challenge to continuity editing. Almost every shot cuts away from one figure to another or cross-cuts two actions in separate locales. Just as Dreyer has no qualms about joining a moving shot to a static one, so even a simple action gets interrupted.

Given the refusal to use characters' presence as a way to link shots, the neutral white background often becomes the only continuity factor across the cut. Thus on many occasions, a character is seen moving just into the frame or just out of it, the shot lingering on empty space after or before the cut, as if the frame were only the trace of the character's passage through space. This effect becomes most percussive during the final slaughter of the crowd. Dreyer makes the smoke another depth-effacing factor in the frame and then cuts on the basis of the smoke's ability to erase or reveal figures. For instance, the last frame of logs at the stake will be swathed in gray or white smoke; the first frame of the next shot will be similarly blanketed in smoke until a figure emerges into visibility. During this last sequence, the void of the frame gains a texture of its own as actions are punctuated by rhythmic bursts of white space.

Apart from revealing itself as an activity of construc-

68

69

70

71

tion, the film's editing frequently refuses the most elementary principles of classical continuity. The usual series—long shot/medium shot/close-up—is either truncated or eliminated. Jeanne is established in the courtroom, torture chamber, and cell by oblique means: either a long shot shows us the space before she enters, or she is hidden by an object (bedstead, chair) in the long shots. On one occasion, the "master shot" comes after the scene has ended (fig. 68); at other times, the establishing shots don't establish. Densely crowded at the horizon, the exterior long shots conceal the principal action to a drastic degree (figs. 69–70). When Jeanne is taken to the churchyard, the composition makes the space virtually as illegible as any long shot can be (fig. 71).[3]

More often, however, we are denied any establishing shots which would permit us to relate Jeanne's space to that of the other characters.[4] Occasionally in the same frame with Massieu or a soldier, almost never in the same frame with a judge, Jeanne inhabits a space apart. It is not just that in several scenes we can only infer the relative distances and positions of the characters. More important, we can no longer assume that a constant, homogeneous set of spatial relations exists. At the beginning of the first scene, Loyseleur is on one side of the room; halfway through, he appears on the other side, although we are never shown his change of position. When the soldier leaps up to attack Jeanne, the glances cue us that he is on her right, but we later discover that he is—not *actually* but *also*—on her left. The principle of cutting away (eliding such actions as de Houppeville's arrest, Jeanne's fainting, and her immolation) no longer permits us the soothing establishment and reestablishment of narrative space. The uncertainty at work within each composition bleeds across most of the cuts as well.

Jeanne d'Arc's cutting offers a good example of how a text can at once cite a norm and work to subvert that norm. Beyond a doubt, one essential principle of the film's cutting is the eyeline match. With the transformation of the tableau comes a promotion of the face: if the decor is largely a void, if there is seldom an establishing shot or a match on action, the glance must take up the burden of defining spatial relations. Classical continuity integrates eyelines: if shot one shows X looking off to the right and shot two shows Y looking off to the left, we will infer (all other things being equal) that they are looking at each other. Now, most of the eyeline cuts in the film adhere to this principle. Jeanne looking off left/her interrogator looking off right: the cut reassures us of a stable axis of action between the participants. Thus the film assimilates and cites the classical norm. But since there remain many cuts which do not obey the norm, eyeline cutting no longer guarantees a stable narrative space.

Sometimes, the film's eyeline confusions are fleeting.

72

73

At the start of the torture scene, a pudgy priest looks down right at Jeanne and she looks up right "at" him; the cut violates the dictum of opposed eyelines. Later in the same scene, a bolder disruption occurs during the glances which Jeanne exchanges with Cauchon (figs. 72–73). In other scenes, the eyelines violate geography with permanently disorienting results. When a soldier steals Jeanne's ring, the camera position leaps back and forth across the putative axis of action, so that we cannot assemble a coherent scenographic space. Similar ambiguities rule other scenes. Whom is the gravedigger watching when he removes his hat? In the churchyard, is Cauchon addressing Jeanne or the crowd? When Cauchon stands above Jeanne in her cell to hear her recantation, where is he in relation to the door? In the absence of establishing shots and identifiable decor, the eyeline cuts break the 180° principle and make the scenes' spatial relations difficult to reconstruct. Most radically, there is the scene of the guards' mockery of Jeanne, which breaks the 180° rule so often that virtually every new shot contradicts the one before, every eyeline disorients us as to characters' positions. Although I once wrote disparagingly that "the mockery episode muddles viewpoints and directions of glances and movements unaccountably,"[5] the scene's inconsistencies are characteristic of the whole film's desire to subvert traditional scenic space.

To try to exhaust the film would only exhaust the reader's patience. Since it is impossible to explicate each example here, my claims can best be tested by examining any scene on an editing table. Each sequence contains an astonishing number and variety of false eyeline matches, which constantly make spatial relations at least ambiguous and often downright inconsistent. What is important for my argument is that such editing requires that the conventional procedure be cited within the film: if *every* cut violated the 180° rule, that violation would quickly become contextually intelligible. The dynamism and uncertainty of the editing stem from the constant play between an embedded norm and violations of it.

If the preceding argument has seemed disproportionately to emphasize what the film does *not* do, that is because the film's spatial system not only works against the classical paradigm and the principle of tableau construction in the earlier films, but also works against *the establishment of an internally coherent narrative space.* Flat areas, figures which float in a vacuum, characters hovering at various points around the frame, a weightless camera, inconsistent figure positions, movements, and glances: like no film Dreyer made before this, as surely as any film by Eisenstein or Vertov, *La Passion de Jeanne d'Arc* foregrounds perceptual contradiction. The stylistic dynamism of the film springs from its discontinuities; the viewer must deal with problems of relating cinematic space to narrative logic. The dynamism is not, however, boundless; the film also seeks to check its disparities by specific unifying operations. The contradictions remain, but set in tension against a drive for narrative continuity and closure.

SUBJECTIVITY

One strategy for unifying the film immediately suggests itself, and although it is incorrect, it is worth analyzing briefly. All the film's disparities might be read as representing Jeanne's point of view. In this context, "point of view" can mean either of two things:

1. Features of the *mise-en-scène* can be read as suggesting Jeanne's spiritual attitude: e.g., the flat space, the shifting framings, the overall stylization of the film's world can be taken to indicate some state of Jeanne's consciousness. This I shall call *Expressionist* subjectivity.
2. Features of cutting and camerawork can be read as representing Jeanne's perception: e.g., camera angles and movements can be taken as embodying optical vantage points. This I shall call *Impressionist* subjectivity.

Upon these two possibilities a previous critical essay of my own bases its analysis. I want now to argue against this reading and show that it reduces the complexity of the film.

Expressionist subjectivity will not occupy us long. Seen at its fullest flower in German Expressionism, this conception of filmic point of view usually seeks to show that all the furnishings of the film—setting, lighting, costume, spatial relations—project the mental state of the protagonist. It seems to me that the interpretive principle of Expressionist subjectivity is applicable only when the narrative structure of the film overtly thematizes subjective attitudes, as *The Cabinet of Dr. Caligari* does by its frame story. The film must posit an objectivity "outside" these distorted visions in order to define the subjective passages as such.

When such thematization is lacking, as in *Jeanne d'Arc*, what can we say about the claim that "the way stylistic abstraction allows the film to be 'not merely visual but spiritual' reflects Jeanne's decision to define herself not by an earthly mission but by her visionary commitment"?[6] Such a reading explains too much and discriminates too little. The idiosyncrasies of any film can be justified as proceeding from the mental state of a character. And if the film is subjective through and through, how to distinguish between the overall structure of the film and moments of greater or lesser subjectivity? The defender of the Expressionist position on *Jeanne d'Arc* must show how, say, the upside-down shots of the populace, or the *mise-en-scène* in shots from which Jeanne is absent, can symbolize a character's mental state. Not only does the Expressionist reading blur the film's specificity; such an explanation must be seen as symptomatic of a desire to close the film comfortably around the idea of personality, to assimilate the film to a psychological-realist aesthetic.

Impressionist subjectivity is a more complex position. Here the critic seeks to show that the cutting and camerawork correspond to the optical experience of a character (in this case, Jeanne). Impressionist point of view allows the critic to make the more modest claim that only portions of the film are structured around character perception. "The camera follows Jeanne's glance as it sweeps along the circle of judges; she looks toward the wafer; then she looks at the recantation. Dreyer's use of close-ups and economical visual symbols, linked by point-of-view, perfectly realizes Jeanne's dilemma."[7] In another sequence, "point-of-view shots and dynamically edited close-ups constitute the most intense presentation so far of Jeanne's experience."[8] Undeniably, certain films utilize stylistic devices to mark elements as optically subjective, so what can be said against the Impressionist point-of-view position?

Only, I think, that one must distinguish conventional from unconventional cues for optical subjectivity. For instance, the accepted figure for point-of-view editing is:

> Shot of looker *(a)*.
> Shot of thing seen *(b)*.
> Return to shot of looker *(a)*.

We also assume that is X is looking off at one thing, we will be informed by a shift in X's glance when he or she is supposed to look at something else. And we assume that the angle of shot *b* will correspond roughly to the angle of the looker's position and glance. Yet *Jeanne d'Arc*—again including the point-of-view norm as a point of stylistic departure—violates all these conventional cues.

1. The film makes extensive use of what Edward Branigan has called "multiple point of view," or what I shall call interlocking point of view.[9] Here the shots violate the *aba* pattern in this way:

> *a*. Shot of character X looking.
> *b*. Shot of what X sees.

74

75

76

77

c. Shot of character Y looking (not necessarily at the object in shot *b*).

In *Jeanne d'Arc,* from the twelfth shot on, this structure is insistent. Jeanne turns sharply to look right; cut to a tracking shot of the chain-clad book being carried; cut to a shot *not* of Jeanne but of de Houppeville, watching either the book or Jeanne or both. This cutting undermines the spatial stability presupposed by optically subjective cutting. Such interlocking point-of-view patterns pervade the film.

2. With equal frequency, the film disturbs the stable relationships among glances. We have already seen how troubling the eyeline-match cutting becomes; now we must consider whether the direction and angles of the glance consistently motivate the cuts.

   i. In the *aba* pattern, the presentation of a new object should correspond to a shift in the character's glance. But in *Jeanne d'Arc,* this will not necessarily happen. In her cell, for instance, Jeanne's answers have been so unsatisfactory that Cauchon denounces her and the priests rise to file out. Jeanne is staring upward; cut to low-angle shot of the scribe closing the book; cut back to Jeanne, still looking upward. So far, so good: a conventional *aba* pattern. But the next shot is of *another* area of the room (Cauchon and the priests filing out) and the next shot of Jeanne exactly repeat her glance. By conventional cues, Jeanne cannot be looking in precisely the same direction and seeing different things.

   ii. In the *aba* pattern, the object in shot *b* will be presented from an angle approximating that of the glance in shot *a*. In the conventional structure, eyes turned *upward* in shot *a* will be echoed by the *low-angle* in the subjective shot *b*. (Indeed, one of the features distinguishing point-of-view cutting from the ordinary eyeline match is the implicit fidelity of the angle onto the object seen.) But *Jeanne d'Arc* constantly violates this convention as well. The glance in shot *a* often does not fit the angle of shot *b*. In the torture chamber, the various angles on the torture wheel, although in alternation with shots of Jeanne's stare, are seen from angles different from her angle of vision. A more striking example can be traced through the accompanying illustrations. Jeanne looks up (fig. 74) and we see the priest from a low angle (fig. 75). In figure 76, Jeanne's glance shifts to a slightly down-ward one. Yet the following "subjective"

78

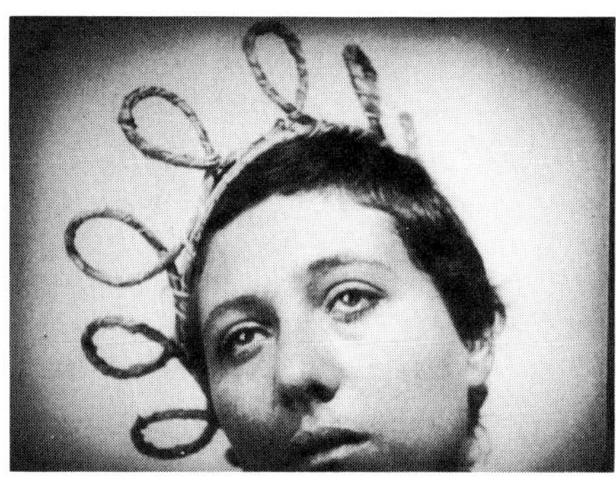
79

80

81

82

shot is from an even steeper *low* angle (fig. 77). This testing of the assumptions of glance and camera angle again exemplifies the film's refusal of spatial stability.

In the light of all the unresolved point-of-view structures I have just mentioned, the argument for Impressionist subjectivity loses force. True, the film alludes to the conventional optical point-of-view pattern no less significantly than it cites the 180° rule and the ordinary eyeline match. But surely we ought to infer from the film's dissonant point-of-view operations that it does not seek to render a character's experience. We can reapply an earlier argument: in failing to recognize the play which the film sets up with respect to subjectivity and in trying to pin the film down to some optical realism, we "naturalize" in psychological-realist terms the very surprises and bafflements which should disorient us. The contradictions in point of view in *Jeanne d'Arc* resemble that strategy of the modern writer mentioned by Jonathan Culler:

> *The ubiquity of such naturalization and recuperation is a problem for the artist. . . . What he must do if he is to outplay naturalization is to create a text which continually makes us aware of the cost at which we naturalize, which flaunts the difference between verbal surface and naturalizing interpretation so that we see how much richer and less banal the former is than the latter. . . . The poet or novelist succeeds in challenging naturalization not by going beyond the bounds of sense but by creating a verbal surface whose fascination is greater than that of any possible naturalization and which thereby challenges the models by which we attempt to comprehend and circumscribe it.*[10]

My dispute with claims for the film's subjectivity can conclude with one more visual example, one which bares the device of contradictory point of view. When the bullish guard views Jeanne through cupped hands, telescope-fashion (fig. 78), we get, logically enough, an iris representing his vision (fig. 79). Then the guard puts his hands down and observes her normally (fig. 80), but the next shot shows her still within an iris (fig. 81). And even this inconsistent view is "interlocked" with a shot of Massieu, also looking at her (fig. 82). In this scene, we get a sense of the price we pay for the comfort of labeling such perceptual play "subjectivity": the film's texture makes such a reading uncomfortably arbitrary. Dreyer's film puts the intelligibility of subjectivity into question.

A DIALOGUE OF TEXTS

If "point of view" in its various guises cannot unify the film, what can? Are the stylistic deformations of *La Passion de Jeanne d'Arc* integrated within a coherent narrative structure?

Not, at least, as far as time is concerned. Certain temporal features of the narrative are no less disorienting than the spatial ones. As a critical category, story duration is clear enough: it is the posited length of time consumed by the action (e.g., two years). Plot duration would then be the length of time which the action consumes in the film (e.g., two hours on the screen). But *Jeanne d'Arc* abolishes story time as an operative category. What story duration can we construct on the basis of the 110 minutes of *Jeanne d'Arc?* How "long" does the story action—the trial and the burning—last? Certainly not more than a week, or even a few days, but we cannot set precise limits.[11] We might be tempted to say that all the action consumes a few hours during one day, but even "day" is hardly a relevant concept for the film; the film's world has no clocks or calendars; this world does not even *wear.* As Jean Sémolué has put it: "Here time is lived in its pure progression."[12] The result is to invest in screen time the sovereign authority for the film's duration. The overall action, in effect, takes as long as the film *shows* it taking. To the disruptions of space, then, there correspond ambiguities of time.

Yet we understand the film when watching it. Troubling as it is, we grasp it and respond to it. So there is a pattern to be perceived. What is it? I suggest that the organizational center of the film is the developing narrative situation of the character Jeanne. This is not to say that the film's stylistic workings can be explained through character psychology; rather, I propose that Jeanne's narrative position counterbalances the fragmented diversity of the film. The protagonist mediates between the dynamic heterogeneity of the film's motifs and the stability of an overarching causal structure. Jeanne as protagonist is the formal device working against the disunity of time and space.

Our previous acquaintance with her story confirms this. In the first shot, hands turn the pages of a book. The shot is emblematic: we come to a familiar tale, equipped with considerable knowledge. Jeanne's peasant ancestry, her religious impulses, her military fervor, and her heroic death: Dreyer assumes that we know all this, takes it as the "pre-text" of his film, and frees the narrative of an expository apparatus. We are expected to recall that Jeanne fought to drive the English out of France, that she trusts that her alliance with King Charles will be honored, that the clerical court is in league with the occupying army. Since we know all this, the film may organize itself around the last phase of Jeanne's life, and create that radical compression of action for which the film is so celebrated. Most important, we know how the story will end. Knowing the outcome of the action endows the film with the determinism so characteristic of Dreyer's work: instead of inscribing predictions of the outcome *into* the narrative as prophecy (as in most of the early films), *Jeanne d'Arc,* like *Leaves from Satan's Book,* explicitly bases itself upon a text outside its own boundaries. (Actually two texts, as we shall see.) In addition, the opening of the book promises us that Jeanne's story has been already completed, finished, written, and that however extreme the stylistic discontinuities, the film will ultimately cohere. Jeanne as historical figure assures the passage between stylistic eccentricity and narrative homogeneity; because the viewer's representational position is made unclear, she or he is thrown back upon Jeanne's story as the one certainty in the film.

The fact that Jeanne is the thread which we follow through the narrative suggests why psychological interpretations so attract the critic. She is, after all, a firmly fixed character, with assigned motivations, goals, and feelings, all of which are expressed in many ways. By almost universal consent we have here one of the cinema's profoundest excavations of personality; every action of mind and heart can be read off the face. Sémolué writes: "These emotions are not only explicated, *they are.* Never have we known characters on the screen so intimately."[13] Within a more theoretical argument, Jean Mitry asserts that the normal close-up expresses but does not signify, whereas in *Jeanne d'Arc,* the facial close-ups signify *"as the very sign of what they express."*[14] Thus the film offers images which symbolize pure states of the soul.

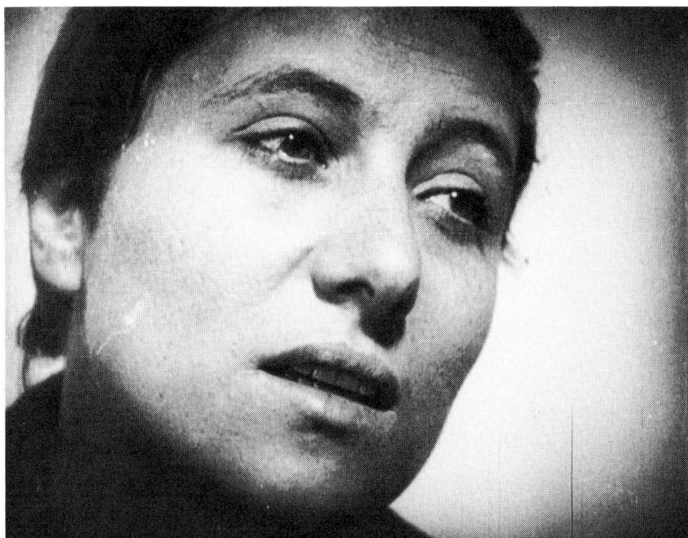

83

84

In his distinction among agent, character, person, image, and figure, Stephen Heath has proposed that the "character" in film can unify the text or split it apart. In Heath's terms, Jeanne is at once agent (the performer of an action), character (an expressive individuality), person (the continuing presence of the body), and image (the focus of narrative economy). Jeanne is not, however, a "figure" in Heath's sense, for a figure is "a point of dispersion, a kind of disarticulation," the bearer of "a radical heterogeneity."[15] In the open force-field of *Jeanne d'Arc*'s space and time, Jeanne is the point of convergence, the axis around which the spectacle turns. Just as without Jeanne there would be no narrative, without her presence the framings, the flatness, the cutting, the camera movements would shatter the film into a thousand fragments. The disparity of the film is the strain between Jeanne as unifying force and the contradictions of space and time.

Moreover, if Jeanne's story is the macro-action behind the cause-effect chain, the film furnishes a constant chain of micro-actions which guarantees narrative direction and a localized causal coherence. If Jeanne as character were a completely fixed point, her stasis would soon disturb narrative linearity. By a brilliant strategy, the film secures her constancy through minimal variation. Hence the second, positive function of the close-up: not only to break apart spatial relations but also to magnify the minute changes of Jeanne's expression. Every attack by her adversaries provokes a response, however slight; every reply she furnishes is accompanied by the flicker of a new expression. At this level, the fullness of Jeanne's character is expressed through a microscopic cause-effect chain composed wholly of nuances. (Compare figs. 83 and 84.) Béla Balázs rightly found in *Jeanne d'Arc* "a drama of the spirit" enacted in "duels between looks and frowns."[16] As a result, the spatial uncertainty from shot to shot is accompanied by one of the most naked narrative conflicts ever filmed. What the close-up as spatial fragment destroys, the expressive face seeks to rebuild. The plenitude of Jeanne's character as a focusing unity and the tiny second-by-second fluctuations of expression are structural necessities.

Let us assume, then, that Jeanne as legendary figure and expressive character seeks to pull together the film's tendencies toward fragmentation and that narrative logic gives her unifying function a causal and temporal direction through a series of micro-actions. We still must specify what propels that movement, what opposes the film's spatial uncertainties. The central principle has been suggested by Jean Sémolué: "If *Vampyr* is conceivable in the first person, *La Passion de Jeanne d'Arc* remains perpetually a dialogue."[17] Indeed, we can consider the premise of the film's cause/effect chain to be a "dialogical" clash of Jeanne and Another, an opposition of voices in a vast alternation. Saturating the film from top to bottom, the principle of dialogue regulates the division into scenes, the interaction of characters, the role of objects, the editing of shots, and the exchange of words. Dialogue becomes the chief means by which the unifying function of Jeanne is reiterated across the construction of the narrative; dialogue seeks to override the film's visual disparities by the force of a general intelligibility.

Dialogical alternation can be observed in the shifts of locale. If we break the film into seven sections, on the basis of change of setting, we arrive at a scheme which alternates scenes outside Jeanne's cell with scenes inside it: (1) the court; (2) the cell; (3) the torture chamber; (4) the cell; (5) the cemetery; (6) the cell; (7) the castle courtyard. In each locale, every scene is structured around a rigorous pattern, a kernel of cause and effect which breaks the scene's action into five stages (see chart, pp. 88–89):

1. The participants assemble.
2. The authorities engage in dialogue with Jeanne.
3. Jeanne or an ally challenges the authorities.
4. The authorities attack her or her ally.
5. The participants disperse.

Usually, these five phases are followed by a transitional passage which explicitly contrasts specific elements through crosscutting. The order of these phases is not invariable, but the general pattern is so pervasive that it becomes a major force in unifying the film.

The pattern is well illustrated by the first sequence of the film. The scene begins with the assembly of soldiers and priests and the arrival of Jeanne. Thereafter, stages two through four (dialogue/challenge to authorities/counterattack by authorities) are repeated three times. First, Cauchon and his assistant question Jeanne; she challenges the English; a soldier springs up to attack her. Secondly, after another series of questions, Jeanne declares that she has saved her soul; a priest comes forward and spits in her face. The third variation alters the order of the phases: *first* the authorities attack (Jeanne's one defender is removed by the soldiers), then the judges ask more questions and Jeanne responds decisively. At this point, the court is adjourned and judges and prisoner disperse. A transitional passage makes characteristic use of crosscutting in order to juxtapose the image of Jeanne in her cell with the image of the judges forging a letter outside.

The pervasiveness of the kernal action can be seen from the accompanying chart. The very layout sufficiently suggests the principle similarities and symmetries among scenes, but a few variations deserve comment.

1. In one respect, the assembly phases alternate regularly: in odd-numbered scenes, Jeanne is brought to the judges, and in even-numbered scenes the judges come to her. But sometimes one priest enters Jeanne's cell first for a brief exchange (Loyseleur in scene 2, Cauchon in scene 4). Outdoors (in scenes 5 and 7), both Jeanne and judges meet before the populace. In scenes 1 through 5, Jeanne obeys the judges' summons to assemble, but in scene 6 she calls them, and in scene 7 her decision draws the people back to the castle.
2. In the questioning phase of each sequence, we find considerable variation. Interrogators differ from scene to scene until the crucial shift in scene 6, when Massieu and Jeanne engage in an exchange about her forthcoming death. In scene 7, the immolation replaces the questioning segment.
3. In the earliest scenes, we can pinpoint each of Jeanne's challenges in a line of dialogue ("I am certain that the English will be driven out of France, except those who die here. . . ." Her reward is to be "the salvation of my soul!"). Sometimes, however, her decisive action is performed silently: refusing communion (scene 4), signing the recantation (scene 5). As she is bound to the stake in scene 7, her last word—"Jesus!"—testifies to her decision, but an ally issues the challenge: an old man shouts, "You have burned a saint!"
4. As we would expect, the attacks mount in severity, but they also shift in tactic and object. In the first scene, the soldier is kept from striking Jeanne, and d'Estivet spits upon her, while the violence of the army and the Church emerges in the attack on her ally de Houppeville. Jeanne is assaulted by another soldier, and mocked by the guards (scene 2), threatened with torture and bled (scene 3), and tempted with communion (scene 4). After signing the recantation, she is sentenced to life imprisonment (scene 5). Since she has accepted the authorities' goal—her death—they have nothing with which to assail her, so scene 6 contains no attack upon her. Finally, as Jeanne is burned in scene 7, the object of attack becomes the populace which supports Jeanne and which the army drives out of Rouen.
5. The scenes' participants disperse by order of the authorities (scenes 1, 5, 7) or when Jeanne initiates the breakup by her fainting (scene 3), her refusals (scene 4), and her withdrawal of the recantation (scene 6).
6. With one exception (the link of scenes 2/3), the se-

quences are joined by transitional passages wherein crosscutting brings Jeanne and others into a "dialogue" across time and space. Apart from their localized structural importance, these crosscut segments illustrate how obsessively the film's chain of cause and effect depends upon juxtaposing Jeanne and Another, constantly interrupting her unifying presence. In these sequences we get, then, a baring of the dialogical principle itself. While Jeanne sits in her cell, the judges forge a letter from King Charles (1/2); while Jeanne is bled, the priests hover outside on the stair (3/4); while Jeanne's hair is cut, the people celebrate (5/6); while Jeanne takes communion, the soldiers prepare the stake and the crowd gathers (6/7). To some extent, the function of these passages is to contrast narrative motifs, and this function is continued in the very last shot: the flaming stake stands in the foreground, a cross surmounts a church in the distance.

Despite such variations, the kernal cause-effect chain demonstrates that here, as in Dreyer's early films, characters' actions are placed within an overriding impersonal pattern. The kernal narrative action permits the viewer to plot the vicissitudes of the drama against a very limited set of possibilities, assuring causal intelligibility.

The concept of "dialogue with Jeanne" rules every one of these scenes. The film's characters function as participants in a series of confrontations with her, as we can see by lining up the opposing forces. On the one side, there are most of the priests (led by Cauchon) and the English army (led by Warwick), with Nicolas Loyseleur as go-between. On the other side there is Jeanne herself, who has a few allies among the priests and among the crowd. It is worth noting that no explanatory intertitles characterize these figures, and that (with some exceptions) the dialogue does not differentiate one from another. As a result, the characters' traits and motifs emerge from physical details; if we are to make sense of the film, we must construct that intelligible entity we call "character" from narrative expression and gesture. Not only the words but the physical beings of the characters enter into dialogue. The film builds upon a narrow set of physical polarities: old (priests, gravedigger) vs. young (Jeanne, Massieu, Ladvenu, the children in the crowd); men vs. women; flesh (Jeanne's especially) vs. metal (the soldiers' weaponry, the torturer's apparatus); cassocks vs. soldiers' uniforms (which, until the end, even Jeanne wears); worked skin (the wrinkled, mottled priests) vs. smooth skin (Jeanne, the young priests).

The purely visual nature of these antinomies is reinforced by the film's refusal of the most common means of identifying a character. It is astonishing that, with the exception of Jeanne herself, no character is *named* in the film. (We can glean names only from the credit sequence.) Roland Barthes has suggested that in literature, "when identical semes traverse the same proper name several times and appear to settle upon it, a character is created," and certainly in cinema the proper name is important for unifying a bundle of traits into a character.[18] But in cinema we also have images of bodies, those vessels of behavior that play an indispensible role in our identifying the concept of "person" in life and "character" in film. In *Jeanne d'Arc,* figures are marked not by name but by physiognomy, costume, station, behavior: the viewer recognizes not a character named Cauchon but the fat old bishop with the warts, not Massieu but the dark, spectrally handsome young priest. The reduction of personality to physicality has led many commentators to see in *Jeanne d'Arc* the very apogee of silent film art, and certainly Dreyer's film takes its place in a physiognomic tradition that includes the 1920s Soviet films and American comedies. For our purposes, we must stress how the film's abrupt, even jerky opposition of one body or behavior to another furthers the dialogical strategy of the film.

The clergy's lengthy interrogations of Jeanne conform to the same principle. Even here the concept of dialogue cuts deeper then sheer talk, for apart from the clash of words and viewpoints, the visual construction of each interrogation arises from the alternation of action and reaction. The absence of matches on action means that there are almost never two successive shots of the same character. Instead, if shot *a* shows Jeanne, shot *b* will show a judge or an object. Gestures which another film would present without interruption are constantly broken by wedged-in shots of other elements. As Jeanne faints, there is a quick cutaway to a priest looking on. De Houppeville's abasement before Jeanne is interrupted by shots of Jeanne and the other judges. When Jeanne withdraws the recantation, shots of soldiers bringing rocks for the stake alternate with shots of staring priests. It is important to distinguish such cutting from that in the films of Eisenstein. Although the latter's films often fragment an action through editing, the fragmentation is frequently a matter

	Participants assemble	Authorities engage in dialogue with Jeanne	Jeanne or ally challenges authorities.
(1) COURT	Judges and Jeanne assemble.	Cauchon and assistants question Jeanne.	Jeanne predicts that English will lose.
		Cauchon and assistants question Jeanne.	Jeanne claims that God has promised salvation.
			De Houppeville declares her a saint.
		Cauchon questions Jeanne.	Jeanne claims she will be rescued.
(2) CELL			
	Loyseleur arrives.	Loyseleur returns ring.	
	Other priests arrive.	Priests interrogate Jeanne.	Jeanne avoids traps.
	Guards arrive.	Guards taunt Jeanne.	Jeanne refuses to speak.
(3) TORTURE CHAMBER	Jeanne enters chamber.	Judges demand her to sign recantation.	Jeanne refuses to sign.
(4) CELL	Cauchon and other judges arrive.	Judges offer Jeanne communion.	Jeanne refuses to sign.
(5) CEMETERY	Crowd, judges, soldiers, and Jeanne assemble.	Priest gives Jeanne sermon; allies urge her to submit. She signs recantation.	
(6) CELL	Cauchon and judges arrive.	Judges and Massieu ask Jeanne why she has changed.	Jeanne announces her acceptance.
(7) COURTYARD	Crowd gathers and Jeanne comes out.	Jeanne is bound to stake; Massieu extends cross.	A man shouts: "You have burned a saint!"

Authorities attack Jeanne or ally.	**Participants disperse.**	**Transition which contrasts elements.**
Soldier threatens Jeanne.		
D'Estivet spits on her.		
Soldiers and Church remove de Houppeville.		
	Court adjourns.	Jeanne in cell / judges forging letter.
Soldier takes Jeanne's ring.		
Loyseleur reads forged letter.		
Judges refuse to let Jeanne hear Mass.	Judges leave.	
Guards abuse Jeanne.	Massieu dismisses guards.	
Judges threaten Jeanne with torture.	Jeanne swoons and judges leave.	Jeanne bled / judges on stair.
Communion withdrawn and Jeanne berated.	Judges leave.	Jeanne weeping / judges on stair.
Cauchon reads sentence; soldiers attack man.	Crowd disperses.	Jeanne's hair cut / people at fair.
	Judges leave.	Jeanne's communion / crowd and soldiers.
Soldiers assault crowd as Jeanne burns.	The army drives the crowd out of Rouen.	Cross / stake.

of abbreviating or distending a movement through (mis-)matches on action. In *La Passion de Jeanne d'Arc,* the fragmentation proceeds from the systematic alternation of shots containing *different* elements. Thus Dreyer carries the crosscutting of his earlier films into every scene.

The dialogical editing construction flings together characters and objects. Has any film more vividly made objects a part of the drama? The nubby crown of reeds, the smooth cross Jeanne clasps, the thick ropes, the dull sheen of the pan that catches Jeanne's blood: every object in the film has a distinct weight and shape and texture that identify martyrdom with an awful tactility. Nonetheless, the compositional principles are severe. A scene will restrict itself to only one or two emblematic objects, which are inserted into the alternating pattern of the dialogue. The soldiers' association with metal results in a striking series of images: when the soldiers file out of court, shots of their spears moving rightward are intercut with shots of priests' faces rising into the frame. Alternating shots likewise integrate the communion wafer into scene four, the torture wagon and the skull into scene five, the bits of hair shorn from Jeanne into scene six, and the logs at the stake and the birds in the sky into the final scene. In such ways, alternating editing selects a very few objects for narrative "dialogue" with the characters' actions.

In addition, of course, some of these objects recur from scene to scene and become woven into the large-scale structure of the narrative. The cross motif appears first as the chains lashed around the Bible, then as the crosspiece on Jeanne's cell window, then as the shadow the window casts on the floor, then as the grave markers and as the crosses atop the churches, and, in the last scene, as the crucifix extended to Jeanne by Massieu; at all points, the motif is intercut with Jeanne. Her crown of straw wends its way through various scenes—it is tossed in the air by her guards, clapped onto her head, cast aside by attendants, and swept up with bits of her hair. Most pervasive of all are those written materials inserted in the course of the action: the forged letter, the recantation which Jeanne initially refuses but finally signs, the "Apostate" parchment nailed to the stake.

Significantly, all these motifs—cross, crown, messages —reinforce a second text upon which the film's narrative depends: the tale of Christ's suffering and death. The outcome of the film is programmed from the beginning, not only because we know the historical Jeanne but also because we know the story of the Passion. The cross and the crown of straw, virtually the only objects associated with Jeanne, unambiguously guarantee that narrative parallelism reiterated in the film's original title: *La Passion et la mort de Jeanne d'Arc.* The written messages that run through the narrative, some of which also refer to the Christ story (e.g., the "Apostate" inscription at the top of the stake), lead directly to yet another way in which the principle of dialogical construction ensures coherence and formal unity.

For the minute-by-minute movement of the narrative depends upon a dialogical clash of *texts.* Dreyer realized this: "For me, it was before all else the technique of the official report which governed. There was, to start with, this trial, with its ways, its own techniques, and that technique is what I tried to transpose to the film. These were the questions, these were the answers—very short, very crisp."[19] With only one exception (a privileged one, as we shall see), there are no explanatory or commentative intertitles, and the resulting dosage of dialogue titles has encouraged the view that this is "a sound film struggling for speech." What the complaint overlooks is that the concentration upon characters' spoken and written words defines the narrative as a battle of discourses. Throughout the film, saying is opposed to remaining silent; question is opposed to answer; the free word is opposed to the enforced word (Jeanne will not say what the authorities demand); speaking is opposed to writing (the scribe labors busily through almost every scene, transforming Jeanne's words into that record which is the book opened at the film's outset). The very "talkiness"—better, the "literality"—of the film is thus indispensable to a conflict of representational systems.

On one side of this conflict, the authorities use representation as a commodity to be transferred and circulated. The exchanges of question and answer which define the courtroom situation are only the most apparent instances of the judges' economic use of discourse. And for this economic function, writing is indispensable. In forging the letter, the authorities reduce King Charles's relation to Jeanne to a sheet of paper capable of being swapped for her trust. More strikingly, they propose, by transforming Jeanne's word into a written record, to schematize her as a historical, hence controllable entity. Just as Cauchon must *read* the charges and the sentence, so the scrupulous demand that Jeanne *sign* the recantation indicates the Church's awareness of the authoritative exchange value of the written word: a woman's life traded for the word that names her, an ecclesiastical trial fulfilling a political bargain. ("I wish," says Warwick, ". . . that she should not die a natural death. I paid a high price for her.") It is Jeanne's signed recantation that Loyseleur offers to Warwick, as if it were a bill of sale.

On the other hand, however, Jeanne's word is not primarily a commodity. Illiterate, she is closed off from the written contract. Hers is the expressive, personalized word, an inspired speech opposed to the ossification of the written record, transcending the systems of political and religious exchange. She does not, though, realize that her word transcends history. In the beginning of the film, she sees her mission and her being as resolutely historical. Coaxed by promises of surviving to fight her enemies, she signs the recantation, thereby submitting herself to the exchange on the judges' terms. But the alien, estranging quality of Jeanne's submission is present even in the very act of signing: Loyseleur must guide her hand through the signature she cannot manage, and she adds to this inscription not a word but an image, two strokes of the pen making a cross on the page. We find in *Jeanne d'Arc* echoes of the"logocentrism" which, Jacques Derrida suggests, recurs throughout Western thought, and which elevates the mystical expressiveness of the spoken word (further sanctified in the film by the mystically expressive face) above the static repressiveness of writing.[20]

If we are left with a dialogue not only between speakers but between two ways of saying, can we claim that the film univocally favors Jeanne's way? We must not lose the film's strain here. To a great extent, *La Passion de Jeanne d'Arc* remains a true dialogue, putting into tension the spoken and the written word. That tension, indeed, manifests itself in the film's very surface. The film's many titles create an oscillation between the dynamic image of a speaker and the remains of speech. To wish that the film had sound is to want to remove one of its most productive contradictions. For one thing, the titles assist the breakdown of narrative space, as Michel Marie has observed: "Paradoxically, the very profusion of intertitles articulated with respect to a visual *découpage* almost entirely based on *inserts* (close-ups of faces and objects) results in creating a purely abstract cinematographic space, without any logical relationship with the discourse's place of reference."[21] Moreover, the dialogue titles foreground the crucial difference between speaking and writing: lips move and then we read what they have already said. Through *Jeanne d'Arc*'s insistence on the principle of dialogue, the archaic dialogue title gets recharged with formal significance. As writing, the intertitle becomes only the trace of Jeanne's dynamic speech and necessarily clashes with the very immediacy which that speech embodies. Only as a *silent* film could *La Passion de Jeanne d'Arc* squeeze the conflict between speech and writing into the smallest crevice of its texture.

This conflict reminds us that ironically the entire narrative depends upon the very record that the authorities kept; the book which existed solely to insert Jeanne's words into the Court's circuit of exchange is now used to reactivate that circuit in the very projection of the film. The historically authentic trial text must be presented to us in all its frozen materiality if the principle which it represents is to be questioned, put in dialogue with the image's spiritual word. In a sense, the film's images become a cinematic gloss, a running commentary upon the trial record. We err, then, if we see the film's intertitles as unwarranted intrusions, for in the juxtaposition of image and text, *La Passion de Jeanne d'Arc* plays out to the fullest the conflict between its voices.

Yet if the film's contradictions—both spatial and representational—are not wholly canceled, they are strongly qualified by the unifying principle of Jeanne herself and, in particular, her defining attribute—saintliness. A traditional conception of the hero here aims to halt the play of ambiguities. The film's ending instates Jeanne as the victor in the battle of discourses. What assures this victory is not only the transhistorical aspect of her speech—the spontaneity which certifies the spiritual expressiveness of the spoken word—but also the way in which the film's narrative structure confirms her prophetic vision.

The turning point is the moment at which she recognizes the similarity between her existence and the story of Jesus (the similarity that the audience has already recognized). When Jeanne sees her crown of straw swept out by the barber, she recognizes both her betrayal of Christ and her likeness to him. In denying her recantation, in canceling the bargain and taking back her word, she assures us that our reading of her situation was the correct one. In the dialogue with Massieu, her earlier pronouncements are now analyzed, and found to have been unwittingly prophetic. She *has* been sent to save France, but the salvation will not be a military one. Her king *will* rescue her from prison, but He is not King Charles. The "great victory" she had predicted will be her martyrdom; her deliverance, death. By that paradoxical gesture characteristic of religious discourse, secular speech is turned inside out and found to contain that visionary word supposedly beyond the contingent and historical. In the scene with Massieu, Jeanne rereads the narrative; now she and the film speak with the same voice. In later films, this strategy will become familiar to us as typically Dreyerian: the revelation of the authoritative word, the unearthing of a text which has determined the narrative action. Now we can see how the film uses character psychology as only one element in an impersonal causal system. Jeanne's centrality is reaffirmed by the film's fulfillment of her prophecy, the spontaneous word is the true one (religiously but also narratively), and the film seeks to contain its contradictions by dovetailing her reading of her life with the reading compelled by the narrative. Here the hero unifies the narrative by becoming the character whose explanations make the fiction most intelligible.

The pull of unity against heterogeneity is nowhere better illustrated than in the finale. Jeanne is burned, the crowd revolts, and the soldiers brutally drive the peasants out of Rouen castle. I have already pointed out the acute spatial dislocations of the sequence's unbalanced framings, the disorienting cutting on the smoke, the upside-down camera movements. We can now see how this sequence also strives to close the film around Jeanne. The clash of written and spoken discourses ends: the executioner nails to the stake a paper reading: "Heretique relapse, Apostate Ydolatre"; but Jeanne has the last word in the dialogue with her cry of "Jesus!" Our and Jeanne's reading of her life as a path toward martyrdom is instantly corroborated by the spontaneous voice of the crowd: "You have burned a saint!" The soldiers attack the people. While spatial fragmentation threatens to burst the film apart, the sequence is saturated with repetitions seeking narrative coherence. Shots of Jeanne alternate with those of the slaughter, Christian icons flood shot after shot: crosses, crucifixes, church towers, birds, the stake all assure us of the intelligibility of Jeanne's death. Finally, the scene's extreme disruptiveness calls forth the ultimate check: an unclaimed voice enters the film for the first time. After the last image, the stake in the foreground standing against the cross in the distance, there appear words which cannot be attributed to a character:

> *. . . and amid the flames the white soul of Jeanne rose heavenwards, that soul which has become the soul of France, as Jeanne herself has become the incarnation of imperishable France.*

The sentence collapses the historical/spiritual dialectic of the discourses in the film: both nation and martyr achieve immortality. As in *Vampyr,* such omniscience is possible only for the sourceless voice of the title. By position and past tense, the title firmly ties the ending to the beginning: the book that was opened is now closed.

But, we must finally ask, what book is this? The ambiguity nags us, for though it is possible to put the first shot of the book outside the narrative time of the film (as I have done in asserting it to be the surviving trial transcript), we may also situate the first shot within the narrative, as part of the first interrogation scene. If we do, the book continues to perplex us. Is it a volume of trial records opened to a fresh page, or is it that Bible upon which Jeanne swears to tell the truth? The uncertainty can never be resolved: the book's function is to remain ambiguous, collapsing (as the last title does) the spiritual and the historical, narrowing the distinction between Jeanne and Jesus. The calculated hesitation between identifying the text as Jeanne's word and identifying it as God's word preserves the heterogeneity at work in the narrative, and nonetheless insists that the weight of the film comes finally to rest in Jeanne's conviction of her saintliness.

This chapter has sought to illustrate a paradox. If the critic seeks unity at all costs in *Jeanne d'Arc,* the film resists, flaunting discontinuity and contradiction. Yet if the critic wants to show total fragmentation, the film suddenly pulls itself into coherent patterns. It may be that every narrative film strains between rigor and dispersion. But if it is also true that at some point every film cracks, *Jeanne d'Arc* emphasizes its fissures much more boldly than do most. Critics have typically overlooked the film's disturbing qualities and favored its unifying ones. This chapter has proposed seeing the film more dynamically, as an intersection of systems in which forces for narrative unity seek to hold together powerful stylistic contradictions. This "seek to" insures the continuing interest of *La Passion de Jeanne d'Arc.*

Vampyr

The difficulty of discussing Dreyer's *Vampyr* has been less a subject of critical writing than an unacknowledged premise. Reading critical commentary on the film, one would think of it as a fascinating but easily assimilable horror film; reading between the lines, one can see that it causes more analytical problems than almost any Dreyer work. Lapses into vagueness are the symptoms: "One has the impression of continual movement, intensifying one's sense of a world of instability and shifting shadows where nothing is fixed or certain" (Robin Wood).[1] "Somehow the whole [opening] sequence, with its dissolving surfaces as though people were literally being seen through a glass darkly, and its profound silences broken only by the unearthly tolling of the bell and the remote echo of a human voice, is like a mysterious ceremonial of death" (Tom Milne).[2] "The people in [*Vampyr*] glide slowly through a vague, whitish mist like drowned men. . . . the film is pervaded by nightmare obsession, and it shows a deadsure, calculated use of every means at [Dreyer's] disposal" (Ebbe Neergaard).[3] Such evocations avoid coming to grips with what is most obvious to the viewer: the film is a very difficult one simply to follow. To admit that *Vampyr* is a "hard" film is not a confession of Philistinism but a basic aesthetic datum which the critic must confront and examine. As we saw in *La Passion de Jeanne d'Arc,* acknowledging a work's particular opaqueness or impedances is often the most direct route to grasping its salient properties.

THE ABSENT CAUSE

Consider, for example, one of the most puzzling segments of the film. David Gray, seeing the shadow of a gravedigger, is led to explore a decrepit building. He watches the shadow of the peg-legged soldier move on its own. Glimpsing an old woman walking down a corridor, he flees. He watches the shadow return to the soldier's body. He hears the old woman ask the soldier, "Where is he?" Shadows dance jauntily on the wall; we glimpse the old woman again. Gray discovers a coffin beside a discarded doctor's shingle. He passes through a consulting room. Meeting a gnomish man who looks like a cross between Albert Schweitzer and Mark Twain, Gray asks if there are children here. The old man says no. "But," says Gray, "there are dogs." The old man responds, "There are no children and no dogs. Good night." And he shows Gray out. On first viewing, it is probably impossible to grasp the rather simple "story" underneath this sequence: the vampire Marguerite Chopin has arrived looking for her assistant, the doctor.

What has happened here? Recognizing this sequence as "hard to follow" goes straight to the point: the plot (the set of events as narrated) does not clearly present the story (that hypothetical concept of the "actual" events which we construct as implicit background to the plot). Indeed, much of *Vampyr* is built so as to make the following of story events exceptionally difficult. The modern cinema has made such effects common, as when *Nicht versöhnt* or *La Guerre est finie* radically reorders story events, and we have already seen how Dreyer's early films experiment to some extent with such shiftings of order. But *Vampyr* yields a different set of strategies for troubling the story. For in such a sequence as this, the *order* of events in the story has not been disturbed. Yet by introducing the old woman, the doctor, and his assistant before we can posit a *causal* relation between them and the old chatelain seen in the previous scene; by presenting major characters at one remove (as shadows, voices, distant figures); by crosscutting; by inserting retarding devices (the dancing shadows, the coffin, the empty examination room, the "children and dogs" dialogue); and finally, by presenting the entire building's contents through Gray's exploration of it—in such ways, the film carefully obfuscates the story by means of the plot.

Form has been made difficult. We have, then, first to examine the film's strategies for relating plot so obliquely to story.

As a starting point, here is the film's story. In the village of Courtempierre flourishes the vampire, Marguerite Chopin, a woman who has died unrepentant, and who now returns from the grave to prey upon the living. She is assisted by the village doctor and his peg-legged henchman. One of her victims is Léone, the daughter of an old chatelain. Distraught, the chatelain one night calls upon a visitor to the village, David Gray, to intercede if he should die. That same evening, Chopin orders her minions to kill the chatelain and to induce Léone to commit suicide. Gray sees the peg-legged soldier murder the father. Dying, the chatelain gives a heart-shaped locket to Gray and his other daughter Gisèle. The chateau coachman goes for the police. Gray begins reading the book on vampirism which the father has bequeathed him. In the meantime, Chopin lures Léone outside and is about to attack her, but when Gray and Gisèle arrive, Chopin flees. The coach returns, bearing the body of the coachman, who has been murdered. Once Léone is inside, she is seized by blood-lust, and is about to attack Gisèle when the nurse intervenes. The doctor arrives at the chateau to tend to Léone, and on the pretext of saving her induces Gray to give blood. While Gray is sleeping, the doctor leaves poison for Léone to take. An old manservant in the chateau, alerted to Chopin's vampirism by the book, awakens Gray and brings him to Léone's room just in time to prevent her involuntary suicide. The doctor flees, taking Gisèle prisoner. Gray rushes outside, where he collapses and has a dream depicting not only Gisèle's whereabouts but also his own death. The manservant and the awakened Gray go to the graveyard and drive a stake through Marguerite Chopin's corpse. The curse on Léone is immediately lifted. The doctor and his assistant are now haunted by a spectre of the father. The peg-legged assistant dies, while the doctor escapes to a flour mill. Gray rescues Gisèle, while the manservant traps the doctor in a cage and suffocates him in a torrent of flour.

To schematize *Vampyr* this baldly is already to hint at how problematic story and plot become in the film, but we may start by noticing what has been selected for presentation in the plot. Consistently, at the level of the events themselves, consequences are shown but causes are concealed. Most broadly, the plot postpones revealing the source of the contagion: it is not until very late in the film that the old vampire is identified as Marguerite Chopin, buried in the village cemetery. But the same principle operates even more strongly scene by scene, for here causes are completely suppressed. Typically the film picks out *late* phases in an implicit sequence of actions. We do not see Chopin's first attack(s) on Léone, only the old chatelain worrying as to whether the wounds will heal. We do not see Chopin decide to induce Léone's suicide, only her delivery of the poison to the doctor. We do not see the chatelain's decision to visit Gray, nor the plan to murder the chatelain; we see only the visit and the murder. The death of the coachman, Chopin's luring of Léone, the summoning of the doctor, the doctor's leaving the poison for Léone, and the abduction of Gisèle are all similarly elided.

Now of course few plot constructions present all story events, but we have here a consistent pattern. An event is presented which, by explicit reference or implicit logic, is seen as a consequence. But the cause is absent. More important, the absent cause is usually not ultimately identified. Not only are the causes concealed at the moment we recognize the effect; the causes are usually *never* explained. The identification of Chopin as the culprit turns out to be virtually the only certain assignment of cause which *Vampyr* permits. We do not know how Chopin seduced Léone out of the chateau, how the coachman was murdered, how Gisèle was carried off, what governs the dead father's return, and so on. Both psychological and physical motivation remain obscure. From even this cursory investigation of such story events as have been selected, we may notice that what makes the film difficult is what will emerge as a generative pattern for the plot as a whole: the absent cause. (We shall see later how other narrative patterns work, by recoil, to override the absence of causes among narrative events.)

It might be argued that *Vampyr* is simply a horror film, and that its uncertainties are motivated in ways traditional to that genre. Certainly the film does solicit a reading as a vampire film, but it resists being assimilated to any norms. As a contrast, take Tod Browning's *Dracula* (1931), surely as canonic a vampire film as exists. Compared to *Vampyr*, *Dracula* is perfectly coherent. Browning's film exposes its narrative premises at the very outset, during Renfield's visit to the inn. Thereafter, causation is lawlike and certain: Dracula can become either a wolf or a bat, he sleeps during the day and prowls at night, and so on. The film carefully motivates the insertion of genre conventions and ratifies them by the "scientific" explanations of Professor von Helsing. Although a thorough study of the horror genre remains to be made, *Dracula* shows that the classical vampire film does not rely upon the type of narrative uncertainty that Dreyer creates in *Vampyr.*

Since in *Vampyr* the absent cause is often assumed to be supernatural, it is also possible to situate the film in the genre of the "fantastic," which makes inexplicable causes its *raison d'etre.* Tzvetan Todorov suggests that the fantastic genre is initially defined by "an event which cannot be explained by the laws of this familiar world." Thus the hesitation between natural and supernatural explanations defines the "fantastic."[4] Similarly, Sorin Alexandrescu finds that the fantastic tale insists on keeping disjoint the natural/supernatural semantic fields.[5]

Mark Nash has shown that in at least one respect *Vampyr* belongs to the genre of the fantastic: the film's systematic play upon point of view creates a hesitation about the causes of events.[6] Yet the film remains, I believe, somewhat unassimilable even to the fantastic genre. Both Todorov and Alexandrescu claim that the hesitation characteristic of the fantastic genre is unstable: by its end, the tale must choose either a natural explanation (which makes it a tale of the "uncanny") or a supernatural one (making it a tale of the "marvelous"). Nash seems to suggest that *Vampyr* indeed settles into a stable ending, one "accepting more conventionalized rules of editing, closing the work with an impression of 'smoothness,' spatio-temporal continuity."[7] There are two difficulties with this position. First, the ending is far from a model of smooth spatio-temporal continuity. Secondly, the final scenes are no less problematic causally than what went before. What makes the dead chatelain's face reappear to haunt the doctor and Justin? What shuts the door of the mill-cage to trap the doctor? What force makes the gears grind to a halt in the very last shot? All the way through, *Vampyr* poses such unanswerable questions: the film *continues* to hesitate over its enigmas. Such hesitation weakens the sequential relations of story events and, by making events in the plot impossible to link with causes, extends the troubling strategy of the plot.

In the sequence in the doctor's lair we noticed yet another means for making the story difficult when we commented that various elements served to retard the revelation of the segment's principal story points. For example, Gray does not immediately observe the exterior of the building: he first sees the gravedigger's shadow. Similarly, he does not immediately encounter Marguerite Chopin, but first sees the peg-legged shadow. He sees the old woman speak to Justin only after he has watched the shadow leave the body. The dancing shadows again delay revelation of Chopin. Gray does not see the doctor until after the ironic joke of the coffin and the *Docteur du Médécin* sign, and after Gray's exploration of the doctor's quarters. Such materials are inserted to retard the principal step-by-step progression of the story. Roland Barthes calls such major steps "cardinal" functions, or "nuclei," and such inserted materials "catalyses," since they "fill in the narrative space separating the hinge-type functions."[8]

In fact, the specimen sequence's use of catalytic functions is typical of the film as a whole. First, the catalyses are not simply random; usually, they connote death (the spiked angel sign at the inn, the man with the scythe, the picture in Gray's room, the gravedigger's shadow, the coffin, and the skulls and potions). When death is not specifically connoted, at least an eerie inexplicability is, as in the case of the peg-legged shadow or the dancing shadows on the wall. But these images' connotations do more than evoke atmosphere. They also foreshadow imagery which will later be taken up by the cardinal functions, or main plot. The most obvious example is probably the way in which the peg-legged soldier's shadow is seen again during the murder of the old chatelain; but we may also note that the man with the scythe takes a boat, as Gray and Gisèle will do at the end; that the etching in Gray's room prefigures the suffering of Léone, the mourning at the chateau, and the skeleton that Marguerite Chopin will become; that the gravedigger's shadow and the coffin prophesy the burials with which the last sections of the film will be occupied. Somewhat similarly, through cutaways the angel sign and the gravedigger's shadow are pried loose from their niches in story-space and raised to the level of ominous emblems to be inserted in later sections. Most interesting of all is the way in which Gray's dreams, in recapitulating all the death-filled catalyses preceding them, also point ahead to the resolution of the main action.

The plot, then, inserts these death motifs between the cardinal functions not solely for atmosphere but also to build up a reserve, as it were, of connotative energy to be discharged in a later phase of the narrative. Often, however, the cardinal functions are so extended, the space between them so saturated with catalyses, that the story is not only delayed but shunted to one side, as if it were less important than the intervening material. By their number, their arresting nature, and the disproportionate time spent on them, such catalyses further loosen the causal relations between events in the story. Barthes affords an explanation of why this happens: "These catalyses are still functional, insofar as they enter into correlations with the nucleus, but their functionality is toned down, unilateral, parasitic. . . . Catalyses are no more than consecutive units, while cardinal functions are both consecutive and consequential."[9] In *Vampyr,* the pure consecutiveness of the inserted material, growing out of hand, finally blurs the consequential relations among cardinal functions. Indeed, since it is *only by means of* such consequential relations that we can *recognize* the cardinal functions, in *Vampyr* we cannot always grasp what the principal story action *is.* We are easily sidetracked and baffled.

A good example of this bafflement comes at the very beginning of the film. The first twenty-six shots depict Gray's arrival at the inn. After the first explanatory title, we get a shot of Gray walking up from the river. He seeks entry to the inn and is at first thwarted. While he waits for the door to be opened, he glances back to the river. Cut to a long shot of a man with a scythe going down to the bank. Gray is admitted to the inn, but shots of his progress through various rooms and passageways are repeatedly interrupted by shots of the man with the scythe. Alone in his room, Gray looks out the window and again sees the man with the scythe. Is the story's action, then, to involve Gray with this man? No, since the man is never seen again. Gray then starts to explore the inn and discovers a dwarfish, disfigured man upstairs. Is the film to be about this sinister inn? No. And so on. We are constantly led astray, until when the old chatelain leaves the parcel for Gray, we grasp gratefully at a bona fide cardinal function. But this is considerably weakened, too, for instead of following it immediately with an explanation of why the old chatelain has turned to Gray for help, the action shifts to Gray's exploration of the doctor's lair. From the start, then, *Vampyr* prepares us for a "flattened" narrative, in which inserted materials not only create atmosphere, not only abstractly foreshadow story events, but also at certain points overwhelm the cardinal story functions and deflect our attention from them. The principal story becomes half-hidden, as obscure as the misty landscapes throughout the film.

Finally, the retardation of story material is obviously related to the absent cause. The retarding elements block revelation of the truth (for if the truth were revealed, the narrative would end). The mysteries posed by the key turning in the lock, the doors which open and close of their own power, the spectral leading figures, and the rest are never solved; the catalyses switch the main narrative questions to one side and immerse us in a host of unanswerable ones. A triple economy is thus at work: by retarding the plot, obfuscating the story, and raising questions which the story cannot answer, the catalyses accumulate an even greater weight as discrete entities.

The temporal composition of the plot further suppresses causal agencies. Most broadly, the plot spans a single night, running from dusk to dawn, and, since it contains no flashbacks, it already limits itself to showing the effects of causes initiated before the plot commenced. This strategy is considerably extended by the way the film's crosscutting affects temporal duration. By crosscutting different action strands, the film constantly slips away from rendering the complete duration of story events. Many sequences are thus made elliptical.

Ellipsis is also a characteristic of the classical cinema, but not usually *within* the scene, as is the case in *Vampyr.* For the temporal ellipticality of *Vampyr* makes it difficult to assign causes (directly the opposite of crosscutting's function in the classical cinema). For example, the shadow of the gravedigger crosscut with Gray's exploration of the doctor's lair blocks our knowledge of how Gray gets from spot to spot in the building; the panning shot of Léone's empty bed inserted into the sequence of Gray's first reading of the book *Vampyre* makes it uncertain as to what has caused her departure; cutaways to the angel and cloudy sky interrupt several actions; the crosscutting of the old manservant and Gray's first dream obscure the means by which the servant reaches Gray's room; even at the very end of the film, the crosscutting between Gray's rescue of Gisèle and the doctor's burial in flour does not permit us to understand what stops the mill's machinery. During every ellipsis, that is, important events occur; thanks to the crosscutting we must assume there are causal connections in the story, but the plot does not show them to us. Thus *Vampyr*'s crosscutting avoids the smooth sequentiality of traditional scenic construction, creating time gaps during which the absent cause can operate.

There is one more principal strategy by which *Vampyr*'s plot is made oblique in its relation to the story, and this depends upon the presence of David Gray himself. He is a curious protagonist. He "does" comparatively little in relation to the principal story action: it is the manservant who discovers how to eliminate Marguerite Chopin and who kills both her and the doctor. Though Gray does prevent the doctor from poisoning Léone and does rescue Gisèle, his behavior is less important to the story than to the plot; he exists less to act than to mediate. Possessing neither past nor future, lacking any definite traits of character, Gray is the thread which stitches the film together, the consciousness which structures the unfolding action. Tomashevsky notes that, "The protagonist is by no means an essential part of the story. The story, as a system of motifs, may dispense entirely with him and his characteristics. The protagonist, rather, is the result of the formation of the story material into a plot. On the one hand, he is a means of stringing motifs together; and on the other, he embodies the motivation which connects the motifs."[10] Gray observes: he sees the vampire and her minions, he witnesses the murder of the old chatelain, he sees the arrival of the doctor and of the dead coachman, and he discovers Gisèle as a prisoner. Gray travels, revealing and linking the various locales in the film. Gray reads, he offers his blood, and he dreams. All these activities motivate and structure the revelation of the story material. Even his rescue of Gisèle (when she is no longer in danger!) functions in counterpoint to the presentation of the doctor's death.

It should be plain, though, that Gray's consciousness is far from the most direct relay of the story. In fact, Gray as a structuring device further obfuscates the basic string of events. In our example of his exploration of the doctor's lair, we saw how the nuclei of the story action became considerably difficult to grasp when presented as his itinerary. Indeed, Gray's nighttime perambulations motivate the roundabout introduction to the story situation as a whole. That Gray is peripheral to the main action makes his viewpoint an ideal vehicle for pushing plot still further away from story.

It is, moreover, Gray's viewpoint which motivates one of the essential editing devices in the film: point-of-view or semi-point-of-view cutting. As in *Jeanne d'Arc,* Dreyer alternates shots of a person looking at a phenomenon with shots of that phenomenon itself (sometimes seen from the person's vantage point). Gray's investigation of the inn, the doctor's lair, and the chateau; his awakening by the old chatelain; his witnessing of the murder; his reading of the book: such episodes are based upon Gray's vision. (We shall see this device laid bare in the subjective vision of burial in his second dream). For the first half of the film, only Gray is given this point-of-view editing. Later the principle is distributed, so that, in a crucial shift, Léone, after the vampire's attack, stares greedily at her sister, and Dreyer constructs the scene around Léone's viewpoint. Still later, the doctor's being haunted by the father and becoming entrapped in the mill are presented through his point-of-view shots. We shall see later how this distribution of viewpoints fulfills important narrative functions, but for present purposes we may note, first, that the repetition of this pattern helps us grasp the film as unified; we accept the point-of-view editing, like crosscutting, as a major constructional principle, and gear our expectations accordingly. More important, the point-of-view editing situates a single consciousness (usually Gray's) as the principal mediation between us and the story events. Restriction to a character's vantage point makes what occurs outside that ken somewhat uncertain and ambiguous. Unlike Jeanne d'Arc, who centers the film causally, Gray as focal point reinforces the absence of cause, since by remaining with him we can *see* only effects. Making Gray the protagonist makes gray the story.

Vampyr's selection and organization of story events by ellipsis, retardation, and viewpoint can now be seen as governed by a basic principle: the disruption of cause-effect relations. Yet by a narrative recoil, this disruption is eventually overcome in the course of the film. Before we can discover how such a recoil operates, though, we need to examine perhaps the most brilliant and disturbing aspect of the film: its construction of space.

CONTRADICTORY SPACES

Early in *Vampyr,* David Gray pauses to examine a picture hanging in his room in the inn. In close-up, the camera moves upward and clockwise across the picture (fig. 1). The camera movement reveals, in turn, several figures grouped around a deathbed: two men, one in prayer, the other gnashing his teeth; then a weeping woman; then a weeping couple; then a priest, arm raised to deliver the last rites; then a skeleton rising beside the bed and brandishing a dagger above the dying man. At this point, Gray turns away.

From what we have examined so far, we can assign several functions to this picture. Another of those portents of death that fill the first sequence of the film, the picture

1

retards the cardinal actions and fills in the pattern of Gray's investigation. We can also see that the picture prefigures those later scenes wherein characters gather around Léone's bed to weep and pray for her. But what must also be noticed is the picture's function in offering itself as a distinct mode of spatial representation. The moving shot traces an effect (the mourners' reactions) easily back to a cause (the dying man). The composition of the picture is fixed a priori; the figures are frozen, the tableau space is stable. This shot constructs a representational system within which spatial relations mutually cohere; not only much painting but most classical cinematic style relies on this assumption of a spatially unambiguous event. But here this assumption emerges only to be attacked, for spatial coherence is precisely what *Vampyr* aims to undermine. The film refuses to establish space in the fashion of the classical Hollywood cinema: i.e., unambiguously, consistently, and with a clear relation to narrative logic. What we have instead is as profoundly discontinuous a space as in *Jeanne d'Arc.* In *Vampyr,* space is fluid, plastic, uncertain; its unfolding foils and baffles us; the revelation of space, rather than situating us more comfortably, disorients us. The picture, then, acknowledges the background against which the film's own work must be read; it cites the norm which the film strives to violate. While narrative operations refract the implicit story, the film's style deforms normal cinematic space. We can best understand how this happens by confronting the arguments of the man who raised the integrity of profilmic space to the level of an aesthetic mandate: André Bazin.

For Bazin, our natural attitude to the world is immediate and is constituted by, among other features, concreteness and continuity. An object in our experience has a "thereness" that solicits our attention to it as a unique presence. As such, objects participate in the world; they have weight, cast shadows, block one's vision, in short, exist independently of our personal projects. Moreover, time and space situate such entities in a continuum. Time is "a succession of concrete instants of life." Space is continuous both before us (in depth) and behind us, as well as on either side of us. Upon such a phenomenology Bazin builds a theory of filmic representation. He suggests that the artist will be able to capture (via the photochemical process which parallels the subject's being-in-the-world) the concrete continuity of existence. *Vampyr* controverts this. But, as the presence of the picture in the inn suggests, the film *needs* this continuum as a shadowy alternative; it implicitly posits concrete continuity as the norm, all the while working to dismantle it as a representational system.

Such dismantling is most apparent from the way *Vampyr*'s editing flagrantly disrupts the spatio-temporal continuum. Like *Jeanne d'Arc, Vampyr* depends on a crosscutting which perpetually fragments narrative continuity. The crosscutting frees up the spatio-temporal relations, making the film more perceptually opaque. From the very start, it juxtaposes spaces whose precise relationship has not been defined: David Gray's arrival at the inn is interrupted by cutaways to the old man with the scythe, while his wanderings are juxtaposed with repeated shots of the crooked angel that surmounts the inn. As in *La Passion de Jeanne d'Arc,* we are here in neither the seamless, "sutured" space of the classic Hollywood cinema nor in the nondiegetic space of, say, the early sections of Eisenstein's *October.* The old man and the angel emblem are within the narrative space but not precisely situated there. In the economy of the plot, these early cutaways function to present a cluster of atmospheric and prophetic motifs, but in the visual structuring of the film, the cutaways rupture spatio-temporal coordinates. In the second part of the film, the doctor's bleeding of Gray is intercut with the manservant's reading of the book *Vampyre,* and the stylistic consequence is that the labyrinthian space of the chateau is even further broken down. To the very end, the crosscutting of

2

3

4

5

Gray's and Gisèle's escape with the doctor's suffocation does not even retrospectively establish spatial relations; it simply closes the film on the graphic parallelism of fog and sifting powder. In sum, crosscutting is not only a vehicle for the narrative suspensions we have already examined but is also a prime factor in sabotaging a sense of continuity, for to recognize *Vampyr*'s disjunctions we must keep, as a paradigmatic substitute, the Bazinian spatio-temporal coordinates in the back of our minds.

Crosscutting is only the most apparent way in which *Vampyr*'s editing ruptures Bazinian phenomenal continuity, for within (supposedly) spatially homogeneous scenes, the editing is no less disruptive. When the old chateau master calls on Gray at the inn, the two men are never seen in the same frame, and the eyeline cues (Gray looking off left, the old man looking straight out at the camera) are angled in an unorthodox fashion. When Léone and Gisèle face each other, Dreyer jumps to and fro across the axis of action. Transgressive shot/reverse-shot editing confuses us as to who receives the heart-shaped locket from the chatelain (figs. 2–5). Even the point-of-view editing we've already examined contributes to the destruction of phenomenal space, for not only does the cut split subject from object, but the film's habit of rarely integrating the two into the same shot permits us no comfortable vision of the whole space. (Here again, *Jeanne d'Arc* is echoed.)

In such ways, editing within the scenes becomes as spatially discontinuous as the crosscutting which juxtaposes discrete spaces; again, if we are to perceive the rupture, we must call upon our customary acceptance of classical continuity. To take only one example, when Gray initially appears at the inn, point-of-view cutting blocks our understanding of the overall space. Several times, Gray watches the man with the scythe, but no master shot ever establishes the two men as being in the same frame, and even the sound of the ringing ferry bell is not motivated realistically (by, say, decreased volume in shots taken inside the inn). Moreover, the shots of the scythe man sitting in the boat are taken from the side opposite to that which Gray sees, thus breaking the 180° rule and creating a *false* point-of-view pattern. In the light of the disorienting editing devices, it is ironically appropriate that in the next shot Gray discovers on the wall of his room a picture which incarnates the stable space that the film already lacks.

To all of this, Bazin would protest that by its very nature editing shatters the continuum of the profilmic event. What Bazin opposes to the disjunctiveness of editing are techniques which guarantee a faithful rendering of the concrete integrity of the world. He suggests, for example,

6

7

8

9

that deep-focus cinematography, the long take, and camera movement permit the director to record an event in all its "real" continuity in space and time within the shot. Bazin goes still further to claim that the fantastic in film (his example is *Le Balon rouge*) needs this "realistic" framework: "If the film is to fulfill itself aesthetically we need to believe in the reality of what is happening while knowing it to be tricked" [*sic*].[11] Yet *Vampyr*'s style continues to challenge such a phenomenology. For even *within* the shot, *Vampyr* continues the editing's task of tacitly assuming concreteness and continuity while at the same time questioning the perceptual and aesthetic presuppositions underlying such a "natural attitude." But how can this questioning be carried out *within* the shot?

We may begin an answer by noticing how the concreteness which Bazin prizes is nullified by the film's stylistic workings. In previous and subsequent films, as we have seen, Dreyer used stark decor to abstract an object by the elimination of contingent detail. But previously the tableau shot had depended on crisp, clear lighting. In *Vampyr*, though, lighting leaves locales or objects ill defined. Most outdoor shots are veiled, diffusing the light thickly; often the shots are so indistinct that one can barely pick out the subject—e.g., Gray crossing a field, Marguerite Chopin bending over Léone (fig. 6). Dreyer carries the same principle further by interposing semi-opaque surfaces between characters and camera. The various windows through which Gray peers—the window at the inn's bar, the chateau's veined and shuttered parlor windows, the ground-glass at the door of the room in which Gisèle is imprisoned, even the glass plate in Gray's coffin—all have different refractive effects, obscuring the image to various degrees (figs. 7–9). Similarly, the fog which envelopes the fleeing lovers at the end is as texturally dense as the sifting powder which suffocates the doctor at the mill.

More profoundly, the lighting of the images questions the very solidity of the "actual presence" of the object represented, invoking Bazinian assumptions only to negate them. For Bazin, shadows and reflections must be paradigmatic signs of the actual, since by means of light they testify to the existence of a concrete cause. But in *Vampyr* we find shadows and reflections without bodies to cast them. The cause-effect assumption, linked to a certain "natural attitude" toward light, is thus negated and we are put in the presence of a "supernature," wherein objects have only the traces of their concrete existence. Indeed, it is only a short step to noting that in Bazin's system, cinema as photography ("light-writing") is itself a tracing, a shadow, a reflection, and then find, in Dreyer's use of *light-*

10

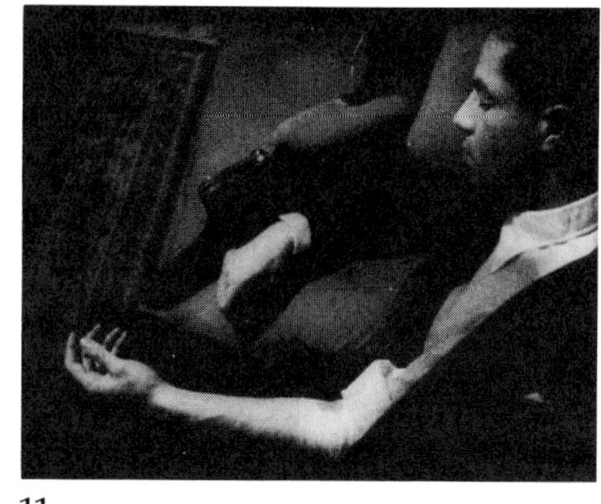
11

12

13

14

15

ing which severs object from effect, an alternative way of seeing cinema: a tool for dismantling the "natural attitude."

Bazin's assumption of the spatio-temporal continuum becomes a subject of still greater stylistic play. For Bazin's aesthetic, the space within and outside the frame is assumed to be of a piece; hence his critique of montage, which is said to fragment the a priori spatial continuum. Bazin ignores the possibility that space can be represented in cinema as if it had no "real" origin; that one can construct it, build it up through camerawork, *mise-en-scène,* editing, sound and overall structure. *Jeanne d'Arc* provides a classic instance of the construction of one sort of discontinuous space; *Vampyr* offers another. We may see, for example, in the diffuse and opaque shots already noted, an alternative to traditional ways of defining the planes within the frame; the suppression of depth cues (e.g., contour and overlap) makes such images spatially "illegible" to a considerable extent. Indeed, when Dreyer does give us an image with a semblance of depth, it is usually to dislocate us further: for instance, the shot of the doctor greeting the vampire is framed from an angle that does not permit us to discern the doorway on the right side, so that the doctor seems to be pulling the old woman straight out of the wall (fig. 10). Even more jarring are the jumbled depth cues in the shot of Gray after the bleeding; he seems to be observed slightly from above, but the rug and floor behind him and his chair slope much more steeply than traditional perspective would allow (fig. 11).

Furthermore, the imposition of a regular geometric pattern "over" the shot often renders the spatial relations secondary to purely graphic ones: repetition and development of the grid pattern (seen in windows and the mill cage) and the rectangular pattern (echoed in the recurring doorways and culminating in the images of the coffin and the cage) build up a structure of graphic motifs which dominate the more strictly spatial relations (figs. 12–15). The inn,

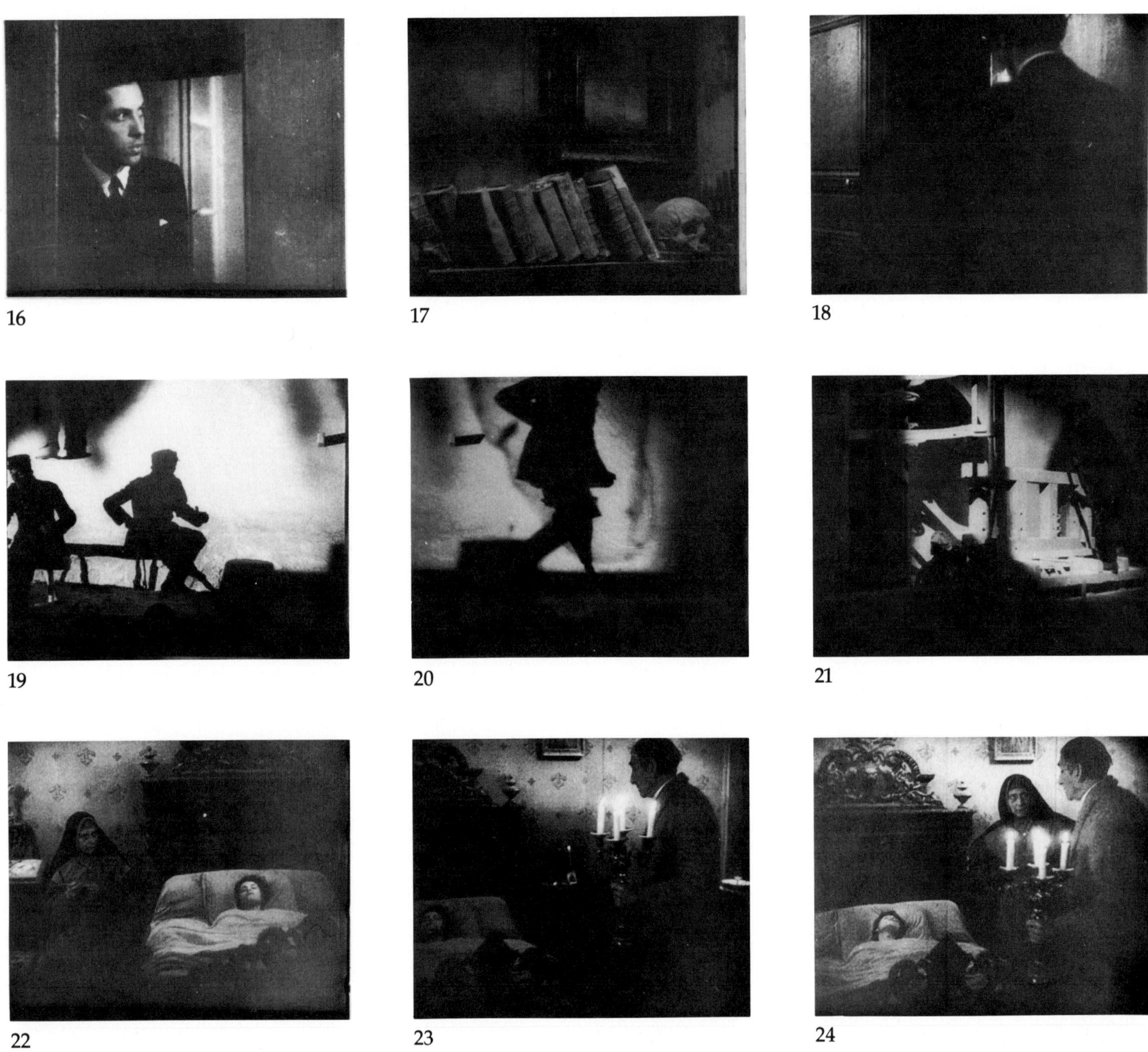

16 17 18

19 20 21

22 23 24

the doctor's lair, the chateau, and the mill often seem to be less independent locales than variants of a core of abstract configurations. It is, then, often difficult to map the space within the frame along the coordinates of our world; what we have is a labyrinth unrolling in accord with an abnormal logic. At this point, Bazin would say that Dreyer has succumbed to "expressionism," using lighting and purely geometric patterns to divorce the image from reality.

When we turn to more subtle spatial structuring in *Vampyr,* however, we find a surprise. For the very representational means which, according to Bazin, guarantee spatial and temporal continuity, function here to create precisely the opposite. The moving camera, for one thing, is supposed to verify the spatial homogeneity of the event presented. Of Renoir's reframing technique, which "respects" the continuity of dramatic space, Bazin notes that the film's *mise-en-scène* becomes off screen as well as on screen, that the one is indissolubly part of the other, and that each exists along a single continuum, mutually consistent and "real." ("The rest of the scene, while effectively hidden, should not cease to exist.")[12] But in *Vampyr,* camera movement permits no uniform "reality" to exist off screen. Gone is the stability of the Dreyer tableau. The camera edges away from compositional coherence. *Vampyr*'s camera movements construct space with no regard for phenomenal continuity.

The most glaring—and persuasive—examples are those in which *Vampyr* flatly defies the assumptions of spatial continuity off screen. When David Gray enters the doctor's office from frame left, the camera leaves him to pan and track right to another door; Gray now comes into the frame *from the right* and exits through the door (figs. 16–18). Almost immediately the same effect recurs: Gray sees the peg-legged soldier's shadow cross the room from the right to left but the soldier comes in to join it *from frame right* (figs. 19–21). Again, in the chateau, the camera pans right from the nun on the left side of Léone's bed and frames the old chatelain coming to the other side; the nun reenters the shot almost immediately from off frame right (figs. 22–24).

The effect is to turn off-screen space into a zone of uncertain status; we must ask throughout the film "*Who* is there?" and "*Where* is he or she?" Figures leave the frame and reenter at unexpected moments; characters spring into the shot when we had no idea that they were even nearby. Returning to his room, Gray shuts the door, and the camera tracks in to the door handle as Gray leaves the frame. But his hand immediately reenters to twist the key; we did not realize that he was just outside the frame line. Similarly, when the camera tracks right to Gisèle asking, "Why does the doctor come only at night?" the old manservant is walking at the same speed as the camera moves but just outside the left edge of the frame. (Only his hand gives him away.) At one time or another every character shares the shadowy off-screen existence made possible by Dreyer's exploitation of the ambiguities of camera movement. This is what has been so often sensed: the film's obsessive obliqueness, its refusal to address the "action" head-on. If, as we have seen, we cannot firmly trust the space represented within the frame, still less can we feel secure about the spatial relations off screen. Such is the consequence of Dreyer's strategy of dismantling that stylistic system which presupposes a stable spatio-temporal continuum.

This uncertainty about off-screen space is initiated from the very start of the film, in which we find crystallized several of *Vampyr*'s characteristic tactics of spatial disorientation. After the introductory title has named Courtempierre as the general locale, the opening shot pans slightly with Gray as he ascends from the river and looks upward; cut to a shot of the angel figure against the sky and a pan to the sign announcing "Hotel." Already Gray's glance, in motivating the cut, has split up the space in which he and the inn are situated. (Compare the classical Hollywood practice of beginning on an establishing long shot of a building, and letting the character come into the already defined space.) These two shots are followed by an even more problematic one: Gray is knocking at the inn's barroom door, but the camera is now *inside* the inn and tracking toward him. Not only does this shot announce the camera's refusal to remain unequivocally inside or outside a defined space, but it also initiates the pattern of seeing Gray framed—in doorways and windows, on staircases, inside coffins.

As Gray turns to the right, we get what we would have expected sooner: a shot of the inn's exterior. But far from stabilizing space, the shot warps it. Since Gray has turned his head, we expect that the next shot's panning movement across the roof represents his point of view. But the shot reveals nothing. The camera simply tilts down to a lighted window just as Gray enters the frame (no longer his "point of view") from the right. He knocks at the window, and the light goes out. Off-screen space (here that *behind* the set) is thus marked as a site of the absent cause. We suddenly hear a voice: "Who's there?" We judge it to be from the window we see, but we are wrong. Gray steps back and looks up. Cut back to the roof, over which the camera had cursorily panned, to reveal a sort of trapdoor-window, now open, a woman's head poking out. She gestures right, calls, "Go around the other way," and shuts the window. In these two shots, the camera reveals its capacity for duplicity; it will not always supply causes for

25

26

27

effects (the camera will not go inside to reveal why the light went out) nor will it remain subservient to the narrative dominant (the appearance of the woman).

Shot seven echoes shot five, for now we see Gray arriving before another door of the inn, but again from the *inside*. By jumping back and forth from outside to inside, the film blocks our attempts to map either the inn's exterior geography (where is the "other way" Gray must take?) or the internal layout (how does the woman get down to the doorway?). Unlike the stable space of the picture in Gray's room, cinematic space has fluid boundaries that can not only organize what is within the frame but also imply—sometimes deceptively—what lies outside.

If the camera *never* followed the narrative dominant, it would be easier for us to adjust. But the camera frustratingly adheres to the story often enough for us to recognize when it strays off on its own. In the segment introducing the doctor's lair, for example, we have already seen how the plot obfuscates cause-effect linkages in the story by expanding retarding elements and organizing most of the segment around Gray's investigation. We can now see how the camera movement aids in delaying and disconnecting story sequence. No fewer than five times the camera moves away from a figure and glides off on its own, dwelling on "atmospheric" elements and giving short shrift to the cardinal story point. At one moment the camera pans away from the peg-legged soldier, following only his shadow, before revealing him talking to Marguerite Chopin. At another point, the camera drifts away from Gray to track along a wall of dancing shadows before briefly glimpsing Chopin again. In another shot, when Gray emerges from a trapdoor, the camera coasts diagonally away from him across a coffin to a *Docteur du Médécin* sign before swiveling back to reveal Gray already in the recesses of a corridor (figs. 25–27). Instead of centering on the dominant characters the camera frequently moves *away* from them, disturbing our ability to grasp narrative logic.

Or consider a later sequence in the film. When the face of the old chatelain flashes upon the window, the doctor and his peg-legged soldier-assistant flee to the hall. The soldier races off to the right, the camera panning with him, as he struggles to open a door (fig. 28). The camera pans away from him to the left to catch the doctor rushing into another room and slamming the door behind him (fig. 29). Lights and shadows burst upon the doorpane (fig. 30). The soldier comes into the frame from the right and frantically tries to open *this* door. There is a cut back to the flashing face. The next shot resumes showing the soldier's attempt to enter the room where the doctor is hiding. He fails and so rushes back out frame right (fig. 31), but the camera doesn't follow him; instead it fastens its attention upon the door as flashing lights slide across it. We might assume now that the soldier has left the building. Abruptly a cawing sound is heard as the doctor opens the door and races out into the corridor, the camera panning right to follow him (fig. 32). The camera tracks in as the doctor opens the door which the soldier could not (fig. 33). A clatter is heard from off screen, the doctor dashes out of the frame left, and a scream is heard. There is a whip pan right, revealing a staircase, the soldier lying upside down upon it, dead (fig. 34). Useless to ask what caused the soldier's death, or what occurred in the first room the doctor entered. In playing hide-and-seek with the story, the camera refuses to trace out the causal skein, to chronicle story time, or to map out story space.

28

29

30

31

32

33

34

The significance of such camerawork is considerable. Classical Hollywood cinema has encouraged us to see the camera as motivated by the cause-effect chain of the story. There, for example, a character's change in position must either be clearly shown or "cheated" via editing or sound; if a character leaves a room, we must *see* or *hear* him or her leave. We assume that the camera will almost invariably show the story's dramatic dominant. But in *Vampyr* the moving camera attends only intermittently to the story. The camera is thus made an *independent* factor in the film; narrative time and space are no longer glued to camera time and space. Out of the causal logic of the narrative, the camera confines itself to registering only certain effects—panic, shadows, or death. Story time is deliberately stretched, retarded; the camera reveals events at its chosen rate. And out of the story space, the frame carves its own "plot," sometimes far removed from the dramatic dominant. If *Vampyr* can be considered a major film, it is because of Dreyer's understanding that the camera need not be subservient to narrative causality, that the film may foreground the active role of the camera in constituting and questioning cinematic space.[13] If, again, someone protests

35

36

37

38

39

40

41

that such stylistic problems are ingredient to the horror genre, *Dracula* is there to show that the classical horror film is representationally coherent. Browning's film never misleads us about narrative space; in fact, many of *Dracula*'s most important scenes—e.g., von Helsing's discovery that Dracula casts no reflection in a mirror—depend upon a consistent scenographic space.

Perhaps the most striking moment of *Vampyr*'s camera activity occurs when Léone is brought into the chateau after Chopin's attack upon her. Given that Dreyer used an actual building for shooting, the complexity of the shot's spatial dislocation, temporal ambiguity, and deflection of spectator attention is all the more remarkable.

Fig. 35: The shot begins with a view of the double windows of the chateau hallway. Outside the nurse and the manservant are dimly visible bearing Leone's body. A servant flits into the frame from the right and the camera tracks semicircularly leftward with her.

Fig. 36: Continuing its leftward circuit, the camera follows the servant as she opens the French doors and begins to enter. The camera leaves the servant and continues to move leftward, passing more windows and a pillar before framing a double door.

Fig. 37: The double door, emphasized by the cessation of the semicircular movement, is kept center frame while the camera now tracks back from it. Such emphasis generates the expectation that someone —probably those bearing Léone—will come through it. But such is not the case.

Fig. 38: Whereas figures 35–37 have integrated lateral off-screen space into the visual "plot," figures 38–39 now pull in the space *behind* the camera as well. As the track backward continues, the old servant woman bustles in frame left (from where we do not know), comes down the corridor a short distance, and moves a chair away from the right wall. Now the nurse and the old manservant enter frame right and, with the old woman, carry Léone's body down the hall. The cumulative disorientation flows from several deflected expectations. At first, we might expect that the camera will stay with the servant girl, but it instead shifts our attention to what turns out to be an irrelevant door.

Fig. 39: The camera continues its backward tracking through an adjoining room, still keeping the group centered, usually framed in successive doorways.

Fig. 40: Drawing back through a doorway, the camera pans away from the group to reveal Gray and Gisèle on the staircase, watching. We did not know for certain that they were in the chateau, let alone on the stair. Again, they were part of that global space behind the camera, but when or how they got there is uncertain.

Fig. 41: After the servants carry Léone upstairs and out frame left, Gisèle follows. Gray hesitates and then goes down the stair, the camera panning right to follow him as he goes back into the room and casually shuts the door on us. Since figure 37, that corridor has been the principal means of our grasping the story space, and now our vision is brusquely curtailed; after no fewer than five glimpses of and through doorways, the shot ends upon a door as blankly uncommunicative as the pair which seemed so important earlier.

According to Bazin, the long take and the moving camera stabilize space. But in this shot, as in the others I've discussed, the camera conceals areas and characters' whereabouts. Writing of Eisenstein's editing in *Ivan the Terrible,* Noël Burch astutely observes that the editing literally constructs the space: "We no longer have any sense of a surrounding space endowed with independent existence from which a sequence of shots has somehow been excerpted. Rather . . . we see a setting that is the sum total of all the perspectives of it embodied in the successive shots."[14] *Vampyr* demonstrates that this same obliteration of profilmic space can occur in the phases of a single shot; out of a real building the camera movement has carved a perplexing space. The camera can no longer be trusted; it will suppress information, swerve away from the story action, and at times lead us astray. What more forceful way to undercut the Bazinian "natural attitude" than to use his privileged techniques to obliterate the very profilmic event which those techniques claim to represent?

It is, finally, in the light of such camerawork that we may explain the disturbing effect of that celebrated episode in Gray's dream wherein Gray's double, in the coffin, watches, frozen, his own funeral. For the corpse's eye view in this sequence bares the device not only of Gray's point of view but also of the film's very act of constructing space. Through the window of the coffin we (and Gray) see the

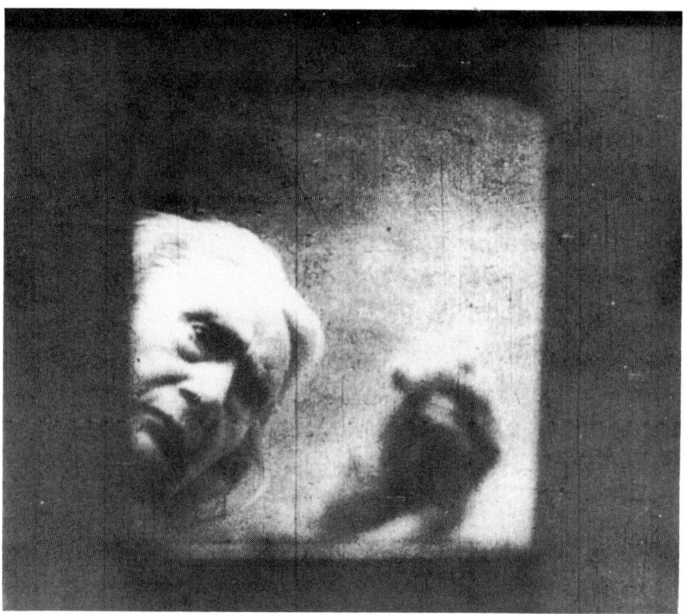

42

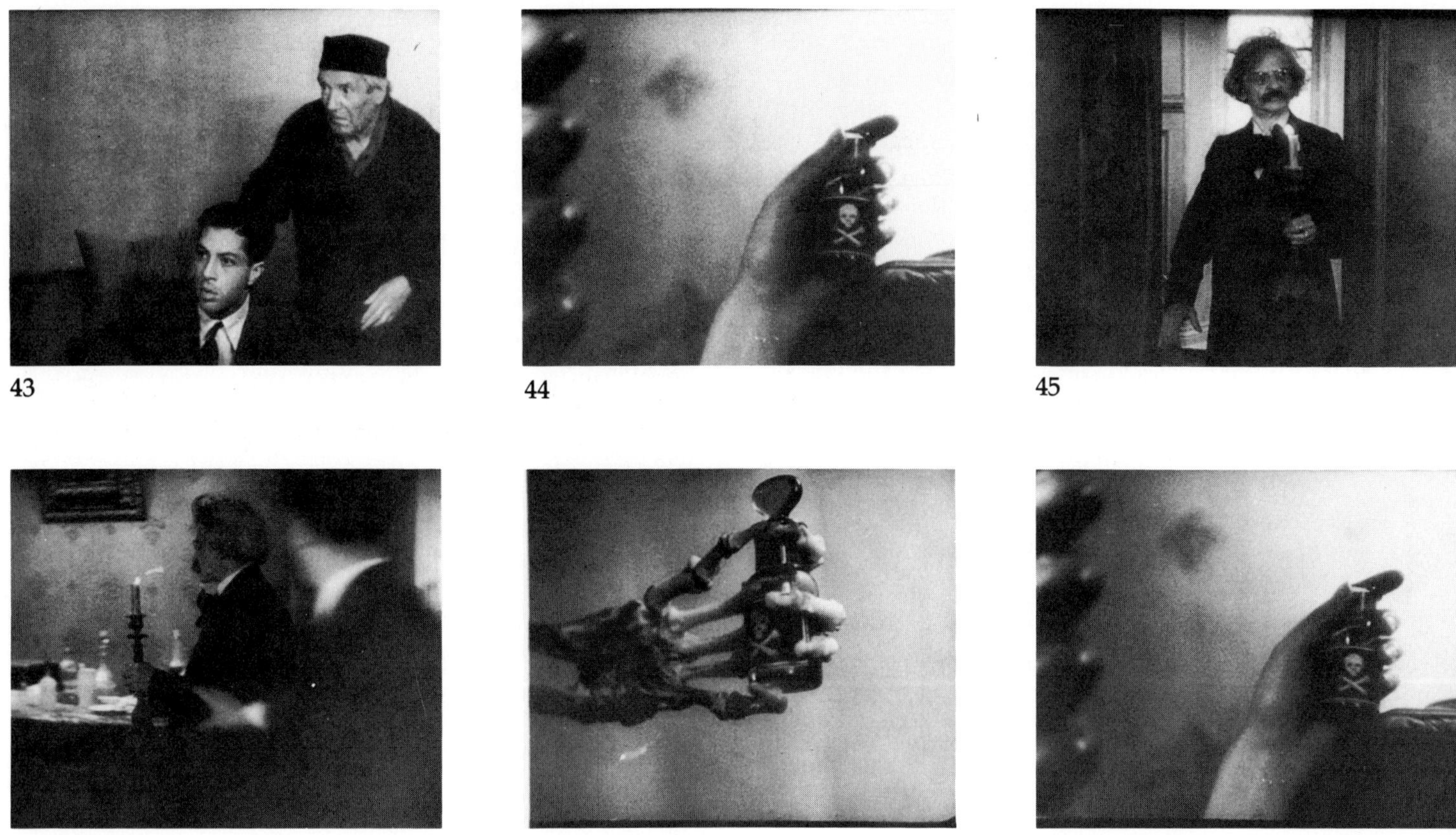
43 44 45 46 47 48

soldier glancing down at us, then a tool fastening the coffin lid down, and then—abruptly—the face of Marguerite Chopin appears and peers down at us (fig. 42). Just as throughout the film we have not been able to determine confidently who is present outside the frame, we have had no idea that Chopin was even in the room. The small window of the coffin, the frame for Gray's vision, decisively demonstrates the limitations of Bazin's "window on the world." One can see in this sequence a negation of classical representation itself. Though he errs in description, Barthes makes a fruitful suggestion in this regard:

> *In the theatre, in the cinema, in traditional literature, things are always seen* from somewhere. *Here we have the geometrical foundation of representation: a fetishist subject is required to cut out the tableau. . . . In order for representation to be really bereft of origin and exceed its geometrical nature without ceasing to be representation, the price that must be paid is enormous–no less than death. In Dreyer's* Vampyr, *as a friend points out, the camera moves from house to cemetery recording* what the dead man sees: *such is the extreme limit at which representation is outplayed; the spectator can no longer take up any position, for he cannot identify his eye with the closed eyes of the dead man; the tableau has no point of departure, no support, it gapes open.*[15]

Though Gray's eyes are in fact open (accentuating the role of witness which he has played throughout), Barthes's paradox is not lost: the seeing but dead subject is the contradictory limit of that representational system which stabilizes space around the pivot point of the observer. And it is precisely that stability which Dreyer seeks to undermine.

If it is through specific devices of editing and camerawork that *Vampyr* invokes and subverts the phenomenal continuum of traditional cinematic representation, we can find a brief segment which well illustrates the cumulative force of all these means working together. About two-thirds of the way through the film, Gray has allowed the doctor to bleed him and has been taken into an adjacent room to rest. The manservant awakens him: "Something terrible is happening!" The men look off left (fig. 43). There follows a close-up of the top of Léone's head; the camera then pans right to the poison bottle (fig. 44). Her hand comes in from the left, clutches the bottle, and carries it back (pan left), *out of the frame* (presumably to her mouth, but as in the doorway shot, the camera puts the chief dramatic action off screen; we cannot know if or when she will take the poison). Moreover, the cut from the two men's glances may seem to imply they are watching her, but—given the geography articulated in earlier shots—the cut creates a spatial mismatch. The next shot continues to disintegrate space. In a medium long shot, the doctor saunters into the bedroom from the main entrance, looks off to the right, and calmly moves left towards Léone's bed (fig. 45). A moment later Gray bursts in from frame right (fig. 46). But the framing of the shot conceals the reasons for Gray's delay and his position prior to the doctor's entrance (especially since the room in which Gray was sleeping would be off frame *left*). The camera pans with Gray as he darts to the bed, seizes the poison from Léone, and wipes her lips. Abruptly the camera pans right to reveal the open doorway as the servant trudges in from off right: during the moment Gray went to Léone's bed, the doctor escaped. When the camera does adhere to the principal story movement (will Léone be saved?) it misses another significant action.

Thus the unified space of the deathbed picture which hung in Gray's room finds its opposite in the fragmentation of this deathbed sequence. In the picture, the mourners, the priest, even Death and the sufferer inhabit a closed, centripetal continuum which the camera confidently traverses. But Léone, the doctor, Gray, and the manservant move through ambiguous, open zones. The modernity of the film's strategy becomes apparent when one recalls how that picture in Gray's room is echoed thirty years later in the pointlessly precise maps which decorate the spa in *L'Année dernière à Marienbad* and which are contradicted by a style of editing and camerawork that destroys the representation of phenomenal space and time. In those shots which show a character in one locale and in one costume and which track away to reveal the same character elsewhere and dressed differently, Resnais pursues that line of inquiry opened by *Vampyr.*

The deathbed sequence, by no means exceptional in the film, does concisely illustrate how *Vampyr* uses crosscutting, point-of-view editing, figure placement, lighting, and treacherously unpredictable camera movement to construct a space which disorients us with respect to the narrative. As in *Jeanne d'Arc,* the continuity prized by classical Hollywood cinema is cracked open by a formal system which operates by a principle of contradiction.

NARRATIVE RECOIL

Vampyr's difficultness, then, stems from a strategy of suppressing causal events in the story and constructing a spatio-temporal field which deviates from that of the story events. If this were all, though, *Vampyr* would be a much more unwatchable film than it is. The fact that it is not completely impenetrable, that we can grasp it to some degree, suggests that we need to balance our earlier efforts and consider how the film's difficulties are countered by structures of intelligibility. Not that the film's overall economy of forces erases the disturbing effects of the devices already discussed. Instead, like *Jeanne d'Arc, Vampyr* harnesses its disjunctions, organizing them in a certain way. Most generally, this consists of constructing narrative patterns in the plot itself which postpone our questions about the relationship of plot to story. The intelligibility of the film stems from coherent plot structures which seek to override the troubling aspects. This is the film's recoil, its effort to organize its own disruptions.

Abstractly considered, the plot presents the struggle between two forces for the possession of an object. The object is the young woman Léone. On the one side is the vampire, Marguerite Chopin, who desires Léone's death; on the other side is Léone's father, who desires that she live. Each side is supplemented by a cluster of atmospheric indices, objects, and locales. Chopin's power is associated with night, shadows, skulls, poison bottles; she holds sway over the decrepit warehouse. The father's power is associated with light and day, with candles and the book *Vampyre;* his milieu is the chateau. The struggle between the father and Chopin is determined by the opposition *life/death*. The film offers a series of variants upon the paradoxical theme of "Death in Life/Life in Death": *the living live* (e.g., Gisèle and Gray); *the living die* (the father, the coachman, the doctor); moreover, *the dead live* (Chopin initially and the father, as a spectre at the end); and *the dead die* (Chopin at the end). Chopin, posited as dead, is actually living, and must be "brought back to death." In contrast, the father is killed, but is brought back to life. Especially important is the way in which even two definitely "living" characters are pulled into this zone of uncertainty. Léone, though alive, is throughout the film on the brink of death. And after Gray's bloodletting, he splits into three bodies and, when one is encased in a coffin, he is simultaneously frozen in death and fully sentient. Indeed, the somnambulistic rhythm of gesture and walk of every character implies a trancelike state halfway between the living and the dead.

Apart from the symmetrical oppositions and parallels, the father and Chopin share one feature: both operate by means of the absent cause. For the bulk of the film, as we would expect, Chopin is seen as the dominant center of such an absence: virtually all the enigmas mentioned above are associated with her powers. It is significant, however, that the father is introduced as having similar powers: he is able to divine Gray's presence and to enter locked rooms. At the end of the film, moreover, the father returns from the dead as a spectre. What we have, then, is a struggle between two forces—the death-principle and the life-principle—*both* of which are seen as inexplicable, rooted in the absence of cause.

These two forces, each seeking to possess Léone, never meet directly; it is their intermediaries who clash. Chopin operates through the doctor and the peg-legged soldier, while the father is served by David Gray, the chateau servant, and his daughter Gisèle. (As we shall see, the first section of the film is occupied with establishing these intermediaries as such by reiterated exchanges.) As the object desired, Léone remains a victim throughout, but at certain points her function is also "distributed" to Gisèle and Gray. The equivalences of the two sisters are carefully established: a title introduces them as a pair ("Here . . . live the two daughters"); and the father visits each of them in turn. Near the end of the film, moreover, when the doctor has failed to subdue Léone, he captures Gisèle in her place, and now each daughter is seen in bed as at the beginning (but now Gisèle is a prisoner lashed to a bedstead). Finally, the lifting of the curse from Léone is paralleled by Gray's rescue of Gisèle from the doctor's lair. Gray is also briefly equated with Léone, and this more gradual shift is, as we shall see below, crucial to much of his function in the plot.

Vampyr's plot, then, generates specific patterns of action, one being the careful symmetries of opposed forces. Another such pattern is a progression toward confronting the state of death. At the start of the film, twilight is falling and Gray encounters a series of death portents. Later Gray witnesses a death (the chatelain's), witnesses a bleeding and slow dying (Léone's), and is himself bled. Next, in a dream vision, he sees himself dead, then sees death "through a corpse's eyes." He is taken to be buried; recovered from his vision, he witnesses one interment (Chopin's). At the end, we witness another burial (the doctor's death in the mill). Only after the film has, so to speak, *lived through* the state of death does the sun rise to dispell the gloom. Thus the plot submits Gray (and the viewer) to the trajectory of premonition/dying/death/burial. But running alongside these actions is a series of commentaries, an authoritative intelligence linking the actions and guiding our understanding.

We can see the film as falling into three parts. Part one consists of Gray's investigation of the inn, the father's visit to his room, Gray's investigation of the doctor's lair, and the murder of the father. Part two consists of Marguerite Chopin's attack on Léone, Léone's greedy contemplation of Gisèle, the return of the dead coachman, the doctor's bleeding of Gray, and the attempt to poison Léone. Part three is comprised of the first dream, Gray's thwarting of the poisoning, the second dream, the staking of Chopin, the death of the peg-legged soldier, the rescue of Gisèle by Gray, and the death of the doctor in the mill. Why these divisions? Although there are not always clear-cut spatial units, we can find at least one temporal justification and two causal ones. First, three stages dominate the chain of actions. By the end of the first part all the major characters have been introduced, the initial conflict has been established, and the dominant project (saving Léone from poison) has been presented; the second part traces the attack on Léone until it reaches its highest pitch, culminating in the prepared poisoning; the third part reverses the conflict and resolves the action with the deaths of Chopin, the soldier, and the doctor. More important, however, this conventional *découpage* of the action is reinforced by two idiosyncratic strategies. For one thing, each part has its characteristic motif: in part one, the motif is that of *giving an object in exchange for loyalty;* in part two, it is that of *bleed-*

ing; in part three, it is *burial.* These motifs tend to cluster, to accrete in each segment and not to recur in other segments. This partition is further dictated by insertions or embeddings within the film. Part one is characterized by the presence of explanatory intertitles outside the narrative; in part two these materials have vanished, to be replaced by the more realistically motivated inserts of passages from the book *Vampyre;* in part three we find neither titles nor texts, but instead embedded dreams, which play a role similar to that of the other inserted materials. As we traverse these three parts, we shall trace the multiple roles of Gray as explorer and expiator, reader of the prophetic Word and dreamer who becomes prophet.

Part One

Gray's arrival at the inn initiates several significant events, but even before he walks into the film, the first of four intertitles has already appeared. We need to notice how odd it is that a sound film uses such explanatory inserts. They function as a major set of formal devices in this section of *Vampyr.* How do the titles relate to the plot action? Here is a schematic outline.

TITLE 1: *There exist certain beings whose lives seem tied by invisible bonds to the supernatural. They love solitude . . . They dream . . . Their imagination is developed to such a point that their vision reaches further than does that of most other men. David Gray's personality was thus mysterious . . . One night, lured as usual by fantasy toward the unknown, he arrived very late at the inn which is by the river in the village of Courtempierre.*

Gray enters the inn, goes to his room, starts to investigate the inn, and returns to his room.

TITLE 2: *What a wondrous night! Everything seemed unreal, unusual, fantastic–what a strange omen–David Gray has retired, but an atmosphere laden with mystery keeps him awake.*

Gray is awakened and visited by the old chatelain, who leaves the small parcel.

TITLE 3: *Is this a phantom? Is it a dream? Would it not be instead some poor creature seeking his help?*

Gray leaves the inn and is led by a sprite to the doctor's lair. There he sees the shadows, Chopin, and the doctor. After Gray leaves, Chopin gives the doctor a bottle of poison for Léone. Gray sees two more sprites.

TITLE 4: *David Gray follows the mysterious shadows who lead him to a clearing–where among the trees stands a lonely chateau–here, far from the world, live the two daughters of the unknown man whose desperate appeal reached David Gray.*

The old chatelain looks in on his daughters. Gray arrives at the chateau, witnesses the murder of the chatelain, and summons help. The chatelain dies.

What do these intertitles do? Chronologically, they segment the entire first part, sandwiching each sequence of actions. Temporally, they cover ellipses in story duration. Logically, they mark the organization of the plot, foregrounding the protagonist ("David Gray") and the dominant action sequence (the plight of the old chatelain and his daughters). Psychologically, they supplant the entire mental apparatus of the classical cinema: the recounting of events prior to the narrative's opening and the characters' psychological motivation are absorbed by the intertitles. (Gray as *seen* is a psychic tabula rasa.)

Most striking, though, is the prophetic power of the titles: they predict what we will see next. The titles constitute an independent voice which controls the film's unrolling. This voice can pronounce general statements, articulate the emotions of the protagonist, guide our perception of the film's action, reiterate primary plot sequences (e.g., title 4 reminds us of the old chatelain's function), transfer point of view (e.g., the shift to the chatelain after title 4), and predict subsequent action. In short, we have the characteristic omniscient voice of Dreyer's films, an external commentary of great authority. We cannot disbelieve what the voice says about Gray's past, about his sleep, about the chatelain; we cannot suspect that the voice will not be confirmed by the subsequent action. *Vampyr* accepts this voice as the ultimate source of meaning, beyond question or reproof. For this reason, the intertitles become of great importance, for such is their authority that the action becomes an illustration or corroboration of the titles, rather than vice versa. Furthermore, in the first part, it is this unexplained but authoritative voice which at the level of plot counters the absence of causes at the level of story. It helps make the film intelligible by providing *from the outset* a power which has the capacity to transcend the disparities of this diegetic world. In the film's first section, this capacity is only implied; but later we find the voice inhabiting first a text and then a body, both of which master the absent cause.

Wedged between these titles, the scenes of part one operate to develop specific narrative functions and oppositions. Consider, for example, Gray's arrival at the inn in the first scene. This might appear a somewhat uneconomical segment, since neither the inn nor the servant nor the man with the scythe reappears directly in the later action. (Compare the way *Dracula* saturates a similar opening with characters who vociferously establish the forthcoming intrigue.) Yet we have also already seen the crucial role of the first scene in marking out the uncertain spatial coordinates of the film and in presenting motifs which both retard the dominant story action ("Gray takes a room at the inn as night falls") and prophesy subsequent imagery (e.g., the servant with the candle foreshadowing the servants in the chateau, the picture prefiguring Léone's deathbed, or the skeleton which we shall later see as Marguerite Chopin). The first sequence is a microcosm of the images and gestures upon which the film will expand: Gray drifts, eyes bulging, through a landscape initially defined as that of death.

If this first scene, fulfilling the prediction sketched in the first title, delineates the environment and the protagonist of the ensuing film, and second scene begins to establish the system of parallel narrative roles occupied by the characters. Gray has entered his room, glanced around it, peered out of the window, pulled down the shade, left his room, reentered the room, and twisted the key in the lock. Now, awakened, he is confronted with a series of actions which curiously mimic his own: the key turns in the lock, the old chatelain enters, slowly surveys the room, goes to the window, raises the shade, and comes to the bed. After leaving the package, the chatelain departs, turning the key to relock the door. This series of actions (entering-looking-lowering/raising the shade-leaving) roughly parallels the two characters; in the overall economy of the narrative, it marks the chatelain's importance.

The parallel actions also permit us to measure differences between the men. Gray is the passive witness, sharply separated from what he sees by framings which keep him apart from the chatelain. The chatelain, on the other hand, acts. Pointing to the sky, he stops short, then comes to Gray, looks almost directly at the camera, and says: "She mustn't die . . . do you hear?" This is the father's interdiction, the purpose of the plot being not to violate it. In this death-laden atmosphere Gray is enlisted in the project of saving "her" (Léone) from death. As if to pledge Gray's support, the chatelain leaves a parcel for him, writing upon it: "To be opened after my death." Needless to say, this parcel must be opened (*Vampyr* is not so unconventional as to keep it wrapped); in order for it to be opened, the old man must die. Thus his primary roles are charted out: the father exists to pronounce the inviolable commandment, to confirm support by *giving,* and to die. The narrative affinity established between the chatelain and Gray is thus made a bargain.

The parcel requires some additional commentary. The first of the three loyalty-assuring gifts which rule the second, third, and fourth scenes, the parcel is literally marked as a source of significance. The chatelain's handwriting, the first written sentence we see in the action proper, links his paternal authority to that of the sourceless titles. Furthermore, the parcel contains *Vampyre,* the book selected to guide Gray, and the object through which the father's death will guarantee his daughter's life, the text through which the dead father will "speak," as if by supernatural ventriloquism. Thus the parcel is at once deed and testament, the father's inscription of the promise of his own death but also the means by which his interdiction will persist beyond the grave. This text will turn out to be the revealed word, the means of mastering the absent cause.

After the third intertitle, describing the uncertainty that leads him to heed the call for help, Gray follows the shadow along the river to the doctor's lair. The scene establishes Marguerite Chopin as the principal antagonist by means of Gray's investigation: he follows the peg-legged shadow and sees Chopin; leaving Gray, the camera glides across dancing silhouettes to Chopin, who orders them to stop; Gray watches the soldier rise and cross to Chopin. As if tracing the capillaries of a web to the spider at its center, Gray and the camera move again and again from the fringes of this world to seek the core, an origin for these causeless effects, the vampire herself.

Marguerite Chopin's control is further asserted in the second loyalty pact in the film, when she gives the doctor a bottle of poison. The gesture points both forward and backward. The camera movements (a leftward pan shot moving from the vampire's hand carrying the bottle and extending it to the doctor, and a close-up which again moves down a shelf of bottles to the doctor's hand putting down the poison) anticipate Gray's first dream and Léone's suicide attempt. At the same time, the doctor's accepting of the poison parallels Gray's receipt of the parcel, pairing them off as intermediaries for the principal antagonists.

In the final scene of part one, the primary project of the narrative is at last identified. The nondiegetic voice of the titles identifies the chateau as belonging to Gray's visitor. Again, as an illustration of the titles, we see the chatelain look in on Gisèle and Léone. The space of Léone's room is as warped as that of the doctor's lair: when the father looks in on Gisèle, the camera simply pans left from him to her sleeping and then back right to him, but when he looks in on Léone, the camera traverses an impossible geography by moving from the nun to the father entering and going to the bed, followed by the nun coming in from the right (as Gray and the soldier had in the doctor's lair). Chopin's power is revealed by Léone's delirious sobbing ("The blood! The blood!") and the father's order to await the doctor's arrival (the latter firmly cementing the previous scene to this and foreshadowing later scenes). As Gray approaches the chateau, the father prepares to retire. Gray, now in his role as witness, sees the shadow of the soldier inverted on the ceiling (the soldier himself will die inverted on the doctor's stair). The chatelain is shot and slumps to the floor, clutching the doorknob.

Part I does not end, however, with Gray's entry into the chateau. Not until the chatelain gives away the heart-shaped locket is the last exchange completed. Gray and Gisèle, recipients of book and heart, are enlisted in opposition to Chopin and the doctor. With this scene's end, the terms of the father's inscription are met: he is dead, and the parcel may be opened. Thus the extradiegetic voice of the titles is replaced by the embedded diegetic voice of the book entitled, provocatively, *Vampyre.*

Part Two

As the intertitles headnote each section of part one, so photographed passages from the book *Vampyre* mark off phases of part two. And even more strongly than in part one, the first five excerpts of written material anticipate the images which follow, so that images form a running verification and fulfillment of the text.

Passage 1: The book defines vampires, links them to Satan, and explains that they rise at night to prey upon the living.
IMAGES: Léone is missing.

Passage 2: The book describes how vampires bite the victim's neck to suck blood.
IMAGES: Léone is bitten by Chopin, then rescued by Gisèle and Gray.

Passage 3: The book tells of how the vampire's blood-lust is contagiously transferred to the victim, and how she may seek to kill others.
IMAGES: Léone studies Gisèle, preparing to attack her.

Passage 4: The book describes how a vampire once took a village doctor as her accomplice.
IMAGES: The doctor arrives, examines Léone, and bleeds Gray.

Passage 5: The book describes how a victim is driven to suicide and thus joins the vampire among the damned.
IMAGES: The doctor prepares to induce Léone's suicide.

Subsequent, longer passages explain events prior to the opening of the film (naming Chopin and tracing a plague to her), and even more powerfully determine later actions by explaining to the reader in the film (and the audience) how the vampire must be eliminated.

By the end of part two, then, the contagion has been assigned a history and a name. At this point, reference to the book *Vampyre* ends, since it has fulfilled its role as the second of those authoritative voices which interrupt, gloss, and predict the film's action. Moreover, it is significant that the book is given the title *Vampyre,* the plural of the title of the film. The book situates itself in an authoritative role similar to that of the voice of the intertitles. As we have seen in other Dreyer films, the action here is interpreted by a text which ensures its coherence; as the transcript of Jeanne d'Arc's words corroborates the unity of the film, so the film "*Vampire*" embeds within itself a confirmatory text which situates the narrative with respect to "vampires" as a category. The book cannot err.

Part one is echoed in another way in part two. In the former, the act of giving/receiving as a pledge of loyalty stood out against the background of the constant entrance/exit motifs. In part two, against the background of the constant reading of the text, what stands out is an act already announced in Léone's nocturnal cry of "The blood!"—the act of bleeding. No sooner has Gray begun to read *Vampyre* than Gisèle sees Léone outside, walking as if in a trance. As they run out, Marguerite Chopin bends over Léone. When she is taken inside, the contagious blood-thirst reemerges when Léone scrutinizes Gisèle. Later, when the coach returns, the dead coachman slumps over and, as Gray and the servant stare, drops of his blood spatter to the ground. The bleeding motif reappears, when the doctor arrives at the chateau and demands that Gray save Léone by giving his blood. Confirming the book's assertions, the vampire's death drive is established as a draining of blood, the life that the father's forces seek to preserve.

The doctor's bloodletting also marks the changing function of Gray. The opening of the book *Vampyre* generates a new narrative role: the reader-learner. This role is first filled by Gray, who reads passages 1–5 and becomes our chief channel for the flow of the authoritative voice. But when the doctor proposes a bloodletting, Gray takes on the role of Léone-surrogate. (This has been prepared earlier when the point-of-view cutting reserved for Gray is transferred to Léone.) Explicitly, the doctor claims that bleeding Gray will save Léone; implicitly, Gray submits to the doctor as Léone has submitted to Marguerite Chopin. This symbolic transfer introduces Gray to Léone's state: dying. In part three, we shall see the logical consequence, wherein Gray undergoes the state of death and burial. Here, his acceptance of the bloodletting grants him the vision which constitutes his first dream. The manservant has taken over the role of reader-learner (he reads passages 6–8, learns the identity of the vampire, and will succeed in staking her in her grave and in killing the doctor), but this does not vitiate Gray's new function. Gray's willingness to undergo the experience of dying permits him to fulfill the father's second inscription on the book: "Only you can free us from our affliction."

Part Three

The enigma has been solved: the servant has learned that Marguerite Chopin is the vampire. The book is put aside, its purpose achieved. But the doctor has left the bottle of poison within Léone's reach. The servant, seeing him strolling on the upper landing, runs to get Gray. Gray, however, is in the throes of delirium. His dream announces the final replacement of the authoritative voice: progressively naturalized and internalized, the voice passes from the extradiegetic intertitles to the diegetic book *Vampyre,* and then to Gray's inserted dreams. His two dreams define part three as the visionary fulfillment of the powers of this voice.

Consider, for example, the brief but significant first dream. It consists of only two images—a skull rising and turning and a skeleton hand clutching the poison bottle and moving right (fig. 47)—but those two images testify to the powers which Gray now possesses. The pulsating light associates Gray's vision with the father, recalling the abrupt fading up and down of light during the chatelain's first visit to Gray's room. Apart from its traditional connotations, the skull has been associated at the outset with Marguerite Chopin, while the image of the hand reiterates her passing of the poison to the doctor in part one. (Gray did not witness this; the gesture has been kept apart from his consciousness so that the dream may indicate insight and not mere recollection.) So Gray's vision identifies the vampire as effectively as has the text, but at one remove, by connotation.

The dream has prophetic powers too. Only two shots after the close-up of the skeleton's hand with the poison, we see *Léone's* hand reach up in close-up to clutch the same bottle (fig. 48). Gray's dream has acquired the explanatory and prophetic powers of the intertitles and the texts, but through the image, not the written word.

At the same time as the first dream assumes the function of the "voice," it continues the sabotaging of Bazinian phenomenal space. In the classical Hollywood film, dream is dream and waking is waking, and a system of punctuations (fades, music, misty dissolves, etc.) is called in to distinguish the two. In *Vampyr,* these marks are violated by making the dream space of a piece with the waking space. In Gray's first dream, the light pulsates rhythmically behind the skull and the skeletal hand; but in shots of Gray sleeping, the light continues to pulsate *behind Gray himself,* and when the servant wakes him, the flashing light abruptly stops. In putting forth Gray as the new vessel of authoritative vision, the film sees this vision as overriding differences of inner and outer, subject and object.

The second vision follows, soon, but only after Gray has thwarted the doctor's poisoning of Léone and after the doctor has abducted Gisèle (the latter action presented, of course, only in its consequences). Gray follows a sprite outside, runs through a meadow, and falls. He limps to a bench to rest. Strictly speaking, this may not be a dream (since we aren't shown Gray falling asleep), but because it is formally parallel to the delirious vision shown earlier, I shall call it "the second dream." It begins rather simply: a double of Gray detaches itself from Gray's figure and moves, translucently, off on its own. What does this dream do? How does it function in the narrative?

Most strikingly, it constitutes a story within a story, a metadiegesis formally parallel to the "voice" of the intertitles and the book. As Tzvetan Todorov has remarked, such a metadiegesis is a putting forward of the essential properties of the surrounding narrative.[16]

As an embedded narrative, the second dream operates on two strata: the *pattern* of the actions recapitulating, as if in shorthand, Gray's essential gestures in the first part of the film; the *substance* of the actions predicting events which will appear in the last section of the film. Poised at a critical moment in the film as a whole, Gray's dream retards the action by replaying (through a connotative shorthand similar to that of the first dream) what has come before and sketching what will come after.

Consider first the recapitulative function. In the dream, Gray's double walks along a field, pauses at the stone wall, enters the doctor's lair, sees the coffin and himself in it, goes to a doorway and peers in, sees Gisèle lashed to a bedstead, and, as the doctor and the soldier return, hides by climbing down through a trapdoor. As the doctor and the soldier prepare the coffin for burial, the focus shifts from Gray's double to his "triplet," the Gray in the coffin—through whose eyes we see the coffin lid screwed on and the coffin borne outside to the church. Passing the bench, the procession fades out as Gray's original body fades in where he had rested, and the vision is over. (Again the dream and the dreamer inhabit the same space.) This series of actions summarizes Gray's function throughout the first part of the film. For Gray's normal activities have been to drift, to pause at thresholds, to penetrate interiors, and to peer through doorways and windows. Now, in a condensed, almost parodic version, the dream represents Gray the prober and witness: the man who has been seen from the very start framed in the rectangles of doorways is now boxed up, and the eyes that have stared so often through windows now strain to penetrate the pane of glass over his coffin.

More particularly, when we lay out the sequence of actions in the dream, we find a distinct homology with Gray's first visit to the doctor's lair. In both, bells toll, Gray arises from a sleep, walks through a landscape, pauses at the stone wall, enters the doctor's lair, sees the coffin, investigates the doctor's first-floor rooms, views the doctor from the foot of the staircase, encounters the doctor, his assistant, and Chopin, and finally leaves. Thus the dream recapitulates major narrative gestures of Gray's early visit. Moreover, the sequence of actions had earlier been interrupted by local metaphoric expansion (the gravedigger, the skulls); now the entire chain is seen as one extended metaphor: the earlier visit is revealed as Gray's initiation into the world of the dead. Passing through those doorways, glimpsing Chopin—all the narrative strategies we have examined throughout—all these are exposed as a penetration into a state of death and dying. What the second dream reveals, in short, is that the absent cause is nothing other than the mystery of death, knowledge of which the vampire, the old chatelain, and now Gray possess.

The dream also foreshadows events by enunciating a motif paralleling the motifs of exchange and bleeding in the previous parts: that of burial. Early in the sequence Gray hides under the trapdoor—never to reemerge. The triplet Gray is nailed in his coffin and taken to the churchyard; the tolling bells of the first part reemerge as the churchbell in this sequence. After Gray's dream has brought the coffin near the church, the dream ends, and Gray helps the servant open Chopin's tomb. His dream is at once confirmed and negated: here is a grave and burial, but now *he* peers down at *Chopin* suspended in living death in her coffin. She is staked, the curse upon Léone is lifted, and Chopin's tombstone is slid back into place. Later, at the very end, we see burial again: the doctor, trapped in a mill cage, is engulfed and suffocated in a shower of powder. Gray's dream thus forms the premise for successive burials, stages which might encourage us to inscribe part three with the words which Gray's double sees on the coffin lid: "Dust thou art and to dust thou shalt return."

Prophetic, too, is Gray's vision of Gisèle. Just as his earlier dream had connoted Léone's poisoning and suicide, this dream identifies Gisèle as captive. Both sisters are seen in bed; both are saved by Gray. In all, then, the prophetic second dream yields further proof that through obedience to the father and submission to death, Gray has assimilated the power of the titles and the book to overcome the absent cause.

Indeed, part three in its entirety establishes the victory of the forces of the father over those of Chopin. Obliquely, her death is certified by yet another authoritative text, the inscription on her tombstone ("Marguerite Chopin . . . Good Lord grant her eternal mercy"). More directly, when the dead chatelain returns as a spectre, his furious, oversized face terrifies the doctor and his assistant. Reappearing immediately after Chopin has been staked, the father becomes the new "living dead" of the film and his presence replaces Chopin as the principal manifestation of the absent cause. Thus we do not know what force brings him back from death, slays the peg-legged soldier, or closes the mill cage's door on the doctor, but all these incidents reveal a power as great as that wielded by Chopin.

The father's allies further ratify his power: the loyal manservant sets in motion the machinery that will kill the doctor, while Gray rescues Gisèle. The shots of the couple escaping through a dense fog to a bright sunrise complete the elimination of the sway of the vampire. But to the very end the film insists that the father's power remains as mysterious as that of Chopin: the last shot shows the mill gears grinding to a stop, halted by no visible means.

Paradoxically, then, *Vampyr*'s difficultness is necessary to its making itself intelligible. As in *La Passion de Jeanne d'Arc,* two formal gestures are made by the film. The first is that of disruption. The narrative posits an uncertainty at its core—an absent cause—and we submit perceptually to the ambiguities of a space and time divested of much that is comforting and familiar. But the occluded plot-story relations and the opaqueness of the film's spatial structuring clash with *Vampyr*'s counter-movement, whereby the film works to overcome the absence of cause which it initially posited. This counter-movement depends upon revealed words and images. The titles possess the authority to transcend the disparities of the narrative, while the book and the dreams function to invest in Gray, surrogate for the dead father, a power to master the absent cause. Such mastery amounts to reasserting the father's power. Thematically, the film's counter-movement presents mastery over death through submission to it, aided by prophetic text and vision. We are given a set of guidelines by which to read the film's ambiguities and discontinuities. Muddled, we are fortunately flung upon the titles, the book, and the dreams, and we cling to them as we are tugged through the film. The film thus seeks to subdue its own disruptions.

The film's counter-gesture is as overpowering as those made by the impersonal narrative patterns of Dreyer's previous films. Discontinuities rattle against a superstructure that reiterates the film's *own* pressure: the titles emanating from a sourceless authority, the text bearing a title close to that of the film itself, the dreams that recapitulate and predict plot events. To some extent this counter-movement rehabilitates the narrative, making it easy prey for Christian or Freudian allegory. But it is a merit of *Vampyr,* I think, to leave the gap between its questions and its explanations problematic. The enigma of the absent cause is reiterated, not dispelled, at the very end. A dense, shadowy work, the film insistently challenges our perception, forcing us to struggle to grasp its spaces, its time, its logic. The complexity of this spectatorial activity makes *Vampyr,* in all its snares and bafflements, the fascinating film that it is.

Day of Wrath

Day of Wrath is probably Dreyer's most popular film, which already indicates something of the problems it poses. Stylistically, it is a calmer film than *La Passion de Jeanne d'Arc* or *Vampyr.* A tale of witchcraft, passion, and murder, it has more melodramatic appeal than *Ordet* and *Gertrud.* Is the film then a moment of equilibrium in Dreyer's career? Yes, but not in any simple way. Our sense of the film as a retreat after *Jeanne d'Arc* and *Vampyr* issues from its tendency to pose problems more at the level of narrative structure than at the level of spatial unity. But the film does strongly challenge our perception at the temporal level. We can most usefully begin with an examination of the narrative's dynamics: how the story seeks coherence and what pressures work against this.

FORCES FOR UNITY

Day of Wrath is the story of how, in seventeenth-century Denmark, Anne falls in love with the son of Absalon, the old pastor whom she has married. A subplot involves Herlofs Marte, an old woman accused of witchcraft and persecuted by the church elder Laurentius. After Herlofs Marte is executed, Anne and Martin share a furtive idyll. When Anne tells Absalon of the affair, the old man dies. The pastor's elderly mother Merete accuses Anne of witchcraft. When Martin abandons her, Anne finally confesses to having been in Satan's power and is burned as a witch.

For our purposes, we can break the film into sequences (see chart on next page: numbers in parentheses refer to the shots in each sequence). Compared to *La Passion de Jeanne d'Arc* and *Vampyr, Day of Wrath* is relatively easy to segment. Our sense of an orthodox construction is increased when we see that the film falls into two large parts. The first, comprising about a third of the running time, is concerned with the pursuit, trial and execution of Herlofs Marte (segments II–X). The second part of the film (segments XI–XVII) focuses on the relationships among Absalon, Anne, Martin, and Merete. The proportions balance; the early part subordinates the family romance to Herlofs Marte's plight through the device of making the family witnesses to her progress to the stake, while in the second part of the film, her plotline becomes subordinated to the family romance and survives only in the form of the dying Laurentius. The two plotlines connect through a pair of devices. First, Absalon as the village pastor presides over all cases like that of Herlofs Marte. Second, Herlofs Marte knew Anne's mother, who was also reputed to be a witch. This gives her access to Anne ("I helped your mother") and to Absalon (who spared Anne's mother in order to marry Anne). The secret of the dead mother thus links the Herlofs Marte plot to the main plot and implicates the family in the old woman's fate.

A glance at the segmentation will suggest several ways in which the narrative encourages us to seek closure. Most generally, the relatively small number of characters (six in all) presents a limited number of interrelationships. After the initial scenes in the rectory conveniently assemble five of the characters, there is a strict combining of them in the scenes which follow. By the end of the film, three of these characters (Absalon, Herlofs Marte, and Laurentius) have died, leaving only three principals—all of whom are gathered together for a confrontation in the final scene. If we read the film seeking closure, we are rewarded in that by the conclusion, nearly all the major narrative strands have been tied up. Herlofs Marte has been killed and has in vengeance killed Laurentius; Anne has eliminated Absalon as a barrier between her and Martin; Martin, persuaded that Anne is a witch, has abandoned her and allied himself with Merete; and Anne has confessed to witchcraft.

Yet another contribution to closure is the way that the subplot involving Herlofs Marte foreshadows what will happen after the conclusion of the film. *Day of Wrath* begins with Herlofs Marte being accused of sorcery. She flees, hides, is discovered, confesses, and is burned. After this, Anne begins to practice witchcraft. The film ends with *her* accused and confessing. The progress of Herlofs Marte has mapped out the process of interrogation, torture, and execution which Anne will undergo. The two parts of *Day of Wrath* thus enact Ambrose Bierce's double definition of a witch: "1) An ugly and repulsive old woman, in a wicked league with the devil; 2) A beautiful and attractive young woman, in wickedness a league beyond the devil." The last shot of the film announces that Anne has indeed been burned by surmounting the cross with two sloping bars—the same figure that runs through the *mise-en-scène* of Herlofs Marte's immolation. Finally, the film achieves closure through the characteristic Dreyer device of prophecy—here motivated by characters' supernatural powers. Herlofs Marte makes two predictions: if she dies, Laurentius's death will soon follow and Anne will go to the stake. Both prophecies eventually prove correct, the film thus validating—for the sake of closure—the old woman's power. Later, Absalon tells Laurentius that he will soon join him in death; returning home, he reflects that, "In my innermost soul, I felt my death had been determined." There are several other closure factors at work, but these features already suggest the tight unity which the narrative seeks. Later, however, we shall see that nearly every one of these forces for closure is questioned, and the reading of events which I have proposed is undermined.

Our segmentation permits another principle of construction to strike the eye immediately. Like *La Passion de Jeanne d'Arc* and *Vampyr*, *Day of Wrath* is based upon an insistent principle of alternation of plotlines, of characters, and of locales. At an intersequence level, for example, Anne and Martin's first forest idyll (segment VIII) rests between the torture scene (VII) and Absalon's visit to Herlofs Marte in prison (IX). Even more insistent is the narrative alternation within sequences established by crosscutting. The family awaiting Martin's return (IV*a, c, e*) is juxtaposed to Herlofs Marte's flight (IV*b, d*). Against Martin and Anne's nocturnal escape to the forest (XII*a, c, e, g*) there is Absalon's solitude in the rectory (XII*b, d, f*); against the couple's trip down the stream (XIII*g, i, k, m, o*) there is Absalon's visit to Laurentius (XIII*h, j, l, n*). Anne and Martin's love play (XIV*a, c, g, i, k, m*) is counterposed to Absalon's leaving Laurentius (XIV*b, d*) and traveling through the storm (XIV*f, h, j, l*). Finally, Merete's vigil by Absalon's corpse (XV*a, c, e*) is alternated with Anne's search for Martin in the fog (XVI*b, d, f*). But what compositional purposes does such alternation serve?

For one thing, the alternation enhances the fairly rigid temporal delineation of the action. Without flashbacks or flashforwards, the plot moves chronologically; the only deformation of sequential order occurs when the crosscutting exhibits simultaneous events. (While Anne and Martin go boating, Absalon visits Laurentius, and so on.) As for the overall duration of the plot, the story events consume two or three months, in the early summer of 1623. From this period, the plot has selected five days to show. At the beginning, Herlofs Marte is captured on the same day that Martin returns home (segments II–IV). The following episodes, depicting Herlofs Marte's interrogation and torture by the Church and Anne and Martin's walk through the forest, consume a second day.[1]

I. Dies Irae prologue (1).
II. A hand writes the accusation (2–3).
III. Herlofs Marte flees from her cottage (4).

IV. *Rectory:* *a.* Anne chastised by Merete and soothed by Absalon (5–15).
Outside: *b.* Herlofs Marte flees (16).
c. Anne meets Martin (17–25).
d. Herlofs Marte flees (26).
e. Anne and Martin trick Absalon (27–34). Concealment and discovery of Herlofs Marte (35–73).

V. A hand writes the order (74).

VI. *Sacristy: a.* Absalon questions Herlofs Marte (75–97).
Cathedral: b. Anne and Martin hear the choir (98–103).

VII.	*Torture chamber:*	Herlofs Marte confesses (104–19).			
VIII.	*Forest:*	Anne and Martin walk (120–30).			
IX.	*Prison:*	Absalon visits Herlofs Marte (131–33).			
X.	*Churchyard:*	Herlofs Marte is burned (134–70).			
XI.	*Rectory:*	*a.* Absalon warned by Merete (171–209).			
		b. Absalon tells Anne of her mother (210–28).			
		c. Anne summons Martin (229–35).			
			Forest:	*a.*	Anne and Martin (236–37).
XII.	*Rectory:*	*b.* Absalon alone in study (238).		*c.*	Anne and Martin at spring (239–41).
		d. Absalon sits by fire (242).		*e.*	Anne and Martin (243).
		f. Absalon (244).		*g.*	Anne and Martin lie down (245).
XIII.	*Rectory:*	*a.* The family prays (246–52).			
		b. Merete upbraids Anne (253–65).			
		c. Merete and Martin (266–67).			
		d. Anne and Martin at embroidery (268–75).			
		e. In his study, Absalon and Merete (276–84).			
		f. Absalon joins Anne and Martin, who leave for the river (285–87).	*Forest:*	*g.*	Anne and Martin run to river (288).
		h. Absalon called by Laurentius (289).		*i.*	Anne and Martin ride in boat (290–93).
		j. Absalon leaves (294).		*k.*	Anne and Martin ride in boat (295).
		l. Absalon comes to Laurentius's deathbed (296–98).	*River:*	*m.*	Anne and Martin leave boat (299–303).
		n. Absalon consoles Laurentius (304).	*Grass:*	*o.*	Anne and Martin talk (305).
XIV.	*Rectory:*	*a.* Waiting for Absalon (306–11).	*L's house:*	*b.*	He is dead (312).
		c. Anne shows sketch to Martin (313–26).		*d.*	He is dead (327).
		e. Martin and Merete (328–33).	*Outdoors:*	*f.*	Absalon journeys home (334).
		g. Anne comes to Martin (335).		*h.*	Absalon on way home (338).
		i. Anne and Martin (337).		*j.*	Absalon on way home (336).
		k. Anne and Martin (339).		*l.*	Absalon on way home (340).
		m. Anne and Martin (341).			
		n. Absalon, Anne, and Martin (342–61).			
		o. Absalon and Anne; he dies (362–88).			
XV.	*Rectory:*	*a.* Merete keeps vigil (389).	*Forest:*	*b.*	Anne seeking Martin (390).
		c. Merete by coffin (391).		*d.*	Anne finds Martin in fog (392).
		e. Merete by coffin (393).		*f.*	Anne questions Martin (394–96).
		g. Martin assumes vigil and forces Anne to swear (397–407).			
XVI.	*Sacristy:*	At the funeral, Anne is denounced by Merete and confesses (408–35).			
XVII.		Dies Irae scroll concludes (436).			

On a third day, Herlofs Marte is burned, Absalon tells Anne of her mother's transgressions, and Anne seduces Martin (segments X–XII). After an unspecified interval, there occurs that crowded day during which Laurentius dies, Absalon confronts Anne and dies, and Martin begins to doubt her (segments XIII–XV). After another short interval, on a fifth day, the final scene by Absalon's coffin takes place. Within each day, the alternation permits the film to skip over certain stages of the action. (While Herlofs Marte is prepared for torture, we view Anne and Martin in the cathedral.) The elision is often quite significant: twice the crosscutting conceals the time it takes for Anne and Martin to have intercourse. Like *Thou Shalt Honor Thy Wife,* which compresses a month into two days (one at the beginning, one at the end), *Day of Wrath* achieves that durational concentration so characteristic of Dreyer's films. Hence the need to pack each selected day as densely as possible by showing different simultaneous events in alternation.

Alternation of sequences and parts of sequences unifies the film in another way: by keeping the general narrative point of view omniscient. Though in certain scenes we share Anne's vantage point on events (we shall return to this), much occurs that she never witnesses. Only the audience sees and knows all. The creation, if not of a narrator in any rigorous sense, at least of an overriding narrative intelligence, counterposing certain scenes for our scrutiny, intensifies the closure and internal determination of the film.

Supported by such omniscient point of view, alternation encourages us to construct parallelisms. The parallels reinforce the general thematic oppositions of the film: every alternation builds up an opposition between closed, dark interiors and open exteriors, between age and youth. Most pointedly, this contrast emerges from the juxtaposition of Anne and Martin, in natural surroundings, with the torture of Herlofs Marte, or with Absalon's solitude, or with Absalon and Laurentius, or with Merete. Crosscutting permits Dreyer to play on a subtle range of similarities and differences. Consider two segments. While Anne and Martin drift in the boat, Absalon visits the dying Laurentius, and crosscut alternation produces many echoes and interferences between the two lines of action. Martin asks: "How shall we end up?"; and both Absalon and Laurentius pose the same kind of question. Martin lies cradled against Anne; Absalon assures Laurentius that he is as "soft and snug as in your mother's arms." Anne describes the tree bent over the water in monistic terms—it cannot be separated from its reflection—and, gently clasping Martin's hand, she claims that they too are bound together. In the alternating scene, Laurentius speaks of splitting his soul from his body and begs for Absalon to grasp his hand. When Absalon seeks to comfort Laurentius with the reminder that he, too, will soon die, Dreyer cuts back to Martin, his father's son, saying, "Anne, if we could die together now. . . ." Already the film has worked out, within the general age/youth opposition, differences between Anne and Martin that link him to his orthodox elders. These differences are confirmed later (segment XV), when Anne runs through the fog calling for him: Martin sits, grimly silent and still, exactly like Merete keeping vigil over Absalon's corpse. The likeness is confirmed not only by her words ("Martin will keep vigil tonight") but also by his words (Martin's "only thought now" is for Absalon). Even the local texture of the cutting tends to support such parallelisms: the compositions often work to compare specific figures, as in the dissolves which compare Herlofs Marte to Merete (shots 4/5) or which "match" Herlofs Marte with Anne and vice versa (shots 16/17 and 25/26), or which contrast the inquisition record with a leafy branch (shots 119/120). In all, the alternating structure permits comparison at every level, from the most general thematic features to details of dialogue, gesture, and even graphic qualities.

The principle of alternation that rules the cutting between different locales functions within the spatially homogeneous scene as well. As in *La Passion de Jeanne d'Arc,* Dreyer usually cuts from one face to another. If one character is in movement off screen, the on-screen character's turning face and shifting glance signal it. For example, the first time that Anne meets Martin, the two are never shown in the same shot: their eyes meet, they talk, they go to the dining table, and the scene simply alternates shots of each one. If more than two characters participate in the scene, Dreyer selects one character—Merete, Anne, Herlofs Marte—and uses alternating cutting to segregate her from the others. Anne in particular tends to be chopped out of scenes. An outsider in the world of the rectory, an isolated observer in the cathedral and at the execution, Anne is frequently severed from the action by means of alternating editing. In one scene, a lengthy alternating series of shots has already juxtaposed the couple in the rectory with Absalon's walk home. When Absalon enters the rectory, his arrival shatters the spatial unity between Anne and Martin. Before, they shared the same frame; now they separate, and Anne leaves the frame altogether. A new shot shifts the angle to reunite the three, but Anne immediately goes out of the frame again. At the stove, she is framed in her own separate medium shots, while Martin helps Absalon to sit down. Anne brings some beer, and again all three are in the same frame, but again she leaves; and for the rest of the scene, Anne remains utterly isolated. Thus the intimacy Anne offered Martin is replaced by Martin's filial devotion, and this devotion shuts Anne out.

The presence of alternating cutting should by now impell us to ask to what extent the interior scenes possess spatial unity, for we have already seen how in *La Passion de Jeanne d'Arc* and *Vampyr* alternating cutting tends to crack the scenographic space. And it must be admitted that although most characters' eyelines are classically matched in *Day of Wrath,* the glances are often angled "incorrectly" from shot to shot. Yet the scenes in *Day of Wrath*—and particularly the scenes in the rectory—have a much stronger sense of spatial unity than comparable scenes in the two earlier films. One obvious cause is the greater number of true establishing shots; even if in close-up the glances crisscross, we are constantly reoriented to the action by long shots. But the film has another, somewhat unusual tactic for unifying the narrative space.

In one of his courses at the Soviet State Cinema Institute, Sergei Eisenstein approached the problems of staging and editing. The specific task which Eisenstein set his students was the presentation of an episode from Haiti's anticolonialist struggle in 1802, the attempt of the French to capture the leader Dessalines. First, in plotting the *mise-en-scène,* Eisenstein demanded that the overall setting (a banquet hall) be analyzed into areas in which specific actions would take place. Thus one portion of the scene would occur near a stair, the next in the center of the hall, a third at the table, and so on. "You must," he told his pupils, "work out a scheme of where and on what spaces—zones of action—each section is to be played. The division between the sections of the story must also be rendered spatially; each action fragment must have its own allotted space and develop upon it."[2] So far, this is standard staging practice. But when it comes to filming and editing the staged action, Eisenstein suggests that the theatrical proscenium view is not to be respected. Camera-work and cutting are not restricted to a single orientation to any zone of action. "In the cinema . . . [there] exists the feasibility of observing the action from all four sides."[3] In the Dessalines exercise, then, Eisenstein does not hesitate to break, again and again, the "axis of action" of Hollywood practice; although he warns against disorganized fragmentation, he stresses the *need* to violate the axis in order to produce varied shot patterns. This means that the action "flows *around* the camera, that is, around the spectator. To get this effect, the camera can not only dissect a view from inside the circular *mise-en-scène* but can also as though flank it from the outside."[4] Although the result of Eisenstein's project will diverge sharply from Hollywood's spatial layouts, nevertheless in his exercise, the narrative motivates the apportioning of scenic zones as well as a fluid, shifting series of camera and editing orientations to those zones.

No better term than "circular" could be found to describe Dreyer's scenography in *Day of Wrath.* The film reminds us how Dreyer's films, from the start of his career, are intimately linked to that tradition of chamber art that includes Hammershøi and Vermeer. The director who compared cinema to architecture finds human-made space, especially the closed chamber, to be the primary site of action. Furthermore, in *Day of Wrath,* as in *Thou Shalt Honor Thy Wife,* the chamber is a familial space. After Jeanne d'Arc's cell, the monks' court, Léone's sickroom, the doctor's warehouse, Dreyer returns to the family parlor. The rectory parlor stands at the intersection of the family's activities: Anne's bedroom, Absalon's study, Merete's bedroom, and the corridor to the outdoors all give onto the rectory parlor. Topographically, the parlor is meeting place and microcosm for the family's social activities. (Note that only Anne is alone in the parlor for very long.) With its prayer stall, its windows looking onto nature, its staircase leading up to the loft, the parlor appears as an abbreviated anthology of several motifs in the plot. And in the course of the narrative, the parlor will function, progressively, as a setting for reunion, concealment, sexual intrigue, and murder; the last time we see it, it has become Absalon's crypt. But the parlor as the arena of this domestic drama must be made narratively intelligible. So let us concentrate momentarily upon how, despite violations of the 180° rule and the eyeline match, this chamber space becomes comprehensible.

1 2 3 4 5 6

That the rectory parlor can be reduced to a systematic floorplan already suggests that we are far from the fractured space of *Jeanne d'Arc* and *Vampyr.* Within this room, several different areas, Eisenstein's "zones of action," are clearly marked and reserved for specific events. At one corner of the dining table, Anne plays out a scene with Merete and Absalon (IV*a*); at the opposite corner of the room, near a linen cupboard, she first sees Martin (IV*c*); in another corner, she leads Herlofs Marte up to the loft (IV*e*); and so on. What differentiates Dreyer's handling from Eisenstein's is that the latter conceives his Dessalines banquet hall as a setting to be used only once in the film, and thus to be exhausted, dramaturgically speaking, in a single sequence. Dreyer, as we would expect, is more parsimonious. In no sequence of *Day of Wrath* is *every* zone of the parlor utilized. Instead, each scene emphasizes a distinct area of the playing space—the dining table, the linen cupboard, the loft stairway, Absalon's prayer-stall, even the empty center of the room (where Absalon's coffin will be put). Only by the end of the film has virtually every inch of the parlor been utilized.

The dramatic motivation for the breakdown of the parlor into areas is apparent enough—Martin must be seated at the table, Herlofs Marte must be concealed in the loft, and so forth—but the pressure of narrative intelligibility also determines our orientation to each zone of action. One orientation (through camera position and editing) views the table against the background of the windows, so Absalon meets Martin or the family holds morning prayers within the warm daylight. In contrast, Dreyer will sometimes film the dining table from a completely opposite standpoint, the camera, as it were, assuming the position of the window, and situating the table against the open space in the center of the parlor. Such an orientation is

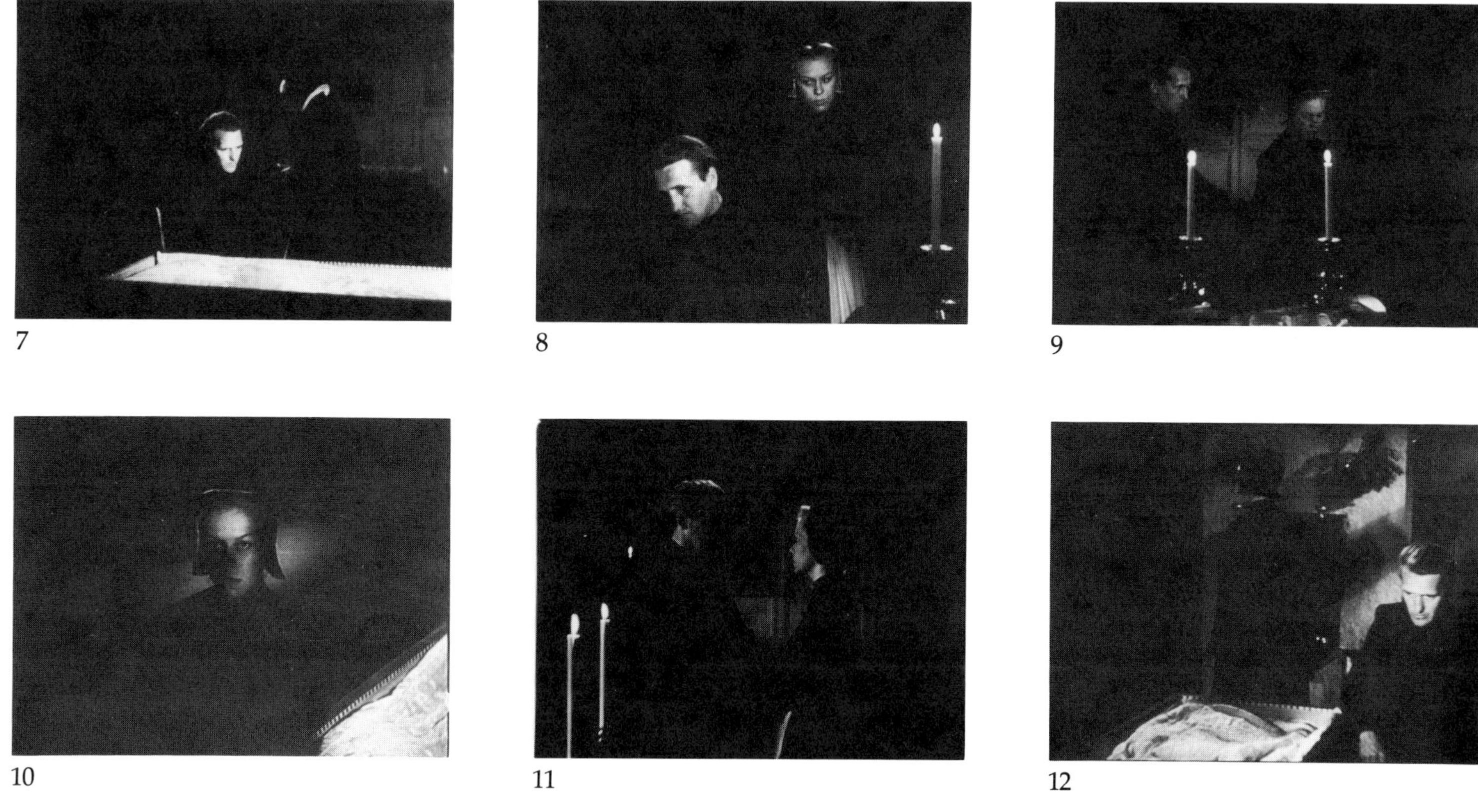

7 8 9

10 11 12

used for the night scene during which Anne summons Martin. Within a sequence, our standpoint on the action will shift as well, as when the morning prayers at the table are initially viewed against the windows, and the later incident between Anne and Martin at her embroidery is seen against the opposite wall.

Once the zones of action are established, narrative logic overrides what are, strictly speaking, incorrectly angled eyelines. More important, the mobility of orientation onto the playing areas permits disjunctive editing to isolate certain details. Often Merete is treated in a spatially disjointed manner, but since she is absent from most scenes, she must be set up as a significant aggressor, and off-the-line cutting cooperates with her behavior in so marking her. For the sake of a narrative parallelism, Dreyer systematically violates the axis of action in the scene in which Absalon leaves Anne alone and she summons Martin. Absalon draws back from Anne, moving to frame right, Anne on frame left (fig. 1). There is a 180° shift, switching their locations as he stares into her eyes and judges them "so marvelous, innocent like those of a child" (fig. 2). The crossing of the axis of action reveals, for the first time in the scene, the windows and trees outside, through the windows on the other side of the table. The discontinuity is stressed by another 180° cut, which returns us to the original position (fig. 3). But almost immediately, after Absalon is gone, Martin comes to Anne and kisses her (fig. 4); and another 180° cut switches us around again (fig. 5). As Martin calls her eyes "fathomless and mysterious," Anne is again seen before the window and the couple is framed so as to mirror the earlier shot of Anne and Absalon (fig. 6). Thus father and son, elder and lover, are concisely contrasted: a narrative parallel arises from the jump in orientation.

The two last sequences in the rectory parlor (segments XIV and XV) carry to a conclusion the tendency of the action in each zone to be observed from a variety of positions. The first of these sequences is organized, reasonably enough, around Merete's circular sewing table. It is at this table that Merete mends the clothes, that Anne seduces Martin, that Absalon joins the couple, and that Anne reveals the truth to Absalon. This complex series of actions is shown from virtually every side, bringing into play every wall of the parlor and placing the characters at the center of a mobile architectural space. (An obvious comparison is the 360° scenographic space developed in the films of Yasujiro Ozu, although Ozu's style differs from Dreyer's in many other respects.)

The last sequence in the rectory anchors its composition around a rectangle, Absalon's coffin, but the principle of circularity continues to operate. Martin is initially seated in a chair at the foot of the coffin. After Merete leaves (fig. 7), he moves to another chair at the coffin's head, and Anne enters. She passes behind him (fig. 8) on her way to yet another chair. Martin goes to her and asks about Absalon's death. He then urges Anne back to the coffin to swear her innocence, and the camera follows them to the head of the coffin (fig. 9). When Anne kneels to swear, the camera shows us the fourth edge of the coffin (fig. 10); when she rises, we see the fourth wall of the parlor (fig. 11). The camera then follows the couple as they complete their circuit of the coffin. Martin returns to his first chair and Anne leaves (fig. 12). Such systematic changes of camera orientation permit us to construct an intelligible scene because, as Eisenstein puts it, the action "flows *around* the camera, that is around the spectator."

According to one of his students, Eisenstein also noted that camera movement can supply a great flexibility of orientation to the zones of action. In *Day of Wrath,* narrative controls. Often a character (Anne, Merete) will look off to one side and the camera will pan to reveal Martin arriving; he becomes, in fact, associated with this kind of anticipatory pan shot. Eisenstein's notion of allowing the action to flow around the spectator can be seen at work in other camera movements. Generally speaking, the camera will track in an arc in one direction and pan slowly in the other—against the grain, as Edward Branigan has put it—thus giving a spiralling twist to the scenographic space. More specifically, three of these semicircular camera movements are paralleled to one another. In the torture chamber, the camera tracks leftward, revealing first the judges, then the scribe, then the torture apparatus, and finally Herlofs Marte. In Laurentius's house, the camera leaves Absalon in the doorway to move along the walls of two rooms, wheel left, and back up, framing Laurentius in his deathbed. At the outset of the film's final scene, the camera follows the boy choir to the gathered elders and then to the group around Absalon's coffin. While there is much to be said about these three shots, it is enough for the moment to note how, coming at the beginning of their respective scenes, these shots establish the various playing areas for the action. In these shots, three walls are revealed, glances and turns motivate the directions of the movement, the camera coasts along independently of any one figure, and its trajectory determines a "spatial teleology"—the end of each shot pays off with a tableau. If we add to these shots the lateral tracking movements which follow Anne through the church corridor and which trace Herlofs Marte's escape from her cottage, it becomes evident that every interior scene in the film, in the rectory or elsewhere, contrives one way or another of constructing a unified, narratively intelligible space.

THE ABSENT CAUSE

Closure, temporal concentration, omniscient point of view, parallelisms, a coherent familial space—all these forces determine the film's world as unified and homogeneous. But narrative causality, the relation of event to event, is hardly so clear-cut. In *Day of Wrath,* actions spring from three causes: the social, the natural, and the supernatural. Curiously, character psychology as a source of action becomes identified with one or more of these three rather impersonal causes. Moreover, each of these causes is given a concrete expression in the film's *mise-en-scène.*

Day of Wrath represents society neither as economic production nor as the state. Instead, the social is identified as a religious institution. The first action that we see (the accusation of Herlofs Marte) is performed by the Church, thus setting in motion the entire narrative machinery of the film. What sort of institution is the Church? It is identified with dispassionately repressive law (witness the torture of Herlofs Marte), and with death: it performs no festive rituals, only interrogations, execution, last rites, funeral ceremonies. The *mise-en-scène* defines the social as the realm of the *chamber*—the rectory (with its bars and grids in the decor), the cellarlike torture chamber, Absalon's sacristy, Laurentius's home. All the chambers in the film except Herlofs Marte's are also associated with the Church.

Opposed to causation of a social order is causation of a natural order. The growing love between Anne and Martin is presented as the response to social constraint, an outburst of natural energy. Whenever the lovers seek solitude, they must go outdoors, to the sunny forests and streams or the moonlit countryside. The allure of the realm of nature is strongly marked by the light streaming into the rectory, revealing the leafy trees outside the window.

Characters in the film are defined in terms of such causes. The behavior of Laurentius and Merete, for instance, is seen to spring from the narrow severity of the Church—the one in his merciless badgering of Herlofs Marte, the other in her disgust for Anne's vitality. The major characters, though, stand at points of intersection between the social and the natural. Absalon the parson is erected as the pillar of the society, but he has betrayed the Church by his desire for Anne and his freeing of her mother. Thus his actions proceed from a tension between natural and social impulses. Of course, as both priestly and secular Father, Absalon occupies an important symbolic role in relation to Martin and Anne: to deceive him is to transgress the vested authority of the social. And this is indeed Martin's point of conflict. The son's duty to his father and his father's society is set against the lover's attraction to Anne, and this conflict will culminate in the film's final scene. It is the struggle between such causes that motivates most of the film's causal lines—e.g., Absalon's secret betrayal is revealed by Herlofs Marte, which in turn provokes Anne to learn of her mother's power; Martin's deception of Absalon is played off against his social duty.

Yet the film relies on causation of a third sort. If the social is defined as the Christian Church, the supernatural is necessarily defined as witchcraft, and as we would expect, it occupies a problematic causal position. Our first impulse is to interrogate the film. What bestows upon Herlofs Marte the power to curse Laurentius and to prophesy? How does Anne achieve the power to "summon" Martin? Or to wish Absalon dead? It would be easy to go on at length about whether Anne has convinced herself of her power (a psychological reading) or whether she "really" has witchly powers (a symbolic reading), but this encloses us within the terms of the film's own operations, offering us no standpoint from which to grasp these operations, no alternative but to repeat in an endless play of ambiguity what the film itself "says." A remark of Fredric Jameson's is pertinent here:

> *In matters of art, and particularly of artistic perception, in other words, it is wrong to want to* decide, *to want to* resolve *a difficulty: what is wanted is a kind of mental procedure which suddenly shifts gears, which throws everything in an inextricable tangle one floor higher, and turns the very problem itself (the obscurity of this sentence) into its own solution (the varieties of Obscurity) by widening its frame in such a way that it now takes in its own mental processes as well as the object of those processes. In the earlier, naive state, we struggle with the object in question: in this heightened and self-conscious one, we observe our own struggles and patiently set about characterizing them.*[5]

We must, in other words, map the terms of the film's equivocations, the conditions of its hesitations, its varieties of Obscurity.

From this vantage point, the functions of the supernatural as a cause become clearer. As in *Vampyr,* the supernatural is the site of the narrative's causal excess: it constitutes an absent cause, the place of a hesitation about causes. In one sense, the supernatural motivates events which cannot be motivated by social or natural causes. Thus the supernatural often replaces purely psychological motivations. In another film, Absalon would inadvertently overhear Anne wishing he were dead, but here he is walking home and feels "as if Death brushed past me." In another film, Laurentius might die of a guilty conscience, but here his death simply fulfills Herlofs Marte's curse. The supernatural, then, tends to obliterate personal psychology as a cause.

The supernatural's force as a cause might be seen as motivated by a loose notion of realism. I have often heard people say of *Day of Wrath* that the pervasiveness of witchcraft in the film is a reflection of the beliefs of the milieu depicted.[6] And it is true that the film, set during the worst years of the European witch-hunts, relies on a general historical awareness of the Church's persecution of witches. More specifically, in 1575 the Danish Lutheran Niels Hemmingsen published a treatise which so excoriated witchcraft that King James of England found it authoritative. Certain events in the film are faithful to what we know of the witch-craze. But what is significant is that at crucial points Dreyer's film refuses to define a position with respect to the historical phenomenon of witchcraft. Gone is most of the paraphernalia of traditional witch-lore: the witch's ability to confound neighbors, the witches' sabbath, etc. (Compare Christensen's *Hexen.*) Although the apparatus of Church repression is well summarized in Laurentius's interrogation, the film remains silent about the various causes which historians have proposed for the witch-craze (religious strife, the rise of the medical profession, the retention of pagan religious customs). Similarly, it is true that Herlofs Marte uses herbal remedies, but they are "herbs from under the gallows." The question of whether she is simply a lay healer or someone dabbling in magic is left open. The film similarly refuses to specify why, in the first scene, a woman has sought out Herlofs Marte. Historically, "witches" often attended to peasant women, but we cannot know whether Herlofs Marte's client has come seeking medical or supernatural aid. The *shifting* status assigned to the supernatural blocks our reading it as a direct reflection of some historical reality.

Indeed, we must look at the supernatural as cause exactly because of its shifting status. The supernatural cause permits slippage and play between "natural" causes and sources of action which the film cannot overtly confront. In *Day of Wrath,* whereas the Church stands in for the socioeconomic, the supernatural constantly merges with the sexual. Early in the film, the inquisition scene is presented as a theatre in which men watch the stripping and torture of Herlofs Marte. By the time that the presence of the supernatural has been motivated by Anne's dead mother and Herlofs Marte, witchcraft becomes one side of the dialectic of natural/supernatural, the purpose of which is to displace perpetually the problem of woman's sexuality. A tale of intercourse and incest seeks to become a tale of the insoluble mystery of love and evil. But it never completely succeeds; there is a steady shuttling to and fro.

The principal site of that shuttling is, of course, the character Anne. On the one hand, her behavior incarnates the "natural": she flings herself into Absalon's arms, and she demands a child from Martin. Martin has thoughts but she has "dreams." Sexuality is here identified as an organic natural drive for affection and procreation. But at the same time, sexuality as desire, and especially as violation of the social order, exceeds this natural position and becomes identified with supernatural power. (This, in fact, echoes the Church's position; and at the close of the film, Martin can understand Anne's power over him only *as* witchcraft.) All the questions we asked earlier indicate how the specific narrative consequences of Anne's actions are the result of the hesitation between these two strategies for deferring the problem of Anne's sexuality. Now let us try, as Jameson suggests, to characterize more closely how our oscillation between these strategies is systematically produced by the film's *mise-en-scène.*

There are, for instance, Anne's movements and costumes. The film represents Anne's development through subtle shifts in the speed and rhythm of her movements. At the outset, Anne moves slowly and rigidly, stopping often; her straightness is only broken when she bows to cry or rushes impetuously to embrace Absalon. But she becomes less statuesque and more catlike, as when during the storm she glides around Martin in a sinuous spiral: eroticism mingles with the supernatural: her prowl through the darkened rectory connotes both voluptuousness and sorcery. A similar play is present in the use of costume, typical of Dreyer's sparse style. That Herlofs Marte's flesh strikes us as shockingly naked recalls how determinedly most characters here are *covered* by their clothes. Of this absence of skin Raymond Durgnat has remarked: "All the respectable bourgeois citizens of *Day of Wrath* are clad in long black angular garments which encase their bodies like coffins. They are all dead from the neck down."[7] From the neck up, though, Anne blooms. Dreyer concentrates on slight alterations of Anne's collar, cap, and hair. We first see her wearing an angular black cap; Martin arrives as she is donning a white collar. At the morning prayer scene, after her lovemaking with Martin, she wears a softly curving lace bonnet and a curving collar. By the time the couple sit in the tall grass, Anne is letting her curly hair hang free. This last development of naturalness/supernaturalness/sexuality links her to the only other woman who wears her hair free—Herlofs Marte, the witch.

Anne's costume changes serve primarily to draw attention to what Dreyer called "that landscape one can never be tired of exploring"—the face. As in *Jeanne d'Arc* and *Vampyr,* the eyes define the face's expression. Glances hold the scenes together from shot to shot, and no glance matters more than Anne's. Her look is at once the sign of natural love, the vehicle of her witchcraft, and the expression of sexual desire. Martin's arrival marks the motif: when he appears, Anne is looking in a mirror and she turns and comes to him in a series of shots which stress the force of her gaze. That gaze is overtly discussed in segment XI. Merete asserts that Anne has her mother's dangerous eyes; Absalon finds them "childlike—pure and clear"; Martin perceives them as harboring "a trembling, quivering flame." For the characters and for us, Anne is a text to be deciphered, and her glances are the cues for us to "read" her in one way or another. Again and again, a scene will be broken by inserted close-ups of her looking intently at someone. The light falling across Anne's face insists on the eyes; as she moves, shadows form a cowl around her glance. True, Merete and Absalon, figures of authority, are established by their penetrating looks (Merete is the first "looker" we encounter in the film, fixing Anne in her scowl) and Absalon and Martin can, like Anne, even look without looking *at* anything in particular. But only Anne's eyes can break from the social exchange of glances into a lover's gaze or into the raptures of supernatural vision. When she summons Martin, her back is to him; her eyes turn upward, staring (through the window? through the roof?) at something which we cannot see. (That same upward look will return at the end of the film, though to very different effect.) The eyes become invested not only with witchly force but also, and especially, with sexual energy.

The shadows enveloping Anne's face are part of another system which oscillates between "natural" love and "supernatural" force—that of the interior lighting of the film. We have already seen how much *Day of Wrath* owes to Dreyer's chamber-art qualities, but here Dreyer's lighting reaches a level of complexity not seen in his earlier work. Sometimes light transforms a room so as to remind us of the world outside, as when sunlight filters through windows. But other chambers—Herlofs Marte's cottage, the torture chamber, the nocturnal rectory, the sacristy—become steeped in a lighting marked as "supernatural." While Hollywood films after *Citizen Kane* often turned to the solid blacks and brilliant whites of arc-lamp illumination, *Day of Wrath* (presumably shot using incandescent lamps) employs a diffused lighting, a wide range of grays, and soft shadows that are dark without being opaque; the film is lit neither "high key" nor "low key." In fact, Dreyer generally avoids the Hollywood "three-point" lighting system (the use of key, fill, and backlight on a figure, which is lit independently of the set as a whole). Instead, in *Day of Wrath,* the sets and figures are, for long shots, lit as a single unit. Seldom does any backlighting separate figure from ground (if backlighting is present, it edges only the face), and often there is no filler light either. Most noticeable is a general lack of motivation for lighting effects. For example, Dreyer uses steep downward lighting for night scenes in the rectory. True, the Hollywood style often utilized high lighting sources, but either crosslights prevent our noticing the source or else the source is motivated (as window, skylight, or whatever). In *Day of Wrath,* although in "realistic" terms the illumination comes from candles, light slants sharply down from above, as if the rectory roof were perforated.

Or as if the walls were transparent. For in *Day of Wrath* we discover a highly unclassical lighting technique that would stay with Dreyer for the rest of his career: what we can call the "glowing-wall" technique. A soft light, from no apparent source, is spread across a wall, leaving an irregular darkness around it. But figures in front of the surface will cast no shadows on it, and indeed they will often be edge-lighted as if the light came *through* the wall. One result is to leave the edges of the shot as serrated as the masked and vignetted frames of Dreyer's silent films. Consider, for example, the film's second shot (fig. 13), with the glowing background behind the hand with the pen. But the more powerful consequence is the eradication of any realistic motivation for the illumination. What, for instance, creates the glowing walls of the torture chamber, as in the shot of Laurentius interrogating Herlofs Marte (fig. 14)? In Herlofs Marte's house, one patch of light comes from the window, but what of the one on her hair (fig. 15)? In *Ordet* and *Gertrud,* the glowing-wall technique will reappear, but it is significant that in *Day of Wrath* such carefully unmotivated lighting from above and "through" surfaces functions to imbue the various chambers of the film with a supernatural aura.

One should not infer from such area lighting, though, that a chiaroscuro is statically laid across the decor, like the traceries in *Morocco* or the web-motif in *Suspicion.* In *Day of Wrath,* the blocks of light and darkness become visible only when a character passes through them. The steepness of many light sources is often not apparent in the static shot; figure movement is required to reveal the unexpected patches and angles of illumination. Even as simple a task as crossing a room or going to a door (figs. 16–17) becomes a stream of optical transformations, inducing the character to penetrate a three-dimensional network of darkness and light. This effect is most pronounced at night, when the rectory's volume is shot through with a light evoking

13 14 15 16 17

the supernatural. As Anne circles Martin, she passes through thicknesses of light and shadow which are never projected onto the floor but which endow her with an aura at once mysterious and sexual.

The prominence of Anne's eyes has a role within this system of unmotivated lighting. Often we see Anne's face in areas of soft shadow. Sometimes she moves into shadow, motivating the illumination. But sometimes shadows flit uncertainly across her face. Most explicit, of course, is the leaf-shadow motif. During her flight, Herlofs Marte passes through the shade of a tree, whose tossing branches cast speckled shadows on her. Just before her death, strapped to the ladder, she curses Absalon and the shadows of leaves again fall across her face. This motif is transferred to Anne. When she calls Martin and when they kiss, the shadows of leaves tremble upon her face, yoking Herlofs Marte's supernatural powers to Anne's sexuality. The leaf shadows become, as it were, the supernatural/sexual "negative" image of the "positive, natural" image of tree branches that dominates the lovers' first outing. By the penultimate sequence, shadows appear without any motivation whatsoever. Kneeling by Absalon's coffin, Anne swears to Martin that she did not kill Absalon, but as she does so, a dark shadow slides across her face, from no physical cause. In such moments, the face truly becomes a landscape, one which is transformed through lighting into a *scene;* better, the face becomes the support for an overt "writing" in light and shadow.

So Anne is, evidently, the problem of the narrative. Although tradition urges us to read her actions as psychologically motivated, the "absent cause" supplied by witchcraft displaces personal psychology. The oscillation between the natural and the supernatural should be seen as the film's strategy for postponing sexuality (yet, paradoxically, confronting it at every moment, confronting it in the only terms the film can). But is the oscillation endless? In the final scene we find all the components of this hesitation—Anne's movements, her costume, her glances, her lighting. Abandoned by Martin, she stands confronting Absalon's corpse and confesses that she killed him and ensnared his son with the aid of Satan. Is her confession an adequate conclusion? "Is she a witch?" Has she collapsed, succumbed to society's determination to define natural desires as supernatural wickedness? (As Bazin puts it: "The despair at the end could as well indicate confession as a lie."[8]) Or does psychology remain absent to the last? Does the film, that is, continue to hesitate between the natural and the supernatural to the very end? Or does it finally settle on a reading which places Anne, *solves* her? Before we can examine this complex final scene, we need to consider some aspects of the film which we have so far ignored.

THE SCROLL

The film begins without a credit sequence, only a title: *Vredens Dag* in Gothic script, with a cross in shadowy superimposition. To a lugubrious melody a scroll unwinds up the screen. On the right side of the scroll is inscribed a text. On the left side of the scroll, a series of woodcuts depicts the Day of Judgment: Christ dividing the earth, a city in flames, angels weighing souls, the jaws of hell. The cross remains superimposed. Only after seven illustrations and seven verses does the scroll start to fade out over the beginning of the penultimate stanza: "Day of wrath, from the strap of Satan. . . ."

We have already seen that Dreyer's films are built around such authorless texts, timeless messages addressed to no one in particular. They function most obviously as closure devices, and in *Day of Wrath* the scroll returns, expectably, at the end, entirely unrolled, its text complete. But we have also seen, in the early films, how such texts tend to serve as an ahistorical determination of the film's structure, how the written word guides us in the reading of the film. In *Jeanne d'Arc,* Dreyer sets in dialectical confrontation, one such exemplary text—the transcript of Jeanne's trial—with an altogether different medium—the film image itself—to construct a tension between the dead social word and the living expressive word. In *Vampyr,* the intertitles and the diegetically motivated book organize the film and transmute their authority into Gray's prophetic dreams. *Day of Wrath* bears all these tendencies. The scroll programs the ensuing film for us—not only in its narrative unfolding but also by diagrammatically setting several representational systems against one another.

The text of the opening immediately poses a problem. It both is, and is not, the Dies Irae. *Vredens Dag,* or *Day of Wrath,* corresponds to the Latin "Dies Irae," and the music supplies the traditional Dies Irae melody. But the verses are not translations of the Latin poem which has come down to us. The film manages to draw upon the entire tradition of the Dies Irae while presenting an unorthodox written text. (English-language prints have mistakenly translated the Latin poem and attached it to the illustrations.)[9] A literal translation follows, accompanied by the appropriate woodcuts (figs. 18–24):

DAY OF WRATH: WRITTEN TEXT

1. *Day of Wrath, as the dark night*
grasps hold of the ends of the earth,
the sun stands, surrounded by darkness.

2. *Day of wrath will stand with sulfur,*
flames will fall upon us,
the lovely castle of the world perish.

3. *Day of wrath with a thunderous mouth*
awakes us from the pale slumber
announces to us our galling moment.

4. *Day of wrath's trumpet blow*
calls the dead and the living
opens the hollow lap of the grave.

5. *Day of wrath, arranged by God,*
the horrible slate of the Devil
is shown before the court of the Lord.

6. *Day of wrath breaks out the verdict;*
lightning shall press some like
the sinful flow of their deeds.

7. *Day of wrath, O see them stand*
small as grain before his throne,
dressed in shame and sinful desire.

8. *Day of wrath, from the strap of Satan*
lifts up the sin-burdened body,
the crushed soul to Heaven.

9. *Day of wrath, listen to our penance,*
the sorrow's holy flood of tears;
Save us, Jesus, by your blood.

18 19 20

21 22 23

24

The formal and thematic advantages of this version stand out obviously enough; the verses introduce motifs for use in the narrative to come. The light/dark imagery (verse 1), the flames (2), the act of judgment (5), the fear of damnation (6), and sinful desire (7) all recur significantly in the ensuing film. The judged souls stand before the throne; later Martin and Anne discuss whether Absalon is standing before God interceding for them. The last trumpet summons all souls, just as Anne's mother supposedly had the witch's power to call "the quick and the dead." Numerous references prepare for the film's use of sound, especially for that off-screen sound which will threaten Herlofs Marte and Anne. From this standpoint, the verses establish the gloomy repressiveness of the Church in the film. But this addresses only the inscription; why the images? And why text, images, and music together? To get a better purchase on the functions of these elements, we need to consider how they combine.

First, the scroll unwinds a *series* of images and texts, and that series represents a chain of narrative events. The story of the Last Judgment, as told in Revelation, is here "plotted" through the two channels of pictures and written language. As we would expect, the result conforms to the principles of narrative: events are linked chronologically and causally. The first cause is supernatural, God Himself. Darkness falls, our vain civilization is destroyed, the last trumpet summons the living and the dead, souls are weighed, the verdict is given, and the damned are shoveled into hell. Motifs, both pictorial and verbal, stitch the events together; throughout, the scroll makes the act of judgment into what Barthes calls an "action sequence," analyzable into discrete narrative segments. Even the music adds narrative force. The melody has undergone so much quotation—particularly in Romantic tone poems—that it now carries representational weight, irrestistably summoning up the day of judgment and the knell of damnation. All that the scroll lacks is narrative closure. Though we might think the events to have concluded with the act of judgment, the fact that the scroll continues unwinding, revealing a bit of another image and text (fig. 22) as the screen fades to black, promises more to come.

Several consequences crowd upon us. Before the film's own narrative has commenced, the Dies Irae scroll models for us another narrative operating on stable, unified principles. And as an *already* completed narration—like *Jeanne d'Arc*'s trial transcript, the scroll is a finished object at the very start—the scroll prepares us for its return and completion. Whatever the disparities of the narrative to come, then, the scroll places them within an integrated master-text. Like *Vampyr, Day of Wrath* uses the authoritative word to hold localized ambiguities in check.

The Dies Irae scroll programs another set of structures—sonic ones. The musical notation and the nondiegetic orchestral accompaniment for the scroll's unwinding foreground the role of sound, especially music, in the film to come. The musical implications of the Dies Irae are realized through its reinscription into the film's action. Though the scroll initially positioned it outside the film's narrative world, the Dies Irae, as music and text, reappears in the narrative. In the church, Anne and Martin pause to listen to the boy choir rehearsing the Dies Irae in preparation for the immolation. As the couple go out, the sequence ends with a shot of the musical score on the choirmaster's stand. Off screen, the boys' voices pipe; on screen, the shadow of the choirmaster's conducting hands falls across the sheet. At first glance, this would seem to link the Church to the transcendent position of the scroll. But immediately the soundtrack cancels the possibility of reading this performance as asocially spiritual. For as the shot of the sheet music dissolves, the sound of the *next* sequence bleeds over into this shot, and Herlofs Marte's anguished shriek is "conducted" by the choirmaster, completely synchronized with his cues and tempo. That scream gives the lie to the rehearsal's complacent piety. ("I hear her shrieks all the time," Anne has remarked earlier.) Though the Dies Irae melody is first identified as transcendent, the soundtrack places the performance firmly within the repressive social mechanism.

The Dies Irae reappears at the immolation of Herlofs Marte, a sequence which points up the functions of sound in the construction of the film. Off-screen noises, the plastic textures and timbres of the sound, and the dense polyphonic mesh of dialogue, music, and noise, make the sequence the performance of an ensemble piece, an oratorio for choir, bell, flames, and female soloist.

At the start of the sequence, the image track lays out the scene through glances. From the rectory loft, Anne watches Herlofs Marte brought out. Martin declines to watch the immolation and comes to join Anne as she turns from the window. No establishing shots define the characters' positions; the setting and the relationships are indicated through cutting and camera angle. Nine shots of Anne, the looker, alternate with eight shots of various objects of her glance. As Anne views Herlofs Marte, Dreyer adheres to her point of view through eyeline matches and high-angle compositions of the old lady and Laurentius. Anne looks to screen left, and we see the elders looking on as Martin rises and leaves. Anne's eyes follow Martin's walk across the courtyard and then return to Herlofs Marte, now bound to a ladder. Distraught, Anne turns away, goes to a seat, and will watch no more. As a whole, the sequence of her witnessing these events is bracketed, front and end, by two full shots from inside the loft. Although point of view is no longer subjective in the remainder of the sequence, the scene continues to build upon the spatial premises established in this early phase.

Cutting and angle of view do not, however, overwhelm the soundtrack. This early phase of the scene is accompanied by three sonic lines which become the ground bass of the sequence. As Anne enters the loft, we hear the one sound that will continue through the entire sequence: the muffled tolling of the off-screen churchbell. Monotonously steady, the bell articulates a metric pulse for all successive "melodies." As Anne appears at the loft window, we hear the sound of the onlooking crowd, now a soft babble. (Handled in Bressonian fashion, this crowd remains off screen during the entire scene.) In the next shot, the smoke and flame of the stake crackle on the soundtrack, to remain menacingly audible for the rest of the sequence. Three shots, three sonic lines. Moreover, all are noises issuing from a source within the scene's space and thus all implicitly define spatial relationships. The two channels, image and sound, complement each other: the shots portray loft, yard, elders; the sounds evoke the onlookers and the bell tower; only the shot of the stake and the sound of the flames duplicate information between channels. When Martin joins Anne in the loft and the crowd's clamorous chants and the sound of the flames vanish, the pause is not there merely for verisimilitude: the brief quiet helps demarcate the end of the scene's initial phase. Henceforth the couple will only *hear* what occurs outside; their refusal to look stresses the action's sheerly sonic significance.

The scene's second phase centers on Herlofs Marte's shrill arguments with Laurentius and Absalon. Lashed to the ladder, she demands to speak with Absalon. He ignores her threats to denounce Anne, and as he prays the executioners lift the ladder. Visually, this section of the scene parallels the initial phase. A pair of identical shots (Herlofs Marte from a high-angle long shot) bracket the segment. Within the segment, shots of the characters alternate. Herlofs Marte replaces Anne as the point-of-view character: four shots of her looking alternate with four shots of Absalon approaching her, hands folded in prayer.

Sonically, the initially introduced elements continue and become the background for new "lines." After the pause with Anne and Martin in the loft, the crowd's chant and the flames return as constant off-screen noises. Against this dense fabric, the character's dialogue stands out, and it, too, develops in markedly acoustic terms. Herlofs Marte tells Laurentius to fetch Absalon. Laurentius: "What for?" Herlofs Marte, louder: "I want to speak to Absalon!" Laurentius: "Can you denounce someone?" Herlofs Marte, shouting: *"I want to speak to Absalon!"* Laurentius's off-screen questions, and Herlofs Marte's request, thrice iterated, throw into relief her act of speaking and its steadily increasing volume. As the accompanying frame enlargements (figs. 25–36) and sound chart indicate, this phase of the sequence concludes on an even stronger and sharper increase in volume and pitch. To Absalon's indifference, Herlofs Marte shakes her fist at him, and shrieks that she will denounce Anne (shot 162, fig. 25). Absalon does not reply, but the soundtrack answers her: in the next shot (163, fig. 26), the off-screen flames hiss and bark even more loudly and, while the crowd murmur continues, other voices begin to shout: "Lift—her—up! Lift—her—up!" The executioners bend to the task and start to raise the ladder (shot 164, fig. 27).

The final phase of the sequence carries the sound-image relations to a paroxysmic climax, playing upon leaps in pitch, abrupt silences, clashes of tone qualities, and—as we would expect—the reappearance of the Dies Irae. Now the flames appear against the background of the church (shot 165, fig. 28), creating a juxtaposition that will soon be commented upon by the soundtrack. In shot 166 (fig. 29), Herlofs Marte is raised, slowly arcing up out of the frame, and as she rises not only does her voice jangle against the darker, lower tones of the off-screen chanting but her screams rise in pitch, synchronized with her upward movement. Absalon, turning and making the abrupt gesture of the conductor giving the downbeat, suddenly cues a new sonic element. On a cut, silence. The babble, the shouts, and the flames are gone.

Earlier, as Martin left the churchyard, the choirboys were brought in, filling the frame which he vacated. Now they begin to sing the Dies Irae (shot 167, fig. 30). Their high, sweet tones abruptly cancel the harsher shrieks of the old woman. The camera pans across the boys to the choirmaster, and as he comes into view, an off-screen adult chorus—never firmly anchored diegetically—accompanies the boy choir. Here the first two lines of the Dies Irae are linked to the circumstances of performance, but immediately they begin to function in a fashion characteristic of the sound's attempt throughout the film to undercut the social sanctity of the Church. For the next shot (168, fig. 31) repeats the image of stake and church, but the off-screen song links the execution of Herlofs Marte to the Last Judgment, when the sun is "surrounded by darkness." This hesitation between the Dies Irae sung diegetically (in the scene) and nondiegetically (the adult choir commenting upon the action) will dominate the last few shots.

Absalon's stabbing gesture, decisively signaling silence and cueing the choir, has bared the performative, musical construction of the scene. As this ensemble piece draws to a close, the soloist launches into her final passage, against the accompaniment of the reverberant beat of the bell, the rasp of the flames, and the choir's song. The executioners stand poised (shot 169, fig. 32), and Absalon again gestures downward sharply, cueing the scene's final passage. The executioners push the ladder over. Herlofs Marte claws at the air and topples into the flames (shot 170, fig. 33). Just as her upward arc was duplicated by the panicky rise in pitch of her shrieks, so as she falls her scream plunges down the scale.

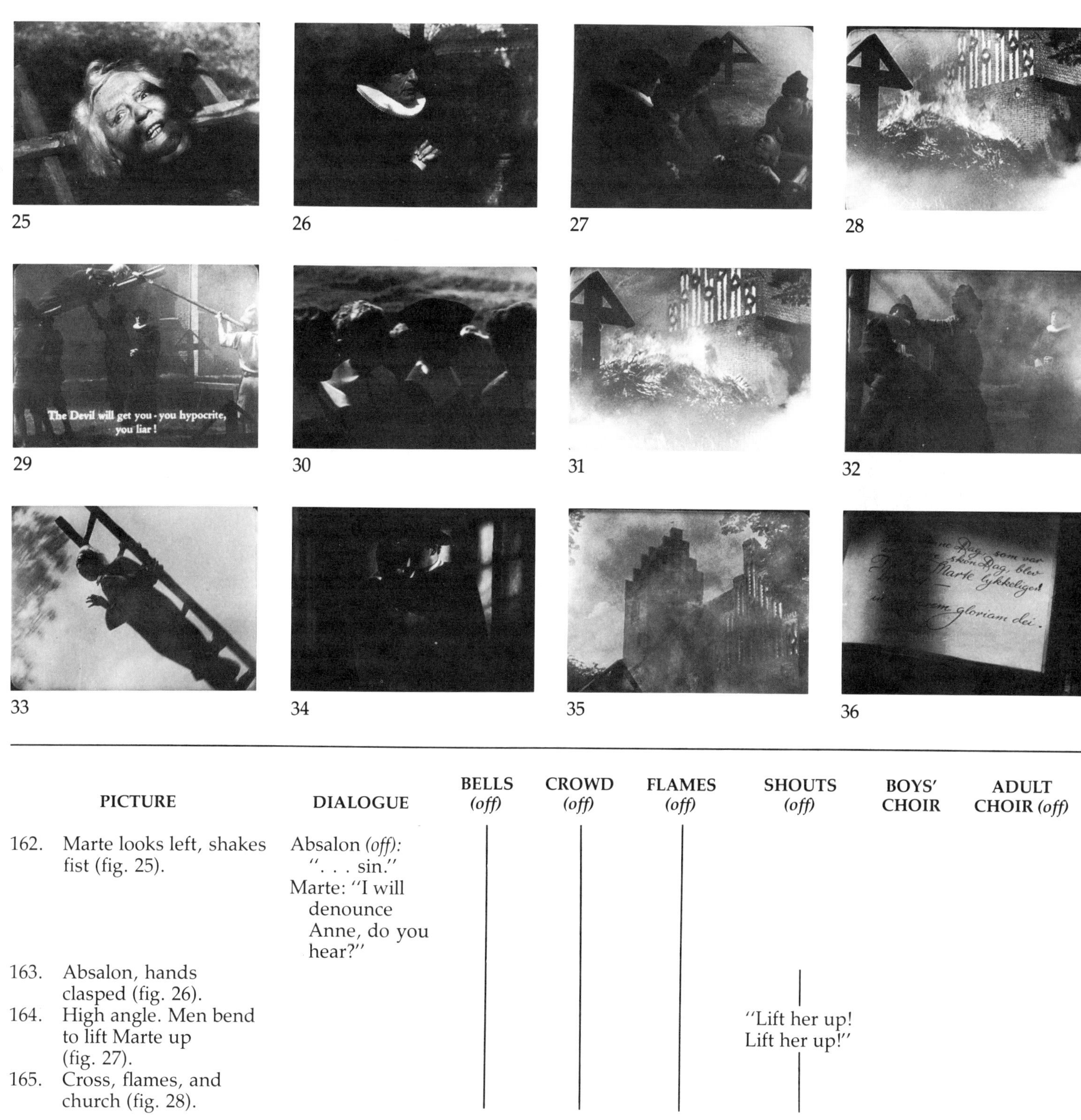

25 26 27 28

29 30 31 32

33 34 35 36

	PICTURE	DIALOGUE	BELLS *(off)*	CROWD *(off)*	FLAMES *(off)*	SHOUTS *(off)*	BOYS' CHOIR	ADULT CHOIR *(off)*
162.	Marte looks left, shakes fist (fig. 25).	Absalon *(off)*: ". . . sin." Marte: "I will denounce Anne, do you hear?"						
163.	Absalon, hands clasped (fig. 26).							
164.	High angle. Men bend to lift Marte up (fig. 27).					"Lift her up! Lift her up!"		
165.	Cross, flames, and church (fig. 28).							

	PICTURE	DIALOGUE	BELLS (*off*)	CROWD (*off*)	FLAMES (*off*)	SHOUTS (*off*)	BOYS' CHOIR	ADULT CHOIR (*off*)
166.	The men push the ladder up (fig. 29). Absalon gestures rightward.	Marte: "You shall suffer for this!" (goes off screen) "The Devil will get you, you hypocrite, you liar!" (*off*) screaming.						
167.	Choirboys. Pan right to leader (fig. 30).						"Day of wrath, as the dark night grasps hold of the ends of the earth,	
168.	Cross, flames, and church (fig. 31).						The sun. . .	
169.	Man supports ladder; one turns right. Pan with him to reframe Absalon. He makes a sharp downward gesture. Man turns back and with others topple ladder (fig. 32).						(*off*) . . . stands surrounded by darkness. . . . (*off*) Day of wrath with sulfur. . . .	
170.	Pan, arcing down as Marte topples into fire (fig. 33).	*scream*					(*off*) . . . will stand.	
171.	Anne moves to Martin; they embrace (fig. 34).						(*off*) Flames will fall upon us. The lovely. . . .	
172.	Pan up from flames to church steeple and smoke (fig. 35). fade out fade in						(*off*) . . . castle of the world will perish. Day of wrath with thunderous mouth. . . .	
173.	End of document: "On this day, when nature sang the praises of our Lord, the sinner Herlofs Marte expiated her crimes at the stake. In majorem gloriam Dei" (fig. 36).		*fade out*		*fade out*		(*off*). . . awakes us from our pale slumber. . . ."	

Her last "solo" is accompanied by the second verse of the Dies Irae. The verbal image of sulphur supplements the flames we see in shot 170. Her death is sonically re-marked by a shot (171, fig. 34) of Anne embracing Martin in the loft—their responses based wholly on the sound of the scream—and Anne's sobs are as abruptly juxtaposed to the old woman's voice as the boy choir's song had been. While we see Anne and Martin, off screen the choir sings, "Flames will fall upon us." The line links not only to the execution and to Anne's future in witchcraft ("Send me to the stake and Anne will follow"). "Flames will fall upon us," said the scroll: the Apocalypse will spare no one, all souls will be judged. Through the cutting and the addition of the adult chorus, the verse is freed from its source in the action, and turns against the society depicted. Such a turn concludes the sequence: while the camera pans up the church steeple from the stake (shot 172, fig. 35), we hear the prediction that "the lovely castle of the world [will] perish" on God's Day of Judgment. And the steady pulse of the bell throughout it all is referred to in the next verse about the Judgment Day's "thunderous mouth": the term used *(malme-mund)* carries in Danish the connotation of church bells. The Dies Irae sung *by* the Church, thus "generalized," becomes a condemnation *of* and warning addressed *to* the Church.

But the sound does not cease until after the sequence has been written up, translated into the official record (shot 173, fig. 36). Absalon's account of the immolation not only again foregrounds the musical-ensemble aspect of the scene but also signals the desire to define nature as an extension of the social will, to encompass it in a careful description. "On this day when nature sang the praises of our Lord . . ." But we have seen that it is not nature but society that conceives this as a laudable day, and we have also seen that the friction between the Dies Irae and the images already works against a literal, supplementary relationship. And even now, the words heard over Absalon's writing (the Day of Wrath "awakes us from our pale slumber") identify the community as the object of forthcoming judgment. The succeeding line, left tacit, is "announces to us our bitter moment," opening into the phase of the film involving Anne.

What has happened, then, to the Dies Irae? Defined initially on the scroll as outside the diegetic world of the film, it enters the narrative only to be pried loose from a secure univocal meaning. The boys rehearse it, but what the conductor conducts are Herlofs Marte's screams. In the immolation scene, the Dies Irae begins as part of the social matrix, but the editing and the uncertain placement of the unseen adult chorus push the piece into a more abstract, commentative role. By the end of the immolation, the Dies Irae has again become an asocial master text, an echo of the unrolling scroll, in which we read the vanity and repressiveness of the social formation.

The presence of text, image, and sound in the opening scroll does one more thing. It puts on exhibit two pairs of representational systems—written language and musical notation on the one hand and images and sounds on the other. In the Dies Irae prologue, these systems harmonize in an asocial, ahistorical transcendence. Music, pictures, and words determine each other, each one paralleling the others. The ensuing film, however, shatters this harmony, revealing disparities and frictions among these systems. Within the narrative world that we see, writing becomes radically differentiated from images and speech, the former being generally identified with the frozen sterility of the social world, the latter elements being associated with the more vital experience of natural and supernatural forces. The interaction of these representational systems is traceable within *Day of Wrath*'s narrative structure.

After the scroll has faded out, the narrative begins with the writing of a text. Whereas the Dies Irae text is already written, its production unknown to us, this other text is presented as undergoing the act of production (the film's second moving image is of the quill dipped in the inkpot). This text is not the authorless, ahistorical Dies Irae but a dated and signed document stating that Herlofs Marte, denounced as a witch, must be seized and brought to court. Eminently social writing: the shots emphasize not the author as individual (we see only a hand guiding the pen) but the act of inscription as a pro forma ritual. As in *Vampyr,* such written texts are interspersed through *Day of Wrath's* narrative—five insertions in all, cooperating with the alternating division of scenes—but the functions of the texts are not as entirely predictive as such texts are in the earlier film. These writings stand as what Fernando Lazaro Carreter calls "literal messages" or "ritual language." These are public records, lacking a definite addressee and aimed at preservation; other examples are contracts, edicts, and funerary inscriptions.[10] Literal messages are meant to last, to certify for the future how an event occured. They tacitly claim to report specific happenings adequately and objectively. The question in *Day of Wrath* is: how adequately and objectively?

Social writing is seen as inadequate because (unlike the book *Vampyre*) it misinterprets or distorts what it reports. Immediately after the document announces the public denunciation, we see the accused herself, as Herlofs Marte gives her customer a potion. Off screen the chants and bells signal the approach of the witch hunt. The old woman, terrified, flees through her home into her barn and out through her pigsty. Already, albeit minimally, the detached language of the writ has been set against concrete human behavior. Narratively, the formal certainty of the document is qualified by an ambiguity: whether or not Herlofs Marte's sorcery works, people seek her out to try it. Stylistically, the abstract treatment of the act of writing is counterposed to the spatially and temporally concrete action of Herlofs Marte. A single shot renders the entire scene, with a lateral and parallel camera movement following her through her home; her prolonged pause after hearing the bell foregrounds the passage of time, as does the camera movement itself. In sum, though the text does not specifically seek to record the actions we see and hear, Dreyer has by juxtaposition of document to scene brought out that opposition between the abstract social mechanism of writing and a concrete, spatially and temporally "lived" experience.

In the course of the film, the social nature of such documents becomes more and more specified. The second text, like the first, is relatively unlocalized narratively: it orders Absalon to win over the soul of Herlofs Marte. Causally, it motivates the ensuing scene (segment VI) in the sacristy. As a text, the declaration functions in the machinery of the Church's judicial process, defining a structure of social roles. And again we are forced to compare the text's expression with the scene that we witness: the letter's drab pieties, ordering that Absalon "exhort her to confess the full truth that she may not die without penance," are given the lie by Absalon's suppression of the truth about Anne's mother.

The conclusion of the sequence in the torture chamber (segment VII) becomes a still more penetrating demonstration of how inadequate social writing is to the concrete event. The film's third written text, which ends the sequence, explicitly purports to sum up the action. Herlofs Marte has been subjected to strappado, scrutinized by the elders, and badgered by Laurentius, but the record curtly notes: "After having denied it, and after being put to the question, Herlofs Marte freely surrendered to the benevolent abjurations and preaching of the Saints' College and freely admitted to having taken part in sorcery and black magic." The social ceremony of writing is at last precisely located: Absalon walks slowly to the scribe and signs the document, attesting to its adequacy. Yet we have earlier seen Absalon conceal the truth about Anne's mother and Herlofs Marte's knowledge of it; what authority can his signature have now? A wedge has been definitively driven between the concrete event and its transcription. Written language must now be doubted; its very inadequacy, in fact, makes it a valuable social tool. It seems to record, to preserve ritual documents, when it actually represses.

The repressiveness of the "literal message" is finally and ironically specified after the immolation. "On this day," writes a pen on a page, "when nature sang the praises of our Lord, the wicked Herlofs Marte expiated her crimes at the stake. In majorem gloriam Dei." The writing is socially specified when the next shot reveals Absalon as the author. He has concealed the truth from his peers and now the only record of the event is his "literal message." Inadequate and unfaithful, his account becomes the final and definitive instance of the social repressiveness of writing. When Absalon solemnly places the pen in its inkpot, the gesture parallels that of the hand taking up the pen at the film's beginning, and simultaneously closes the series of written documents that runs through the first third of the film.

What opposes social and inadequate writing? Speech and images. The transitional element is the poem. When Martin arrives, Absalon begins to read from a book a song about a maiden and an apple tree: "A maiden she sat in an apple tree/A lad he chanced to pass by. . . ." Martin completes it: "She stretched—the bough it bended/Within his arms she landed." The verse of course functions as another determining prophetic text, preparing for the alliance between Martin and Anne. The poem, also, significantly, is never shown, only recited. Delivered from the constraints of the document, the poem enters into a living circuit of communication among the characters. Later, after Martin and Anne have committed adultery, Anne asks permission to read from the Bible and selects the Song of Songs: "I am the rose of Sharon and the lily of the valley. Like the lily among thorns, so is my beloved among the daughters. As the apple tree among the trees of the wood, so is my beloved among the sons. I sat down under his shadow. . . ." Anne transmutes the scriptural word into the living word, an expression of her new vitality and voluptuousness. So concrete have the texts become that she can cite them later—first, the Song of Songs while she and Martin sit in the grass; later, more ambiguously, "the song about the two of us" while the couple await Absalon's return to the rectory. Thus against social writing and the notated Dies Irae are set the recitation of the Song of Songs and the apple-tree folksong.

37

38

39

40

The most powerful contrast to social writing remains, however, the system of embedded images that dominates the latter two-thirds of the film. If Absalon tends to be identified with the written, Anne is identified with the pictorial. First, she *sees.* The first half of the film emphasizes Anne as witness during Absalon's interrogation of Herlofs Marte and during the immolation. In these sequences, the film's omniscient point of view is suspended in order to channel narrative information through Anne's eyes. And Anne's first encounter with Martin, as we have seen, relies upon her sighting of him, as conveyed through her glance in a mirror and eyeline-match cutting. Indeed, her first point-of-view shot (and the first in the film) enmeshes Martin in a grid, puts him into a composition (fig. 37). This initiates Anne's second role: she *makes* images. Her embroidery depicts a woman, back coyly turned, walking down a flowered path. When Anne sits before it, her glance installs Martin in the pictorial matrix of the needlework, thus linking his face to the woman's body (figs. 38–39). When her pattern for the embroidery is later revealed, we find that Martin had held the place designed for the image of a child. Indeed, the images of Martin and Anne *on either side* of her embroidery rack reproduce those replicas of artists sighting through grids in order to construct correct perspective upon a picture plane (fig. 40). The lovers are bound to each other in and through the relations of pictorial representation.

Throughout the film, Anne stitches image to image, drawing surrounding elements into the unfurling fabric of representation. In the scene at the river (segment XIII), she points out a tree to Martin. But we see only the tree's reflection. "It yearns after its own reflection in the water. The reflection and the tree cannot be sundered" (fig. 41). The

41

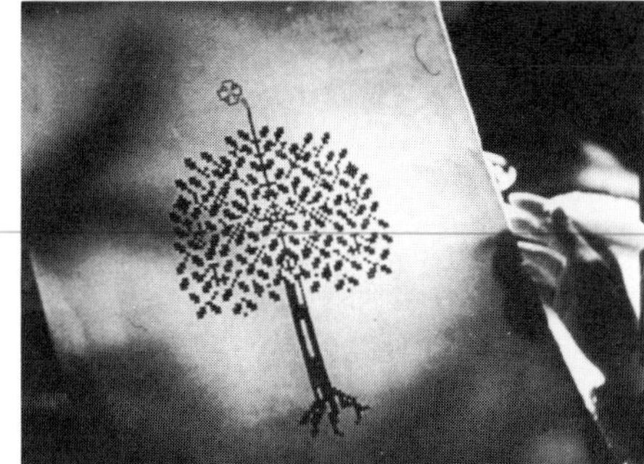
42

43

most direct reference is to the couple themselves, yet the remark and the image lay bare the film's conception of pictorial representation. First, the image is a reflection of the real, bound to it immediately in a way that social writing cannot be. Second, the image expresses vital human traits; for Martin, it is "bowed in sorrow, it grieves over us"; for Anne, it is bowed "in longing." Reference and expression, reflection of reality and revelation of feeling: the image enjoys a privileged relation to the world and the human that writing, locked within its frozen ceremonies and routines, cannot attain. That the couple disagree about how to read the image's expressiveness only reminds us of the film's insistence on the undecidability of the causes of actions. And that the images link to the recited passages from the folk song and the Song of Songs (motifs of flowers, trees, seduction, fertility) is to be expected: if writing is duplicitous and socially repressive, the image is located outside social constraint, being a sheer effect of nature.

Logically enough, the last image that Anne creates is explicitly paralleled to social writing. While the storm tears at the rectory, Anne is inside drawing a picture (fig. 42), using a quill pen and inkpot similar to that used by the authorities and Absalon. The image condenses the earlier motifs—like the woman and child, it is a pattern for her embroidery; like the folksong, the Song of Songs, and the reflection in the water, it represents an apple tree; like all the others, this image manifests a natural expressivity, revealing Anne's love for Martin: "My apple tree has only one blossom." Significantly, just as Martin could not grasp the meaning of the tree's reflection, so now he sees the drawing as depicting a pear tree. And his allegiance to the social is immediately confirmed after Anne has left the parlor; we next see him seated at her table, thoughtfully *writing* (fig. 43).

It is only in the context of the interplay of representational systems which is initiated by the Dies Irae scroll and sustained through the ensuing film that we can now return to consider the final scene of *Day of Wrath.* Not only does this last scene display, microcosmically, the interaction between narrative coherence and disruptions which were examined in the first part of the chapter, but it also indicates the crucial *relation* between the narrative's patterning and the representational systems.

The scene is this. Singing choirboys circle the room and file out past the church elders, Merete, Absalon's bier, Anne, and Martin. Martin thanks those assembled and makes the formal declaration of Absalon's death. A priest takes over the ceremony but is interrupted by Merete, who accuses Anne of murder and witchcraft. Martin shrinks from Anne and goes to his grandmother's side. Anne is asked to swear on the coffin that she did not kill Absalon. She starts to swear, but stops and confesses that she killed him "with the help of the Evil One." After a shot of her at the bier, the image returns to the scroll with which the film began, and the final verses unwind and fade out, leaving only the cross design. In a final gesture, onto the top of the cross fade two sloping bars (fig. 44).

In the course of the last sequence, space is mapped characteristically. Alternating editing sets, first, Martin against the elders, then Merete against Anne and Martin, and finally Anne against all the rest. The "circular" *mise-en-scène* reappears first in the form of the tracking shot (the camera moves laterally, following the boys around the room) and later in the ping-pong panning shots which link Martin and Anne, on one side of the coffin, with Merete on the other side. The cutting also establishes the film's characteristic variety of orientations to a zone of action. The setting is in fact the sacristy (the locale of Herlofs Marte's first interview with Absalon in segment VI*a*) and the boys go out the door through which Anne had peeped during that interview. Generally the camera stays on one side of the action (as in the rectory scenes), so the eyelines are invariably true. But when the cloth covering Absalon's

44

coffin is peeled back, the orientation shifts 180° to show his face, and this shot is alternated with a medium shot of Anne's face. Moreover, the framing and cutting at the end of the scene establishes Anne as even more isolated than in the rest of the film, her figure floating against the glowing white walls.

The narrative functions of the final scene in supplying a certain closure are evident. What must be examined is how the scene and the epilogue handle the problem which Anne poses for the narrative, the slide between the natural and the supernatural in relation to sexuality.

The frame of reference remains initially social. In this chamber a church ritual is enacted; the gathered elders again form an audience for a public ceremony, the theatricality of the scene stressed by the most stark tableaux in the film. Moreover, the social nature of the group is defined by the plethora of father-images. While off screen Martin says, "God gave me a father," we see the stern, intently listening elders, their faces encircled with replicas of Absalon's stiff collar. Most important of all, Martin's speech offers, for the first time in the film, a spoken "literal message," an articulated "document." (It is perhaps for this reason that the film omits showing Absalon pronouncing the last rites over Laurentius.) Dreyer makes the aural nature of the act apparent by diction (Martin's "One word more . . . ," Merete's "I will speak now") and by a shot of a listener cupping his hand to his ear. Martin now swears, formulaically, that Absalon died of natural causes; thus speech, earlier an articulation of the natural, is surrendered to social constraint.

The social frame of reference, though, does not mean that the hesitation of Anne's sexuality has stopped. All the signs of that hesitation rush in. The costumes eliminate more flesh than ever before—even hands are hardly visible—but six close-ups pinpoint Anne's face, with hood and lighting emphasizing her expression and her eyes. Her reactions to Martin's speech, to Merete's denunciation, to Martin's withdrawal are manifested solely through eyes and lips. She is asked to swear. As she stands over the corpse of her husband, her face is wrapped in a shadow. Appropriately, the last two cuts of the scene are eyeline matches, relaying our attention from her glance to Absalon's face and back again. Thus by the time she speaks, the first time in the scene, we are already enmeshed in an interplay of the natural and supernatural, the slippage of sexuality. Even now, the film refuses to stop the oscillation between the two poles.

What happens next propels the film onto a new level. In the penultimate image, a seventy-five-second medium shot with only eyes and lips moving, Anne is made to transcend altogether the terms of the film's hesitation. Looking down at Absalon, she makes her confession, shadows encircling her face. With Anne, speech keeps its expressive status ("So now you have your revenge . . ."), but like Martin's address to the elders, Anne's speech has a social addressee—the (dead) father, what Julia Kristeva calls "the paternal function as support of all unity: unity of naming, unity of society."[11] Her confession acknowledges the terms of the social, but these will soon be surpassed. After a pause, she looks left and slightly downward—at Martin?—and says: "I see you through my tears, but no one comes to wipe them away." The statement recalls the moment after she had first summoned Martin and he had brushed off her tears. More important, the blockage of vision starts to sever her from the terms of representation and of sight that have defined both her natural and supernatural roles. A solo boy soprano is heard, nondiegetically, on the soundtrack. The erotic problem is being transcended through a decisive repudiation of the narrative dialectic of social versus natural, natural versus supernatural. Anne shuts her eyes and slightly smiles. Stockstill, she opens her eyes and slowly raises them. Anne has done this once before, in summoning Martin, but now "no one comes." The look, *at nothing,* breaking once and for all from the gazes of the social and natural worlds, defines her entry into a new realm.

Immediately, a representational system comes in to complete the surpassing of the narrative problem, and it is that asocial, atemporal, now asexual system of the Dies Irae. The scroll, interrupted in the prologue at the moment of its greatest despair (the sinners stand before the throne to be judged for their "shame and sinful desire"), concludes itself with an abrupt gesture of blessing (figs. 23–24):

Day of wrath, from Satan's strap
lifts up the sin-burdened body,
the crushed soul, to Heaven.

Day of wrath, listen to our penance,
the sorrow's holy flood of tears;
Save us, Jesus, by your blood.

The image supplementing the first verse shows the repentent soul carried to Heaven; the second shows men and women kneeling at the foot of the cross. The movement is to grant mercy, to absolve . . . what? *Whatever Anne has done.* The question of what she *has* done—our questions about her powers and her motives, in short our (and the film's) hesitations—are negated and surpassed by fiat. The Dies Irae, the voice outside the film, in its harmony of image, language, score notation, and music—a representation always present, representation outside contradiction—"solves" Anne.

When the scroll has completely unwound, it fades out, and the cross that has been superimposed over it remains. The final scene has been crowded with cross images, all identified as part of the social panoply of the Church; but this last cross hovers in an eternal fixity. Situated in the before-and-after of full presence, the cross is the stopping point of meaning, the single model from which the scroll issues. A final movement identifies the film's conclusion with this ultimate end of meaning: the cross becomes the witch emblem. Since this latter motif had originally appeared in the scene of Herlofs Marte's immolation, its recurrence signifies the close of the narrative: Anne is burnt. But the final figure is also stressed as a *variant* of the cross. Like the last sequence of *La Passion de Jeanne d'Arc,* which halts the film at the reiteration of Jeanne's sanctity and treats the stake as a rough version of the cross, the ambivalent emblem completes the transformation of Anne into a holy witch. But, in contrast to *Jeanne d'Arc,* this transformation occurs *outside* the film, in a realm which transcends the narrative world and its problems of causality. A credit sequence would disturb this transcendence by repositioning it within sociality, and so no credits appear. Authorless, outside time, *Day of Wrath,* like the Dies Irae scroll which it "performs," purports to come from nowhere.

PROBLEMS OF RHYTHM

All of the foregoing has necessarily spread out the film for dissection. But besides the problems thrown up by its narrative, *Day of Wrath* confronts us with another difficulty, one we have encountered before but in rather different form: the problem of reading the film perceptually. In *Jeanne d'Arc* and *Vampyr,* narrative intelligibility is put into question through spatial and temporal disjunctions. *Day of Wrath,* possessing an already problematic narrative, is much more continuous spatially and temporally. Yet it initiates a problem of legibility that will return through the rest of Dreyer's career: that of rhythm. *Day of Wrath* is a slow film.

Just how slow it seemed initially may slip our minds. Today the film is readily watchable (it presaged the tempo of the 1960s "art film"), but we should remember that in its day many audiences found it intolerable. The Danish press criticized it so harshly that Dreyer was forced to defend its *longueurs.* "A macabre screen melodrama in slow motion," wrote one American observer. "The bridging passages have a way of dragging, particularly for audiences geared to the staccato pace of Hollywood offerings."[12] Bosley Crowther asserted: "The tax of his slow and ponderous tempo upon the average person's time is a rather presumptuous imposition for any motion picture artist to make."[13] Apparently *Day of Wrath* was the *Gertrud* of 1943.

Since film rhythm is a matter of patterned duration, we can distinguish durations in a narrative film at no less than seven levels. First, there is the duration consumed in accomplishing a story event. (It takes less than a second to fire a pistol but years to learn to sing opera.) Second, there is the duration of the story events *as rendered in the plot.* How much time is granted these events in presentation? (Does the pistol shot last twenty minutes as presented in the plot? Does the woman learn to sing opera in a montage sequence lasting a few seconds?) Third, there is the duration *between* story events. Evidently, if the situation changes precipitously from minute to minute, a different rhythm will result than if the situation drags on for years without a ripple. Fourth, there is the duration between story events as presented in the plot. A film's tempo will often be speeded up by the elimination of the "dead time" or negligible filler between major story events; this is common in the classical narrative cinema. Taken together, these first four types might be called "narrative rhythm." Fifth, there is the duration of each shot in relation to every other shot: the old saw, for example, is that the shorter the shot, the quicker the editing tempo. Sixth, since camera movement occupies time and entails a certain velocity, camera movement may have its own durational, hence rhythmic, properties. Finally, there is rhythm in its original sense, as applied to the patterns of sound in a film. In sum, a film's overall rhythm is the complex result of the relations among all these durations.

How does this seven-part scheme shed light on the problems of *Day of Wrath?* First, many story events themselves tend to be slow. A few swift actions—Anne's and Martin's flight through the rectory, their running through the forest, Herlofs Marte's plunge to her death—stand in sharp contrast to the generally slow tempo of other events. The delivery of lines, the gestures of the figures, their turns, their walks, all are deliberately paced.

At the level of plot rendition, Dreyer refuses to condense the duration of such story events. Stasis is rendered directly: recall the opening sequence in Herlofs Marte's cottage, when she stands stock-still for several seconds, simply listening; or the final shot of Anne, only eyes and lips moving in a medium shot lasting over a minute. Even in a scene wherein different people move in different directions, to eliminate any sense of bustle the camera concentrates on one figure (as at the end of the prayer session in the rectory parlor, when all rise and the camera picks out Absalon to follow). The already considerable duration of story events is accentuated by the plot's *holding* on those events.

Day of Wrath also insists on a considerable duration *between* story events. Except for the crosscutting scenes, these intervals are often retained in the plot. Here we return to what Roland Barthes calls those "catalyses" that are wedged in between principal actions, that " 'fill in' the narrative space separating the hinge-type functions."[14] At the level of plot, *Day of Wrath* utilizes quite small-scale catalyses. For instance, almost never does anyone in the film move *and* talk at the same time. A movement—say, walking across the room to another character—is followed by silence, *then* speech. Walking and pausing become the film's catalyses, stretching out the distance between major events. Moreover, if a character slowly moves to speak with another, the camera will usually follow that movement rather than cut away. One recalls Dreyer's praise of Sjöström's handling of the farmers in *Ingmar's Sons:* "They used up an eternity to come from one end of the room to the other."[15] If one person pauses in a speech or movement, that pause is not ellided but held. The most apparent marking of such pauses is the repeated device of panning from one character to another. When, sitting at her embroidery, Anne turns to Martin, Dreyer pans rather than cuts to Martin, then pans back to catch Anne getting up. Later, Anne meets Martin in the church, and she halts a few steps from him, the camera panning to pick him up. When Absalon visits Laurentius, he pauses in the door, and the duration of the pause is weighted by the camera's slow survey of Laurentius's home. Most intensely, near the end of the film, Martin interrogates Anne about Absalon's death. The two are in profile and as they talk the camera pans from one face to the other, rendering visible the pauses in their talk.

One result of such catalyses is similar to what we saw at work in *Vampyr:* to emphasize catalyses is to downplay causality and stress *consecutiveness.* When causality is distended, time seems to pass before our eyes. More important, here time passes much more slowly than in classical narrative films. Barthes rightly calls catalyses "the areas of security, rest or luxury"[16] between cardinal functions; but we must not rest too long. Splinter an action into too many components and they will draw disproportionate attention to themselves. In *Day of Wrath,* the unusual length of the catalystic passages gives them a difficult prominence.

What of editing and camera movement? Both techniques, as we know, play central roles in working out story space; what of story time? It is evident that *Day of Wrath* does not have the editing rhythm of an *October;* Dreyer's film is slow even in the context of the Hollywood long-take cycle. According to Barry Salt, "The Hollywood mean A.S.L. [average shot length] went up from about 8 or 9 seconds in the late 1930s to about 10 or 11 seconds in the period 1940–1945, and finally to around 12–13 seconds in the period 1946–1950."[17] (Though, as Salt admits, this sample is probably askew, it leans to the longish side.) *Day of Wrath* has a significantly slower editing tempo; made in 1943, the film has an average shot length of 14.8 seconds. A mechanical computation of shot lengths reveals only one component in the overall rhythm of a film, but undoubtedly the lengthiness of the shots in *Day of Wrath* cooperates with the emphasis on the duration of story events and the intervals between them to increase the sense of slowness.

The camera movements have a similar rhythm. Though sometimes the pans are fairly quick, the lateral tracking shots tend to move slowly, sometimes, as we've seen, at the same rate as the characters, sometimes relatively faster (the tracking shots over the stationary elders in the torture chamber). Sometimes too the camera moves even more slowly than the characters do. The funeral scene opens on a medium shot of the singing choirboy. He turns to march left, and the camera begins to track laterally to follow him, but he moves more quickly than the camera and so leaves the frame; then another boy passes slowly through the frame; then another, and so on. Dreyer called such movements "long, gliding close-ups that follow the players in a rhythmic way, feeling their way from one to another."[18] According to the classical Hollywood paradigm, all this camera movement should be "a complete waste of screen time," a "loss of pace" (Reisz and Millar on Hitchcock's *Rope*), since no narrative purpose is directly served. Instead, the camera systematically scans the scene, its movements stressing their own duration in relation to the duration of figure movement. The camera's rhythm—constant, calm, with no sudden accelerations or braking—departs from the rhythm of the figure movement and becomes a process which we perceive in its own right. Again duration becomes palpable.

As for our last category—the rhythm of music and noise—I have already suggested the importance of several scenes' quasi-musical construction. Here we ought simply to note how the ponderous rhythm of the opening Dies Irae tune establishes a solemn musical rhythm that is picked up in the bell of the witch hunt, clanging steadily off screen in the first scene in Herlofs Marte's cottage. When she stops simply to listen to the bell, its monotonous beat comes forward to dominate the pace of our perception of the scene. The same rhythm is reiterated at the end of the film: during Merete's accusation, the bell returns on the soundtrack to mourn Absalon's death and to announce the beginning of Anne's ordeal. At the very close, the boy's voice on the soundtrack repeats the same rhythm, serving now as wordless spacing between lines of the scroll's last verse.

Our scheme suggests that *Day of Wrath* seeks a slow rhythm on every level, from slowly paced story events and their rendition as such, to the inclusion of many catalystic actions (walking, pausing) between these events, to the long take, the music, and the deliberate velocity of camera movement. What are we to make of the problems which this strategy poses for the viewer?

For Dreyer himself, the matter seems to have been relatively simple: the sound film must be slower than the silent cinema. "Then the tempo was racing, with scenes rushing across the screen. I have purposely tried to create a calmness in the scene which is a natural one for the talking film."[19] But as we would expect, Dreyer justified this slowness as necessary for the development of the narrative. "The drama creates a rhythm that in its turn supports the mood of the action," and a slow rhythm will "emphasize and support the monumentality the writer has aimed at in his play."[20] It is not far from this account to the view that such a rhythm is correlated to the psychological states of the characters, an explanation implicit in Philippe Parrain's study of Dreyer.[21] As I have argued in chapter five, the concept of verisimilitude, especially of the psychological sort, is misplaced in application to Dreyer's late style. We shall make *Day of Wrath* more interesting by considering the effects that Dreyer's rhythm has on the viewer's experience.

To my knowledge, only Donald Skoller, in the prefaces to his English translations of Dreyer's essays, has tried to come to grips with this. Skoller emphasizes that the rhythm of Dreyer's late films must not be judged by verisimilitude but by our perceptual attitudes. "Because the flow of the action is deliberately impeded . . . attention is permitted to accrue upon the sufficiency of information present in the given moment: the *presence* of the present is heightened."[22] Skoller's emphasis on attention and concentration is accurate, and our analysis of the film's attenuation and marking of duration bears out his claim. What are the *functions* of this impedance? Skoller says that these "visual *retards* . . . shift the experience to a more subjective, penetrative dynamic, beyond accustomed intensity. . . . This contributes not only to the intensification of the experience offered—familiar or not—but allows a grasp of nuance, of implications and connotations, to refine our total perception of the scene: our sense of what is happening or of what simply *is* becomes more accurate."[23] Surely the stress on perception, intensification, and nuance is right enough, but without a larger theory of aesthetic perception and function, this account remains sketchy (no example or evidence is offered) and can easily slip into subjectivism (hinted at in Skoller's subsequent claim that Dreyer puts us "at a new level of consciousness"[24]). The critical method which this book has been utilizing suggests a more specific function of the viewer's role in Dreyer's films.

The Russian Formalist Victor Shklovsky emphasized the importance of delay in the artistic text. "The technique of art is to make objects 'unfamiliar,' to make forms difficult, to increase the difficulty and length of perception because the process of perception is an aesthetic end in itself and must be prolonged. Art is a way of experiencing the artfulness of an object."[25] To deal with art's tendency to prolong our perception, Shklovsky proposed the concept of "stairstep construction," that principle whereby delaying devices are set up within the text, as Kristin Thompson puts it, "to turn the action away from a straight path . . . to deflect and tangle the structure of the work."[26] Shklovsky considers repetition, rhyme, tautology, and parallelism all devices of stairstep construction, but the most salient for our purposes is the one he calls retardation. Here the action does not halt, but slows down significantly: Shkovsky even writes it as a formula: "If, for the realization of any problem a force of A^m is required, then it is presented in the form A^{m-2} A^{m-1} A^m."[27] The result of this device is an extension and heightening of our awareness of the work's aesthetic specificity; retardation aids the text in offering a difficult—Shklovsky says "fractured," "splintered"—perception.

Now every artistic text displays stairstep construction and many display retardation in one form or another. But "one form or another" is precisely the point. The analyst will find that within different genres, schools, periods, and styles, the retardation devices will vary. Certain norms of retardation will appear and be canonized, while others fall into disfavor.

The concept of retardation helps us see the significance of the slow rhythm of *Day of Wrath*. In this film, the disjunctions of *Jeanne d'Arc* and *Vampyr* are for the most part gone: narrative logic is not attacked through contradictory temporal and spatial structures. But the film's style does not become "normal" either. The *discontinuity* of the two previous films is replaced by *very slow continuity*. The film resists being read, no longer because of incompatible spatial cues but because of an attenuation of the time of the text. The slowness of events, the catalyses between them, the gravity of the rhythm of editing, camera movement and sound, all retard the momentum of the film. The Hollywood norm handles retardation almost wholly at the level of cause-and-effect logic (rape delayed until the cavalry comes to the rescue, the killer revealed after the detective's investigation). In *Day of Wrath*, on the contrary, *mise-en-scène* and camera movement are systematically utilized to slow our reading process down and, in an important way, block the flow of narrative meaning. The rhythms of *Day of Wrath* refuse to be unified narratively. We cannot interpret the long walks, the pauses, the camera movements as "significant" in some way (representing psychology, historical setting, atmosphere). Instead, we must recognize that such rhythmic devices are in a literal sense quite empty, barren of significance; they *mean* nothing. Which is not to say that they have no function. They force us to shift our reading down several gears to the level of what Shklovsky calls "not of course a march set to music, but rather a dance-walk which is sensed, more exactly—a movement constructed only so that it may be sensed."[28] Such a shift in our perception is necessary to the process of "theatricalization" that comes to prominence in *Ordet* and *Gertrud*.

Despite its popularity, then, *Day of Wrath*, in its play on narrative, its problems of representation, and especially its rhythm, throws up a challenge to comprehension which might be formulated in terms similar to those which T. W. Adorno applied to *Wozzeck*: "The stringency of a structure that is not quite transparent to the audience enables quality to transcend the realm of assumed comprehension."[29] The trait of being "not quite transparent" will be made even more stringent in the films that follow.

Ordet

Ordet may be about a mystery, but in many ways it is the most obvious film Dreyer ever made. Avowedly "symbolic," *Ordet* is easy to read: it declares itself to be about the clash of different kinds of religious faith and their reconciliation through a simpler, "natural" faith. This readability, however, is precisely what I want to examine. What holds this obviously symbolic narrative together? How is the narrative intelligibility of the film affected by the film's spatio-temporal strategies? To give some answers to these questions, we need to consider the easy unity proffered by the film.

THE MIRACLE

Ordet ("The Word") is set in the Jutland countryside of Denmark. Two families are separated by religious beliefs: the Borgens subscribe to a life-affirming, here-and-now creed while Peter Petersen belongs to a sect which emphasizes self-denial and preparation for life in heaven. The youngest Borgen son falls in love with Peter's daughter, and the families are offered the chance to be reconciled, but Peter refuses to mix his family with another faith. When Inger, the young wife of the Borgen household, dies in childbirth, the two families are united in mutual sorrow and forgiveness. Peter gives his daughter permission to marry Anders. Aided by the faith of the child Maren, Johannes, a young Borgen who has believed himself to be Jesus, commands Inger to return to life. She does.

Much of the stalwart homogeneity of the film is created by devices of unity so familiar to us by now that I need only mention them. *Ordet*'s action is concentrated into a night, the next day, that night, and another day. The film has five interdependent causal lines, each corresponding to a member of the Borgen family. The first two sequences introduce the problems of two Borgen sons and their father. Johannes, gone mad from studying for the ministry, believes he is Jesus. Mikkel, on the other hand, does not believe in God at all. Old Borgen also has a crisis of faith, chiefly because of Johannes's madness. In the third sequence, Anders's desire to marry Anne is revealed. The task of the film's action is to solve all four problems, which it does by means of a fifth line of action involving Inger, Mikkel's wife. Her death in childbirth makes peace among the disputing religious factions, brings Anne to Anders, and brings Johannes back to sanity; her resurrection at the film's finale unites Borgen and Peter in a common faith and wins Mikkel to a belief in God. These interdependent plotlines run in generally parallel fashion, thanks to Dreyer's familiar tactic of crosscutting from one locale to another. The result looks like the accompanying plan.

This plan of the film makes it evident that the alternation among locales outside the Borgen house (segments II*a*–*r*) is replaced, during the night of Inger's childbirth, by alternations between areas of the house (sickroom/parlor) and even alternations between areas of the parlor itself. As in previous Dreyer films, the alternating crosscutting produces not only suspense but also narrative parallels. Shots of Mikkel at work outdoors, for instance, reinforce his unassuming pragmatism by showing phases of a single chore, his reed cutting, from departure (shots 17, 18) through loading (28) to unloading (referred to in 31). More important, Inger's centrality is reinforced by inserted shots of her at work or lying on the operating table. The segmentation also makes clear the larger parallels across the film: the comparison of the initial search for Johannes (I*a*) with the later one (III), or the comparison of his abrupt breach of family peace (I*b*) with his entry into the death room (IV*h*); the rhyming of Borgen's trip to Peter's house (II*k*) with Peter's trip to Borgen's (IV*a*, *g*); the parallel religious disputes between Borgen and Peter (II*n*) and between the parson and the doctor (II*s*, shot 56). And Dreyer's familiar pattern of narrative replacement is enacted as well: Maren's natural faith replaces Inger's, Peter offers Anne as the new Inger, a sane Johannes substitutes for the baby who died at birth.

Important as all these alternations and parallels are, we come closer to the film's dominant principle of unity when we examine the use of causality and closure. It is obvious that a conception of Christianity, in one form or another, motivates all the plotlines. One explanation offered for Johannes's madness is his overzealous study for the ministry. Mikkel's alienation from his father springs from his distaste for old Borgen's religion. What separates Anne

I. **Night** (1–16).

a. Johannes goes out and the men pursue him (1–14).

b. The family have coffee and discuss Johannes (15–16).

II. **Day** (17–63).

BORGENSGAARD	*OUTDOORS*	*PETER PETERSEN'S*
a. Kitchen: Anders asks Inger's help (17).	*b. Yard:* Mikkel on wagon (18).	
c. Kitchen: Inger hums (19).	*d. Road:* Anders walks (20).	
e. Parlor: Inger tries to persuade Borgen (21–25).		*f. Parlor:* Peter warns Anne about Anders (26–27).
	g. Field: Mikkel with load of reeds (28).	
h. Parlor: Johannes encounters parson (29).		*i. Parlor:* Peter refuses Anders (30).
j. Parlor: Parson meets Borgen (31).	*k. Road:* Borgen and Anders drive (32).	*l. Parlor:* Borgen and Anders arrive (33–34).
m. Parlor: Doctor arrives (35).		*n. Parlor:* Borgen and Peter talk (36–37). *Kitchen:* Kirstine reads to Anne and Anders (38–40). *Parlor:* Borgen and Peter argue (41).
o. Sickroom: Doctor and Mikkel (42).	*p. Road:* Borgen and Anders drive back (43).	
q. Sickroom: Inger on table (44).	*r. Road:* Borgen and Anders drive back (45).	
s. Sickroom: Doctor operates (46). *Parlor:* Discussion of Inger (47–52). *Sickroom:* Inger, gasping (53). *Parlor:* Parson arrives (54). *Sickroom:* Borgen and Mikkel by Inger's bed (55). *Parlor:* Doctor and Parson talk; Johannes predicts death; Mikkel announces that Inger is dead (56–58). *Sickroom:* Inger dead (59–60). *Parlor:* Johannes offers to revive her (61). *Sickroom:* Johannes faints (62). *Parlor:* Mikkel and Anders carry Johannes to his room (63).		

III. **Night** (64–73).
- *a.* Death certificate (64).
- *b.* Johannes leaves (65–66).
- *c.* Search for Johannes (67–72).
- *d.* Death notice in newspaper (73).

IV. **Day** (74–114).

		a. Parlor: Peter sets out for Borgensgaard (74).
b. Funeral booklet (75).	*c. Road:* Hearse driving (76).	
d. Coffin room: Borgen and Anders light candles (77). *Parlor:* Mourners sing (78). *Coffin room:* Mikkel enters (79).	*e. Courtyard:* Hearse arrives (80).	
f. Coffin room: Parson arrives and speaks (81–86).	*g. Courtyard:* Peter arrives (87).	
h. Coffin room: Mikkel collapses; Peter brings Anne in; Johannes arrives; Inger resurrected (88–114).		

---

and Anders is their fathers' determination not to let their children marry outside their sects. Inger prays for help in changing Borgen's mind. Johannes's dialogue is crisscrossed with scriptural quotations. Addressing Borgen indirectly, Peter instructs his congregation to sing, "Sinner turn no more a deaf ear." In the kitchen, Kirstine reads to Anne and Anders from an illustrated Bible. More broadly, the death and resurrection of Inger must be read as divinely caused. The thematization of the religious motif goes further, since every character embodies a distinct mode of faith: the parson (institutional religion), Johannes (mad faith), the doctor (positivist skepticism), Mikkel (agnosticism), and Maren (natural faith). Most protracted, of course, is the dispute between Borgen and Peter, a debate between Grundtvigism (a brand of Danish Lutheranism emphasizing vital Christianity) and Inner Mission (a sterner evangelical sect). Thus virtually every gesture in the film is freighted with Christian significance.

With equal obviousness the Christian religion supplies the closure for the film. The narrative sets as its task the overcoming of social problems of belief by demonstrating two transcendent powers: mortality and faith. In one way, doctrinal squabbles are swept aside by the brutal fact of death. Inger must die so that Peter will permit Anders to marry Anne, so that Johannes will recover his sanity, and so that Mikkel will be plunged into despair. But Inger must also be brought back to life as the tangible proof of the power of innocent faith (Maren) guided by a faith free of institutional shackles (Johannes). The film's drive toward resolution, its suffering/death/resurrection pattern, is required to overcome the social problems of faith through a Christian principle of closure: miracle.

All of which is to say that in *Ordet* narrative principles characteristic of Dreyer's work are transposed into their most explicit forms. The absent and impersonal cause is now brusquely collapsed into God. Trust in the Word, the writing which guides the characters through the world of absent causes, has never been more powerful: not only do the characters quote Scripture to one another, not only does the Bible itself prophesy the narrative action (fig. 1), but the overall narrative of the film rests upon the Christian pre-text. Johannes becomes a walking text; like his namesake St. John, he transmits the Word of the title, the *logos* governing the film's logic. *Ordet* is not an allegory in any strict sense, but its unity becomes intelligible only as a retelling of Gospel. As in other Dreyer films, the visible action becomes a fulfillment of an authoritative, eternal text. For the film to cohere, the viewer must accept a narrative causality premised upon Christian precept. (Inger must die so that others may be reborn; but then *she* must be reborn.) The resolution of this religious narrative requires a miracle. It is not that Dreyer is "a religious director" and has found in *Ordet* the perfect narrative. Just the opposite: Dreyer's typical narrative unity finds in *Ordet* its most thoroughgoing justification—religion. Christianity becomes Dreyer's most overpowering formal device.

If the narrative draws on such potent forces, what could trouble it? In the next two parts of this chapter, I shall suggest how the film's mode of representation pulls it away from any simple or direct transmission of this Christian tale. Yet *Ordet*'s narrative itself, for all its unity, is not free of inner difficulties.

As in Dreyer's other films, problems are engendered by the film's very need to unify itself. The four lines of action are resolved by the fifth, Inger's death and resurrection. Yet someone must perform the act of resurrecting her. The film's problems crystallize around two questions. How to *motivate* the necessary miracle? How to *represent* it?

A miracle must violate natural or scientific laws. Thus it cannot be motivated "realistically," as verisimilitude.[1] So the miracle must be motivated compositionally—by functioning within a system of motifs. The miracle must become a necessary component of the film's narrative.

In part, *Ordet*'s conclusion is motivated by the characters' constant discussion of miracles. Religious alignments are reiterated in the views which different characters adopt toward miracles. Borgen has lost his hope in miracles, the parson asserts that God deliberately withholds them, and so on. More important, the film predicts the miracle through an image: the Bible illustration depicting Christ raising Lazarus (fig. 1). Here, independent of any character's opinion, the narrative inserts a motif foreshadowing the outcome. In another way, though, the miracle is motivated by particular human agents—initially Johannes, then the child Maren.

To consider Johannes as a character raises problems that are apparent the first time you watch the film. Audiences often laugh at his somnambulistic movements, deflected gaze, and high-pitched voice. Critics have been caught off guard: Tom Milne dismisses the actor's portrayal of the "gibbering idiot" as "irritating and singularly unconvincing."[2] But the strangeness is necessary. Since the official church and the sectarian squabbling must be incapable of resurrecting Inger, Johannes must initiate the miracle. The film needs a figure to mediate between social religion and spontaneous faith, and this mediation demands that Johannes be isolated from the social world of old Borgen, Peter, the parson, and the rest. His madness and the stylized representation of it are crucial.

The isolation of Johannes is established in the early portions of the film. Throughout the first sequence, when he is glimpsed wandering into the pasture, Johannes functions chiefly as an absence through which the other Borgens are introduced. For one thing, Dreyer sets up a false eyeline match. Father and sons look right; Johannes looks left and refers to "You, and you, and you. . . ." But a pan left reveals Borgen and his sons now *behind* Johannes, looking left. These two shots define Johannes as always an object of sight. His speech in this scene and the next further separates him from the social world of the narrative in that he simply quotes scripture (The Word is not *his*.) This end-stopped prologue establishes Johannes's estrangement as an agent of miracle. If a character typically possesses traits, desires, wishes, Johannes is not a character. He is, rather, a formal need of the text, a manifestation of *Ordet*'s demand for Christian legibility and narrative closure.

Yet Johannes must not be simply mad; madness will not guarantee a miracle. He must be motivated as a *holy* madman. This the text achieves by means of his prophecies. He

1

interrupts Inger and Borgen's coffee drinking: "A dead body in the big parlor!" During the night of Inger's childbirth, he sees "the man with the scythe" enter Inger's room and leave with the dead child; he tells Maren that Inger will die and that he will resurrect her. In retrospect, even his first sermon on the hill and his claim that his candles "will brighten the darkness" constitute veiled prophecies.

But a difficulty crops up. Johannes cannot be omnipotent, unless the narrative is prepared to acknowledge him as the Christ he claims to be. Two strategies keep Johannes in check. First, the narrative distributes the powers of prophecy to other characters, Inger in particular. At various points she asserts that Johannes will be himself again, that Mikkel will believe someday, that she will bear Borgen a grandson, and that God will answer Borgen's prayers. Even the doctor confidently predicts that a knock on the head will set Johannes right again. Thus the film absorbs Johannes's prophecies within a larger system of predictions which both ratify his claims and prevent him from becoming deified. The narrative keeps its fool from becoming too holy in a second way: by finally revealing his madness as helpless. When Johannes believes himself Jesus, he cannot revive Inger. Thus the film curtails Johannes's powers, keeping him as a narrative wild card, a necessary but potentially disruptive agent.

Yet—again—when Johannes loses his madness, he falls into the social world of inadequate faith. The narrative needs a new agent of miracle, and the child Maren is brought in to fulfill this function. Introduced quite late in the film, she relays Johannes's supernatural powers to the final scene. Her faith accepts as fact Johannes's claims that Inger will die and he will resurrect her. (Even the child's name is motivated—old Borgen's dead wife was named Maren, as is the woman who gives testimony at Peter's meeting). Maren is put in the narrative to check her uncle; if Johannes is necessary but disruptive, Maren manifests the narrative's drive toward unity and closure. In this light, the scene in which the two sit together in the parlor functions as a crucial transition. Johannes now doubts his power to resurrect Inger ("I may not be able to do it") and seeks to persuade Maren that it is better that Inger is dead. But Maren insists on the resurrection, anticipating closure: "I am looking forward to it." We shall see later that at the stylistic level this sequence operates to foreground the arcing camera and analytical editing; but narratively the dialogue helps motivate the miracle through a transfer of power. Maren is established as a narrative force; the problematic Johannes is replaced by a much more conventional figure of unity: the pure, faithful child.

If Christianity, Johannes's alienation and holy prophesies, and the child Maren strive to motivate the miracle that concludes the film, we are still left with the question of how that miracle may be *represented.* To answer this question, we need to examine how *Ordet*'s spatial and temporal systems operate with and against the film's narrative structure. Two principles, which I shall call "theatricalization" and "sparseness," will help us see how the film represents Inger's resurrection.

THEATRICALIZATION

Once we raise the issue of *Ordet*'s representational strategies, we look immediately to the theatre as a model. And indeed, *Ordet* is "filmed theatre," but of a peculiar sort. To describe the problems posed by the film's style, we need to understand the nature of its theatricality. André Bazin has some helpful suggestions here.

Bazin distinguishes three sorts of filmed theatre. First, there is "canned theatre," which simply records a stage performance. There is also the conventional adaptation, which "opens up" a play by making it into "cinema." The adaptation replaces dialogue scenes by images, shows on screen what stage exposition conveys indirectly, and breaks the single set of a theatre performance into many locales, "ventilating" the play. For Bazin, such adaptation practices may make a good film (e.g., *Boudu Saved from Drowning*) but the film has bypassed the problem of representing theatricality as such. Assuming that theatricality consists of conventions of text (the play is dialogue) and of spatial localization (the stage is a microcosm), Bazin posits a third alternative: "staging a play by means of cinema." Neither canned theatre nor adaptation, this alternative seeks to retain theatrical conventions of dialogue and setting. The start of Olivier's *Henry V* carries us to an "Elizabethan" performance of the play; Olivier, says Bazin, "is not pretending to make us forget the conventions of the theatre. On the contrary, he affirms them."[3] Similarly, Cocteau's *Les Parents terribles* finds a cinematic equivalent for the spatial concentration of the play by making into an apartment what was a single room in the stage version.[4] This is not ventilation, Bazin asserts, but finding a set of cinematic equivalents for the theatrical qualities of the original; you do not record the play on film or transform the play into film but you *transpose* the play for a new instrument, you score it in the key of cinema.

Since *Ordet* is neither canned theatre nor a straightforward adaptation, does it belong to the third type of film which Bazin identifies? I shall argue that it does not, that it belongs to a fourth category which we must construct; but we can construct this category only thanks to Bazin's theorizing.

Bazin's case for staging a play by means of cinema assumes a homogeneity between play and film realization. The film must "retain the dramatic force of the play in a medium that reflects it."[5] This is possible, Bazin believes, because cinema possesses an ontological realism based on photography. Theatre is an art, but cinema is a medium. Cinema can find equivalents for stage conventions because its realism opens onto an infinity of possibilities. To take one of Bazin's most famous metaphors: if the theatre is a crystal chandelier (contained, artificial, autonomous), cinema is the roaming flashlight of the usher (free-floating, fluid, boundless).[6] Filmed theatre, then, can consist of playing the flashlight over the chandelier, highlighting this or that aspect of theatricality. Cinema's nature equips it to become the "humble servant" of theatre.[7] The corollary of this view is that the viewer's reflection on theatre is a pleasurable one.

But if one denies Bazin's theory of cinema's fundamental realism and considers the medium as a set of formal possibilities, there is no need for the relation of play and film to be so peaceful. What if the film pulls itself out of gear with the play, setting up a *disparity* between the text and the cinematic representation? Instead of point-for-point equivalences, we find the refusal of two formal systems to mesh. Since Brecht, we have realized that a production can criticize its source, but that may be only the extreme edge of a practice whereby a film can mark a certain distance from its text by preserving a relative autonomy for its cinematic systems. I shall call this strategy "theatricalization."[8]

A clear, if extreme, example may be found in Straub/Huillet's opera film *Moses and Aaron*. Since one convention of opera is that people sing the text, Bazin would favor a cinematic handling that stresses and respects that convention. But *Moses and Aaron* announces from the start that it has no such intention. The first shot is a lengthy close-up over Moses' shoulder in which the framing does not permit us to see the act of singing. Thus the expressivity and histrionics characteristic of opera are eliminated, and we become aware of a framing deliberately chosen to impede our grasp of the opera as opera. Unlike Olivier's and Cocteau's films, *Moses and Aaron* refuses to subordinate cinematic space to a clear transmission of the conventions of the stage text. The result is neither fish nor fowl, too theatrical to be a true adaptation, too obtrusively cinematic to be a satisfactory equivalent for the convention of the sung text. By creating interferences between play text and cinematic representation, theatricalization produces problems of reading.

In what follows, I shall try to show that *Ordet* exemplifies this fourth type of filmed theatre. It should come as no surprise to learn that the film sets up a distance between play text and cinematic style, since from the tableaux of Dreyer's earlier work onwards, his films have tended to pull narrative structure somewhat apart from spatial and temporal structure. In *Ordet*, the split is between a closed, highly motivated narrative and its "performance" in the *mise-en-scène* and the filming. In *Ordet* the play text is challenged by the film's spatio-temporal systems.

In order for theatricalization to draw a distance between text and film, the text must be signalled as existing prior to the film. Whereas Dreyer habitually selected little-known works as sources, with *Ordet* he was filming one of the most frequently staged Scandinavian plays of the twentieth century. Gustav Mollander had adapted the play to cinema only a decade before. Yet even if the viewer were unaware of the source, the opening establishes that this is a *performance.* The title credit identifies Kaj Munk as author of *Ordet* (fig. 2) and no lists of cast or crew intervene to contest this. Moreover, the design of the title credit reproduces Munk's manuscript title and signature, establishing the play as being like Jeanne d'Arc's trial—already transcribed and completed. Here Dreyer's usual reference to the written word intersects with theatricalization's need to establish the play (Munk's written *Word*) as distinct from this performance of it. The actors' somewhat formal declamations of their lines continue the stress on performance throughout the film.

Theatricalization is also created by the film's style. *Ordet* uses sound, *mise-en-scène,* camera movement, and the long take to separate text and representation of text. These de-

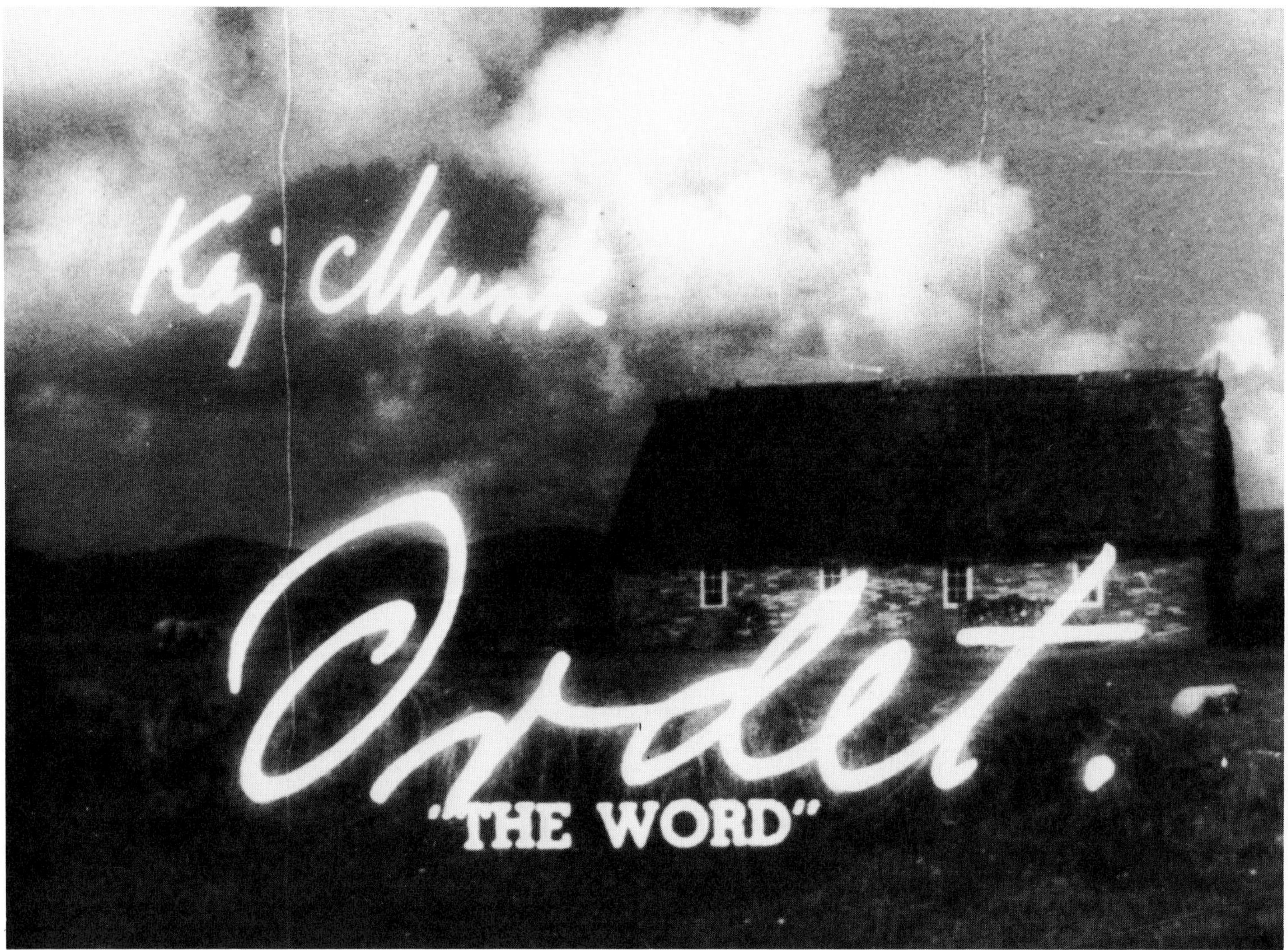

2

vices cooperate in pulling the staging and filming away from the play text by creating a relatively independent system that foregrounds the duration, the spatial construction, and the internal development of the shot.

Shot duration

In one scene, Inger praises the new parson, but old Borgen has reservations: "It takes him too long to reach the amen." The line anticipates and parodies what most viewers leaving the theatre will say about Dreyer and his film. *Ordet*'s narrative system is attenuated to a degree rare even today. What Mollander's 1943 adaptation of the play could squeeze into one hundred minutes, Dreyer stretches to 129 minutes (and Dreyer claimed he cut the play's dialogue by two-thirds). The "theatrical" feel of *Ordet* issues in part from its retardation of the play's rhythm. Using the categories we applied to *Day of Wrath,* it would be easy to show how *Ordet* possesses an even slower tempo on every level, ranging from the intervals between story events to the rhythm of the music. What is worth examining is how theatricalization produces the retardation unique to this film. How, in other words, does the principle of theatricalization slow down the viewer's reading?

One tactic will be familiar to us. Throughout this book we have noted how the decor in Dreyer's films is habitually barren, allowing for the emergence of tableaux. Not surprisingly, the same starkness rules *Ordet*'s settings. The white walls of the Borgens' and Petersens' homes let pictures, decorations, and furnishings stand out in relief; in general, the sets are more sparsely furnished than in any Dreyer film since *Jeanne d'Arc.* (We shall even see, at the end of the film, a development of the decor toward the pure white ground of *Jeanne d'Arc.*) As in *Day of Wrath,* the "glowing wall" technique further isolates objects in patches of decor. *Ordet*'s frames are so cleansed of content that they forbid our eye to rummage around within them. We are forced to grasp the total composition because there is so little detail to deflect our attention. As a result, the sets, while functioning to locate the narrative action, begin to construct *mise-en-scène* as a system distinct from the narrative relations of the play text.

If theatricalization demands that staging and filming be allowed to develop their own distinct systems, the long take offers rich possibilities. In promoting the shot from a private to a captain, so to speak, the long take tends to assume the role of a large-scale formal component in a film. As the *long* take, its most salient feature is its duration, and it can emphasize this by developing its own structure, its own rhythm. Given historical norms, a shorter shot will not usually persuade us to ask, "When will it end?" or "How will it end?" or "Isn't this a repetition of something that was just shown?"

It is no accident that in *Ordet* Dreyer makes extensive use of the long take for the first time in his career. In *Vampyr* and *Day of Wrath* the length of a few shots stands out within a generally traditional *découpage. Day of Wrath,* a slow film for its day, has 436 shots, or one every 14.8 seconds. But *Ordet* has only 114 shots, and almost half of these occur in the opening and closing scenes (sections I and IV). Across the entire film, the average shot lasts about sixty-five seconds; within the central three sections, the average shot consumes over a minute and a half. This means of course that several shots run a very long time, ranging from a minute or two to seven minutes. Even in the 1950s, when the long take became popular, such long takes were rare. Putting aside the *tour de force* of *Rope,* Hitchcock did not come close to such lengthy shots, even in *Under Capricorn* (average shot duration, 48 seconds). We have seen that a film's rhythm is not reducible to the length of its shots, but certainly in its historical context *Ordet*'s long takes stand out as extraordinary stylistic devices. The primary function of these long takes, I suggest, is to foreground *the shot itself* as a component of cinematic perception.

Ordet's long takes stress shot duration. Obviously, the rarity of cuts emphasizes both the cuts and the internal amplitude of the shot. More strongly, the long take in *Ordet* deliberately slackens the pace of the narrative action. We are now back at Reisz and Millar's critique of *Rope,* but with a different emphasis. In their discussion, they point out how Hitchcock wastes precious time panning or tracking from one point of interest to another. *Ordet,* like *Day of Wrath,* uses camera movement and shot duration to move through what Reisz and Millar correctly call "dramatically meaningless intervals."[9] Unlike Hitchcock, however, Dreyer seldom moves his camera through empty space; Dreyer usually follows one character or another. Typically, two or more people have a dialogue exchange and one moves away; the camera follows that figure until he or she encounters another character and becomes involved in another dialogue. To take a simple example, the first shot-sequence at Peter Petersen's house begins with the camera framing him, sitting crosslegged and sewing (fig. 3). When Anne enters, the camera leaves Peter and tracks with her (fig. 4), but when she encounters Kirstine (fig. 5), Kirstine is followed and Anne leaves the shot (fig. 6). When Kirstine leaves, the camera picks up Anne again (fig. 7), follows her to Peter (fig. 8), then ends by framing Peter as at the start (fig. 9).

In this shot, as in others, what is "dramatically meaningless" is the interval consumed in moving from one grouping to another. This is a good example of how *mise-en-scène,* camera movement, and the long take function together durationally. The characters are scattered around the room, not compactly organized. Since the figure seldom speaks while in motion, the walk itself holds no particular narrative significance. Moreover, in Reisz and Millar's examples from *Rope,* there is a certain internal segmentation of the shot: a pan from Rupert to the boys could conceivably be split into two shots joined by an

3

4

5

6

7

8

9

eyeline match, thus eliminating the camera's trip across the room. (I am not saying that *Rope should* be chopped up this way.) But because *Ordet*'s camera almost always moves with a figure, there is no point at which the shots could be interrupted. Like the long takes of musical performances in Huillet/Straub's *Chronicle of Anna Magdalena Bach,* most of *Ordet*'s long takes exist as durational chunks, unsegmentable. Thus *Ordet,* much more frequently than *Day of Wrath,* uses the long take to stretch out catalyses between principal narrative actions. The tendency of camera movement to make duration palpable (what Jean Mitry calls "presentification") is here elicited through an insistence upon intervals.[10] Together, *mise-en-scène,* camera movement, and the long take create retarding, narratively empty passages which stress sheer duration, consecutiveness rather than causality.

Furthermore, *Ordet* develops a temporal possibility only latent in *Day of Wrath:* the selective filling of such empty movements by sound effects. Since *Ordet* was shot with direct sound, the noises already have a strong presence. Teacups clink, floors creak, and wash snaps sharply on the line. Sugar lumps clunk as old Borgen stirs his coffee, and Inger's rolling pin positively rumbles. Other noises come from off screen: Borgensgaard is characterized by the clucks, bleats, and whinnies that seep in from outdoors, while from outside Peter's home we hear children playing and a barking dog. In one respect, all these sounds function as realistic detail. But most sounds come forward during camera movements. While the camera moves, we hear people's footsteps or, from off screen, horses clopping, or Karen calling the hens. The duration of the sounds thus becomes more evident by virtue of their strictly governed role as *insertions* within a specific interval.

Two sounds particularly stress the duration of the shot. There is the clock, whose ticking measures the time consumed by a camera movement or figure movement. There is also the frequent sound of the film apparatus itself. In *Two People,* the clatters of dolly and crew were audible but not integrated within a formal strategy. In the context of *Ordet*'s foregrounding of shot duration, the squeaking of the dolly audibly records the camera movement we see, marking it as a determinate gesture in time.

A long take need not foreground shot duration, but in *Ordet* the sparseness of the decor, the movement of camera and figures, and the insertion of sounds force us to acknowledge the time passing within the shot, to see the shot as a durational block.

Shot space

Ordet stresses the space of the shot as well as the duration of it, and it does this in ways which are sometimes familiar, sometimes novel. As in *Day in Wrath,* the action of *Ordet* occurs predominantly in a single interior setting. Like Absalon's rectory, the Borgen farmhouse is a familial space where several lines of action intersect. The parlor is accordingly blocked out into zones—the table, the window, the desk area, and so on—around which scenes are organized. In our examination of *Day of Wrath,* we saw how Dreyer tended to vary the camera's orientation to these zones of action from sequence to sequence. The same strategy is at work in *Ordet;* by the film's end we have seen every side of this room.

In *Day of Wrath,* however, the orientation is usually defined through editing patterns. Here, with the predominance of the long take, we are oriented to this or that zone of action through camera movement: the gliding tracking shots frame or reframe each area of the parlor, of the kitchen, and of the adjacent bedrooms. The process recurs in Peter Petersen's parlor, all four walls of which are eventually shown to us. *Ordet* carries to a further extreme *Day of Wrath*'s use of the moving camera to construct a *circular mise-en-scène*. The chamber aesthetic of Dreyer's work is here pushed to a new level, as the camera continually wheels around within the domestic interior. How do camera and figures behave in this circular chamber space?

Discussions of camera movement in cinema usually distinguish between the camera movement which follows a moving subject and that which moves on its own, independent of subject movement.[11] So far, this distinction has served us well, especially in our analysis of *Vampyr.* But for *Ordet* such a distinction is too gross. We may tend to assume that camera movement which clings to subject movement becomes "transparent" or negligible and that the camera which moves on its own is more significant, commentative, closer to the eye of an omniscient narrator. These two positions have been neatly rehearsed in critical disputes about *Ordet.* For Philippe Parrain, most of Dreyer's panning and tracking movements are motivated by subject movement; in the late films especially, "the camera primarily follows the characters, submitting itself to their displacements: suppleness, naturalness, discretion are the criteria which rule its movements."[12] For Robin Wood, however, nothing could be less modest or submissive than Dreyer's camera, which "remains a rigorously detached observing eye, its movements dissociated from those of the people it watches. . . . *Ordet* seems director-dominated to an extent that deprives the action and actors of all spontaneous, individual life. The impression of Dreyer behind every gesture, every camera movement, is inescapable."[13]

I shall try to show that these two positions are excessively schematic, that it is possible for the camera's movements to "follow the characters" and at the same time to create stylized, relatively autonomous patterns of its own (*not* of "the director's eye"). This means asking more precise questions. What characters are to be followed, and when? What kind of camera movement follows the figures? How does the camera movement set up anticipations and rewards of its own, creating a miniature, teleological form unrelated to the narrative? How does each moving-camera shot interlock spatially with adjacent shots? The answers to such questions all point to *Ordet*'s tendency to foreground the long-take shots as formal components distinct from the play's text.

To understand how the camera movements operate, we should first observe how *Ordet*'s multiple plotlines create a new problem for the chamber aesthetic. The room becomes crowded; the Borgen parlor is more thickly populated than the rectory parlor in *Day of Wrath.* How will camera move-

10

11

ment, in the context of the long take, solve the difficulty?

One conventional solution is to vary the distance of figures from the camera. Consider two prominent long-take films of roughly the same period as *Ordet:* Hitchcock's *Under Capricorn* (1949) and Antonioni's *Cronaca di un amore* (1950). Like *Ordet,* both these films use the long-take camera movement in crowded scenes, but such scenes utilize extreme variations in figure size. Within any given long take, some characters will be seen in extreme long shot, some in medium shot, some in close-up; camera movement plays off the constantly changing scale of the moving characters. During most of *Ordet,* however, the figures are in long shot or *plan-américain.* On the whole, Dreyer adheres to the architectonic premise of his tableau construction and refuses to lose the overall framing quality of the chamber by drastically shifting the scale of the figures. For example, during the scene in the pigsty, Hitchcock would dolly in for a medium shot and Antonioni would stage the scene in depth; but Dreyer composes the scene as a flat, perpendicularly observed tableau, and then pans back and forth to subordinate Inger and old Borgen to the lines of the surrounding architecture (figs. 10–11). In this rigorous a context, when a character steps into medium shot, it is a major event, and not until the last scene will there be a sustained series of close-ups; it is as if this common cinematic resource had been hoarded, parsimoniously, for its most explosive effect.

So the problem remains: how does camera movement construct the space of the crowded chamber? Dreyer tries several solutions, some more radical than others. Our initial distinction helps us a little here: sometimes the camera moves independently of the characters, motivated by an off-screen sound (e.g., Mikkel hears his father coming and the camera leaves Mikkel to pick up old Borgen just entering) or by a look (as when Borgen, Inger, and Mikkel glance off right and the camera moves right to reveal Anders). As we've already seen, though, Dreyer generally uses figure action to impell the camera to move. Even in a scene containing several characters, at any one moment usually only one character will be shown moving. The camera will follow him or her as a leading edge shifting from one group to another. A simple example occurs when Anders asks Mikkel and Inger to help him win Anne. Mikkel is seated, and Inger stands rolling dough at the kitchen table; each remains in the same spot during most of the shot. It is Anders who strides back and forth from one to the other (no fewer than five times!), motivating the camera's to-and-fro movements. In more complicated scenes, such as the one in Peter's parlor already mentioned, Dreyer will set characters moving successively, with the camera "feeling its way," as he put it, from one to another.[14] In the film's second scene, after the men have brought Johannes inside, old Borgen is the target which the camera follows rightward to his pipe rack. He pauses and the camera continues to move rightward to pick up Johannes entering the room. The camera then follows Johannes to the window. After he leaves, Inger comes into the shot and the camera now follows *her* leftward, back to the parlor table. Throughout the film, the camera movement creates a situation wherein characters communicate movement one to another, like billiard balls in slow motion.

Furthermore, the camera does not follow *every* moving character. Often one character will lead the camera to a second one, then although a third might pass through the shot, the camera stays with the second figure until, perhaps, a fourth character enters. For example, while the doctor and the parson sit at the table, old Borgen moves in and out of the shot, but he is not followed; only when the doctor stands up and leaves the frame does the camera begin to trace old Borgen's movements. It is, then, inadequate to ask whether the camera "follows the characters": the tendency of only one character to be moving, the transmission of movement from figure to figure, the camera's habit of lingering on characters before deliberately selecting what next to follow—all complicate the simple formula.

A major result of following only one character during each camera movement is that most characters in the scene slide off screen. This affords a chance to create the sort of spatial uncertainty we have already seen at work in *Vampyr.* However clear our orientation to particular areas of the setting, the way characters behave when off screen is often troubling. Spatial ambiguities are, of course, most strongly motivated (and least bothersome) in relation to Johannes. The film's framings construct around Johannes a privileged zone, a portable limbo progressively modified through the course of the film. In the first eleven shots, Johannes is completely separated from the family, locked within his own space by the editing (itself quite disorienting, as the false eyeline match in the pasture suggests). On the hillside, the camera pans right to link Johannes with his father and brothers in the same shot but not in the same frame. After he wanders off, however, cutting separates them again. Once inside the house that night, with the family at the table, the camera moves away from them to Johannes and his candles—again, however, not in the same frame with his family. After this, Johannes's privileged zone will be opened up, first when old Borgen herds him back to his room (the two are in the same frame for a fraction of a second) and then during the parson's visit (Johannes is only intermittently alone in the frame).

During Inger's childbirth, Johannes begins to be seen in the frame with the others, but he still bears traces of that off-screen limbo he has inhabited, and Dreyer insists on the resulting spatial ambiguities. Johannes materializes briefly behind Mikkel to intone "God be with you," before vanishing again. Similarly, when old Borgen sits at the table alone, Johannes drifts in from the left and out right, destination unknown. Often—as when Mikkel comes out to tell Borgen that Inger has died—we are disconcerted to see that Johannes has (perhaps) been silently present off screen for the entire shot. He is only firmly integrated into the space of the family when he is taken in to confront Inger's corpse. Here, for once, the privileged space he inhabits is broken by three shots putting him unambiguously in the same spatial framework as the other characters. Soon, though, the camera reiterates Johannes's separation: during his escape from his room, he and Anders are not shown in the same frame. When he disappears altogether and people search the countryside, we reach the culmination of his shadowy off-screen status.

If only Johannes occupied such indeterminate space, we might find the device a powerful source of narrative unity. Yet at one point or another the camera movements tease every character into ambiguous realms off screen. *Ordet*'s shots lead us to ask, again and again: Who is there? When the camera travels with Johannes to the window sill, we hear Mikkel's voice say: "Why do you put the candles there?" But Mikkel was not established as being in the scene. Similarly, after old Borgen has sent Maren off to bed, he goes to the left wall, where the camera discloses Mikkel leaning, aghast, on the doorsill of Inger's sickroom; we had no idea that he was there. On both occasions when old Borgen tells Karen to prepare something for the doctor, we discover that she is in the room only when the camera draws her into the frame.

Because of this uncertainty as to who is there, we are often unsure of the direction of off-screen characters' movements. A clear instance occurs during the parson's first visit. He and Mikkel look off right, and the camera tracks right across the parlor to reveal Inger, old Borgen, and the children eating. But almost immediately the pastor enters the new composition, which suggests that he and Mikkel walked almost as fast as the camera moved, yet they perversely hung back just off screen left. Later in the

12

13

14

15

same shot, the camera pans left with old Borgen to the parlor table and Inger comes in (almost immediately) from the right; she has been walking just off screen. More complex examples utilize a device from *Vampyr,* the off-screen space behind the camera. When we first see Inger in shot 5, she is on the left side of the room (fig. 12); but when she enters the frame to take away Johannes's candles, she comes in from the *right* side (fig. 13). One later scene bares the device of space behind the camera by framing the doctor and the parson at the table and showing old Borgen enter the shot first from the right, then the left, several times (figs. 14–15). Such passing around behind the camera avoids the coherent spatial relations characteristic of the classical Hollywood scene. The classical representation of space seeks to frame all the relevant features of setting—hence the "establishing" shot—but in *Ordet* the relation of setting to frame is pulled out of kilter; there are hardly any establishing shots in the traditional sense. Our orientation to the tableau is now challenged by disorientation of frame edges and character location. *Ordet*'s camera movements open up gaps and difficulties within these tidy interiors.

A specific sort of camera movement creates yet another spatial deformation, one that the "following characters/moving independently of the characters" distinction ignores. *Vampyr, Day of Wrath,* and *Two People* had already exhibited a tendency toward peculiarly rotational camera movements. When David Gray surveys the doctor's offices, when the camera explores the room to reveal Gisèle's absence, when Anne crosses the rectory parlor, or when Absalon visits Laurentius, the camera *arcs in one direction* and *pans in the opposite direction.* In *Ordet,* virtually every moving-camera shot has recourse to the arc-and-pan movement. The transitional film here is Dreyer's short documentary *Thorvaldsen* (1948). An exploration of the various relations of camera movement to an object, the film favors circular motion, with statues revolving on turntables and the camera spiralling slowly around them. The result is a powerful sense of three-dimensionality, achieved through the kinetic depth effect.[15] By the time of *Ordet,* Dreyer no longer had to build curved dolly tracks and could simply use a crab dolly to shape every shot in a rotational way.[16] Often *Ordet* organizes the arc-and-pan movement around objects or relatively unmoving figures. As a result the painterly flatness of lighting, setting, and composition is undermined by a camera movement which throws the objects and static figures into relief, and continuously re-angles the overall lines within the frame. Objects and motionless characters become less painterly, more sculptural. *Ordet*'s most flagrant example, which bares the device, is the shot of Johannes sitting with Maren. The two characters stay in the same spot, but the camera arcs slowly around them in a half-circle counterclockwise, while Dreyer pans against the grain (figs. 16–18). We might be watching a shot of a Thorvaldsen statue; the arc-and-pan movement creates a new, plastic chamber space.

16

17

18

19

20

But the nature of *Ordet's mise-en-scène*—not statues but moving human beings—complicates the effects of the arc-and-pan movement. In a curious reversal, the shots which travel with walking characters tend to flatten them within the overall space. Why? Because even though moving, the figures tend to display a narrow range of their aspects. Even if the characters walk diagonally or turn semicircularly, the arc-and-pan movements carefully compensate so as constantly to display the same side of the figure. For example, the camera gyrates when the doctor walks around Inger's bed, keeping him in roughly a three-quarters view. Or, when Mikkel crosses the parlor to rebuke Johannes, the camera minutely displaces itself so as to present only his profile (figs. 19–20).

Although such spatial effects are difficult to illustrate on the page, their functions can be identified. In general, the camera movements in *Ordet* exceed the "following shots" typical of classical practice (and the very concept of the "following shot"), in that the arc-and-pan combination is narratively gratuitous. (A lateral or diagonal track would do as well.) Another consequence of this type of camera movement is that it permits Dreyer to stay at a fixed *distance* from the characters while still keeping them and the camera in motion. There is seldom a straight track-in or track-out, only a sidelong gliding with the figures. Thus the camera is never forced into patterns which would internally segment the long take, as in Reisz and Millar's *Rope* examples. The arc-and-pan movement helps keep frame space prominent, the figures equidistant from the camera, and the long take blocklike in its unity.

In addition, the camera's treatment of the moving figures interacts significantly with its handling of the objects and static figures. What Dreyer's early films do to chamber space through shot composition is now done through camera and figure movement. In those films, *mise-en-scène* calls attention to the figure composition and its decor. Now the arc-and-pan movement yields a similar result while following moving figures. Camera movement compensates for figure movement by keeping the scale and angle of the figure constant; at the same time, the moving frame animates the setting by giving us constantly changing rotational views. The characters' surroundings—static

21

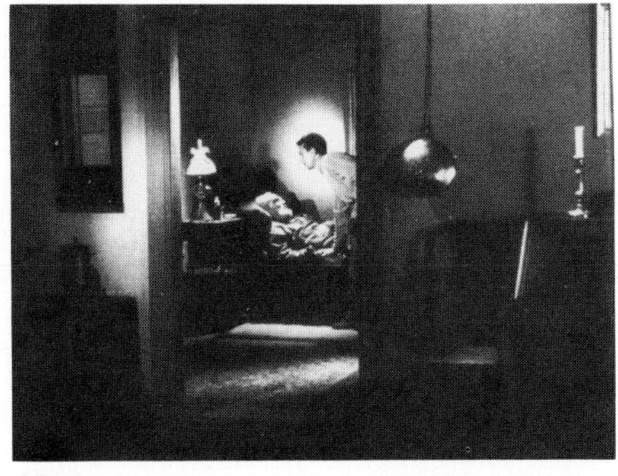
22

23

24

25

objects and people—become prominent, chunky, solid, but the moving character retains a comparative flatness, since it presents fewer aspects than adjacent chairs, lamps, desks, tables, and doorways. Thus the tendency toward the tableau reappears in camera movements which stress the shot space as such.

The teleology of the shot

The result of all these ways of foregrounding the shot as a unit of cinematic representation is the creation of relatively autonomous patterns of time and space. Through the sparse setting, the long take, and camera movement, each shot develops its own teleology: we ask how the shot will develop, who will enter it, where and when it will end. A suspenseful fascination with sheerly temporal and spatial patterns is forced upon us. Like the music of an opera, the shots in *Ordet* "accompany" the narrative, developing alongside the unfolding action. Sometimes, as especially in the treatment of Johannes, the cinematic accompaniment is expressive, "Wagnerian," motivated narratively; more often, the accompaniment is more "Schoenbergian," in that the shots concern themselves only with the cool working-out of their own internal laws, thus constituting parallel systems *relatively independent of narrative demands.*[17]

Let me briefly point out some of these laws. The relative autonomy of the long-take shot is immediately apparent in those shots when camera movement clearly ignores motivation by narrative cues. At certain moments, we hear offscreen sounds and the camera does not move to reveal their sources. Similarly, the camera may play tricks on us, as when Inger sits at the parlor table, praying; the shot frames a door prominently behind her, but no one comes through it. Three shots later, as old Borgen leaves, the camera moves not to reframe him but to conceal him. In such instances, we sense strongly that the camera is pursuing its own arabesque course, which need not coincide with the trajectory of the dramatic action.

More striking because more subtle are the shots which emphasize their own overall patterning. Simple precedents for such patterns may be found in *Two People,* where the longish takes and arc-and-pan movements tend to call a certain attention to their own symmetrical shapes. The final shot illustrates this habit. Husband and wife have both swallowed poison. He lies with his head in her lap. The camera tracks in to her, pans down to him, pans up to her, and tracks back; then the camera again tracks in to her, again pans down to him, and again tracks back to its initial position as the two die. Add to this the incessant creaking of the dolly, and we have something like a rehearsal for the theatricalization of *Ordet.*

Indeed, throughout *Ordet,* almost every long take develops its own rigorous logic. In the very first scene in the Borgen parlor, we encounter a shot which is programmed as thoroughly as a formula. Anders is looking out the window, framed in a doorway (fig. 21). He comes out and goes to wake his father (fig. 22), then goes outdoors (fig. 23). The camera continues on its leftward course to catch Inger opening her door and going to look out the window (figs. 24–25). The shot is balanced by its symmetries: Anders at a window at the shot's beginning, Inger at a window at the shot's end; three walls of the parlor, each with a doorway giving onto an adjacent room; Anders coming out of his room's depth at the beginning, Inger going into her room's depth at the end, and Anders both going into and coming out of Borgen's room in the middle. Apart from concisely introducing us to the chamber space which will dominate the film, the shot creates its own temporal-spatial form, comparable to the one created by the editing in the sequence from *The Parson's Widow* analyzed in chapter four.

The shot is typical of how the film combines camera movement, setting, figure movement, and the rhythm of the long take to create rigorous patterns. Once each shot has been stressed as a unit, it gains even greater formal integrity through rhymes and rhythms of activity and stasis within it. The "dominant" of such patterns will vary. In our first example, movement and geography govern. Sometimes the glance will create a formal symmetry. One shot begins at the left doorway as Mikkel enters to greet the parson. The camera follows them around the table until Mikkel looks off right and the camera moves to the right doorway, through which Borgen, Inger, and the children enter. After the parson leaves, Borgen and Inger come to the table to await Anders's return from Peter's. Again, Mikkel and Inger look off right, and again the camera glides right to pick up Anders entering. Characters' looks have neatly segmented the shot. Or the movement of a single character around the space will often give the shot a marked internal shape. We have seen how Anders's pacings around the kitchen motivate several camera movements; the same effect appears when the doctor's trips from Inger to the surgical instruments and back to Inger produce a regular rhythm. It is now clear why the camera does not follow any and every figure movement: the camera accompanies only those character movements which enable it to construct the patterns we have been examining.

All these examples permit us to identify another law of the long take: the shot will ask us to compare its beginning with its ending. The various stages of shot 47 are illustrated on the following pages. The shot begins framing the table while Karen trims the lamp. Mikkel enters the frame (fig. 26) and we follow him right to the door to meet Borgen and get a pail (fig. 27). He leaves the shot and we follow Borgen and Anders as they walk to the chest (fig. 28). After Anders goes to bed, Borgen walks left back to the table (fig. 29). This completes the first phase of the shot, the first return to the point of departure. Johannes enters and, after talking with Borgen, drifts out (fig. 30). As earlier in the shot, Mikkel rushes into the frame (fig. 31) and we follow him and Borgen across the parlor to the chest (fig. 32). Mikkel seizes linen and dashes out (fig. 33), and again old Borgen shuffles back to the table (fig. 34). The shot ends where it began. The return to previous setups, the repetitions of actions, and the alternation between movement and rest—all contribute to making the shot a highly formalized spatio-temporal entity.

Sometimes, on the other hand, the shot will make a point of *not* ending where it began. When little Maren comes out to see Borgen, the camera's orientation is toward her room (fig. 35). After Borgen sends her off to bed, the camera arcs with him as he goes to the opposite end of the room to console Mikkel (fig. 36), and the shot ends with the image of the door of Inger's sickroom (fig. 37). Here beginning and ending contrast two implicit off-screen spaces by gradually linking the two doors. (The same contrast is stressed in the arcing movement around Johannes and Maren which we have already examined.) In such ways, the shots gather force through their teleological

You do the praying, father !

26 27 28 29 30 31 32 33 34

forms, the implication that they are developing toward the completion of internal patterns.

In his essay on the sound cinema, Dreyer points out how camera and figure movement can create a rhythmic ensemble. Here, twenty years before *Ordet* was made, he anticipates the film's handling of these two sorts of "restlessness."

Characteristic of all good film is a certain rhythm-bound restlessness, which is created partly through the actor's movements in the pictures and partly through a more or less rapid interchange of the pictures themselves. A live, mobile camera, which even in close-ups adjusts flexibly and follows the persons so that the background is constantly shifted . . . is important for the first type of

35

36

37

> *restlessness. . . . Example: the third act of Kaj Munk's* The Word *takes place in the drawing room of the Borgen family's farm. . . . The actors going to and from the sickbed would contribute to creating the two types of restlessness or excitement that condition the rhythm of the film to an essential degree.*[18]

Dreyer correctly seizes upon the scenes taking place during the long, painful night of Inger's giving birth, for in this section of the film (shots 35–63), the shots' tendency to assume complex spatio-temporal shapes is at its height. Distinct zones of the parlor are established—the desk by the sickroom door, the doorway in the left rear, the parlor table, Inger's yarn chair, the back door in the right rear, the door to the children's room, and, on the far right, the door to Anders's and Johannes's room. As in the nighttime circuit from Anders's room to Inger's at the film's beginning, during these later shots characters are constantly crossing from her sickroom to the other side of the parlor and back again. One shot (47) will, as we saw in figures 21–29, begin on the table and trace only part of Mikkel's progress as he dashes in and out of the sickroom with bucket or linen. Another shot (49) will begin on the door to Maren's room, follow her to the table, then follow old Borgen to the sickroom door. Yet another shot (56) begins on the table and moves to the window when Anders and Borgen go to watch the doctor's car leave. What creates the overall to-

ZONES OF ROOM	Sickroom door, desk, and phone	Table	Door	Chest	Yarn chair	Window	Anders's room
	35	47a →	47b →	47c			
		47d ←		→ 47e			
		47f ←					
		48b ←		48a			
	49c ←	49b ←	49a				
					50		
SHOTS	51c ←		51b ←		51a		
	52						
	54a →	54b					
		56a →				56b	
						57	
	58c ←	58b ←				58a	
	61a →				61b		
	61c ←						
	63a →						63b
	63c ←						

38 39 40 41 42 43 44 45

and-fro pattern? A simple chart will clarify the shifts in camera movement. Omitted shot numbers are cutaways to scenes outside the parlor, and arrows indicate camera and figure movements from one point to another.

Now the conditions for the to-and-fro framings of the figures emerge more clearly. Sometimes the camera movement will pick up a moving character at a point already traversed in the previous shot, so that the space covered overlaps; this happens when the area to the right of the table is crossed by Borgen and Mikkel (shot 47), then by Johannes (48), then by Maren (49). More often, a long take will begin on or near the spot where the previous shot ended. Significantly, this occurs even after we have *cut away* to another locale and then *returned* to the parlor. Thus shot 54 begins at the spot where shot 52 left off, as 56 does from 54, 58 from 56, and so on. Not until the very end of the childbirth sequence does a single camera movement encompass the *entire* room: in shot 63, Anders and Mikkel carry Johannes out and Mikkel returns to the sickroom, griefstricken. The diagram makes it apparent that the overall pattern of the scene's camera movements consists of a precise, inexorable *scanning* of the parlor, the camera swinging across this space almost as singlemindedly as does Michael Snow's in ⟵⟶. The sequence's rigorous theme-and-variations form shows that not only does each long take have an internal logic but so does the overall ensemble of long takes. From a parlor, some moving figures, and a mobile camera, there emerges a densely patterned system independent of the narrative.

By now it should be clear that the film's use of camera movement cannot be adequately understood by using only the "following moving characters/moving independently" distinction. Neither Wood nor Parrain could account for the shots we have examined. For Wood, the geometrical camera movements would point to an omniscient manipulation; yet virtually every camera movement is motivated by character movement. But Parrain would be wrong to see in this a subordination of camera movement to the narrative, since the camera does not follow any passing figure but only those "going its way," fitting into its own trajectory. The complexity of the spatial system is perhaps best revealed in the last shot we get of the Borgen parlor, the long track down and along the hymn-singing mourners in shot 78. This is the culmination of the film's exploration of this chamber, recapitulating all the temporal, spatial, and teleological features of camera movement that we have seen at work.

The shot begins as a clear instance of "following the characters." Mikkel enters the parlor by the main doorway and comes to talk with a mourner (fig. 38). The camera then leaves Mikkel and begins a slow arc right and pan left, picking out one seated or standing mourner after another (figs. 39–40) and ending on those by the right wall (fig. 41). We follow no one's movements; we simply survey the guests. The camera then, with a flagrant lack of economy, *doubles back on itself,* arcing left and panning right, again accompanying no one (figs. 42–45). But this new route reveals several things. First, it carries us much closer to the people we have already seen—so close, in fact, that some mourners in the foreground during the first phase are off screen (behind the camera) on the second pass. Secondly, the new path permits the arc-and-pan movement to reveal people who could not be seen the first time around, a woman with a little girl sitting in the corner. (Compare figs. 41 and 42.) This is a good example of how the arc-and-pan can make unmoving objects spring forward sculpturally. When the camera eventually returns to Mikkel (fig. 45), his conversation with the mourner has been completed; along with the (by now ubiquitous) creak of the dolly, this offscreen narrative action helps foreground the duration of the camera movement we've just witnessed. Already we can see the complex effect of a camera movement that is at pains to complete its own spatio-temporal pattern, intersecting with and deviating from the narrative: to return to the opera metaphor, in this shot the camera has been given a formally integral solo.

But the shot is not over. After Mikkel leaves, the camera continues to move laterally left along the wall, past the stove and a few more mourners, to settle on the door of Inger's sickroom (figs. 46–47). This conclusion, as unexpected as it is gratuitous, recalls how previous camera movements had begun at the table or the opposite wall and

46

47

48

ended on the door of this room. Moreover, the camera plays strongly on our expectations here: so many people have passed through this door that we have a right to expect someone to emerge. (No one does.) Finally, this last phase of the shot poses an amusing problem for the "subordinate to the characters/independent of the characters" distinction. At first glance, the camera seems to move autonomously to the sickroom door. But the next shot (fig. 48) reveals Mikkel coming into the sickroom by another entrance. Given the layout of the house, our tracking shot has in effect traced Mikkel's steps to the death room by *following his movements as if he could be seen through the wall* and ending on the door of the room which he enters by another route. The rhythm of Mikkel's walk is sensed and followed by the camera even though he is not visible.

To what end do time, space, and teleological form so stress the shot as a unit of cinematic representation? Our study of other Dreyer films offers one answer: that all these devices permit cinematic time and space to vie with narrative logic for prominence. The flow of the narrative slows, thickens, freezes; the rhythm is broken; the film becomes an example of that "relative immobility" which Brecht claimed to be characteristic of cinema: "It is by nature static and must be treated as a succession of tableaux."[19] Specific to *Ordet*, however, and new to Dreyer's career, is that mode of theatricalization whereby the film splits cinematic "performance" from the play's text. The larger purpose of *Ordet*'s theatricalization must be sought within the need of the film to represent the resurrection of Inger.

SPARSENESS

Ordet is widely considered to be a film whose style is "abstract" in some respect. Usually, the term refers to the bare *mise-en-scène*, but the concept can be widened usefully if we consider "abstraction" in its root sense—*ab-strahere*, to "draw away from." What is implied is a process of sparsening, of selection and simplification. Following this lead, we find that a notion of sparseness helps explain many features of the film—not least the representation of the miracle at the end.

As a theoretical concept, sparseness entails a process of at least two stages.

1. *Reduction*. The classical narrative cinema, as we have seen, subordinates stylistic means to a narrative dominant which deforms them. But these stylistic means remain relatively varied and replete. This does not mean that the classical style's possibilities stretch to infinity; the model is an internally varied, but still limited, norm. For our purposes here, the classical model functions as a background set for a sparser cinema.

Initially, we are tempted to define that sparser cinema as sheer stinginess. Compared to Hollywood's variety of camera distances, Bresson utilizes relatively few. Of the classical cinema's range of camera heights and angles, Ozu typically retains only a low, straight-on camera position. Against the finite stylistic set of the Hollywood cinema, sparse style seems at first simply negation through quantitative reduction.

Such reduction is characteristic of *Ordet*. There is, for instance, the film's general lack of stylistic variety. *Jeanne d'Arc, Vampyr,* and *Day of Wrath* all work with a considerable range of camera distance and angle. *Ordet* seldom varies the camera distance from *plan-américain* and long shot, and there is an obstinate refusal to leave the straight-on angle. We have seen how editing in *La Passion de Jeanne d'Arc* and *Vampyr* plays off several classical norms, but *Ordet* has very little editing at all; viewers are likely to remember the neglect of cutting. For such reasons, the film is often classified as a work of sheer asceticism and rarefaction. *Ordet*, writes Robin Wood, is symptomatic of Dreyer's "progressive stylistic tightening and rigidifying, a movement away from freedom and fluency."[20]

Ordet's reduction operates in another way. If the classical norm subordinates style to narrative form, that means that moments not clearly related to the narrative logic must be excised. Yet we have seen how *Ordet*'s *mise-en-scène*, long takes, and camera movements work to slow the film's rhythm through dramatically empty intervals. The resulting retardation has the effect of planing down narrative elements to the same level as non-narrative ones: the doctor's movement from instrument table to Inger is as important as his diagnosis. The saliency of narrative is reduced by the attenuated surface of Dreyer's theatricalization.

Yet if reduction were all that mattered in the sparse style, Wood's charge of ossification might be apt. If the cliché that "less is more" means anything, it must be that quantitative selection somehow affects qualitative richness. The qualitative move comprises a second stage of the sparsening process.

2. *Foregrounding of the minute.* Stylistic denial produces discrimination. A Gestaltist metaphor is useful; against a cluttered background, a figure can barely be discerned; against a relatively reduced ground, the figure stands out more sharply; and against an absolutely neutral ground, the figure's slightest details yield themselves. Hollywood cinema, for aesthetic and ideological reasons, offers us a relatively reduced ground. Going further, sparse cinema's reduction foregrounds certain qualities of style that are underplayed by the norm. In a film with 500 shots edited in continuity, the cut will not acquire much edge or force; but in a film composed mainly of long takes, such as *Ordet,* the cut is considerably foregrounded. Our threshold of significance shifts, and the nuances of *mise-en-scène,* camera and figure movement, sound, and editing stand out in a rare relief. The reduction is cued by context, as Meir Sternberg suggests:

> *The more revolutionary a work in its conception of the scale of significance, the more does it depend on the operation of the sharply-enclosed, value-determining context of the whole work. For in such revolutionary works it is mainly the quantitative indicator that draws the reader's attention to the modification or even inversion of the conventional hierarchy of significance; or in other words, it is these works that most fully exploit the fact that what is conventionally regarded as trivial can be contextually invested with artistic importance by extensive treatment.*[21]

Stylistically, *Ordet* confronts us not only with denial but also with a sharpened and precise selectivity, a parsimony that tests and weighs its every choice. To stress only what is absent is to miss the figure-and-ground interplay. Against the background of the dominant norms, the systematic refusal of those norms (e.g., shifting angle or cutting within scenes) yields what Juri Lotman calls a "minus-device,"[22] a negating factor which emerges with particular salience. (So we attend to the straight-on angle in itself, or to the long take as such.) Earlier I suggested that for a Formalist theory of art, a work defamiliarizes not only ordinary perception of the world but also our perception of other art works. Parody is simply an extreme instance of the tendency of art works to cite and negate other works. We have already seen how *Jeanne d'Arc* and *Vampyr* assume acquaintance with principles of the classical Hollywood paradigm. In *Ordet,* Dreyer goes further. Granting all the film's systematic refusals, *Ordet* nevertheless reinserts, in small quantities and at judicious intervals, ordinary stylistic devices. Compared with the classical cinema, *Ordet* remains radically spare; but the film goes on to introduce doses of impurities which become strikingly noticeable. In this context, common devices stand out with an uncommon boldness. *Ordet,* in fact, creates a context which defamiliarizes a range of classical devices.

For example, a film may present a narrative episode in one shot or in several shots. If we exclude the brief transitional shots that function within crosscutting patterns, we find that *Ordet* displays a considerable range in the relation of editing patterns to narrative development. It is not surprising that thirteen scenes present their action in a single long take. What is noticeable is that the long take does not exhaust the film's *découpage.* Three scenes consume two shots each, one scene consumes four shots, one comprises five shots, two scenes comprise six shots, one scene consumes ten shots, another fourteen, and another forty. Notwithstanding some differences in running time, the range of results exhibits a fairly selective application of editing to narrative logic.

Sparseness strategies emerge even more saliently when we consider the nature of the shot changes involved. Before part IV, there are only four "analytical" shot changes (i.e., shot changes enlarging or reducing a portion of space shown in the previous shot) and thirty contiguity shot changes (i.e., shot changes revealing space adjacent to that shown in the previous shot). The point lies not only in the rarity of such ordinary stylistic figures. The *distribution* of the devices constitutes a much more powerful index of *Ordet*'s strategy of sparseness. If the ten eyeline matches before part IV were evenly scattered across the film, it would not be so significant as what actually happens: the first scene utilizes six out of the ten eyeline matches, and the other four appear at two quite significant moments afterward. In the first scene, when Anders discovers Johannes missing, the male members of the family follow as Inger watches. The scene is built entirely out of contiguity cuts, either with benefit of eyelines or with simple spatial proximity. In subsequent scenes, when Dreyer cuts to a new space in the same locale, he does not use eyeline cutting. Given the reliance on continguity cutting without glances to motivate the cuts, the two later eyeline-match cuts stand out with special boldness: Inger looking out at the parson entering the church and Anne's point of view on the Biblical illustration. Taken together, the eyeline-match cuts compare Anders, Inger, and Anne as point-of-view charac-

49

50

ters and parallel what they see (Johannes, parson, Jesus) in order to help motivate the denouement. In short, quantitative reduction is accompanied by a *patterned* foregrounding of the minute.

Even the comparative stability of the contiguity cut is eroded somewhat in the course of the film. During the long night of Inger's painful childbirth, the cutting within the chamber space becomes as noticeable as any camera movement seen prior. In the course of the segment (demarcated as II *o*-II *s*), Anders and old Borgen return to the farmhouse, the child dies, Borgen tries to console Maren and Mikkel, and Johannes tells Maren he will try to revive Inger after she dies. It is during this segment that Johannes leads his most ambiguous off-screen existence, for not only does he drift unexpectedly in and out of the frame but contiguity cutting keeps us uncertain as to whether he is present at any one moment. For example, after old Borgen sits back down at the table, there is a cut to a shot of another corner of the room, a shot revealing Johannes kneeling before "the man with the scythe." Retrospectively, we cannot ascertain whether Johannes has just entered the room or whether he has been there offscreen throughout the previous shot. After Borgen and Mikkel go into the sickroom, a contiguity cut to a chair reveals Johannes sitting there, but again we cannot decide how long he has been present. In this scene, the contiguity cut becomes marked as a device by the indeterminacy it creates.

A similar effect arises from the "analytical" shot change, the editing device that situates a spatial fragment within a whole by means of cutting into or out of the scene. Sitting on the chair, Johannes is joined by Maren; Dreyer cuts in to a *plan-américain* of the two (figs. 49–50). The effect is explosive. The second shot is only 24 seconds long (whereas its mates are 204 and 140 seconds respectively). Moreover, this is only the second analytical shot change in the film. (The first was the dissolve from the Borgen farm to the "Borgensgaard" sign, some ninety minutes earlier!) Finally, the cut is gratuitous. Many earlier scenes have begun similarly and have readjusted the camera or figure position to keep the action within a single shot; this abrupt cut violates the reductive norm already established in the course of the film. Plainly, the film here defamiliarizes the analytical-cutting device: one of the most common figures of classical editing is here "made strange" by the context. Since the next shot consists of the arcing camera movement we have already examined (figs. 16–18) and since the next cut (to the sickroom door) is also an analytical one—the last before the final scene—there can be little doubt that in this scene between Johannes and Maren, many of the fundamental principles of theatricalization and sparseness are laid bare.

After Inger has died and Johannes has failed to revive her, one more stylistic device of the classical cinema is brought in to be estranged. The "montage sequence," as normally used, compresses a lengthy process or a set of habitual actions into a short space by excerpting certain typical aspects and linking them through dissolves or other optical punctuations. The montage sequence in *Ordet* represents Johannes's second escape and the family's search for him. But in the sparse context of the film, the sequence stands out as a specimen of the classical norm. Nondiegetic music wells up for the first time since the opening credits. In a film containing long takes, five fade-outs and four dissolves, we now find a sequence presenting six shots in a minute and a half, all linked by wipes. In context, the sequence looks positively flashy. This sequence defamiliarizes another figure of the classical style, adding to the film's practice of judiciously reinserting standardized devices within its scale of significance.

The result of all this is a film which leans toward a "permutational" form, a tendency to cite a range of classical stylistic devices very sparingly.[23] This can be considered a case "where separate portions of a single text are constituted according to different structural laws and a possible paradigm of codes is realized in the different portions of the work in various degrees of intensiveness."[24] *Gertrud* will push the permutational principle even further.

It is only in the context of the process of theatricalization and the strategy of the sparse style that the function of *Ordet*'s last scene can be estimated. From a narrative standpoint, the miracle unifies the film, canceling the problems raised by Johannes as a narrative force. We need to notice, though, that this final scene also accomplishes an important *representational* unification. Whereas theatricalization and sparseness have foregrounded spatio-temporal form as such, the resurrection of Inger reintegrates space and time, *realigns* them with structures of causality. Here, cinematic form returns to a stable articulation of narrative form and helps motivate the miracle.

From this standpoint, it is evident that in two cases, the citation of classical cutting patterns works to prepare for a final alignment of narrative and style. The scene between Johannes and Maren in the parlor (shots 50–51) does, we know, several things, including forcing us to notice the arc-and-pan camera movement. Narratively, the scene is crucial, for here the story is struggling to keep itself unified. Johannes begins to fear that he cannot revive Inger, while Maren insists that he must. Johannes must see his way to the narrative's closure, but Maren is the agent who makes sure that the film can achieve it. In this context, the sudden appearance of analytical editing patterns anticipates the way that cutting will fulfill narrative demands in the death room. Later, the search for Johannes (shots 67–72), edited as a conventional montage sequence, anticipates closure by its very position. Odd as it looks in *this* film, the sequence announces a possible harmony of narrative meaning, image, and music that leads smoothly toward the resurrection.

The final sequence has often been considered a prime instance of Dreyer's stylistic abstraction, and indeed the pervasive white walls, broken by shafts of light and a few pieces of furniture, stress bodies and faces with an insistence similar to that of *La Passion de Jeanne d'Arc*. In the earlier film, however, the abstract *mise-en-scène* is accompanied by abstract, even incoherent spatial relations. In *Ordet*'s last scene, the abstract *mise-en-scène* permits cutting and camera movement to construct an integral and narratively intelligible space.

Some characteristically Dreyerian devices establish the unity of the death room's space. The room is treated as a 360° whole, each half of which is shown during the first two shots: on one side, the two windows (fig. 51), on the other side, the clock and the opposite wall (fig. 52). The clarity of this space is further assured by a centerpiece—Inger's coffin, a fixed reference point for all character position and movement. It is inaccurate to claim that the shots of the opposite wall are taken from the point of view of Inger lying in the coffin,[25] but certainly the presence of the foot of the coffin in such shots creates a unified position from which to map the flow of the action. The coherence of the space is reinforced by two devices not previously used in the film: traditional establishing shots and tracking shots which move straight backwards or forward. Throughout the final scene, Dreyer is careful to signal the presence and location of every character, a practice which seldom occurs in the rest of the film.

Once the space has been laid out, in a manner characteristic of Dreyer's circular *mise-en-scène,* it is quickly made subordinate to the cause-effect progression of the narrative. The characters announce the scene's agenda: "The Vicar will soon be here." "And so, Inger, we shall put the lid over you." "Let the Parson say a prayer." "Any news of Johannes?" The narrative problems are about to be resolved, and at just this point the final sequence rapidly returns to the conventions of the classical norm. *Ordet* rediscovers the match-on-action cut, shot/reverse-shot, the eyeline match, analytical editing, and the close-up. Here are the major stages.

The prayer. The parson comes forward to lead a prayer (fig. 53) and a 180° cut matches his action (fig. 54). This is the only match-on-action cut in the film. The parson now stands at the point from which most shots facing

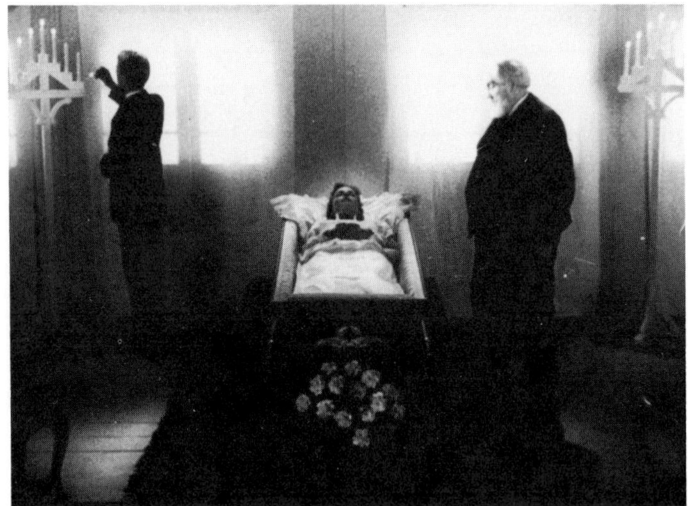
51

52

the opposite wall are taken; even when he steps away, this position remains the perspective of the scene's intelligibility. As the parson admonishes each of the Borgens not to grieve, shot/reverse-shot editing, linked by eyelines, punctuates his speech according to traditional narrative logic ("Therefore, cherish those memories . . . ," "And to you, Mikkel Borgen . . ."). (See figs. 55–56.) When the parson bows to pray, a cut outdoors reveals Peter and his family arriving at Borgensgaard. It is the last instance of crosscutting in the film; from now on, all action will be confined to the death chamber.

The union of Anders and Anne. One long take presents the family's thanking of the parson, the reunion of Borgen and Peter, Peter's giving of Anne to the family, and Mikkel's breakdown. In the next shot, taken from the opposite side of the room, Anders, Borgen, and Maren bid goodbye to Inger while Mikkel sobs beside the coffin. In both these shots, the positions of the seated characters and the movements of the others are clearly established. We always know who is where.

The return of Johannes. A sound from off screen distracts Borgen, who looks off screen. Johannes enters, not only the object of the look but also the wielder of it: his eyeline crosses Borgen's and motivates a reverse shot as Borgen comes to his son. Against a wall so bare that light seems to be pouring through it, the camera moves to frame the two men—the first time that we have seen father and son look at each other (fig. 57).

The resurrection of Inger. With Johannes's entrance, the cutting accelerates: twenty-two shots (a fifth of the film's total) will present Inger's rebirth. Johannes at the foot of the coffin announces that Inger must rot because no one dares ask God to resurrect her: Maren comes in to ask him to hurry up. As we have seen, Maren is the narrative's attempt to replace the madness of Johannes, to contain the dispersion it unleashes. At this moment, in other words, narrative unity reestablishes its control.

And space bends obediently to the narrative's needs. Eyeline-match shot/reverse-shot cutting continues as the parson objects (fig. 58) and Johannes continues (fig. 59). Earlier in the film, during the scene between Johannes and Maren, analytical editing had been introduced in small and isolated doses. Now analytical editing returns in a more plentiful context. Furthermore, the editing is dependent upon the dialogue. There is a shot of Johannes and Maren (Johannes calls on Jesus); a medium shot of Maren ("Grant me . . ."); a return to the shot of the two (". . . the word that can . . ."); another shot of Maren (". . . raise the dead"); back to the two-shot ("In the name of Jesus Christ I bid thee . . ."); and as climax a shot of Inger in the coffin (". . . Arise!"). The resurrection is accompanied by reaction shots of Borgen and Peter and of Maren. Husband and wife, reunited, embrace. As Anders goes to start the clock, the camera follows him. Mikkel tells Inger: "Life begins!" The camera tracks in to the film's first close-up (fig. 60).

Only our analysis of theatricalization and sparseness

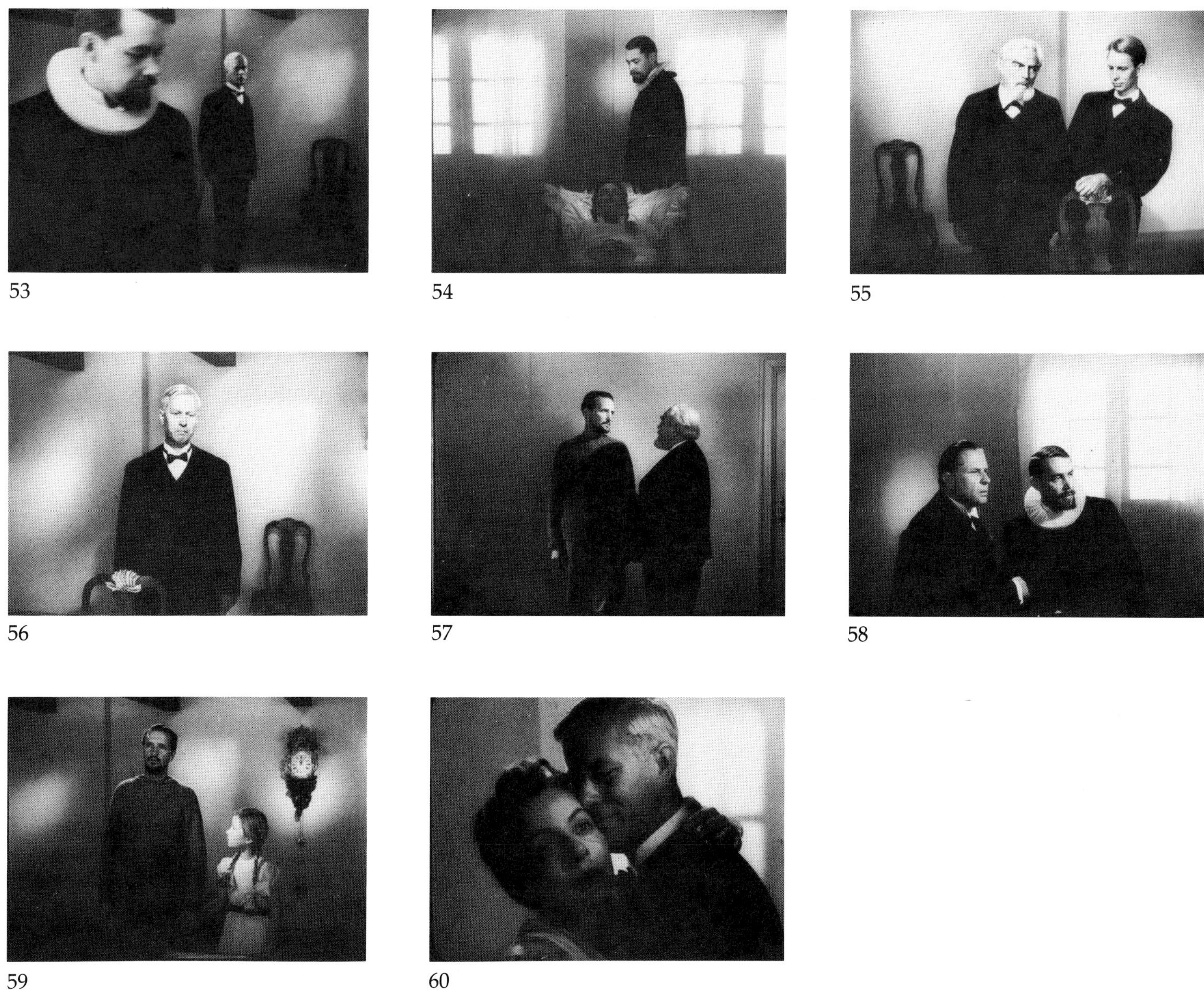
53 54 55 56 57 58 59 60

permits us to see how this final sequence functions to complete and unify the film. Our earlier questions—How to motivate the miracle? How to represent it?—are now revealed as interrelated. The miracle is justified as much by *the style which Dreyer employs* as by purely causal factors. Before this final scene, theatricalization has made spatio-temporal systems relatively independent of narrative logic, while sparseness has defamiliarized traditional stylistic procedures. Now, in a rush, the spatio-temporal systems fuse with narrative logic; now the classical figures of editing and camerawork parade past one by one, reinforcing the action's climax. What could have been a wholesale defamiliarization of the entire *découpage* system of classical cinema (this will be the task of *Gertrud*) has become a return to the familiar. It is not just that the miracle resolves the last of the plot difficulties, returning to narrative stability. The miracle is *represented on film* as a return to cinematic intelligibility, to a space and time responsive to narrative demands, to stylistic figures immediately meaningful. In Inger's resurrection, verisimilitude is violated in the name of narrative order, and the sense of order is justified by the return of conventional filmic comprehension.

Yet there remains a problem: Johannes. Even sane, he proposes that Inger be resurrected. To the end, he is a narrative wild card, moved not by psychological causality but by the narrative's compulsion to end in a way that will satisfy the claims of narrative unity and Christian allegory. The style of the final scene works overtime to motivate the miracle, but Johannes, who announces his function as as formal device, continues to be troublesome. The scene acknowledges Johannes's ambivalence the only way it can—spatially. After reviving Inger, Johannes leaves the frame, going out left. He becomes the only character whose final position in the room remains unknown to us. This tiny gesture poses as slight a problem as one can imagine. Yet even in a scene as massively unified as *Ordet*'s miracle, space refuses to lie completely under the sway of narrative structure.

Gertrud

Gertrud is the most problematic film of Dreyer's career. Its release created a celebrated controversy. The film was booed at Cannes, and snide reviews greeted the Paris premiere: the *Arts* headline pleaded, "Let's let Dreyer sleep in peace"; *Le Nouvel Observateur*'s fake interview described a snoring audience; *Cinema 65* attacked this "two-hour study of sofas and pianos."[1] American reviewers were as stupefied. "In his best films there has always been an underlying human concern that sustained us through any longueur of execution. Here, under the slow, posed pictures, there is nothing but the dated theme."[2] "*Gertrud* is a further reach, beyond mannerism into cinematic poverty and straightforward tedium. He just sets up his camera and photographs people talking to each other, usually sitting down; just the way it used to be done before Griffith made a few technical innovations."[3] If we had to reactivate the unfamiliar qualities of *Jeanne d'Arc,* we need not remind any viewer of the forbidding, estranging qualities of *Gertrud.*

Such critical responses are symptoms of something very important: *Gertrud* will not accept either the norms of the classical cinema or the norms of the "art cinema" (a concept I shall later elaborate). Denying both of these modes, *Gertrud* simply offers itself as empty. The bludgeoning sarcasm of the critics reveals the panic that can seize us when confronted with a film that unremittingly, almost malevolently, refuses to be cinema of any classifiable kind. *Gertrud*'s significance for us today lies primarily in what it does not do.

The first step is to recognize what binds the film together. In analyzing narrative logic, we shall find that even the minimally coherent narrative raises problems of representation. Yet a narrative analysis leaves much unexplained; this will carry us toward a consideration of the film's use of theatricalization and sparseness. At the level of cinematic style, *Gertrud* constitutes a virtual "anthology" film, citing the classical paradigm in a nearly exhaustive manner. But even here we find a remainder, an excess which cannot be justified on narrative or thematic grounds. Perverse as it sounds, the last section of the chapter argues for the important *negative* functions of *Gertrud*'s emptiness.

A MEMORY FILM

"A steady contemplation of a dispassionate loneliness in itself, appalling in its unrelieved restraint."[4] This description of Ralph Vaughan Williams's Sixth Symphony might serve as the ideal epigraph for *Gertrud,* at least if viewed as an ordinary narrative film. *Gertrud* is, according to a straightforward account, about the tragic isolation which a woman imposes on herself, through the failure of her men to match her impossibly zealous standard of love. Certainly the film's narrative logic, its *kammerspiel* qualities, and its use of the impersonal and hidden cause encourage such a résumé. Before we can consider the film's excessive qualities, we must do justice to the several ways in which it proffers itself as readable.

The plot is constructed along two axes. One is the forward movement of Gertrud's decisions to leave her husband Gustav Kanning, to become the mistress of the composer Erland Jansson, and finally to abandon all her men. The second movement is retrospective: flashbacks and conversations reveal story events in the manner of Ibsen's "continuous exposition." Thus the plot moves forward but is accompanied by a constant backing and filling. In the first scene, Gertrud and Gustav lay plans for future actions (going to the opera, attending Gabriel Lidman's banquet) but at the same time they exhume events from the past: their strained marriage, Gertrud's affair with Gabriel. Gertrud's announcement that she no longer wants to be Gustav's wife is accompanied by her post mortem on their life together: "You love power, honor. You love yourself, you

1. Vilhelm Hammershøi, *Solskin i Dagligstuen No. 2 (Sunshine in the Dayroom No. 2)* (1903).

2

love your intellectual life, your books, your Havana cigars. I'm sure you also loved me at times."

Subsequent scenes continue the process. In the park, before Gertrud consents to make love with Erland, they recall their first meeting, and a flashback shows her visiting his studio. In a carriage, Gustav's memory of his love for Gertrud impells him to drop in at the opera. At the banquet, while the student league and Gustav pay tribute to Gabriel's poetry, the plot moves ahead when Gertrud feels faint and is helped to the lounge. The lengthy scene in the lounge is a veritable orgy of continuous exposition, as characters analyze the past, both recent and distant. Gertrud reminisces with Axel about her father, Gustav tells her that he looked for her at the opera, and Gabriel tells her how Erland indiscreetly revealed that Gertrud was his mistress. In the park again, Erland admits that he is tied to another woman and can't run off with Gertrud. In the Kannings' parlor, Gabriel begs Gertrud to leave with him, and by way of explaining her refusal she recalls their affair—motivating the film's second flashback. After Gertrud has left Gustav, the film's epilogue returns again to nostalgia. Axel visits Gertrud in her retreat and their conversation makes a final trip into their days in Paris and into Gertrud's adolescence. Since narrative unity is, for once, not supplied by an omniscient authorial intelligence, the plot depends on Gertrud's development as a character, her gradual change in her attitude toward present and past, her rethinking of her life.

Like *The Magnificent Ambersons, Gertrud* becomes a film of memory, whose plot forces characters to spend most of their time recalling and reinterpreting story events. In harmony with the intimacy of the conversations, *Gertrud* constructs the closed world of Dreyer's *kammerspiel.* The film returns more explicitly than any since *Michael* to the tableau style reminiscent of Hammershøi, the Danish painter of the interior as still life (figs. 1–2). For the only time in his career, Dreyer utilizes a slightly widescreen ratio (approximately 1:1.45), the better to favor two people symmetrically disposed in the frame, talking. Circular *mise-en-scène* is used in the Kannings' parlor, in Jansson's studio, in the banquet lounge, and in the final scene in Gertrud's retreat, which makes a complete circuit of the decor. These sets, Dreyer tells us, were built as closed rooms, and he echoes Strindberg's justification of the chamber theatre as a place in which one can hear a whisper: "It creates an intimacy; the actors eventually

3

4

5

6

begin to feel as though it were their own home: rooms in which they lived."[5] With the exception of the student league's march, all the music in *Gertrud* is literally chamber music, for solo violin, string quartet, or piano.

Gertrud's insistence upon interior space is accompanied by an unprecedented emphasis on doors, the passages into and out of the chamber. Part of the theatrical quality of the film stems from the characters' incessant entrances and exits. One out of every five shots begins with an opening door or ends with a closing door or a vacant doorway. Gertrud in particular is associated with portals. She enters the film framed in the parlor doorway, as if on a proscenium stage (fig. 3) and leaves the scene in the same way. During Gustav's diatribe, the door becomes an overt symbol for Gertrud's sexuality: "For a month now your door has been closed to me." Before she sings at the banquet, the wall behind the sofa is opened to reveal a door (fig. 4; compare the frames from *The President* in chapter four, figs. 37–38). After she has left Gustav, she is framed in the kitchen doorway (fig. 5). It is thus consistent with the film's *kammerspiel* aesthetic that its last shot depicts a closed door (fig. 6): not only does the image represent narrative finality but it concludes the constant to-and-fro passage through domestic space; the chamber is at last sealed.

The film's insistence upon memory also works in tandem with the narrative principle of the hidden cause. What the characters seek in the past is the reason for later events. "Why did you break with him?" Gustav asks. Gertrud will not say. He asks her why she wants a new lover: "What can I explain? I don't understand it myself." When Gustav threatens her, she doesn't recognize him as her husband and can't understand why he is bitter. In the lounge, Gabriel repeats one line as if it were a refrain of Jansson's music: "Gertrud, why did you leave me?"—the same question he reiterates when they meet again in the Kannings' parlor. As surely as David Gray, these characters search for the absent cause.

Never has a Dreyer film devoted itself to the search so verbosely. Embedded in *Gertrud* are several types of discourses explicitly *about* causation. Now the characters themselves lay bare all the usual narrative motivations for closure. Religious discourse: "There must be a God. Without that, everything is incomprehensible." Political discourse: Gabriel will become a cabinet minister since "a little opposition will do the government no harm." The language of psychoanalysis: Axel studies "psychosis, neurosis, dreams and symbols." Philosophical reflection: Gertrud and Axel discuss the problem of free will. Parodying the work of critics hauling out meaning from the Dreyer film, *Gertrud* renders most thematic interpretations useless: the characters have already applied conventional frameworks of intelligibility to their own actions.

Most tellingly, there is the framework of aesthetic discourse, in the form of the art works that populate the film. As in *Michael,* this film about artists invokes its narrative parallels through *objects d'art,* in virtually every medium. We find sculpture (the statue of Venus in the park), photography, painting, weaving (the lounge tapestry), drawing (Gabriel's sketch of Gertrud), dance (the students' march), theatre (Axel's book on Racine), opera *(Fidelio)*, poetry (Gabriel's and Gertrud's verses), and music. Such aesthetic texts are frequently motivated by the narrative. Both of Gertrud's songs represent her feelings for Erland, the first ("Serenade") expressing her desire, the second ("Why am I angry?") her anguish at his betrayal and her recognition that he is incorrigible. Similarly, Axel's book on Racine, the playwright of tragic self-sacrifice for love, alludes to Gertrud's situation. No more troublesome are the ironic possibilities of the artifacts: Gabriel's passionate youthful poems juxtaposed with his present resignation, or Gertrud's painting of a man laboring under a burden. Expressive or ironic, most such citations are explicable through character psychology. It would be a mistake, though, to see the art works as functioning simply to parallel situations. *Gertrud* uses art works to pose the problem of how aesthetic discourse can adequately represent the motive force of the narrative.

Gertrud has recited, to Erland, an account of a dream in which she is running naked, pursued by wild dogs. But she is ready with a reading: "It was then that I realized that we are alone in the world." From psychological concept (solitude) to image (dream) to verbal transcription (speech) runs an unbroken chain of representations. But now Gertrud sits in the banquet lounge with Axel. "My father was a sad fatalist. He taught us that everything is predestined. . . . 'Destiny controls everything.' " She opts for free will: "I prefer to choose *my* husbands." Suddenly she notices the tapestry behind her and the camera draws back to frame it (fig. 7). Gertrud says uneasily: "I had that dream last night." The sudden appearance of the tapestry, with its woman surrounded by wild dogs, cannot be ex-

7

plained through character psychology; the hidden cause has revealed itself as impersonal. If one thinks in terms of psychological origins, where did *this* image come from? The overarching principle of all of Dreyer's narratives—the abstract causal pattern which governs individual action—has manifested itself to the characters. The tapestry challenges the smooth passage from concept to image. At stake is nothing less than the founding and authoritative intelligibility which Dreyer's narratives have always sought to guarantee. This tapestry scene sets the narrative a new question: not, "What is the absent cause?" but, "Once the absent cause is represented, how to interpret it?"

The narrative proposes two answers to the problem, one which Gertrud settles upon, the other toward which the audience is drawn. The tapestry is discovered in the context of Gertrud's advocacy of free will. If the tapestry poses the problem of causality, one could solve it in the fashion of Gertrud's father: everything is determined. Within the world of the film, the characters might posit fate as the reason that Gertrud left Gabriel, married Gustav, took up with Erland, and so on. At some points, Gertrud indeed turns into a fatalist. When Gabriel says that he had to tell her of Erland's indiscretion, Gertrud can say only: "Yes, yes, you *had* to." When Erland admits that he was forced to go to Constance's, she responds: "Yes, yes, you had to. *Had to*—I suppose that's the key word to everything." She finally leaves to go to Paris with Axel, to study scientifically how such things are possible.

By the end of the film, however, Gertrud has rejected simple fatalism. She gives determinism a twist (characteristic, incidentally, of much literary criticism as well). Wanting to preserve personal psychology, she reduces the hidden cause to changeless traits of character: thus fate becomes only character writ large. Representation will *mean* again if we posit childhood as its source. When Axel visits her, she discloses a poem written in her youth: "Look at me./Am I beautiful?/No./But I have loved.//Look at me./Am I young?/No./But I have loved.//Look at me./Do I live?/No./But I have loved." The poem supplies the absent cause, but personalized: "Sixteen-year-old Gertrud wrote my gospel of love." The search for the hidden cause has become a search for the foundation of representation, and the answer which satisfies Gertrud is a simple one. In her youth, her character was determined, her future mapped out. That is to say that there is still a founding concept which provides a source and model for representation.

Gertrud's solution invites us to accept it, for it explains the parallelisms of the film. If character is destiny, then we can account for the way that lovers replay situations. With her old love Gabriel and her newest love Erland, Gertrud passes through the same phases—infatuated devotion; the discovery that she is not loved wholly; and the decision to break with her lover. Dialogue reechoes. To Gabriel: "In you I had found a man with whom I could share my life. . . . What separated us was your work—honor, fame, and money. Love had become a burden to you. . . . You are as cold as stone. I want complete love. . . . It's too late." To Erland: "Here with you I'm alive again. I can't tell you how happy I am. . . . I love you but you don't love me. I no longer want you. . . . Leave me alone, Erland." Even Gustav, her partner in what she considers a purely sensual marriage, gets much the same treatment: "A woman puts love of her husband first, but for him work is more important. . . . Do I exist at all? You're never aware of my thoughts or wishes. . . . The man I choose to live with must belong to me completely. . . . I'm leaving." The symmetrical placement and diffuse lighting of the flashbacks thus function to parallel Gertrud's two affairs, and the doubling of locations (two parlor scenes, two park scenes, two scenes in Erland's studio) reinforce the sense of cyclical reenactment. Parallels of past and present are defined through such stylistic devices as sound bridges (Jansson's voice over the first flashback) and emphatic dissolves which contrast Gertrud "now" and "then" (figs. 8–9). In sum, narrative parallelism is now explained by a pervasive causality: Gertrud's desire for absolute love. From this standpoint the final scene—shot with the diffused light of the flashback—gives Axel the status of yet another lover and reveals that at age sixteen Gertrud's poem had "predicted" her life.

All of these connections come from reading the final poem as full of significance; the search for the hidden cause is finally rewarded by a discovery of the fateful force of human choice. But the tapestry remains unexplained and might encourage a fatalist reading of the narrative. One could argue that Gertrud is deluded, that a cause no less impersonal than that of other Dreyer films holds sway here as well.

What makes both readings inadequate is the remainder that they leave. Both conclusions are at odds with the qual-

8

9

ity which we noticed at the outset. If meaning and representation are full and unproblematic, derived either from the psyche or an impersonal cause, why is *Gertrud* itself so difficult to assimilate to our ordinary viewing habits? To answer that question, we need to examine how the film offers a critique of the adequacies of *cinematic* representation.

AN ANTHOLOGY FILM

Throughout our survey of Dreyer's films, we have seen them pose their own persistent problem of representation: that of a relative independence of narrative logic and cinematic space and time. Against the background of the classical model, the films—in various ways—deflect clear transmissions of story meaning, outrun narrative function, and focus attention on their manipulations of the film medium. For convenience, we can designate as "excess" all these patterns whereby the films systematically escape narrative determination.

Gertrud's difficulty, then, lies not in an incoherent narrative, like that of *L'Année dernière à Marienbad.* As our "obvious reading" has demonstrated, the film's story makes sense in many traditional ways. What is excessive is the way that this narrative is subjected to the work of cinematic representation. We know that Dreyer's films open up a gap between causal logic and spatio-temporal structures. What happens in *Gertrud* is that the "very slow continuity" initiated in *Day of Wrath* and continued in *Ordet* now becomes more than the narrative can bear. Narrative events—dialogue, gesture, character confrontations—become swallowed up in cinematic structures, like pennies tossed into a canyon. The film's structuring of space and time creates that excess described by Roland Barthes: "It is this story which here finds itself in some sort parametric to the signifier for which it is now merely the field of displacement, the constitutive negativity, or, again, the fellow traveler."[6] However readable, even in its ambiguities, the film forces us to notice a disparity between narrative and cinematic form. In one way, *Gertrud* becomes excessive by carrying further certain principles of theatricalization and sparseness already at work in *Ordet.* These principles are the subject of our attention now. In the next section, I shall suggest how *Gertrud* is excessive in another way: in its emptiness.

As in the other late Dreyer films, filmic space and time come forward in *Gertrud* because of inadequate narrative motivation. This permits the play text to be distanced from its performance, shifting our attention to style as a relatively independent realm. Once the shift has been made, the film can foreground certain figures from the paradigm of the classical cinema. But *Gertrud* is Dreyer's most radical film in these respects. Theatricalization is more stylized than ever before, and the process of sparseness moves toward an unprecedented exhaustiveness. Cinema may be the only representational system *not* cited specifically within the narrative, but in its own manipulation of space and time, the film lays bare—with great freedom and arbitrariness—virtually the entire classical model of cinematic representation.

Gertrud measures its distance from Söderberg's original play by means that are familiar to us from *Ordet.* Using even longer takes, the film's camera movements emphasize in more obvious ways the shot as a spatiotemporal unit of construction. Certain shots call attention to how the camera movement marks narrative actions. For instance, when Gertrud sings in Erland's apartment, the camera swings in from a long shot to a medium shot of them at the piano, then spirals back out. Later, when Gertrud is undressing, the camera arcs around the doorway through which she passes and subsequently spirals around the piano, as the earlier rehearsal shot had. Stylistically, *Gertrud* also makes us notice how the long-take camera movements segment scenes internally, as when the camera tracks back or around to stress a completed phase of action. Within the context of the long take, the action gets segmented by the theatrical device of *liaison des scènes*—chopping up the action by the entrance or exit of a character. A classic instance occurs in shot 5, when the arrival, visit, and farewell of Gustav's mother all constitute subdivisions of the shot.

In other ways, *Gertrud*'s theatricalization surpasses that of *Ordet.* In one shot of *Ordet,* Inger and old Borgen talk to each other after coffee. As they chat, they slowly walk to and fro across the parlor, stopping in certain fixed positions and refraining from looking at each other. The shot stands out strikingly in *Ordet,* and it looks forward to the dominant principles of *Gertrud*'s theatricalization. Dreyer's last film drives the stylization of the previous work to a new extreme: the sense of the "performance" of a text was never so strong.

Now speech tends toward recitation. The "poetic" delivery of the lines, stressing the literary flavor of the language, is called to our attention in several ways. As the actors declaim, they make little attempt to slur or vary their rhythms naturalistically. The film constantly treats language as performance. Characters make formal addresses (at the banquet) or recite poems (the students, Gertrud). The film's use of memory motivates the characters' discussing each other's voices (Erland: "How well you sang") and quoting each other to each other, even if some characters forget (Gabriel: "Yes, that sounds like me").

Now, similarly, gesture and figure movement function to accompany, in a musical sense, the already stylized delivery. Sitting, standing, and sitting again build up a steady, wavelike rhythm across each scene. A conversation may have no movements until the very end, as when Gertrud ends her talk with Gustav by rising to leave the banquet lounge, or when, more dramatically, Gabriel breaks down into sobs at the close of his talk with Gertrud. More often, gestures punctuate speech, Kabuki-fashion. Shot four shows Gertrud and Gustav in their parlor, with her sitting at the desk while he stands beside her, his elbow resting on his money chest. Gestures systematically mark the dialogue:

> *Gustav sits on the edge of the desk.* / "Why did you break up with him?" /
>
> *Gertrud raises her hands.* / "Let's not discuss it." /
>
> *Gustav picks up the cigarette pack.* / "No, it's all over now . . ." /
>
> *Gustav looks off and up.* / ". . . You were a free and independent woman. It's quite different." / *Gustav puts down the cigarette pack on the final line.* /
>
> *Gertrud smiles.* / "Is it?" /
>
> *Gustav moves his hand and shoulder slightly.* / "But of course it is. Why do you laugh?" / "I only smile when I think of all those who permit themselves to love and are not great artists." /
>
> *Gertrud stops smiling.* /
>
> *Gustav nods.* / "Oh." /
>
> *Gustav rises and returns to leaning on the money chest, looking out and up.* / "Have you seen my briefcase?" /
>
> "Yes." / *Gertrud unfolds her hands and raises the newspaper page.* / "In the hall." /
>
> *Gustav moves back slightly.* / "Thank you." / *Gustav turns and goes out frame right.*

Slight turns, shifts of gaze, small movements of the hands —in context, these become fixed elements to be wedged into the flow of talk, measuring a distance between text and performance.

"Why must a dialogue scene be bound to the idea that one either sees the people in profile or sees one actor with his back turned around? That way, the *interplay* between the actors can easily be washed out. In a dialogue scene, *both* faces are important."[7] Dreyer touches upon another important aspect of *Gertrud's* theatricalization. Whereas

10

11

12

Ordet utilizes the figures' profile and three-quarter views to a considerable extent, *Gertrud* insists on frontality of figure position. When the figures move they will sometimes turn slightly from us, but seldom do they come to rest in anything but a frontal posture. From the very first shot, Gustav and Gertrud face us, and the second shot—a pan from one to the other—accents the way both favor us with the full-face view. Even though figures turn their backs to each other (as when Erland rebuffs Gertrud in the park), they display their faces to us. Indeed, we might take the attitudes displayed in the embedded art works—the Venus statue, the tapestry—as representing this frontality most classically, in the figure of the frontally viewed nude female (fig. 10). Again, in this context, slight shifts stand out. After the second park scene, we start to see the profile of Jansson and of Gabriel. And the final scene gathers considerable force when the characters deliberately turn their backs to us (fig. 11). (This change is anticipated by another embedded art work: the painting in figure 12, which accompanies Gabriel's plea that Gertrud come live with him "by the sea.") In general, however, frontality assures that nothing is hidden, that this spectacle overtly keeps the spectator in mind.

If theatricalization in *Gertrud* is even more pronounced than in *Ordet,* what purposes does it serve? The film's obsessive rigidity provides that reduced ground so necessary for the sparseness we examined in the last chapter. The long take, the restriction of *mise-en-scène* to monotonous delivery, and the use of punctuational gesture and frontality yield a background against which the film may force our attention onto the minutiae of conventional cinematic representation. To a greater extent than *Ordet,* this film *anthologizes* and thus *estranges* the classical narrative cinema.

The anthological quality of these devices has already been suggested by Noël Burch and Jorge Dana. They maintain that *Gertrud* "deconstructs" traditional codes of shot/reverse shot and frame cutting, of three-dimensional space, and of certain camera movements. Burch and Dana's essay has informed this chapter in ways which will become evident. My argument, however, differs in scope. One of their points—*Gertrud*'s subversion of three-dimensional space—seems to me unjustified, based as it is upon an assumption that classical filmmaking is "illusionistic" (a concept which I regard as problematic). Moreover, Burch and Dana do not examine the entire range of techniques which *Gertrud* anthologizes. I shall try to show that not only camera movement and cutting within the scenes but also other editing devices, lighting, camera position, glances, and the use of sound are laid bare in the course of the film. Finally, although Burch and Dana refer to pertinent traits of the film's system, they nowhere specify these traits systematically. The implicit model for their essay is that of the analysis of contemporary music, but one need only glance at Boulez's dissection of *Le Sacre du printemps* or Babbitt's analysis of *Moses and Aaron* to see that Burch and Dana do not demonstrate *Gertrud*'s "vast and complex network of contrasting elements."[8] My argument, then, seeks to show the systematic exhaustiveness of those citations that follow in the wake of the film's sparseness.

Like *Ordet, Gertrud* displays, one by one, conventional figures of *découpage* relations—the various ways in which narrative may be articulated through editing. The film's work on *découpage* relations begins straightaway at the level of scene-to-scene transitions. *Gertrud* opens without a fade-in and ends without a fade-out; simple cuts open and close the film. Dissolves function solely to signal flashbacks, and even then minute differences are marked: the first flashback uses quick dissolves, the second very slow ones. Within the film, scenes are joined by a cut from

13

14

15

16

17

18

19

the last black frame of the fade-out. Not until the beginning of the very last scene are we treated to a full-fledged fade-out/fade-in. (Only Dreyer would make of this hackneyed transition from darkness to light a major formal event!) Thus the film fastidiously lays out the range of classical "punctuation" devices—cut, dissolve, fade.

Cutting within the scenes presents a veritable repertory of classical figures. Whereas *Ordet* anchored its permutations within the solidity of Dreyer's typical alternating construction, *Gertrud* denies itself this comfort. For virtually the first time, a Dreyer film is not predicated upon crosscutting. No greater evidence of *Gertrud*'s anthological construction could be found than its tendency to cite crosscutting only *once:* the moments when Gertrud and Erland's affair is alternated with Gustav's search for her at the opera house. Now crosscutting becomes no more important than other classical editing figures. Indeed, assuming that two shots within the same locale may be spatially proximate (i.e., revealing no overlapping areas) or spatially overlapping, we find that every classical editing device is cited (however sparingly) in the film.

Proximate cuts. *Without eyelines.* In *Ordet,* during Inger's childbirth, Dreyer cuts from one portion of the parlor to another, without characters' glances assuring continuity. The same effect arises in *Gertrud:* a shot of one area (of the Kannings' parlor, of the lounge) will be juxtaposed with a shot of another.

With eyelines: shot/reverse shot and eyeline match.

1. *Non–point of view.* At three points in the film, Dreyer cites the familiar shot/reverse-shot and eyeline-match devices. In the first section of the film, Gustav and Gertrud discuss her love affair, and Dreyer cuts between the two characters (figs. 13–14). There is a problem, however: while Gustav is looking at her, it is not clear whether she is looking at him. The second instance of shot/reverse shot and eyeline matching occurs in the

banquet scene; as we shall see, this passage is clearer and more conventional in the direction of glances. A similar eyeline-matching effect occurs when Gertrud sings for the vice-chancellor.

2. *Point of view.* Whereas *Ordet* utilized point-of-view cutting at four separate points, *Gertrud* withholds point-of-view cutting among characters until the very last shots. When Gertrud bids farewell to Axel, shots of her looking off at him alternate with shots of him seen from her vantage point (figs. 15–16).

Overlapping cuts. *Static.* Just as *Ordet* reserves analytical editing for the scene of Johannes talking with the child Maren, *Gertrud* utilizes it during a similar scene, when Gertrud and Erland sit on his piano bench (figs. 17–19). The shifts from shot to shot are, however, quite wrenching: Dreyer mismatches Erland's position by crossing the axis of action. Dreyer also uses three "insert" shots in the film: the newspaper announcement of Lidman's arrival, Lidman's scribbled apothegm about women's love, and Gertrud's poem. All three items are identified as objects of Gertrud's look. Apart from their functions as instances of various representational systems, the three elements are inserted into notably lengthy takes and stand out with unusual relief.

Dynamic.

1. *The "frame cut."*[9] When a character leaves the frame, classical practice often ends one shot with the body partially across one frameline and begins the next shot with the body crossing the opposite frameline, entering a new space (figs. 20–21). There are several such cuts in the film, and they display a considerable variety. Burch and Dana point out:

> *A model distinction will be drawn between, on the one hand, a cut "away from" Gertrud, shown on the left of the frame in a knee-length shot, to her reflection in a mirror advancing diagonally from right to left, eventually re-entering the frame in person from the left and, on the other hand, one in which she exits to the right in the mirror and reappears on the left in the shot that follows. A similar difference may be observed between a match which juxtaposes a frame-right exit with a frame-right entrance and another which juxtoposes a leftward exit with an entrance from the right.*[10]

Here the mirror serves to bare the device of frame-cutting, just as it will later assist in revealing the importance of glances in the film.

2. *The match on action.* If we consider the frame cut a separate type, there is only one genuine match on action in the film. In the banquet lounge, Gustav sits down on a sofa to talk with Gertrud, and Dreyer matches his movement across two shots (figs. 22–23). The singularity of the device (as well as its sheer gratuitousness) signals its citational quality.

The exhaustiveness with which these editing conventions are presented exceeds even the range of *Ordet.* (Had *Gertrud* included a montage sequence, the classical paradigm would be complete.) But more important, *Gertrud* goes on to anthologize far more than simply editing devices. One at a time, devices of lighting, camerawork, glances, and sound are exhibited; one by one, they are defamiliarized. The combinatory possibilities of each figure are traced out, and every device is at some point laid bare.

Consider, for one thing, the systematic range of lighting in the film. In any film, lighting can vary in intensity, in direction, and in the motivation of its source. *Gertrud* presents us with lighting of "normal" intensity in most scenes, of extreme darkness in the scenes in Erland's apartment, of dazzling suffusion during the flashbacks and final scene. The lighting may come from the front (fig. 24), from behind (fig. 25), or from several points at once. The light source may be motivated narratively (a lamp, a candle, daylight) or may remain unmotivated (the glowing walls, the patch of light that hovers on the tapestry). (See fig. 7.) Such a range of lighting would not seem very important if Dreyer did not incessantly remind us of the characters' manipulation of light. In his apartment, Jansson goes to a chest and gravely lights the candles before a framed score (fig. 26). At the start of a long scene, Gabriel lights the candles alongside Gertrud's mirror; when the scene is concluded she quietly extinguishes them (fig. 27). When Gertrud claims that the lights in the lounge are hurting her eyes, Gabriel dims them, pointing up the shift to the edge lighting of Gertrud's figure. In such shots, Dreyer's customary glowing-wall lighting is accompanied by an exploration of the various ways in which lighting can shape scenographic space. When spots of light sharply strike Gertrud's face from no discernible source (fig. 18), we must attend to lighting *as* a device, and *Gertrud* makes manifest how those devices are normally used in the classical narrative film.

Camera angle, we say, can be straight-on, high, or low. Camera distance can vary across long shot, *plan-américain,*

20 21 22 23 24 25 26 27

medium shot, medium close-up, or close-up. The camera can also move forward, backward, horizontally (panning or tracking laterally), vertically (tilting or craning), in arcs, spirals, etc. *Gertrud*'s anthological strategy emerges strikingly when we compare its camerawork to *Ordet*'s. As we saw, *Ordet* narrowly restricts its range of camera angles, distances, and movements. *Gertrud*, however sparingly, displays a wider range of alternatives. The camera assumes a high angle on Gustav or Erland, a low angle on the reciting student. Camera distances range from extreme long shots to medium shots to close-ups. While the arc-and-pan camera movements of *Ordet* have not vanished, they by no means dominate. The camera will track diagonally into the marching students, track laterally down the banquet table, and track back from Erland kneeling, or from the tapestry. For the first time in any Dreyer film, there is a crane shot, the camera crossing the banquet hall and rising to frame the marching students. Even the old chestnut of moving the camera "through" a room's wall, as if the set were a dollhouse, gets replayed when Gertrud comes to sing for Erland. Despite the diversity of such camerawork devices, the critical variable is their paucity: most types are executed only once, none more than a few times. Against the neutral background provided by theatricalization, our at-

28

29

30

31

32

33

34

35

tention is caught by the device itself; across the entire film, the devices form a permutation set, a sampling of camera movements typical of the classical paradigm.

The glance is, as we have seen, a crucial component of the classical narrative cinema, and it is nowhere more important than when two characters talk. The classical conversation scene relies upon the convention that although the figures' bodies must be frontally positioned, the characters must look at each other. But *Gertrud*'s insistence upon a frontal *mise-en-scène* deforms the glance in a new way. Given the face-to-camera postures of the characters, we attend extraordinarily closely to their eyelines. It is not only that characters seldom look at each other; it is not even that when their eyes meet or deflect it becomes a gesture. Rather, in *Gertrud* the permutations of *where two characters may look* are displayed with a richness rare in any film. One character looks at another, but the look is not returned (fig. 28). The two participants in the dialogue can look in several different directions (figs. 29–32). A character can roll one eye upward (fig. 33). One character may gaze at right angles to the other (fig. 34). Most remarkably, we can be made uncertain whether one character actually

36

37

is looking at another (fig. 35). By slowing the narrative pace and restricting the *mise-en-scène* and editing devices in the film, Dreyer is able to foreground the range and number of glances at work. *Gertrud* exposes the traditional powers of the glance to carry narrative meaning and to define scenographic unity.

The glance-structure is bared in the penultimate scene in the film. Gabriel lights the candles and stares into the mirror, gazing at the area of the room he can see from his vantage point. But from *our* vantage point, Gertrud is seen entering the room, reflected in the mirror. To see her, Gabriel must turn *from* the mirror (fig. 36). Viewer and characters share a glance, but a ricocheted one. The scene coheres only around our view, laying bare the power of the characters' and viewer's glance to cut out a representational space. A later shot becomes even more explicit: now Gabriel is absent, Gertrud walks away, and only our oblique gaze into the mirror demarcates her space (fig. 37).

All these figures of style—editing, camerawork, the glance—pertain to the image track alone. What of sound? Dreyer's film about musicians exhibits, one by one, an almost exhaustive set of sonic possibilities.

All three principal types of sound—speech, music, noise—occur in *Gertrud,* and we have already seen the variety of chamber instrumentation to which the film's music appeals. There are both on-screen and off-screen sources of sound. Direct sound (used in most scenes) is counterposed to the dubbed sound of Gertrud's two songs, obvious in their lack of room timbre and resonance. In themselves, though, such devices hardly warrant much notice, since it would be an exceptional film which did not include these possibilities. More important, particular elements focus our attention on the soundtrack.

Gustav says of Lidman's poetry that "he speaks so quietly that he forces us to listen," and the line is a motto for how *Gertrud*'s sparseness throws into relief particular sonic devices. There is, for one thing, the film's remarkable citation of the technique of the "voice-over monologue." While Gustav is riding in a carriage, we hear his voice describing his feelings: "Coming home from the meeting I was thinking. . . ." The device sharply ruptures narrative point of view: only in the flashbacks do we have such monologues, and even there it is always Gertrud addressing one of her men in the present. In the carriage scene, however, Gustav addresses *us,* and in the *past* tense—i.e., from a point *after* the narrative action has been completed, a point outside the time of the film. But nowhere else in the film is Gustav identified as a point-of-view character, and certainly not as one recollecting the entire plot in some present frame-story. Sheerly arbitrary, the insertion of Gustav's commentary functions to quote, as it were, the monologue device once and for all.

It is not only dialogue that enters into such relations with the image. If anything, sound becomes more palpable as music. In the classical paradigm, music operates to accompany the action, signaling characters' psychological states or anticipating narrative events. Ideally, the *duration* of the music should not be noticed. (Hence the significance of the fade-in and fade-out on the soundtrack.) *Gertrud* lays bare music's usual accompanying function by timing sound to action with marked precision. For example, Gertrud asks Erland to play his nocturne, and while we hear the piece she goes to his bedroom and undresses. She has staged his performance to accompany her, and the end of the piece coincides with the end of her action. The tendency of the music to consume only as much time as the action does, no more and no less, turns the scene into a specimen of sound/image relations characteristic of the classical cinema.

The significance of sound/image permutations in the film is clearest—as we might expect—in the scenes which most directly foreground sound. One such is Gertrud's performance of a song at Erland's apartment. Here the film plays overtly upon uncertainties about the sound's spatial and temporal source. Is it sound *off* (from an off-screen story source) or sound *over* (from a non-story source)? Is the sound in the present or in the past?

We dissolve to a shot of Gertrud walking down a corridor and knocking at Erland's door, while piano music accompanies her. Our expectation is that the music comes from outside the story, like previous phrases heard as she arrived at the park. It is only later in the shot, when the camera reveals Erland at the piano, that we realize the music to have been not sound *over* but sound *off*. More drastically, at the end of the scene, Gertrud has completed the song and Erland looks up, closes the score and hands it to her. We hear his voice: "How well you sang!" The context cues us to assume that he is saying this to her in the flashback, and indeed it requires a scrutiny of the film frame by frame to reveal that his judgment is ex post facto, made in the present outside the flashback. The quick dissolve back to the frame situation in the park reveals him continuing his comments. At the transitions into and out of the flashback, Dreyer exploits uncertainties about the spatial and temporal source of the sound.

The same scene reveals unusually clear manipulations of the timing of music duration to image duration. Early in the shot, the music (off screen or over?) mimics Gertrud's movements around the apartment. She comes in to a trilling melody. When she stops, so does the music. As she goes to the window, the music resumes. But when she stops beside the piano, the music stops again. At this point, when we realize that Erland's playing is the source of the sound, the perfectly timed halts and starts of the music are retroactively (and inadequately) motivated as the composer's trying out themes, jotting them down, testing others, and so on. During Gertrud's performance of Jansson's "Serenade," the camera spirals in toward the performing couple and spirals out again. We have already seen how, in the absence of figure movement, the camera movement becomes highly noticeable. Now we can observe how the pace of the movement is markedly synchronized with the structure of the song. The song is a sonnet, divided into a six-line stanza and two quatrains. The camera "choreographs" the song into these segments:

Eternally winged	Camera stationary in long shot
child-god	
Once more my heart	
has been caught;	
Once more will I	Camera starts to arc in to piano
be lonely	
In the midde of	
a satisfied flock.	
Here in your	
burning hand	
May happiness	Camera stops, framing couple
reach me.	
The dark has	Camera stationary in medium shot
formed a pearl.	
The night has	
borne a dream.	
Hidden, it will	Camera starts to arc back from piano
grow in me,	
Blindingly white	
and tender.	
The song will resound	
in my heart,	
Painful, sweet,	
and cruel,	
Remembering my	Camera stops in long shot
shining pearl	
Living in its	
dark dwelling.	

The sonnet is halved by the camera movement, with the song's midpoint (lines 7–8) serving as a resting spot for the camera. Before this pause, the camera has tracked in to the performance, its movement timed to halt with the end of the stanza and a cadence in the music. After the pause, the camera starts to move back again, but more slowly, now requiring five lines rather than four to return to its initial position. It is probably unnecessary to add that the song's vocal line is expressively echoed by the arabesque camera movement. In sum, the sequence forces us to attend to how the image can be synchronized quite schematically to sound duration.

The film's citation of the accompanying functions of conventional film music is even clearer in the scene in the lounge after the banquet. Off-screen sound is already stressed by the dialogue ("Lawyer Kanning has finished his speech"). When Gertrud tells Gustav that she was with her lover, he says harshly: "No woman should be that honest!" At this moment, from off screen, the music of a violin and piano edges into the room and the wistful melody runs under the rest of their conversation, continuing after Gertrud has left and Gabriel has entered. Gustav and Gabriel talk in a desultory fashion, and after Gabriel begins to tell of last evening's escapades, the men pause to listen to the music, still audible in the distance. When Gustav leaves, the music stops. Then Gertrud reenters and begins to chat with Gabriel. Again, just as he begins his tale of last night's party, we hear off-screen music: a string quartet and piano playing Jansson's "Serenade." Again the characters comment on the sound, and again as Gabriel and Gertrud talk, the melancholy music accompanies their increasingly melancholy conversation. By the end, action and sound are perfectly synchronized. Three repetitions of the "Serenade" melody come to a close as Gabriel begins to break into sobs; after the last phrase of the melody, he hurries out; as the coda concludes, Gertrud is left looking off screen; when the last note is heard, the shot ends. In narrative terms, the banquet-lounge scene elaborates upon Gertrud's relation to three of the four men in her life. But in terms of cinematic representation, the off-screen music lays bare the emotional cueing and the precise timing of music in the classical cinema. This film about musicians is no less about film music.

All these permutations of editing, *mise-en-scène,* camerawork, and sound emerge against the sparse background of the long take and of frontal, rigid figure behavior. Each category makes manifest *Gertrud*'s anthological ambitions. We can find one more piece of evidence for such ambitions. Like *Ordet, Gertrud* contains a scene which fuses spatio-temporal form and narrative form. In the banquet honoring Gabriel Lidman's return, filmic representation operates to articulate narrative structure in a classical fashion. An introductory tracking shot coasts down the guests and rises to frame the entrance of the marching students. At times independent of figure movement, at times following a figure (footman, marchers), the camera surveys the overall space of the banquet hall. For once, the characters' frontal positions are realistically motivated: the dining table forces them to sit side by side. For once, the stylized delivery is justified—as public recitation and rhetorical pomp. As at the end of *Ordet,* editing usurps the long take (one-fourth of the film's shots occur in this scene). The editing is almost always conventionally correct: eyelines, analytical cuts, and shot/reverse-shot patterns always cohere. (Even two inserted shots of young blonde women watching the proceedings, supposedly from a balcony and staircase, pose no problem when we remember the circular *mise-en-scène* of the chamber and assign them places on the missing fourth wall.) During Gabriel's address, his glance shifts considerably, but this is motivated by the presence of off-screen listeners. Stylized lighting (the anticipatory dimming of the room lights, the torches) and sound (the boys' rhythmic song and the leader's address) function to represent a stylized ceremony. Even the lateral track down the table to Gertrud is justified: the camera catches her as she starts to feel faint. In this classically-constructed sequence, space and time operate smoothly to sustain causal logic. As in *Ordet,* such a scene constitutes a return to narrative legibility.

The important difference from *Ordet,* however, lies in the position of the sequence. In the earlier film, the alignment of narrative and cinematic space and time came at the film's end, consummating the miraculous closure. But *Gertrud* offers no such satisfaction, since the scene which realigns cinematic representation and narrative logic comes one-third of the way into the film. By virtue of this, the banquet sequence does not cap the narrative; the sequence stands as only *another* possibility, an alternate way to make cinema. Here is sparseness carried to the level of the entire film: against the citations scattered through the other scenes, the banquet stands out as a dense cluster of references to the classical system. Once cited, this cluster can be compared with the rest of the film, in which theatrical text pulls away from performance, narrative logic from spatio-temporal representation. In other words, *Gertrud* has swallowed whole the very paradigm that has served as our background for Dreyer's work.

The exhaustiveness of *Gertrud*'s anthological ambitions should not, however, conceal from us the ultimate *arbitrariness* of their operation. It does not matter to the narrative whether Gertrud looks to the upper left or the lower right; or whether a certain pattern of frame entrances and exits appears at one point rather than another; or whether the film's one match-on-action cut represents Gustav sitting down. Even the banquet scene's return to narrative motivation constitutes simply a specimen; classical *découpage* could have reappeared in almost any other scene. This is why the film's repertory of devices, however systematic, remains excessive: what Barthes describes in *Ivan the Terrible* as "the epitome of a counter-narrative; disseminated, reversible, set to its own temporality."[11] This excess permits the film to carry the questioning of representational adequacy beyond issues in the plot. This is part of the film's answer to Gertrud's reading of her life as bound to the full significance of representation, the link of concept and sign and action. By situating the classical model within a larger field of relationships and then exhibiting that model with a dispersive arbitrariness, *Gertrud* displays the conventionality of cinematic representation.

AN EMPTY FILM

Although *Gertrud* is "excessive" in the way that it uses theatricalization and sparseness to compile an anthology of stylistic devices, it is not this excess that so disturbs its audience. Its excessive emptiness does that.

If we conceive art's primary effect as perceptual, we are inclined to think of aesthetic texts as trying to stretch the perceptual process to its limit. "The technique of art," writes Victor Shklovsky, "is to make objects 'unfamiliar,' to make forms difficult, to increase the difficulty and length of perception because the process of perception is an aesthetic end in itself and must be prolonged."[12] In other passages, however, Shklovsky points out that the prolonging of aesthetic perception is usually motivated by the art work. "Stairstep construction," parallelism, and other principles keep our interest while extending the experience. What happens, though, when the art work does not adequately justify prolonging our perception?

Gertrud affords one answer. The film maneuvers us into defining it as significantly *other than* historical norms. We have seen how *Gertrud* defamiliarizes classical cinema by citing it arbitrarily; shortly I shall try to show how principles of unity of the "art cinema" are invoked only to be dismissed. *Gertrud* is an excessive film in that, like minimal art or "Structuralist" cinema, it reduces meaning but prolongs perception. Here cinematic form pulls so far from narrative function that we must confront a work which is, by normal standards, empty.

The critic can treat such an emptiness positively or negatively. Positively, we can fill in the holes. This means seeing emptiness as an aesthetic device performing particular functions. From a Formalist perspective, emptiness could thus become a path to defamiliarizing the text, roughening our perception, and disorienting us. Emptiness would operate in a figure/ground fashion. We provisionally locate the art work against a scale of interest. Armed with those expectations, we scan the art work and are disappointed to find that it does not conform to our scale. But (assuming that we don't simply turn away) the dissatisfaction can become a pivotal step. We shift our scale of interest, starting to look differently—more closely and carefully—and making fresh connections. Nuances now leap to our eye. The emptiness becomes bait, luring us to adjust our expectations. Refocused, our attention now finds the work interesting; the emptiness was illusory.

To some degree, *Gertrud* makes a positive use of emptiness. By prolonging our perception beyond narrative needs, the film foregrounds those figures of cinematic style I have already mentioned. Yet it would be inaccurate to say that the film's discomforts simply drop away once we have perceived those figures. *Gertrud*'s emptiness exceeds even these functions. One would not need a film so long, so talky, so "slow-moving" to run the viewer through the classical paradigm. It is then necessary to examine the film's emptiness as a negative gesture.

In *Gertrud*, excess is related to inadequacies of narrative motivation, and these inadequacies manifest themselves in duration and repetition.[13] For one thing, narrative function can motivate the presence of a device, but not *how long* the device is present—how far, that is, our perception is stretched. For example, it is necessary that Gertrud talk with Gabriel in the lounge, but that necessity does not determine how rapidly the conversation proceeds. It is evident that *Gertrud* utilizes a slow rhythm on all the levels discussed with respect to *Day of Wrath:* story duration as rendered by plot duration (slow speech and movement presented in all their slowness), story intervals patiently rendered by plot (e.g., the long take), lugubrious editing and camera rhythm, and slow sonic rhythm. Thus the film's tempo creates a constant supply of dead spots from which no narrative information is forthcoming.

Excess is also created by repetition. First, the same narrative function may be repeated across *different* materials—various motifs which "all mean the same thing." We might here think of the stream of motifs which manifest Gertrud's love for Erland (elements of posture, expression, gesture, dialogue, lighting, music, setting, art objects), or which characterize Gabriel (citations of his poems, the figure of the "creative writer"). Similarly, the characters' habit of recalling the same story events at different points contributes to the film's redundancy. In the banquet lounge, some dialogue exchanges reveal new information, but many (e.g., Gustav's telling Gertrud about his visit to the opera) simply return to events which are already familiar to us. Later, at the Kannings' home, when Gertrud and Gabriel discuss their past, the conversation and the flashback tell us little that is new. The characters' recollection of the past constitutes the unrolling action as only slightly modified repetitions of earlier events.

Or *unmodified* repetitions. This would carry us to a different sort of repetition, whereby exactly the same motif appears again and again. In *Gertrud,* repetition of this type appears most readily in the dialogue, which spirals around the same points.

Gabriel: Nothing happens the way we think it should.

. . .

Gabriel: Nothing is ever the way you think it will be.
Gertrud: No, nothing is ever the way you think it will be.
Gabriel: You're leaving and so am I. Let's go away together.

. . .

Gabriel: Gertrud, come with me.
Gertrud: No, Gabriel, there is only loneliness left for me.
Gabriel: It is not too late, leave Kanning and come with me.
Gertrud: There is no happiness in love. Love is suffering. Love is unhappiness.

. . .

Gustav: Gertrud, don't leave me. . . . Stay with me. Let's live together.

Such threnodic repetitions saturate the final episodes of the film (normally, the most "interesting" parts), culminating in the final scene, when the poem's final line ("But I have loved") becomes an ostinato.

Axel: Do you remember your saying, "There is no other life than to love"? Do you still feel the same way?
Gertrud: I don't regret it. There is nothing else in life—youth, love, eternal tenderness—quiet happiness, Axel. When I am about to die, looking back on my life, I'll say to myself, "I have often made mistakes but I have loved."

By conventional standards, the point has been made, yet Gertrud continues, speaking of the inscription on her tombstone:

Gertrud: Just two words: *Amor Omnia.*
Axel: Love is all.
Gertrud: Yes, love is everything.

Isolating these strategies of slowness and repetition helps us specify why *Gertrud*'s excess panics us. This prolonging of perception creates a drainage of meaning. Either the narrative is saying nothing or it is saying nothing *new.* This is why Barthes describes cinematic excess as "obtuse meaning," a "signifier without a signified," "expenditure with no exchange." Indifference to narrative function presents us with the problem of reading an empty representation. There are too few obscurities to tease us on: lighting, the frontality of the figures, and the calculated camera movements assure us that at any moment we are seeing all there is to see. No longer the vacant backdrop highlighting a fascinating presence (narrative, style), emptiness can now work against representation. The film's excess demands that we listen seriously to the claim of many viewers that nothing happens in *Gertrud,* or at least nothing much.

A second consequence of *Gertrud*'s excess should be noted. While narrative logic aims for the closed and finite, excess is potentially unlimited. You can prolong a device beyond its narrative function for as long as you like, you can multiply different instances of the same function, you can repeat the same motif incessantly. The challenge of *Gertrud*'s excess is not only that it deflects from the narrative line; we have seen Dreyer use cinema in this way from the very start of his career. Rather, *Gertrud*'s emptiness is problematic because it could be infinite, halted only by the arbitrary demands of consumption (the film must finish). Again, *Gertrud*'s audiences find the right description: "I thought it would never end."

Within this book's frame of reference, a film's emptiness must be seen in historical terms, as a violation of canonized norms. We have seen in detail how *Gertrud* distances itself from the norms of the classical narrative cinema. *Gertrud*'s potentially endless evacuation of meaning must not, however, be confused with the style of another alternative cinema, the "art cinema" of the late 1950s and early 1960s. Although Dreyer's film owes its financial existence and survival to the art-film mode, *Gertrud*'s relation to that mode is difficult.

As a cinematic practice, the art film defines itself against the classical narrative cinema on two grounds: realism and authorship. Against Hollywood's artificiality, the art film marks itself as more authentic, dealing, in particular, with complex, "realistic" characters. Secondly, against Hollywood's commercialism, the art film is an expression of an individual artist. These contradictory demands—for realism and authorial expression—are resolved through the device of ambiguity. If the Hollywood cinema asks us to create a coherent meaning, the art cinema asks us to read the film for maximum ambiguity (richness, subtlety, tension). Yet this ambiguity is always displayed as such, understood as realism, the psychology of complex characters, or the profundity of an authorial vision. Unlike the Hollywood fiction, the art film seeks to create problems for the viewer. But we are to settle those problems by specific reading procedures: a causal gap will be read as realism (life leaves loose ends), inconsistencies will be read as character psychology (real people often behave in contradictory ways), spatial and temporal ruptures will be read as subjectivity or authorial commentary.

Gertrud's obvious stylization blocks any appeal to Hollywood verisimilitude, so we may be tempted to read it as an art film. Realism? We can view the pace as faithful to the life-style of a bored bourgeoisie. Psychological complexity? The characters' talk constitutes the ceaseless self-examination of intellectuals probing their neuroses. Authorial expression? The posed *mise-en-scène*, the comparisons of Gertrud to Venus and Diana, the allusions to *Fidelio* and painting traditions should suffice to construct a rich, ironic authorial persona. Ambiguity, then: Is Gertrud a monster or a martyr? Do the men deserve her reproaches? Is this a feminist or Marxist or misogynist film?

Plainly, however, such reading strategies do not address the perceptual consequences of the repetitions, excesses, and emptiness of the film. To consider *Gertrud* an art film (good or bad) is to ignore its powerful attack on significance. For above all the art cinema's devotion to ambiguity pledges it to *meaning*. The Knight in *The Seventh Seal*, the characters in Bergman's and Antonioni's trilogies, the protagonist of *La dolce vita* all search for the meaning of life, but that search is itself represented as unproblematically meaningful. The slowness of *Winter Light* is charged with the significance of "a world without God"; the lassitude of *La notte* can easily be read as symbolizing the ennui of a decadent class. That John Simon can savor the tempo of *L'avventura* ("a film in which human problems are insistently, though somewhat mutedly, present") and find *Gertrud* "unutterably boring" suggests Dreyer's more aggressive stance.[14] The viewer sought by the art cinema seeks a meaning; the emptiness of *Gertrud* persistently seeks to negate meaning. No realism, psychological complexity, or symbolic richness can justify the film's forceful vacancies. What tempts us to fall back on art-film reading conventions is Söderberg's original psychodrama. But theatricalization as a formal strategy permits the film to cite, bracket, and surpass precisely those commonplaces of alienation, futile passion, and lack of communication upon which Söderberg's text and the art cinema depend. Like *L'Année dernière à Marienbad*, *Gertrud* starts out within the norms of the art cinema but then challenges those norms, outruns them by means of a stress on the perceptual process.

Unlike the art cinema, *Gertrud* avoids signifying emptiness *by* emptiness. That would be to fall into the trap of straightforward representation, of simply making the metaphysical visible. *Gertrud* prefers to *brush past* images of vacancy: characters caught entering or leaving the room, frames just barely empty, paintings with slight content, reflections glimpsed in the mirror. Knowing our desire to make the very absence of meaning significant, *Gertrud* does not utterly destroy meaning; instead, the film proffers meaning only to withdraw it. As one instance, consider *Gertrud*'s use of the cliché—meaning par excellence but meaning easily cut down to size. Gabriel writes verses about how love quenches the lover's thirst, while Axel reflects on whether we have free will and Gustav comforts himself with proverbs ("Take care of the treasure God gives you, unless you want to lose it"). There is also Gertrud's claim to be dew, white clouds, the moon, and the sky. She concludes that "life is a dream." We have already seen how orthodox interpretations of behavior are offered by the characters; the film thereby cites banal readings (religion, myth, Freudian psychology). The very last shot of the film—a closed door—is itself a cliché of cinematic signification: the closed door of the honeymoon suite, the murderer's lodgings, the spies' rendezvous, the child's room, the madhouse, the execution chamber, the sickroom, the attic, the cellar, the tomb. Yet while this most pregnant image invariably impells us to ask what is happening behind the door, Dreyer's film draws us up short. There is no secret, nothing is happening behind this door: like the clichés of language, the image is vacuous. *Gertrud* is not simply about representational emptiness; turning back again and again to cut across the wake of its drift toward meaning, it seeks, intermittently but regularly, to *become* empty.

Seen from this stance, emptiness no longer lures and tantalizes us; it attacks us. Promising nothing, it challenges the security of change, meaning, conclusion. However functional to some degree, *Gertrud*'s boredom is primarily negative, even punishing; the film's refusal of pleasure constitutes nothing less than a threat.

A threat, we should add, to film interpretation and film viewing. If we see *Gertrud* as presenting an aesthetic vacuum, we must see the film as rejecting the representational richness usually associated with great cinema. We cannot glorify the film's theatricalization as signifying a tragedy; to accept the conventions of tragedy—the fall of the hero, inexorable fate—is to accept Gertrud's reading of her actions. Nor can we argue that the film's stylistic sparseness has an ultimately religious meaning, for no religious discourse frames the narrative structure, as in *Day of Wrath* or *Ordet*. By ignoring the vacuity of its moment-by-moment texture, such readings would assign to the film a transcendent cultural value. In large part, the film's persistent emptiness denies the richness and complexity, the meaning and pleasure, of ambitiously humanistic art. *Gertrud* refuses to be a great film. We cannot call it a masterpiece (or a failed masterpiece, or a failure). *Gertrud*'s empty intervals declare it to be categorically against masterpieces.

More than representational richness falls under attack. Since the excess of *Gertrud* sucks out meaning and opens up the arbitrariness of indefinite repetition, nothing less than representation itself—the security of the picture, the stability of the word—is called into question. We are now in a better position to understand some curious difficulties of the narrative. Although Gertrud rests content with identifying the absent cause as character-determining-fate, the film's overall causal pattern (embodied particularly in the tapestry) encourages us to posit a larger, impersonal force at work. Moreover, since the search for the absent cause becomes a search for a source of representation—what is symbolized by the dream, the tapestry, Gertrud's behavior?—this larger force constantly displaces any determinate source for the texts. The absent cause turns out to be only *another* representation, Gertrud's adolescent poem, her "gospel of love." But where, we must ask, did this come from? What founds its meaning?

Earlier Dreyer films had halted us at the threshold of a secure authorial voice, a non-diegetic master meaning: the authorial word of the intertitles *(Vampyr)*, Dies Irae scroll *(Day of Wrath)*, trial transcript and final title *(La Passion de Jeanne d'Arc)*, or Christian scripture *(Ordet)*. But by refusing to situate its narrative within such a framework, *Gertrud* leads from one representation (Gertrud's dream) to another (language) to others (tapestry, poem), and the chain becomes tautological, potentially infinite (continued as it is by the film itself, which replays with a difference all the other representations). Begun in youth (the poem) and stopped by death (*Amor Omnia* on the gravestone), the chain displays not a smooth passage from idea to image but a perpetual circle started and halted arbitrarily. The problem is that of the very nature of representation; the film's own vacancy and repetition manifest that problem in its most palpable form.

Although boredom has had a bad press, it is a crucial device of modern art. Avant-garde works often refuse dominant norms by emptying themselves of meaning, action, identification, suspense—in short, everything of interest. Such works then establish systems that block our assigning the very lack of meaning a meaning (metaphysical or religious insight, parody), for such an operation on our part reestablishes the text within the bounds of the usual. Paradoxically, then, *Gertrud*'s value is most evident in its ability—in 1964, and still today—to bore us. It is doubtless a desperate solution to the problem of cinematic representation: throw so much weight upon the perceptual process of cinema that dramaturgy and symbolic structure will always remain inadequate. Dreyer's withdrawal from contemporary production practice finds its most extreme form here, in a film which achieves its aesthetic identity in large part by negating our ordinary viewing habits.

At the close of chapter eight, I suggested that *Day of Wrath* achieved what Adorno called "the stringency of a structure that is not quite transparent." In *Gertrud*, this structure has become almost opaque. Like *Day of Wrath* and *Ordet, Gertrud* creates a retardation which brakes the ordinary rhythm of film viewing. Now, prolonging our perception without offering a continuous flow of narrative development, the film offers very few of the pleasures of ordinary cinema. It will not do to posit an "active viewer" who "works to produce meaning"; there is little for an active viewer to find, and a film which tries to evacuate significance and drum our senses with excessive repetition is not a good bet for producing meaning. If we want, we can collect tidbits of narrative interest, or read the film as a psychological study, or strain for allegorical resonance. But this is to ignore the pulverizing force of a film striving to become empty.

Dreyer's Uses

The question, "Of what interest is Dreyer's work today?" might be translated into another: Of what *use* is it? How, more specifically, does an analysis of the career and the films open up issues of film as a social practice? The man, his biographical legend, his aesthetic, and his films—how can they be situated with respect to social formations within and outside the institution "cinema?"

AN AESTHETIC IN HISTORY

Available evidence suggests that the ideological position of Dreyer himself was conservative. According to his biographer Neergaard, in his youth Dreyer belonged to the Radical Socialist party, a conservative group radical only in their opposition to military expenditures. As a journalist, Dreyer turned from social issues. By the time he started work for the Copenhagen daily *Ekstrabladet,* Danish newspapers had muffled their political affiliations and had aimed at readers of all persuasions. Dreyer's aviation reportage and witty feature articles are characteristic of the self-consciously clever *Ekstrabladet,* which was less important for its political views than its up-to-date style.[1] "Even when I was with *Ekstrabladet,*" Dreyer recalled, "I was conservative."[2] Given Dreyer's aesthetic, his suspicion of abrupt change—artistic or political—should come as no surprise. "I don't believe in revolutions. They have, as a rule, the tedious quality of pulling development back. I believe more in evolution, in the small advances."[3]

Dreyer's political views, of course, do not settle questions about his films. A work of art is the result of many factors, of which the explicit opinion of the artist constitutes only one. Two other forces are, as we have seen in chapter two, the aesthetic principles enunciated by the artist and the mode of artistic production. Here the picture becomes more complicated. Dreyer's search for the artisan's role in mass-production filmmaking swerved him toward an ahistoricality of style, an avowed concern for the universal and permanent. By situating cinema art outside industrial definitions, Dreyer's aesthetic blocked consideration of the contemporary conditions of film work. What *makes* films and other art works become commodities? As T. W. Adorno points out: "The division of labor is not to be revoked by the claims of universal genius."[4] Four examples from different phases of Dreyer's career may illustrate how his biographical legend did not permit a recognition of the way his production practice was related to concrete historical circumstances.

When *Leaves from Satan's Book* finally appeared in Denmark in 1921, its portrayals of the French Revolution and of the 1918 Finnish Civil War were criticized for their sympathy with counterrevolutionary regimes. The memory of the Reds' loss of the Finnish war was fresh enough for Danish leftists to see in the identification of Satan with the Bolshevik faction nothing less than what one newspaper called "one big scream against the hated Reds."[5] (Georges Sadoul has even claimed—citing no source—that *Leaves* was financed by the White government of Finland and supported by the Danish Radical Party as part of an antibolshevik campaign.[6]) I have found no record of Dreyer's response to such charges, but presumably it would have run along the lines of the answer he gave to a Finn who claimed that the film's settings were inauthentic:

> *[The episode] does not pretend to be a course in Finnish architecture-customs or an authentic chapter from the Finnish war of independence. It is, in all simplicity, a human story about a woman who dies for a holy cause. It can take place in Finland—or anywhere else in the world.*[7]

Such an answer, however consistent with Dreyer's aesthetic views, is ingenuous. After the Russian Revolution, Scandinavian governments looked with anxiety at the rise of Bolshevism, and Finland became an object lesson on the dangers of Red insurrection. *Leaves* identifies the White Finns with patriotic sacrifice: the opening title ("Pro Pa-

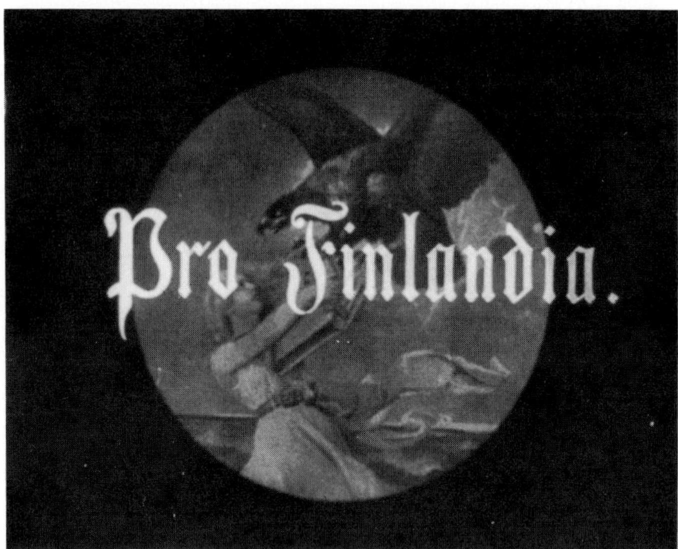

1. *Leaves from Satan's Book*

tria") represents Finland as a woman in white, attacked by the Russian eagle (fig. 1); later the housewife Siri dies rather than surrender to the Reds. More obliquely, the fact that both the French and the Finnish episodes show revolutions leading to repression must be situated with respect to conditions in contemporary Denmark. While Dreyer was preparing the film, the country was shaken by several labor uprisings. During postwar inflation and unemployment in 1918, Danish syndicalists organized several demonstrations, one of which ended in the sacking of the stock exchange. When the leader of the syndicalists was jailed, a general strike was called and sporadic demonstrations left Copenhagen in tumult for days. In 1918 strikes affected almost ten thousand workers; in 1919 over thirty-four thousand.[8] Despite the universalizing impulse of *Leaves,* and despite Dreyer's insistence upon it as a timeless human document, the film takes a stand on issues of mass action and revolution that arose in Denmark at the time.

The Stigmatized Ones, the first film which Dreyer made outside Scandinavia, is so riddled with inconsistencies of production practice, aesthetic precept, and historical situation that we must qualify almost everything we say about it. The film deals with the antisemitic pogroms under the last czar. But it was shot in Germany, with a troupe of emigré Russian actors who had worked with Stanislavsky and who were now with Max Reinhardt. The film sympathetically portrays the sufferings of Jews in the prerevolutionary period. But the emigrés producing the film had fled the revolution, carrying to Berlin horror stories about the new Soviet order, which Dreyer recorded in his terse journalistic style: Bolsheviks flinging passengers from trains, stripping orchards, shooting down men while wives and children look on.[9] In a dizzying turn, the czar's persecution of the Jews in the film becomes an ideological vehicle for the emigrés' experience of Soviet persecution. As a final twist, some of the emigrés who had worked on *The Stigmatized Ones* returned to Russia to work for the Soviet film industry. Again, for Dreyer *The Stigmatized Ones* seems to have constituted only a chance to work in Europe with some actors whom he admired; the political implications of the project apparently escaped him.

So great was Dreyer's attachment to the ahistorical that his productions sometimes became, willy-nilly, interventions on behalf of very different political positions. He writes of *Jeanne d'Arc* that he simply became interested in her, began historical research, and decided to "interpret a hymn to the triumph of the soul over life."[10] He does not note that the canonization of Jeanne in 1920 was one mark of the reentry of religious interests into postwar French governmental policy. Soon the cult of Jeanne d'Arc provided a focus for Catholic and right-wing demonstrators and yielded a symbol for the Action Française.[11] The surge of reactionary nationalism in France during the 1920s finds an echo in the last title of Dreyer's film: "And amid the flames the white soul of Jeanne rose heavenwards, that soul which has become the soul of France, as Jeanne herself has become the incarnation of imperishable France."

At another extreme, *Day of Wrath* stands in a critical relation to the German occupation of Denmark. The film was preceded by some documentaries (*The War on Rats* [1941] and *The Corn is in Danger* [1943]) which audiences had considered subversive commentaries on life under the Occupation. Moreover, *Day of Wrath* opened in November 1943—a critical moment in the Occupation. Sabotage against the Germans was growing. In August there had been a public strike and the government, refusing to acquiesce to Nazi rule, resigned. The Germans disarmed the Danish army; in retaliation, the admiral of the Danish navy ordered his fleet sunk so that it could not be used by the Germans. Hitler had ordered the arrest of all Jews, but the Danes smuggled Jews by boat to Sweden, while the king publicly wore the star of David in defiance of the Nazi order. In this context, *Day of Wrath* could be seen to protest the Occupation tyranny. Yet after the war, when it would have been easy to claim to have made a partisan film, Dreyer calmly insisted that he intended *Day of Wrath* to have no contemporary political references.[12]

In contrast to these four instances, one might glance at the work of Bertolt Brecht, Dreyer's junior by only nine years. Each man began his career in the teens, completed his first major work in 1918, and found his first international success in the years 1927–28. In 1931, while Dreyer was suing La Société Générale de Films for breach of contract, Brecht was in Berlin suing the makers of *The Threepenny Opera*. Whereas Dreyer went to court hoping to win (and did), Brecht, expecting to lose, brought the case in a spirit of inquiry, aiming to display certain contradictions of artistic practice under capitalism. After the case, he wrote an account attacking fourteen preconceptions about cinema, several of which Dreyer espoused: "The cinema cannot do without art," "A work of art is the expression of a personality," etc.[13] Brecht's aesthetic position forced him to consider the concrete social effects of his artistic work. Like Dreyer, he was drawn to the story of Jeanne d'Arc, which he dramatized three times, but each time as a calculated intervention in a social situation. *Saint Joan of the Stockyards* (1932) was in part a response to the rise in unemployment in Berlin in 1930–31. *The Visions of Simone Machard* (1943–44) became an allegory of heroism under the Occupation. *The Trial of Joan of Arc at Rouen* (1952) adapted Anna Seghers's radio play in order to secularize the saint's story: Jeanne's voices are not *vox Dei* but *vox populi,* the cries of oppressed France. The comparison of the two artists is not meant to score points off Dreyer in the name of a fashionable and infallible Brecht. The point is that Dreyer's aesthetic theory could not acknowledge the implications of his work within contemporary situations.

Yet the narrowness of Dreyer's aesthetic principles does not permit us to reduce the films' ideological operations to contemporary situations. The films are too complex for that. *Leaves from Satan's Book* and *The Stigmatized Ones* do not simply rant against mob repression; *Jeanne d'Arc* is not simply a piece of chauvinism, nor is *Day of Wrath* a straightforward protest against tyranny. The problematic aspects of Dreyer's works resist an attempt to see the films as reflecting contemporary ideological positions.

A POSSIBLE CINEMA

Putting aside the biographical Dreyer and his legend, how can we consider the films' ideological work? One place to begin is with the problems of unity and disunity that the films pose. In narrative structure and cinematic representation, in the impersonal and absent cause, in stylistic discontinuity, elongated continuity, theatricalization, sparseness, and boredom; in these formal strategies we must look for Dreyer's ideological uses.

We have one frame of reference within which to theorize such uses. In 1969, Jean-Louis Comolli and Jean Narboni began an interrogation of the ideological presuppositions of contemporary film study: "The question we have to ask is: Which films, books, and magazines allow the [dominant bourgeois] ideology a free, unhampered passage, transmit it with crystal clarity, serve as its chosen language? And which attempt to make it turn back and reflect itself, intercept it and make it visible by revealing its mechanisms, by blocking them?"[14] Comolli and Narboni proceeded to construct a typology of the ways in which films may be related to the dominant political ideology. At one extreme, they claimed, sits the unselfconscious ideological product (e.g., the films of a Lelouch). At the other, there are those films which overtly attack the dominant ideology through a breakdown of traditional cinematic representation. In between, there are several possibilities (political content/bourgeois form, direct cinema, etc.), one of which is appropriate to the work of this book:

> *. . . films which seem at first sight to belong firmly within the ideology and to be completely under its sway, but which turn out to be so only in an ambiguous manner. For though they start from a non-progressive standpoint, ranging from the frankly reactionary through the conciliatory to the mildly critical, they have been worked upon, and work, in such a real way that there is a noticeable gap, a dislocation, between the starting point and the finished product. . . . The films we are talking about throw up obstacles in the way of the ideology, causing it to swerve and get off course. The cinematic framework lets us see it, but also shows it up and denounces it. Looking at the framework, one can see two moments in it: one holding it back within certain limits, one transgressing them. An internal criticism is taking place which cracks the film apart at the seams. If one reads the film obliquely, looking for symptoms; if one looks beyond its apparent formal*

> *coherence, one can see that it is riddled with cracks: it is splitting under an internal tension which is simply not there in an ideologically innocuous film. The ideology thus becomes subordinate to the text. . . . (The films of Ford, Dreyer, Rossellini, for example.)*[15]

Since 1969 the reductiveness of the *Cahiers* typology has become apparent. (Does any film clearly and unproblematically represent a dominant ideology? Can we accept so absolute a split between form and content or signifier and signified?) Yet the passage quoted above echoes Comolli's remark on the "unnatural gaps" between narrative and cinematic form which I quoted in chapter five. The *Cahiers* category is useful because its insistence on the ideological functions of rupture accords with the disparities and tensions which we have found within Dreyer's films.

Not only in production and aesthetic position do Dreyer's films begin from what the *Cahiers* describes as a reactionary standpoint. Everything we have studied as characteristic of narrative structure in the films seeks to keep them in check ideologically, to assure coherent social meaning. In creating intelligibility and closure, the absent cause and the revealed word become motivated as religious predestination. In such films as *Jeanne d'Arc, Day of Wrath,* and *Ordet,* the narrative explicitly sets against the Church a true religiosity that is, in the final analysis, represented by the film's own self-sufficient discourse (the Jeanne d'Arc trial transcript, the Dies Irae scroll, the living word of *Ordet*). Here the practice of eliminating credit sequences *(Day of Wrath, Ordet)* helps sanctify the film as autonomously intelligible, outside history. Here, too, we ought to think of the persistent figure of the father and of the use of the word in ways that reinforce theological conceptions. The search for the concealed text makes the narrative intelligible because the word represents an explanatory principle over and above the world of the film. Religion as a narrative force takes on ideological weight, not only placing the action in an asocial, atemporal frame of reference but also validating it as representation, *theorizing* the film's very production of narrative: religion in a capitalist society, Julia Kristeva emphasizes, is "the privileged place of speculation and the place from which a given socioeconomic formation can elaborate the theory by which it represents its own signifying practice to itself—theory of language and of the function of language."[16]

As for Dreyer's use of tragedy, we can see that the same insistence on authoritative intelligibility has driven him to this mode. Conceptions of tragic inevitability function to overdetermine the film's narrative system. Predictions, parallels, and symmetries find their ultimate fulfillment when the individual's fate is to be represented as predetermined. Of even greater use is a conception of tragic self-knowledge. In *Jeanne d'Arc, Day of Wrath,* and *Gertrud,* the tragic protagonist at first misunderstands herself, failing to synchronize her actions with her "authentic" character. But as martyrdom approaches, the protagonist's acceptance of her fate signifies her recognition of her essential identity. When Jeanne sees her crown and bits of hair swept out of the room, she realizes her destiny. "Your deliverance?" asks Massieu. "My death!" Jeanne answers. When Anne sees Martin betray and abandon her, she confesses: we are to believe that she resigns herself to death. The film asks us to see Gertrud as understanding that although perfect love is impossible, her character will accept nothing less; hence she withdraws from the world. Individual psychology validates the narrative structure; when, in the end, the tragic heroine accepts her fate, her essential nature crystallizes for her; her acceptance corroborates the motive force of the plot, which is in turn corroborated by the outcome. Dreyer's claim that his films center upon psychology and are nonetheless ahistorical now becomes intelligible. In his tragedies, human psychology seeks to become defined through resignation to the inevitability of an impersonal causal scheme.

Conceptions of Christianity and tragedy operate through a specific figure: woman. The female protagonist becomes the site of forces holding the narrative together. Jeanne d'Arc and Gertrud function to center the worlds of their respective films. In *Vampyr,* first Léone and then Gisèle becomes the desired object around which the struggle of the plot takes place. *Ordet* presents Inger as the heart of the household (as *Thou Shalt Honor Thy Wife* had presented Ida). In *Day of Wrath,* Anne shapes the narrative through point of view and her desire for Martin. Yet the place of woman in Dreyer's films is quite ambivalent. From one standpoint, the coherence of the feminine characters is purchased by suppression of their sexuality. One ideological function of the tableau/face dialectic is to postpone systematically the problem of the female body: the body is only a figure in a tableau, eroticism is transferred to facial expression. (*Michael* is the most obvious example.) Usually

2. *Vampyr.*

3. *Day of Wrath*

4. *Ordet.*

the body is wrapped tightly in clothes, presented as what Mikhail Bakhtin, describing the image of the medieval carnival, calls "the limited canon . . . the impenetrable facade"[17] of the body. Carnality asserts itself, grotesquely and intermittently, in images of pain. Often characters force women's bodies into poses no less rigid than those of the tableau itself. *Vampyr* represents Léone as a woman to be pinched and bled, Gisèle as one to be strapped to a bed. Inger lies convulsed on a tabletop, at the mercy of the doctor's scissors. In *Jeanne d'Arc* and *Day of Wrath,* flesh becomes a raw material to be sculpted through torture (Jeanne d'Arc being bled, Herlofs Marte on the strappado). Only a facial shot, the close-up, can cancel such disturbing images. In the face (and all treatment of it through lighting and narrative context of tragic self-sacrifice), the feminine body finds its just characterization. The channeling of corporeal into physiognomic energy sustains Dreyer's avowedly psychological cinema. Once asked if *Gertrud* owed anything to Bergman's *The Silence,* Dreyer responded: "If I were to make a film about two Lesbians, I would not concentrate as much upon the sexual aspect as upon the psychological one."[18] The sexuality of the female body turns into an aesthetic expressivity which supports the unity of the narrative.[19]

Certain of Dreyer's stylistic tendencies also reinforce conceptions of an isolated subject facing a mysterious and impersonal spirit. In a monograph on Dreyer's countryman Kierkegaard, Theodor Adorno has pointed out how the notion of an idealist self was manifested in the recurring metaphor of the interior. For Adorno, Kierkegaard's interior embodied inwardness, with the human subject inhabiting a sheerly personal space, cut off from production. Objects, decoratively arranged, mirror the subject's unchanging essential nature. In Dreyer's chambers, we find the same tendency toward the self-absorption of a subject outside history. "Every single home," reads the opening of *Thou Shalt Honor Thy Wife,* "is a world unto itself. . . ." Most evidently, there are the paintings hanging within those rooms. The chamber's inhabitants sit or stand alongside pictures that double them. David Gray pauses beneath a wispy *fin-de-siècle* portrait (fig. 2). Anne is glimpsed in front of a painting of the crucifixion (fig. 3). Behind the patriarchs of *Ordet* loom images of the founders of their churches, images which echo the old men themselves (fig. 4). Gertrud is reflected in the tapestry behind her, her lovers in pictures of couples by the sea or of a man bending under a burden. The chamber has become a hall of mirrors. From this standpoint, the centrality of art objects in *Michael* and *Gertrud* becomes symptomatic of Dreyer's tendency to impress the social into the characters' surroundings, but at one remove, through decorative objects selected by the characters.

Adorno also suggests that the chamber's furnishings become aestheticized, gaining their significance "not from the substance of which they are manufactured, but out of the *intérieur,* which assembles the illusion of the things as a still life."[20] In Dreyer's films, neither referential realism nor psychological expressivity will justify all the picture frames, tapestries, precisely aligned sofas, fireplaces, woodwork, and cameos upon which the camera lingers. For Dreyer, the chamber is a place of spectacle. Of *The President,* Kirk Bond writes: "There are the bare white walls, walls broken by decorative objects, solid, isolated like gems in a case."[21] Dreyer's chambers put items on display: like museum and shop, the domestic interior is an exhibition space. Yet in Kierkegaard, Adorno argues, the ornaments do not seem alien because they are taken up as religious symbols, creating a second inwardness, the existential subject's religious self-denial.[22] A similar spiritualization occurs in Dreyer's chambers. Hovering ghostlike around the characters, the objects speak of a mystery beyond sense experience. They are there, Dreyer assures us, "for symbolic reasons. Even if the symbols cannot be readily understood."[23] The perceptual strangeness of these bourgeois rooms can signify an obscure but pervasive spirituality. Home or church, the two locales are interchangeable: the chamber becomes a chapel.

In spite of all these determinations, Dreyer's films do, in Comolli and Narboni's phrase, "throw up obstacles in the way of ideology"; the films possess *two* moments. To trace the ideological implications of Dreyer's late films, we need to turn to their gaps and dislocations—that relation of narrative form to cinematic form which has been the center of our inquiry.

One result has already been suggested: a shifting of our attention from the narrative to film style. *Jeanne d'Arc* and *Vampyr,* the one through composition and discontinuity editing, the other through figure movement and camerawork, force us to attend to the structuring of our aesthetic experience. The slackening of rhythm in *Day of Wrath* foregrounds the passage of time in the scene, a strategy continued in *Ordet* and *Gertrud* by lengthening the take, moving the camera, and slowing the figures' movements. In all these films, we must notice filmic representation as a relatively independent system within the text; figures of classical cinema are quoted and defamiliarized. Our viewing of the film must change; we can follow the film only by sensitizing ourselves to cinema as a specific medium. The inadequacy of narrative function to filmic representation thwarts our desire to pass *through* the representation *to* the narrative.

This result could, however, be justified within some conceptions of traditional aesthetics. We ought, the argument goes, to pay attention to the art medium, and Dreyer, like any stylist, is using certain devices to force us to notice the artfulness of the text. To some extent, the description is accurate. Yet the five late films perform a more radical gesture than bringing the medium to our notice. To a certain degree and in certain ways, the problems posed by the films block any immediate consumption—even as "art works." All the characteristic pressures toward disunity operate not only to "crack the film apart at the seams" but also to keep it from being easily assimilated to contemporary aesthetic standards.

So completely canonized have *Jeanne d'Arc* and *Vampyr* become that we may forget how they challenged not only Hollywood norms but also dominant theories of film art. In its time, and perhaps even still, *La Passion de Jeanne d'Arc* emerges as unclassifiable. Financed by an international consortium, the film sought neither an avant-garde audience nor a politically progressive one: according to press reports, the producers hoped to make a commercially popular film which would thwart Hollywood's hegemony in Europe.[24] Yet the film's style assured it of commercial failure. Dreyer rejected both classical continuity devices and avant-garde procedures. Unlike the American cinema, *Jeanne d'Arc* often foregrounds space at the expense of narrative logic; yet it refuses to dismiss or destroy narrative in the various manners of Vertov, Léger, and Buñuel. It neither harnesses its discontinuities to characterization and mood (in the manner of Pudovkin) nor fundamentally challenges the authority of a profilmic event (in the manner of Eisenstein). Its idiosyncrasies drove some of Dreyer's advanced contemporaries to condemn the film as "uncinematic." If cinema was an art of movement, this film's narrow conception of action seemed regressively theatrical. The *morceaux choisis* of the experimental Russian and French cinema took as their subjects violent physical activity (crowds running down steps, train crashes, the raising of Petersburg bridges, machine montages). No one before had confined a silent film principally to the dialogue exchange at a trial. If the film's narrative seemed too theatrical, then the style could seem only static. "Very interesting and beautiful," remarked Eisenstein, "but not a film. Rather a series of wonderful photographs."[25] For Paul Rotha, "The very beauty of the individual visual images destroyed the *filmic* value of the production."[26] Defenses of the film implicitly stressed the same point: *Jeanne d'Arc*'s closest affiliations were with other arts (painting, sculpture, music), not with cinema. Moreover, *Jeanne d'Arc*'s reliance upon intertitles—so central to the film's dialectic of image and language—also violated one of the sacred rules of "pure cinema": that a film must be sheerly pictorial, free of the taint of the word. In its day, the gap between narrative and style made *Jeanne d'Arc* unfashionably unfilmic, embarrassingly impure cinema.

Similarly, *Vampyr* should be located within circumstances of European film theory circa 1930. The coming of sound challenged the "pure film" aesthetic of the 1920s.

The silent film avant-garde all but vanished (*L'Age d'or* and *Zéro de conduite* may have been its last races). American continuity editing easily absorbed sound, and the increased use of camera movement helped clarify narrative space. Directors as different as Clair and Eisenstein sought to make "integral" films which would unify sound with image.

In this context, *Vampyr* becomes no less unclassifiable than *Jeanne d'Arc* had been. Generically, the film links to the German Expressionist cinema and to contemporary American horror films. Technologically, its intertitles and raspy Tobis sound system remind us that it is one of those transitional films of 1927–30. Stylistically, *Vampyr*'s offscreen sounds and complex camera movements are far more disruptive than the contemporary experiments of Mamoulian or Lubitsch. Above all, the breakdown of the relation between narrative structure and cinematic representation violated current concerns about what the sound cinema should be: for such directors as Clair, a visual narrative art appropriately decorated with sonic accents; for certain Soviet directors, an art of contrapuntal sound-image montage. *Vampyr*'s muffled whispers and sobs, its lags in synchronization, and its jerky, unmodulated sound cuts only increase the problems of narrative space and time; it seems much less "smooth" than the contemporary work of Pabst or Clair.

There is no doubt that both *Jeanne d'Arc* and *Vampyr* have lost some of their radical edge through being incorporated into the discourse of the art film. As a category, the art film differentiates itself from the standardized commercial product by representing the "personal vision" of the individual artist; the division of labor of factory filmmaking is now overseen by the filmmaker. We have already seen how Dreyer's biographical legend promoted such a view of his own work, and other factors supplement it. The independent production circumstances of both *Jeanne d'Arc* and *Vampyr,* the mutilation of both films by censorship and the vagaries of distribution, the fact that both films played "specialty theatres" abroad, the canonization of the films by ciné-clubs, the recasting of each film in so many varying versions that it is difficult to recover an original text—all these factors tended to charge *Vampyr* and especially *Jeanne d'Arc* with an aura of high art. That is why it was necessary for us to defamiliarize these classics, to suggest that any unified personal vision is subjected to great torsion by the films' overall functioning. But it is also possible to argue that in the period 1925–30, the art film had not become the routine commodity that it is today. The early art cinema was, in however limited a fashion, a progressive force, in that it permitted directors like Gance, L'Herbier, Epstein, Pabst, and Murnau to work productively within national film industries.

By the early 1950s, however, the art cinema emerged as the mode we know today. The end of World War II broke down international barriers. American film production, beset by the competition of television, tolerated and even encouraged the growth of the art cinema. In this context, *Day of Wrath* (1943) must be seen as an "art film" *avant la lettre,* a prototype. The film's hesitation between natural and supernatural explanations for Anne's behavior anticipates how the art cinema of the 1950s would use ambiguity to foreground character psychology. Yet *Day of Wrath*'s impersonal representational scheme and its retardation of rhythm set it apart from the realist and neorealist alternatives to Hollywood at the time. That today *Day of Wrath* is watchable should not make us forget, as we saw in chapter eight, that during the 1940s the film's power was discomfiting.

The very concept of art cinema comes under direct assault in Dreyer's two last films, as they strive to make themselves unconsumable on any terms. The reason for the change lies in the way that theatricalization answered to the problems set by the sound cinema. Dreyer's aesthetic saw the sound film as leading to a more theatrical sort of filmmaking. "The talking film presents itself like a theatre piece in concentrated form."[27] This was all to the good, Dreyer thought, since during the silent era he had championed a literary-theatrical aesthetic in opposition to the "pure-film" position. But after a fitful beginning, the sound film did not become as frankly theatrical as he had hoped. Swift changes of scene, the selective assimilation of Russian and French cutting devices, and borrowing of techniques from music and radio pushed the cinema toward a narrative expansiveness unlike Dreyer's notion of theatre. Moreover, Dreyer actively sought to distinguish his films from the "film-product." Hence the apparent archaism of the films' return to the theatrical unities. But that very return permitted the films to preserve the essential split of narrative logic (now, the play text) from spatio-temporal form (now, the cinematic adaptation). Once the split is formulated, cinematic representation can prolong the play's text, puncture it, fill it with empty spots, reduce it to a ground for a work upon classical figures of style and ordinary practices of viewing.

The classical Hollywood cinema requires a flow of narrative information which, while varying within certain rates, nonetheless aims for clear comprehensibility and assured consumption. It is not a question of a quantitative measure; the classical causal, spatial, and temporal systems discussed throughout this book create reading conventions based upon a continuous intelligibility. If the classical reading conventions exist at the midpoint of a continuum, we can locate other models at opposite poles. One pole would be the "information overload" cinema, which overwhelms the viewer with too many stimuli, little repetition, and excessively intricate movements and forms. Examples would be some early Griffith Biographs, the single-frame films of Robert Breer, the superimposition films of Stan Brakhage, and certain works by Tati and Rivette. Such films cannot be watched only once; they are designed to be unassimilable on a single viewing. An opposite mode might be called "minimal cinema." If the viewer responds to the information-overload film with a sense of confusion, minimal cinema elicits a sense of boredom. Judged by classical viewing procedures, the film presents too few stimuli, too much repetition, too few complexities. Minimal cinema favors stasis; instead of wanting to slow the film down, the spectator wants to speed it up. (I was once asked to project *Ordet* at a rate faster than 24 frames per second.) Examples of minimal cinema would be some films by Andy Warhol and Michael Snow. Just as definitively as its opposite, minimal cinema refuses certain formal strategies (economy, conciseness, drive) and certain viewing conventions demanded by the classical model.

The slow and sparse pace of *Ordet* and *Gertrud* works against our conventional aesthetic desires in the manner of "minimal cinema." We want a film to be fresh and clear on one viewing, yet we want to be able to return to it, "seeing more each time." (Hence criticism's familiar surface/depth metaphor.) In this respect, the minimal mode may be more radical than the overload one, since the latter seems to promise profundity, abundance, density, almost intolerable richness, while minimal cinema restrains our urge to plumb the depths: everything (such as there is) is on the surface, no more is revealed each time. Hovering on the brink of stasis, Dreyer's late films approach what Jean-François Lyotard calls "acinema"[28]; they start to refuse the very idea of *kinema, moving* pictures, *movies.* Emptiness, latent in *Day of Wrath* and *Ordet,* manifest in *Gertrud,* haunts the late films as the rejection of the need to satisfy any aesthetic canon. Although Dreyer had no overt desire to be radical, his marginal position in film production emerges through the films' refusal to be consumed either as diversion or ordinary art. To this extent, Dreyer severs his work from the art cinema of the 1960s: these films struggle with their own status as commodities.

In the light of the foregoing, Dreyer's career suggests a more appropriate analogy than the work of Brecht: that of Arnold Schoenberg. Granting major differences—that Dreyer never founded a theoretical system, that his most radical works were not of his youth, and so on—nevertheless the filmmaker resembles the composer in working against ideologically determined habits of aesthetic consumption. We need not share Theodor Adorno's loathing of mass culture to agree that Schoenberg's works, by their inhuman autonomy, oppose the ordinary pleasures of aesthetic experience. "With Schoenberg affability ceases."[29] In opposition to mass production and consumption, Schoenberg's pieces and Dreyer's films stand as negations: Schoenberg through the systematized, anti-ornamental piece, Dreyer through representational disjunctions and vacuities. Paradoxically, both men, whose works challenge ordinary comprehension, often sought to justify that challenge by reference to the authority of religion. The Judaism of such pieces as *Kol Nidre, A Survivor from Warsaw, Moses and Aaron,* and *Jacob's Ladder,* and the Christianity of *La Passion de Jeanne d'Arc, Day of Wrath,* and *Ordet* stand out as desperate unifying gestures. It is not accidental that many of the most radical modern artists (Kandinsky, Cage, Bresson) have needed religiosity to motivate formal experimentation and, indeed, perceptual displeasure. (The principal alternative, appealed to by Brecht, Godard, et al., would seem to be politics.) As in Schoenberg's works, however, the forbidding problems of Dreyer's films cannot be resolved by appeal to the holy. Finally, major unfinished works haunt the last years of both artists, and even the finished works have something inconclusive about them. Adorno points out that:

> *Musicians sense that they labor on music and not on works, even if such labor progresses only through works. The late Schoenberg composed not works but paradigms of a possible music. The idea of music itself grows all the more transparent as the works insist less and less on their appearance.*[30]

In a similar way, Dreyer's late films may be said to work

upon film as such, to exist less as summing-ups of a career than as glimpses of what cinema might become.

Dreyer's biographical legend—the stubborn individualist refusing all compromise—may have been a banner for later filmmakers, but "paradigms of a possible cinema" are what we must seek in estimating Dreyer's interest for us now. We do not lack evidence that modern filmmakers have found Dreyer's films important. Alain Robbe-Grillet and Marguerite Duras have acknowledged that their work has been affected by his.[31] Susan Sontag claims that *Brother Carl* was made under the aegis of *Ordet*, a film which "has remained all these years as a kind of ideal experience of my imagination."[32] *Anatomie d'un rapport*, according to its creator Luc Moullet, owes a good deal to *Gertrud*.[33] Michel Delahaye finds Dreyer's hand everywhere, in Hitchcock, Godard, Bresson, Mizoguchi, Straub: "No great film which does not go back to Dreyer, the crux of the modern cinema."[34]

Yet just as we had to avoid excessively simple notions of influence on Dreyer, so must we avoid the same error in considering his effects on other filmmakers. It is not a matter of finding Dreyerian devices in other filmmakers' works, for that simply pries elements loose from their functions in different films. What is at stake is not the borrowing of isolated devices but the functions themselves, the problems and processes that Dreyer's films open up. Influences, writes Tynianov, concern the shifting roles assigned to a given element.[35] Influence is seldom straight or direct; it moves crabwise, like (Shklovsky insists) the knight's move in chess. An artist rarely provides a model to be copied by another artist; an artist opens up a field of problems, launches a theoretical excursion into some possibilities. The problems opened up are not necessarily settled—neither by the first artist (Dreyer did not, as we have discussed at length, solve the problems his work raised) nor by the successors. The successors transform the problem, position the issues within a different context, even reject the initial premises. *Jeanne d'Arc* and *Vampyr* pose problems of spatial and temporal continuity; *Day of Wrath*, *Ordet*, and *Gertrud*, problems of rhythm, theatricality, sparseness, and emptiness; and all of the films, problems of the relation of narrative logic to the spatio-temporal structures of cinema. What is at stake is not direct influence ("I have no disciples") but rather ways in which modern filmmakers have transformed those issues.

It is of secondary importance, for instance, that the young Jean-Luc Godard knew and admired Dreyer's work.[36] What is crucial is that Dreyer's films pose a series of problems which Godard addressed in a film like *Vivre sa vie*. We have already seen how, in *La Passion de Jeanne d'Arc*, a concentration upon faces in dialogue transforms the space of classical editing, disturbing the unity of point of view and shot/reverse shot. In *Vivre sa vie*, Godard returns to this problem by setting Nana's face in dialogue with another. But Godard goes farther, treating each scene as a variant upon the face motif. The opening credits present Nana from three aspects—profile looking left, full face looking at the camera, profile looking right—and the first shot of the first episode concludes the circuit by presenting her from the rear. Thereafter, Godard's camera positions, tracking shots, and editing build up a set of permutations far more schematic than anything in *Jeanne d'Arc*—something much more like the rigorous *combinatoire* of *Ordet* or *Gertrud*. Conversation scenes are filmed from behind one participant (episode 7) or behind both (episode 1); from angled and straight-on subjective positions (episodes 4, 5, 10); over one participant's shoulder in long take (episode 2) or in many shots (episode 10); with a camera that arcs and pans to reframe each speaker (episode 3) or which tracks in and out on a single one (episode 6). Two sequences present virtually every aspect of Nana's face, one by montage (episode 8), the other in long spiralling tracking shots (episode 9). One episode even represents a character's point of view without identifying the character (episode 12). And not until episode 11 (Nana's conversation with Brice Parain) are the cutting and framing of orthodox shot/reverse shot used—having by this point been thoroughly defamiliarized. Thus the famous excerpt from *La Passion de Jeanne d'Arc* in *Vivre sa vie* functions not simply to compare Jeanne with Nana. Neither homage nor imitation, the sequence cites Dreyer's film as a *locus classicus* of how the face and the glance can fragment cinematic space, offering a point of departure for Godard's own stylistic work.

Godard also considered *Vivre sa vie* a "theatrical" film, in that language is central to it: "In my film one must listen to people speaking."[37] No less than discontinuity, Dreyer's strategy of theatricalization has opened up problems for subsequent filmmakers to resituate and challenge. In ways which we have seen, Dreyer's films pose the problem of how to represent theatrical texts, how a film may be a "performance." Dreyer's work has helped change the status of "filmed theatre" in the modern cinema. As Stephen Heath has suggested, classical theory defined cinema *against* theatre (film's "impression of reality," freedom of locale and time). Consequently, a film's stressing of theatrical representation can rupture many of the classical norms: "One way of restating the limits of cinema (of posing its specificity) has been precisely the *theatricalization* of film."[38] Paradoxically, by defining themselves against dominant conceptions of what cinema can or must be (Reisz and Millar disparage the modern "cinema of immobility"),[39] Dreyer's late films define the *heterogeneous* specificity of cinema, cinema as a mixed representational mode. Thus *Ordet* and *Gertrud* belong less with *The Little Foxes* or *Henry V,* say, than with Ichikawa's *An Actor's Revenge* and Oshima's *Death by Hanging.*

And, most saliently of all, with the work of Danièle Huillet and Jean-Marie Straub. As in Godard's films, overt influences are apparent. Straub considered *Othon* to present "a theatre that would be somewhere between Hitchcock and Dreyer," and in an essay he vigorously defended Dreyer's work.[40] Here again, however, the primary issue is that of surpassing, of pushing off in new directions like the knight's crooked move, of transforming the field of problems revealed in Dreyer's work. So it is important that *The Bridegroom, the Actress, and the Pimp* condenses a play text, but in an utterly un-Dreyerian way—by simply reducing it to a frantic, elliptical ten minutes; the film "stages the play by means of cinema" but by framing the stage to reveal the wings and the incomplete flats.

It is similarly important that *The Chronicle of Anna Magdalena Bach* uses tableau compositions and long takes with scant figure movement, but these Dreyerian devices appear within a context that transforms them. Straub and Huillet's film attacks narrative causality in a far more radical way than Dreyer's films do: since the device of the "chronicle" elevates sheer temporal successivity above causality, the segments are far more autonomous, the tableaux (however crammed) still more empty of narrative significance. However much *Anna Magdalena Bach* resembles *Gertrud* (made four years earlier), Huillet/Straub's treatment of musical performance criticizes and revises Dreyer's. The songs Gertrud sings in Erland's apartment and after the banquet, though performed with the stylization typical of the film, are in text and emotional expressivity highly motivated by causal factors in the narrative. But Straub and Huillet pose *in extremis* the problem of musical performance as a representational spectacle by cutting the performance free of psychological causes, by eliminating expressivity, and by not showing any listeners. In this way, the film can represent something *Gertrud* cannot: the *productive labor* of musical performance. Moreover, in *Anna Magdalena Bach,* the "sparseness" prevalent in *Ordet* and *Gertrud* is juxtaposed with its opposite, an "information overload" strategy whereby the narrator's voice-over commentary peppers us with historical data. Thus Huillet and Straub negate and surpass Dreyer's cinema of immobility by setting it within a context that includes its opposite: the static performances stand against an overwhelming saturation of narrative information. In this framework, the film's traditionally narrative scenes become clipped and fragmentary, what Straub called "points" in Stockhausen's sense of elements "existing for themselves in complete freedom and formulated individually and in considerable isolation from each other."[41] Bach is examined as a contradictory figure: the narration and dramatic scenes play between his roles as servant to the nobility and composer for the bourgeoisie, while the isolated performances stress the music itself and its "relative autonomy" with respect to the conditions of production. This account schematizes the complexity of *Anna Magdalena Bach,* but the sketch should still suggest how the film assimilates and yet de-centers Dreyerian principles by situating them within a new field of inquiry, one in which the examination of theatrical representation is carried out in an overtly political context.

The "paradigms of a possible cinema" latent in Dreyer's films depend, then, precisely on his works' tensions and disjunctions. That filmmakers like Godard and Straub/Huillet and leftist critics like those of *Cahiers du Cinema* can cite Dreyer as a model suggest that his films' contemporary significance rests upon how they work upon representation and perception. At one level, the problem is that of the narrative irresolutions of the late films. A hidden and impersonal cause is referred to an initially supernatural authority, then to a sheerly linguistic one (the book, the word) before turning back to become only *the film itself* (the film as the document of Jeanne's trial, the film as the book *Vampyr,* the film as the Dies Irae, as the Word, as the performance of Gertrud's poem-script). Representation has no ultimate meaning; there is only, arbitrarily, the text, ceaselessly and circularly self-referring. What keeps the films from hermetic isolation is the disjunction between such narrative structures and the functions of cinematic space and time—a disjunction which introduces the issue of cinema as a specific art. Adapting novels and plays fulfilled for Dreyer the purpose Walter Benjamin saw for translation: "Expressing the central reciprocal relationship between languages."[42]

It should thus not be surprising that Dreyer's films have become important for certain members of the European avant-garde. "Pure" structuralist filmmakers, totally rejecting narrative, have not found his work as exemplary as those filmmakers for whom narrative and fiction remain important problems.[43] Dreyer's work demonstrates ways in which narrative structure can be challenged through perceptual and representational processes specific to cinema. The difficulties of the tableau/face dialectic, of the discontinuities of *Jeanne d'Arc* and *Vampyr,* of theatricalization in *Day of Wrath, Ordet* and *Gertrud,* all show how cinema can construct its own systems against narrative coherence and spectatorial pleasure. Dreyer's usefulness is that of a director who posed problems which contemporary filmmakers must address, but in other terms than his own.

It would be specious to reduce Dreyer to a failed avant-gardist, as if he couldn't quite become Straub or as if *Gertrud* were merely a trial run for *India Song*. Dreyer's work has its own specific aesthetic interest. Every artist's work contains something of the old and of the new, but seldom in such tense conflict as in Dreyer's films: anachronistic and modern, challenging in their very archaism ("the old-fashioned [rhythm]," he remarked, "can under certain circumstances be the most modern"),[44] embedded in psychological and theological assumptions, but at the same time tracing the possibility of alternatives and oppositions. Here are films whose narrative determinations collide with radical stylistic experimentation, films which exhibit the most traditional regularity only to raise difficulties of a theoretical nature. The autonomy which the works seek springs from Dreyer's marginal production position and conservative aesthetic, but in their period that position and that aesthetic also helped break the films from dominant cinematic practice.

Dreyer's films contest simple ideological transmission in ways already proposed, yet the same films cannot be seen as freed from other ideological determinations. Formal devices do not make a text politically radical. Dreyer's works remain torn by inner conflicts. Like Schoenberg in Adorno's account, like Ozu, Mizoguchi, Tati, and Bresson, Dreyer's historical importance lies in his contradictory in-betweenness. His fascination for us today is that of a director who, in the ways we have analyzed, opens up a problematic distance between dominant cinematic practice and another cinema: a cinema which demands fresh perceptual activities, a cinema which *refuses to be cinema* as normally conceived and consumed. Semicomprehensible, the films of Carl-Theodor Dreyer exist on the margin of unity, meaning, pleasure. Beyond lies the cinema of unintelligibility.

Biographical Filmography

Dreyer's origins are as obscure as many of his films. We know that he was born in Copenhagen on 3 February 1889, but beyond that we must rely upon his own accounts of his youth, transmitted chiefly through his friend and biographer Ebbe Neergaard. Dreyer's mother was Swedish; his father's identity and background are unknown. Dreyer claimed at least once that he was illegitimate.[1] His mother died soon after his birth. We do not even know Dreyer's original name, since he took the name of the Danish family who adopted him. He told Neergaard that this family "consistently let me know that I had to be very grateful for the food I got and I really had no claim on anything because my mother had cheated her way out of paying for me by going off and dying. . . ."[2]

Dreyer as a young man.

According to Dreyer, the family wanted him to repay them by becoming a cafe pianist, but he had no musical talent. A series of office jobs in municipal administration, in a power company, and in a telegraph company—the latter described in the anecdote cited on p. 9—led him to try something different.

That was journalism. Between 1909 and 1912, Dreyer did aviation and nautical reporting for *Berlingske Tidende* and *Riget,* two Copenhagen newspapers. By July 1912, he was working for the daily *Ekstrabladet. Ekstrabladet,* popular for its witty writing in the continental fashion, relied strongly upon feature stories, and in October 1912, Dreyer began a series of articles called *Vor Tids Helt (Heroes of Our Time).* These were feuilletons profiling Copenhagen celebrities. Under the pseudonym "Tommen" ("Inch"), Dreyer

Dreyer as a reporter.

included in his roster of heroes such film figures as Ole Olsen, Asta Nielsen, and many Nordisk directors. Today, the essays seem more mocking than clever.

Heroes of Our Time put Dreyer in touch with the world of film and theatre. He later recalled that one day a film producer complained to him that he had a script problem: he had just locked his heroine in a tower but didn't know how to get a message to her. When Dreyer suggested carrier pigeons, the producer proposed that he write a film.[3] At this time, it was not unusual for journalists to enter the film business: the successful director A. W. Sandberg had been a reporter for six years before Nordisk hired him in 1913. Between 1912 and 1913, Dreyer wrote three scripts for the firm of Skandinavisk-Russiske Handelshus. He then joined Nordisk Films Kompagni, first part-time in 1913, and later full-time in 1915. In all, at least twenty-three films of the period credit Dreyer as scriptwriter.

Bryggerens Datter (The Brewer's Daughter). 1912. Director: Rasmus Otteson. Story/script: Dreyer and Viggo Cavling. Photography: Adam Johansen. Production: Det Skandinaviske Handelshus. First shown: 9 August 1912. Players: Olaf Fønss, Emilie Sannom, Richard Jensen.

Ballonexplosionen (The Balloon Explosion). 1913. Director: Richard Jensen. Story/script: Dreyer. Production: Skandinavisk-Russiske Handelshus. First shown: 6 March 1913. Players: Richard Jensen, Emilie Sannom, Valdemar Møller. Dreyer is said to have played the role of a balloon captain in this film.

Krigskorrespondenten (The War Correspondent). 1913. Director: Vilhelm Gluckstadt. Story/script: Dreyer. Photography: Alfred Lind, Adam Johansen. Production: Skandinavisk-Russiske Handelshus. First shown: 27 April 1913. Players: Emanuel Gregers, Richard Jensen, Emilie Sannom.

Hans og Grethe (Hans and Grethe). 1913. Director: Sofus Wolder. Story/script: Dreyer. Photography: Axel Graatkjær, Rasmussen. Production: Nordisk Films Kompagni. First shown: 1913. Players: Maja Bjerre-Lind, Gerd Egede Nissen, Svend Bille.

Elskovs Opfindsemhed (Inventive Love). 1913. Director: Sofus Wolder. Story/script: Dreyer. Production: Nordisk Films Kompagni. First shown: 7 September 1913. Players: Ellen Aggerholm et al.

Chatollets Hemmelighed; eller Det gamle chatol (The Secret of the Writing Desk; or, The Old Writing Desk). 1913. Director: Hjalmar Davidsen. Story/script: Dreyer. Photography: L. Larsen. Production: Nordisk Films Kompagni. First shown: 15 September 1913. Players: Aage Fønss, Lau Lauritzen, Ella Sprange.

Ned Med Vabnene (Surrender Arms). 1914. Director: Holger-Madsen. Script: Dreyer. Based on the novel *Die Waffen nieder* by Bertha von Suttner. Photography: Marius Clausen. Production: Nordisk Films Kompagni. First shown: 18 September 1915. Players: Olaf Fønss, Augusta Blad, Johanne Fritz-Petersen.

Juvelerernes Skræk; eller Skelethanden; eller Skelethander sidste bedrift (The Jeweller's Terror; or, The Skeleton's Hand; or, The Last Adventure of the Skeleton's Hand). 1915. Director: Alex Christian. Story/script: Dreyer. Photography: C. Fischer. Production: Nordisk Films Kompagni. First shown: 20 December 1915. Players: Aage Hertel, Alf Blütecher, Frederik Jacobsen.

Penge (Money). 1914. Director: Karl Mantzius. Script: Dreyer. Based on the novel *L'Argent* by Emile Zola. Production: Nordisk Films Kompagni. First shown: 1 January 1916. Players: Karl Mantzius, R. Schyberg, Svend Aggerholm.

Den Hvide Djævel; eller Djævelens protege (The White Devil; or, The Devil's Protegé). 1915. Director: Holger-Madsen. Script: Dreyer. Based on the novel *Esther* by Honoré de Balzac. Photography: M. Clausen. Production: Nordisk Films Kompagni. First shown: 25 January 1916. Players: Carlo Wieth, Gerd Egede-Nissen, Svend Kornbech.

Den Skonne Evelyn (Evelyn the Beautiful). 1915. Director: A. W. Sandberg. Script: Dreyer. Based on an idea by Viggo Cavling. Photography: Olsen. Production: Nordisk Films Kompagni. First shown: 23 February 1916. Players: Rita Sacchetto, Henry Seemann, A. Tronier-Funder.

Rovedderkoppen; eller Den røde enke (The Robber Spider; or, The White Widow). 1915. Director: August Blom. Script: Dreyer. Based on an idea by Sven Elvestad. Production: Nordisk Films Kompagni. First shown: 8 May 1916. Players: Rita Sacchetto, Anton de Verdier, Hans Richter.

En Forbryders Liv og Levned; eller En Forbruyders Memoirer (The Life and Times of a Criminal; or, The Memoirs of a Criminal). 1915. Director: Alex Christian. Script:

Dreyer. Based on an idea by Sven Elvestad. Photography: C. Fischer. Production: Nordisk Films Kompagni. First shown: 7 August 1916. Players: Ingeborg Skov, Lauritz Olsen, Frederik Jacobsen.

Guldets Gift; eller Lerhjertet (The Poison of Gold; or, The Clay Heart). 1915. Director: Holger-Madsen. Script: Dreyer. Based on the novel by Carl Gandrup. Photography: Marius Clausen. Production: Nordisk Films Kompagni. First shown: 16 August 1916. Players: Carlo Wieth, Agnete von Prangen, Anton de Verdier, Peter Fjelstrup, Frederik Jacobsen.

Pavilionens Hemmelighed (The Secret of the Pavilion). 1914. Director: Karl Mantzius. Script: Dreyer. Based on the novel by Viggo Cavling. Photography: L. Larsen. Production: Nordisk Films Kompagni. First shown: 8 September 1916. Players: Karl Mantzius, Vita Blichfeldt, Svend Aggerholm.

Den Mystiske Selskabsdame; eller Legationens Gidsel (The Mysterious Lady's Companion; or, The Hostage of the Embassy). 1916. Director: August Blom. Script: Dreyer. Based on the novel by Sven Elvestad. Photography: J. Petersen. Production: Nordisk Films Kompagni. First shown: 15 January 1917. Players: Peter Nielsen, Magda Vang, Alf Blütecher, Vibeke Krøyer.

Hans Rigtige Kone (His Real Wife). 1916. Director: Holger-Madsen. Story/script. Dreyer. Photography: Marius Clausen. Production: Nordisk Films Kompagni. First shown: 23 May 1917. Players: Johanne Fritz-Petersen, Henry Seemann, Bertel Krause.

Fange Nr. 113 (Prisoner No. 113). 1916. Director: Holger-Madsen. Script: Dreyer. Based on the novel by Carl Muusmann. Photography: Marius Clausen. Production: Nordisk Films Kompagni. First shown: 25 June 1917. Players: Alma Hinding, Gudrun Bruun, Svend Melsing, Peter Fjelstrup, Erik Holberg, Peter Nielsen.

Lydia. 1916. Director: Holger-Madsen. Script: Dreyer. Based on a story by Viggo Cavling. Photography: Marius Clausen. Production: Nordisk Films Kompagni. First shown: 9 April 1918. Players: Valdemar Psilander, Ebba Thomsen, Zanny Petersen, Robert Schmidt, Philip Bech, Charles Wilken.

Glædens Dag; eller Miskendt. (Day of Joy; or, Neglected). 1916. Director: Alex Christian. Story/script: Dreyer. Photography: H. F. Rimmen. Production: Nordisk Films Kompagni. First shown: 3 June 1918. Players: Alma Hinding, Ellen Rassow, Anton de Verdier, Philip Bech, Carl Lauritzen, Birga von Cotta Schønberg.

Gillekop. 1916. Director: August Blom. Script: Dreyer. Based on the novel by Harald Tandrup. Photography: Johan Ankerstjerne. Production: Nordisk Films Kompagni. First shown: 9 May 1919. Players: Johanne Fritz-Petersen, Charles Wilken, Gunnar Sommerfeldt, Frederik Jacobsen, Bertel Krause.

Hotel Paradis (Hotel Paradiso). 1917. Director: Robert Dinesen. Script: Dreyer. Based on the novel by Einar Rousthøj. Photography: Sofus Wangøe. Production: Nordisk Films Kompagni. First shown: 10 October 1917. Players: Ingeborg Spangsfeldt, Ebba Thomsen, Peter Fjelstrup, Gunnar Sommerfeldt, Emma Wiehe, Kai Lind, Oda Larsen.

Grevindens Ære (The Countess's Honor). 1918. Director: August Blom. Script: Dreyer. Based on the novel *Kniplinger* by Paul Lindau. Photography: L. Larsen. Production: Nordisk Films Kompagni. First shown: 14 November 1919. Players: Agnes Rehni, Aage Fønss, Gudrun Houlberg, Alf Blütecher.

The following scripts were prepared by Dreyer and sold to Nordisk, but if they were filmed, they appeared under other titles.

De falske fingre (The False Fingers). 1915.
Greven af Oslo (The Count of Oslo). 1915.
Manden i manen (The Man in the Moon). 1915.
Eventyrskibet (Adventure Ship). 1915.
Den døde passager (The Dead Passenger). 1915.
Den stjalne hus (The Stolen House). 1915.
De hemmelighedsfulde gaver (The Secret Gifts). 1915.
Strandrøverne i Grimby eller Strandrøverne i St. Marco (The Strand Robbers of Grimsby; or, The Strand Robbers of St. Marco). 1915.
Rotterne (The Rats). 1915.
Lovens arm (The Arm of the Law). 1916.
Den gylde pest (The Golden Plague). 1916.
Stjalen lykke (Stolen Happiness). 1916.
Pengene eller livet (The Money or the Life). 1916.
The Financier. 1916.
Sindssyg eller ikke (Insane or Not). 1916.
Dødedanseren (Dance of Death).
Manden der lagde byen øde (The Man Who Destroyed a Town).

Of these films, only two—*Ned Med Vaabnene* and *Pavillons Hemmelighed*—have been found.

At Nordisk, Dreyer's tasks were to scout for literary material, to adapt the material to scripts, to write intertitles, and to work with editors in cutting the finished film. In 1911 he married; by 1917 he had a daughter and was living in Fredericks VI Alle, a comfortable middle-class area popular with actors. Eager to direct, he asked the producer Frost: "I hope that you and Nordisk Films Co. will try to exploit this ability and give me one of the projects I am looking for. If you do that, you won't regret it."[4] In 1918 Nordisk gave him a chance to film a novel he had bought as literary consultant.

Præsidenten (The President). 1918.

SCRIPT: Dreyer. Based on the novel by Karl Emil Franzos. *PHOTOGRAPHY:* Hans Vaagø. *ART DIRECTION:* Jens G. Lind (uncredited) and Dreyer. *PRODUCTION:* Nordisk Films Kompagni. *FIRST SHOWN:* 1 February 1919 (Sweden).

Karl Victor v. Sendigen	Halvard Hoff
his father	Elith Pio
his grandfather	Carl Meyer
Victorine Lippert, his daughter	Olga Raphael-Linden
Hermine Lippert, Victorine's mother	Betty Kirkebye
lawyer George Berger	Axel Richard Christensen
the prosecutor	Peter Nielsen
Franz	Hallander Hellemann
Brigitta	Fanny Petersen
Maika	Jacoba Jessen
Victorine's fiancé	Jon Iversen
Vice-President Werner	Axel Madsen

By the time that Dreyer made *The President,* he had seen *The Birth of a Nation* (it played in Denmark in March of 1918) and perhaps also *Intolerance* (which had been shown privately in January of the same year). Jean Mitry has suggested the influence of Sjöström's *Dodkyssen (Kiss of Death,* 1916), and Georges Sadoul that of the German avant-garde theatre.[5] But *The President* already shows a distinctive touch; it is certainly one of the handsomest films of the silent era. Critics complained of the performances—"The acting is undeniably not completely modern"—and years later Dreyer agreed: "I let the actors do what they liked. Later I saw my mistakes on the screen. That's how one learns to direct."[6] Dreyer was particularly proud of the decor. "I worked toward a simplification of the sets. I already had at that time a theory that if you walk into a man's room you get an impression of his personality and character just by looking at the room. Therefore, the President's room was built up from very calm walls and very few furnishings."[7]

Although completed in 1918, the film was first released in Sweden in the following year; not until 9 February 1920 did it premiere in Copenhagen. Why Nordisk held back the Danish release is unclear, but the delay had precedent: in 1920 Nordisk released seven films made in 1918, five films made in 1917, five films made in 1916, and one film made in 1915! This unusual procedure may be explained by the declining fortunes of the firm after 1917.

Blade af Satans Bog (Leaves from Satan's Book). 1919.

SCRIPT: Edgar Høyer, Dreyer. Based on the novel *Sorrows of Satan* by Marie Corelli. *PHOTOGRAPHY:* George Schnéevoigt. *ART DIRECTION:* Dreyer, Axel Bruun, Jens G. Lind. *PRODUCTION:* Nordisk Films Kompagni. *FIRST SHOWN:* 17 November 1920 (Oslo, Victoria-Theatre).

Satan	Helge Nissen
Jesus	Halvard Hoff
Judas	Jacob Texière
John	Erling Hansson
artist	Hermansen
carpenter	Weigel
bookbinder	Gylche
carpenter	Wilhelm Jensen
Don Gomez	Hallander Hellemen
Isabella	Ebon Strandin
Don Fernandez	Johannes Meyer
majordomo	Nalle Halden
Count Manuel	Hugo Bruun
Marie Antoinette	Tenna Kraft
Countess of Chambord	Emma Wiehe
Genevieve	Jeanne Tramcourt
Joseph	Elith Pio
Count de Chambord	Viggo Wiehe
people's commissar	Emil Helsengreen
Michonnet	Sven Scholander
Père Pitou	Viggo Lindstrøm
Fouquier-Tinville	Vilhelm Petersen
Paavo	Carlo Wieth
Siri	Clara Pontoppidan
Rautaniemi	Carl Hillebrandt
Naimi	Karina Bell
Corporal Matti	Christian Nielsen

Long before *The President* appeared, Dreyer had already begun work on a much larger film, *Leaves from Satan's Book.* The project was approved in the spring of 1918, even before Dreyer had filmed *The President.* In the fall, two scripts were written simultaneously, one by Dreyer, the other by Edgar Høyer. (Although the credits claim that the script was adapted from a Marie Corelli novel, there is no evidence of this in the film.) In December 1918 disputes arose between Dreyer and Managing Director Stæhr, whom Dreyer accused of trying to sabotage *Leaves.* Dreyer and Høyer agreed upon a script in early 1919. In March there followed the quarrels between Dreyer and Nordisk discussed on pp. 15–16. Forced to adhere to Nordisk's budget, Dreyer went ahead with the filming. Dreyer recalled that he shot the Finnish episode first and screened it for the Nordisk administration. Olsen approved of what he saw and told Dreyer to go ahead with the film.[8] *Leaves* was finished in 1919.

Like *The President, Leaves* was first released outside Denmark, and Dreyer was aghast to learn that it had been cut and accelerated without his permission (see pp. 16). At the Danish premiere (24 January 1921), Nordisk officials stated frankly that *Leaves* was an attempt to recover some of the firm's glory. The film was treated as primarily Edgar Høyer's work. A successful playwright, Høyer disparaged Dreyer for cutting his script, for lengthening the Christ episode, and for not making enough use of Tenna Kraft whom Høyer had gone to pains to obtain for the role of Marie Antoinette.[9] But in the program accompanying the premiere, Dreyer was acclaimed as the first director to compete with the Americans' and Swedes' refined delineation of character and image composition:

> *So far we in this country have not made any notable attempt to compete in this new field, because we have not had the director whose nature made it possible to steep himself in the individual shot and make it a complete story in itself. We were missing the man who strings pearls, stringing shot after shot in the knowledge that even if the string should break a thousand details would remain as small masterpieces by themselves. Carl Th. Dreyer is the first Danish director for whom the method is the natural one.*[10]

Leaves stirred up religious and political controversy. Some church groups attacked the depiction of Christ as blasphemous.[11] A Socialist newspaper called *Leaves* "one big scream against the hated Reds" and compared it unfavorably with *Intolerance:* "The American capitalist film company can afford to be open-minded, while the Danish film, as often before, sets a record for spiritual narrow-mindedness and poisonous hatred for the workers."[12]

Prästänkan (The Parson's Widow; The Fourth Marriage of Dame Margaret). 1920.

SCRIPT: Dreyer. Based on a short story by Kristofer Janson. *PHOTOGRAPHY:* George Schnéevoigt. *PRODUCTION:* Svensk Filmindustri, Stockholm *FIRST SHOWN:* 4 October 1920 (Stockholm, Rialto Theatre). Shown in the United States as *The Witch Woman.*

Margarete Pedersdotter	Hildur Carlberg
Söfren	Einar Rød
Mari	Greta Almroth
the aspiring pastors	Olav Aukrust and Kurt Welin
Gunvor	Mathilde Nielsen
the gardener	Emil Helsengree
the beadle	Lorentz Thyholt

Nordisk was not prospering. In 1920 its mainstay director, Lau Lauritzen, left. As a result, Nordisk released only eight films that year. Dreyer may well have believed he would have better luck working for Svensk Filmindustri. In 1920 Svensk bought Nordisk's Hellerup studio and hired Christensen to make *Hexen* there; the firm also sent Dreyer to Sweden to shoot *The Parson's Widow* that summer. According to Dreyer, Hildur Carlberg, the actress playing Dame Margaret, was mortally ill during the filming and died soon afterward.[13] Neither Dreyer nor Christensen stayed on with Svensk, most probably because the firm cut production sharply in 1921. Both directors went to Berlin, Christensen to Pommer's Decla-Bioskop and Dreyer to the small firm Primusfilm.

Die Gezeichneten (The Stigmatized One. Love One Another). 1921.

SCRIPT: Dreyer. Based on the novel by Aage Madelung. *PHOTOGRAPHY:* Friedrich Weinmann. *ART DIRECTOR:* Jens G. Lind. *HISTORICAL ADVISERS:* Viktor Aden, Prof. Krol. *PRODUCER:* Otto Schmidt. *PRODUCTION:* Primusfilm, Berlin. *FIRST SHOWN:* 7 February 1922 (Copenhagen, Paladsteatret).

Hanna-Liebe	Polina Pickowska
Jakov Segal	Vladimir Gajdarov

Aleksander "Sascha" Sokolov	Torleif Reiss
Fedja	Richard Boleslawski
the merchant Suckoswerski	Duwan
Klimov, alias Rylovitch, alias Father Roman	Johannes Meyer
Hanna's mother	Adele Reuter-Eichberg
	Emmy Wyde, Friedrich Kühne, Hugo Döblin

For a time after he left Nordisk, Dreyer seems to have kept open the possibility that he might return. He corresponded with the producer Frost until at least 1922, and his permanent address remained a Copenhagen one. His next project, however, seems to mark the break with Nordisk. In the early 1920s, Berlin housed many Russian emigrés—Kandinsky, Horowitz, Pavlova, Piatagorsky, Gabo, Lissitzky, Chagall, Shklovsky, Pasternak, Nabokov. Among these were many of Stanislavsky's troupe, the most famous member of which was Richard Boleslawski. With these actors, some performers from Max Reinhardt's troupe, and some Scandinavian actors (Johannes Meyer, Thorleif Reiss), Dreyer filmed an adaptation of the Dane Aage Madelung's novel *Love One Another.* Planned in early 1921, the film was shot in the summer of the same year. As usual, Dreyer studied hundreds of prints and photographs to get ideas for sets, and much of the decor came from the emigrés' own belongings. *The Stigmatized Ones* was the first of Dreyer's films to attract attention in France, called by Riccioto Canudo "one of those polyrhythmic frescos that the artisans of the screen must soon create."[14]

Der Var Engang (Once upon a Time). 1922.

SCRIPT: Dreyer, Palle Rosenkrantz. Based on the play by Holger Drachmann. *PHOTOGRAPHY:* George Schnéevoight. *ART DIRECTOR:* Jens G. Lind. *EDITORS:* Dreyer, Edla Hansen. *PRODUCTION:* Sophus Madsen, Copenhagen. *FIRST SHOWN:* 3 October 1922 (Copenhagen, Paladstreatret).

the princess of Illyria	Clara Pontoppidan
the prince of Denmark	Svend Methling
the king of Illyria	Peter Jerndorff
Kaspar Roghat	Hakon Ahnfelt-Rønne
	Karen Poulsen, Gerda Madsen, Valdemar Schioler-Linck, Torben Meyer, Musse Scheel, Viggo Wiehe, Mohamed Archer, Henry Larsson, Lili Kristiansson, Zun Zimmermann, Bodil Faber, Karen Thalbitzer, Emilie Walbom, Lars Madsen, Wilhelmine Henriksen, Frederik Leth

In 1922 Dreyer returned to Denmark to film *Once upon a Time* for the theatre owner Sophus Madsen. The original operetta, still a Danish sentimental favorite, had been adapted by Nordisk as early as 1907. Since most of the actors came from the theatre, Madsen rented a Hellerup studio and Dreyer shot the film during the performers' summer vacations. As in *Leaves,* Dreyer worked with Clara Weith Pontoppidan, one of the most popular Danish stars. During the shooting, she called the director "Wonderful. . . . Dreyer is so certain in his style."[15] To economize, Dreyer planned what he called a "Chinese box" system for shooting the sets: the most spacious set would be built, then within that a smaller one, then a smaller one within that, and so on to the smallest set standing at the center of the nested sets. Dreyer hoped to shoot in phases, working his way from the most intimate sets to the largest. Unfortunately, the actor Jerndorff's commitments changed the shooting schedule and the plan was abandoned.[16]

Once upon a Time was lost until 1964, when a Nordisk employee found portions of it in a film vault. What remains are the first half, more or less intact, and unedited retakes from the final scene.

Michael. 1924.

SCRIPT: Dreyer, Thea von Harbou. Based on the novel by Herman Bang. *PHOTOGRAPHY:* Karl Freund (interiors), Rudolph Maté (some exteriors). *ART DIRECTOR:* Hugo Häring. *MUSIC:* Hans Joseph Vieth. *PRODUCER:* Erich Pommer. *PRODUCTION:* Decla-Bioskop for Ufa, Berlin. *FIRST SHOWN:* 26 September 1924 (Berlin). Shown in the United States as *Chained.*

Claude Zoret	Benjamin Christensen
Michael	Walter Slezak
the Princess Zamikoff	Nora Gregor
Switt	Robert Garrison
Alice Adelsskjold	Grete Mosheim
Duc de Monthieu	Dider Aslan
Leblanc, the art dealer	Karl Freund
	Mady Christians, Alexander Murski

Like Christensen before him, Dreyer went to Ufa to work for Erich Pommer. Pommer is said to have suggested *Michael,* and Dreyer claims not to have recalled that Stiller had already adapted Bang's novel in 1916.[17] *Michael* was shot in Ufa's Tempelhof studio, and Dreyer and the set designer dressed the sets from items discovered in Berlin shops. Dreyer claimed to have enjoyed working with Pommer (see pp. 17–18), despite accounts of fights with Christensen. Because Freund was often occupied with planning Murnau's *Der letze Mann,* Dreyer relied considerably upon the assistant cameraman Rudolf Maté.

Letters indicate that Dreyer negotiated with Nordisk to buy the rights to Sophus Michaelis' play *Revolutionsbryllup (Revolutionary Wedding)* for him to film at Ufa, with Nora Gregor to star.[18] When *Michael* was finished, however, Pommer changed the film's ending without Dreyer's consent. The nature of the changes remains obscure, but Dreyer left Berlin after less than a year's stay.

Du Skal Ære Din Hustru (Thou Shalt Honor Thy Wife; The Master of the House). 1925.

SCRIPT: Dreyer, Svend Rindom. Based on the play *Tyrannens Fald* by Svend Rindom. *PHOTOGRAPHY:* George Schnéevoigt. *ART DIRECTOR:* Dreyer. *PRODUCTION:* Palladium Film. *FIRST SHOWN:* 5 October 1925 (Copenhagen, Paladsteatret).

Victor Frandsen	Johannes Meyer
Ida	Astrid Holm
Karen	Karin Nellemose
Mads, the nanny	Mathilde Nielsen
the boys	Aage Hoffman and Byril Harvig
Ida's mother	Clara Schønfeld
the washerwoman	Petrine Sonne
the doctor	Johannes Nielsen

By 1924 Nordisk was feeble and only Palladium Films offered a Danish director any opportunities. Palladium had built its success on Lau Lauritzen's popular comedies featuring "Long and Short," a Danish Laurel and Hardy. *Thou Shalt Honor Thy Wife,* then, was an isolated opportunity for Dreyer. A set of a two-room apartment was built in the studio—complete, Neergaard reports, with functioning gas, water, and electricity.[19] It was this film that se-

Dreyer ca. 1924–1925, at the time of *Master of the House.*

cured Dreyer a reputation throughout Europe, especially in France. The film played at forty-one theatres in Paris alone, and a French film magazine named it one of the best films of the year.[20] *Thou Shalt Honor Thy Wife* is also the only Dreyer film to be remade, as *Tyrannens Fald* (1942), with Karin Nellemose (the daughter in Dreyer's version) playing the mother, and with Mathilde Nielsen again taking the role of Mads.

Glomdalsbruden (The Bride of Glomdal). 1925.

SCRIPT: Dreyer. Based on two stories, *Glomdalsbruden* and *Eline Vangel,* by Jacob Breda Bull. *PHOTOGRAPHY:* Einar Olsen. *ART DIRECTOR:* Dreyer. *PRODUCTION:* Victoria-Film, Oslo. *FIRST SHOWN:* 1 January 1926 (Oslo, Admiral-Palads and Carla Johan-Teatret).

Ole Glomgaarden	Stub Wiberg
Berit, his daughter	Tove Tellback
Jacob Braaten	Harald Stormoen
Tore, his son	Einar Sissener
Gjermund Haugsett	Einar Tveito
the pastor	Rasmus Rasmussen
the pastor's wife	Sofi Reimers
Kari, Bratten's wife	Alfhild Stormoen
Berger Haugsett	Oscar Larsen

Like *Michael, The Bride of Glomdal* harks back to Stiller—in this case, his film *Johan* (1921). Dreyer shot the film in Norway, but the project was co-financed by Svensk Filmindustri. Dreyer told Neergard that he had to work much faster than usual: the actors were on summer vacation from theatre work and there was no time to write a detailed script, so he directed from an outline and the actors improvised day by day.[21]

La Passion de Jeanne d'Arc.1927.

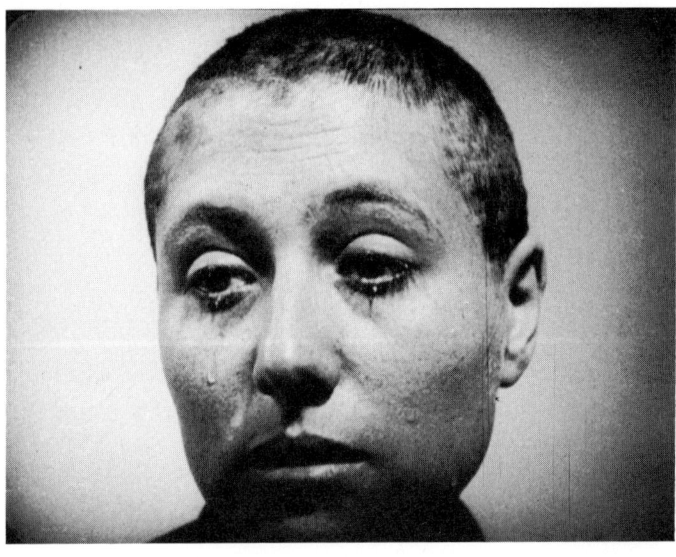

SCRIPT: Dreyer, Joseph Delteil. Based on the original records of the trial. *PHOTOGRAPHY:* Rudolph Maté. *ART DIRECTOR:* Hermann Warm, Jean Hugo. *COSTUMES:* Valentine Hugo. *MUSIC:* Victor Alix, Léo Pouget. *HISTORICAL ADVISER:* Pierre Champion. *PRODUCTION:* Société Générale de Films, Paris. *FIRST SHOWN:* 21 April 1928 (Copenhagen, Paladsteatret).

Jeanne d'Arc	Renée Falconetti
Pierre Cauchon	Eugène Silvain
Nicholas Loyseleur	Maurice Schutz
Jean Lemaître	Michel Simon
Massieu	Antonin Artaud
Jean Beaupère	Ravet
Jean d'Estivet	André Berley
Guillaume Evrand	Jean d'Yd
other judges	André Lurville, Jacques Arna, Alexandre Mihalesco, R. Narlay, Henri Maillard, Jean Aymé, Léon Larive, Henri Gautier, and Paul Jorge

"With the exception of the Société Générale de Films," wrote Paul Rotha in 1930, "there exists no producing company in France which recognizes the artist-mind of the French director."[22] It was this firm which, in the spring of 1926, signed Dreyer to a contract. By October, Jeanne d'Arc was settled as the subject of his first film for the Société. Joseph Delteil had already published a life of Jeanne in 1925, and he wrote a continuity for the film between December 1926 and January 1927; although Dreyer rejected it, Delteil went on to publish his work as *La Passion de Jeanne d'Arc* (1927). Dreyer turned instead to Pierre Champion's 1921 edition of the trial text, and Champion became the historical consultant for the film.[23]

The circumstances of the film's production are quite well known. (See, for a detailed account, my *Filmguide to "La Passion de Jeanne d'Arc."*) Hermann Warm and Jean Hugo spent four months designing the sets. Warm claimed the inspiration of medieval miniatures: "In a Parisian library I found the story of Jeanne d'Arc illustrated by a miniature-painter from the Middle Ages. The simple reproduction of the buildings, landscapes and the people, the naive lines and the incorrect perspective provided ideas for the film's sets."[24] The sets also reflect the style of Jean Hugo's stage designs of the 1920s, which were done in a *peintures illustrateurs* mode based on bare backgrounds, arabesque lines, and simple costumes.

The film's interiors were shot in Billancourt, in an empty Renault assembly shop which Dreyer rented. Sets for rooms were built with walls that could slide away on overhead tracks. Exterior shooting took place in a southern suburb of Paris, near Petit Clamart. The set of Rouen castle was a huge construction of walls, towers, houses, drawbridge, and church. The buildings functioned as changing rooms, toilets, and storage space. Because filming lasted over eight months, the exterior sets were made of cement rather than plaster. To make the walls appear white on panchromatic film stock, the interior sets were tinted yellow, the exteriors pink. Actors appeared without make-up, and panchromatic film registered their facial details with remarkable clarity. Demanding so many low-angle camera positions earned Dreyer the nickname, "Carl Gruyère, l'homme qui fait des trous."[25]

A set design by Hermann Warm.

A set design by Jean Hugo.

Dreyer directing Jeanne d'Arc.

Most of the film's players were experienced stage actors, but Dreyer also cast major parts on facial qualities alone (e.g., Warwick, who was played by a Russian café-keeper). Dreyer demanded the most of Falconetti; at the time, Warm recalls, people joked that Jeanne was murdered twice, the second time by a Dane, a German, and a Hungarian (Maté).[26] Dreyer is said to have relied upon showing Falconetti the rushes of the previous day's work to help her develop her performance. What struck contemporary observers was, first of all, the tactic of shooting in chronological order, and secondly the tension that ruled the set. We often forget how noisy most silent-film production was, with mood music, camera hum, and the director's commands barked through a megaphone. Contemporary

Exterior set from Jeanne d'Arc.

observers were impressed by the stillness on Dreyer's set:

> *Dreyer's method for making the actor perform is entirely personal and singularly tiring. Once the director has chosen the actor (already evidence that in his opinion the actor is good) he no longer tells the actor what he wants from him and he leaves him all alone, in absolute silence, surrounded by those cruel lights which seem to probe to his very heart. And soon, during this contemplation, the nervous tension and the sharpened sensitivity produce the miracle: the actor has seized the personality of the character, he incarnates it. . . .*[27]

The film had an unusually long shooting schedule. Falconetti was announced for the starring role in March of 1927. Filming began in May, and by mid-July the crew had reached the torture-chamber scenes. The Rouen scenes were shot between late August and November. By the end of 1927, at a cost claimed to be nine million francs, filming was completed.[28] Ironically, while Dreyer was filming *La Passion de Jeanne d'Arc,* Marco de Gastyne was making *La Merveilleuse vie de Jeanne d'Arc,* a work emphasizing Jeanne's military exploits. The two productions led to considerable speculation as to how long film companies could milk the Jeanne story, as the accompanying cartoon from *La Critique cinématographique* indicates.

Marivaux and played almost a month there. A fuller version was released in June 1929, causing Artaud to remark: "I am only glad that the screening of the complete version has changed the general opinion of this overwhelming film."[33]

To trace the fortunes of *Jeanne d'Arc* after filming would require an archaeological expedition. The film survives in several different versions, and no one contains all the footage of the others. What led to this curious state of affairs? During his lifetime, Dreyer offered two explanations.

The Copenhagen premiere assembled an upper-class audience in the Paladsteatret, the country's most luxurious theatre. After the screening had finished, Falconetti arose and asked the audience to give thanks to Dreyer, but out of shyness he would not come forward.[29] Later, the Paladsteatret manager was challenged by A. C. Meyer, a prominent Danish socialist, to open the theatre to the city's workers for their response. On 26 April, this was done, and reportedly over two thousand workers saw the film and were asked to write their opinions on cards. Wrote one: "There are women today who are as tortured morally by Society as was Jeanne d'Arc."[30]

The Paris premiere of the film had more difficulties. There was a closed press screening on 26 June, but the film did not open immediately.[31] Contemporary accounts blame the pressures of the archbishop of Paris.[32] The film finally premiered on 25 October 1928 at the newly renovated Salle

1. After Dreyer shot the film, the producers refused to let him cut it. The editing was done without his consent, and he saw the film for the first time at its Copenhagen premiere. In this account, *Jeanne d'Arc* becomes another *Greed.* This explanation loses plausibility in the light of other claims by Dreyer that he edited the film and convinced the producers not to recut it.[34]
2. Dreyer cut the original negative, which was sent to Ufa for German distribution in 1928 or 1929. This negative was incinerated in a laboratory fire. In Paris, Dreyer patched together a new *Jeanne d'Arc* from out-takes. It is this version which has survived.[35] This explanation is plausible, but does not account for the discrepancies between versions.

A third explanation has been advanced by Lo Duca: A fire in Epinay in 1935 burned the print *cut by the Parisian censors.* An *original* negative still survived, and it was this which was rediscovered in 1952. This became the sonorized version currently in distribution.[36] Yet even this print does not contain all the shots to be found in other versions.

As far as I can determine, the matter remains unsettled. All we can say is that, probably from the early 1930s, several versions of the film existed in positive prints, and doubtless many internegatives were drawn from them. How much might we be missing? Contemporary accounts of the Danish premiere describe the film as 2,400 meters long and lasting between ninety minutes and two hours. Years later Dreyer claimed that the film was originally 7,200 feet long (i.e., about 2,200 meters). The print conserved in the Cinémathèque Française (and distributed in the United States by the Museum of Modern Art) is about 2,200 meters long and at silent speed runs about 120 minutes. Arne Krogh of the Danish Film Museum continues to collate all available footage into a single version.

Dreyer was contracted to make another film for the Société Générale, and it was announced that Falconetti would again star.[37] According to Ebbe Neergaard, the firm broke its contract with Dreyer. There is evidence that faced with the coming of sound and the failure of Gance's *Napoléon,* the Société had to cut back production. There is also evidence that Dreyer continued to have business dealings with the firm later in the 1930s.

Vampyr (The Dream of Allan Gray). 1932.

SCRIPT: Dreyer, Christen Jul. Based on the book *In a Glass Darkly* by Sheridan Le Fanu. *PHOTOGRAPHY:* Rudolph Maté, Louis Née. *ART DIRECTORS:* Hermann Warm, Hans Bittmann, Cesare Silvagni. *MUSIC:* Wolfgang Zeller. *PRODUCERS:* Dreyer, Nicolas de Gunzburg. *PRODUCTION:* Carl Th. Dreyer Film Produktion, Berlin-Paris. *SOUND:* Cesare Silvani. *SYNCHRONIZATION:* Paul Falkenberg, Wolfgang Zeller. *ASSISTANTS TO THE DIRECTOR:* Ralph Holm, Eliane Tayara, Preben Birch. *FIRST SHOWN:* 6 May 1932 (Berlin, Ufa-Theater Kurfürstendamm).

David Gray	Julian West, i.e., Nicolas de Gunzburg
Marguerite Chopin, the vampire	Henriette Gérard
the doctor	Jan Hieronimko
Bernard, the owner of the castle	Maurice Schutz
Léone	Sybille Schmitz
Gisèle	Rena Mandel
Joseph, the manservant	Albert Bras
Jeanne, the housekeeper	N. Babanini
the nurse	Jane Mora

Dreyer could not have returned to work in Denmark; Nordisk and Palladium had halted production. In the fall of 1931, Dreyer won his case against the Société Générale and the young Baron Nicolas de Gunzburg (a friend of the Hugos) had offered to support a film. In Paris, Dreyer and Christen Jul composed a script purportedly in reaction against Browning's *Dracula:* "I could damn well make one of those too."[38] The source was Le Fanu's *In a Glass Darkly,* but the adaptation is very free. A few motifs can be traced back to the stories: "The Room in the Dragon Volant" is about a young man who stays at an inn, dreams of burial, and is put into a coffin alive; "Carmilla" is about a vampire woman victimizing a young girl in a chateau.

Dreyer sent his assistant Ralph Holm to recruit a cast, and after looking under Seine bridges and in the Salvation Army Holm returned with a Polish journalist to play the doctor and an actress's mother to play Marguerite Chopin.[39] Under the pseudonym of Julian West, Baron de Gunzburg himself played David Gray. The only professional actor in the cast was Sybille Schmitz, who, although only twenty-two, had already played in Metzner's *Überfall* and Pabst's *Diary of a Lost Girl.* The film was shot in fits and starts over a year, on location in Courtempierre. Dreyer often claimed that on the first day of filming, a light shone askew into the camera, fogging the image.[40] Dreyer liked the effect and insisted that it be repeated for several other shots.

The film was shot with exaggerated lip movements and taken to Berlin for postsynchronization. The eerie score was composed by Wolfgang Zeller, who had scored Reininger's *Prince Achmed* (1926) and Ruttmann's *Melodie der Welt* (1929). The Berlin premiere was turmoil, with boos mixed with applause; according to Neergaard, the

Cast and crew of Vampyr.

cameraman Karl Hoffman and the actor Willy Fritsch shouted at the hecklers, "Paid whistlers!"[41]

Our knowledge of Dreyer's next major project comes from newspaper accounts and the memoirs of one participant, Ernesto Quadrone. As Quadrone tells it, in 1936 he and Dreyer prepared *Mudundu,* a film to be shot in Somalia. Backed by the Turin newspaper *La Stampa* and an emigré Russian producer in Paris, the collaborators worked on a script in Turin and then left for Africa. Over a period of months, they shot several thousand meters of footage, but Dreyer returned to France without completing the film. Here the accounts diverge. According to Quadrone, the producer ran off with the money and Dreyer fell prostrate with malaria and sunstroke. According to Dreyer, the studio conditions were unacceptable, he could not agree with the producers, and he was forced to accept an actress he didn't want.[42] *Mudundu* was eventually completed by Quadrone alone.

Dreyer returned to Denmark and to journalism, writing newspaper pieces under the revived pseudonym "Tommen." Many of his film reviews of this period have been collected in the volume *Om Filmen,* available in English as *Dreyer in Double Reflection.* Not until after the Nazis invaded Denmark was Dreyer able to make another film. To show that he had not forgotten his craft, he directed a government documentary short.

Mødrehjælpen (Good Mothers). 1942.

SCRIPT: Dreyer. *PHOTOGRAPHY:* Verner Jensen, Poul Gram. *MUSIC:* Poul Schierbeck. *NARRATOR:* Ebbe Neergaard. *PRODUCTION:* Mogens Skot-Hansen for Nordisk Films Kompagni, Dansk Kulturfilm, and Ministeriernes Filmudvalg. English version in 1947 in "Social Denmark" series. The film depicts how the Danish social service for expectant mothers helps an unmarried mother take care of her baby before and after it is born.

Dreyer had hoped for foreign offers, but the Occupation blockaded foreign imports and so gave the Danish film industry a greater share of the market. He had been considering adapting Hans Weirs-Jensen's play *Anne Pedersdotter* for a decade, and from his clippings, notes, and books he and two others prepared a script, which was submitted to Nordisk in early 1942. When Nordisk hesitated, Tage Nielsen of Palladium offered to support the film. Dreyer said: "I always counted on coming back."[43]

Vredens Dag (Day of Wrath). 1944.

SCRIPT: Dreyer, Mogens Skot-Hansen, Poul Knudsen. Based on the play *Anne Pedersdotter* by Hans Wiers-Jenssen. *PHOTOGRAPHY:* Karl Andersson. *ART DIRECTOR:* Erik Aaes. *MUSIC:* Poul Schierbeck. *COSTUMES:* Lis Fribert, K. Sandt-Jensen, Olga Thomsen. *EDITORS:* Edith Schlüssel, Anne Marie Petersen. *HISTORICAL ADVISER:* Kaj Uldall. *PRODUCTION:* Palladium Film. *FIRST SHOWN:* 13 November 1943 (Copenhagen, World Cinema).

Absalon Pedersson	Thorkild Roose
Anne Pedersdotter	Lisbeth Movin
Merete, Absalon's mother	Sigrid Neiiendam
Martin	Preben Lerdorff Rye
Herlofs Marte	Anna Svierkier
the bishop	Albert Høberg
Laurentius	Olaf Ussing
Kapellmeister	Sigurd Berg
	Harald Holst

Costing the equivalent of almost sixty thousand dollars, *Day of Wrath* was called the most expensive Danish film to date. Dreyer had hoped to shoot the film in chronological order, but Thorkild Roose's stage schedule forebade it. Nevertheless, Dreyer moved to Hellerup to live near the studio, and he began working day and night.[44] The principal players represented two generations of the Danish theatre world: Roose had been an actor and director for forty years and Neiiendam had begun her career in 1888, whereas Lerdorff-Rye and Movin were relative newcomers and had made films only since 1941. All four were established players at the Danish Royal Theatre.

Dreyer saw in *Day of Wrath* "possibilities for great monumental visual effects—four or five figures as sharply-defined as medieval wood sculptures." He sought a slow pace which he called "deceptive tempo . . . a calmness in the scenes which is a natural one for the talking film, so that the impressions can find a little rest and fasten themselves in the spectator."[45] The tempo indeed deceived Danish reviewers, who disparaged *Day of Wrath*. More prophetic was Bazin: "Like its contemporary *Ivan the Terrible,* this is a film which is not of the moment, a masterpiece at once anachronistic and ageless."[46]

Dreyer circa 1945.

Två Manniskor (Two People). 1944.

SCRIPT: Dreyer, Martin Glanner. Based on the play *Attentat* by W. O. Somin. *PHOTOGRAPHY:* Gunnar Fischer. *ART DIRECTOR:* Nils Svenwall. *MUSIC:* Lars-Erik Larsson. *EDITORS:* Dreyer, Edvin Hammarberg. *PRODUCER:* Hugo Bolander. *PRODUCTION:* Svensk Filmindustri, Stockholm. *FIRST SHOWN:* 23 March 1945 (Stockholm, Roda Kvarn). *PLAYERS:* Georg Rydeberg (Dr. Arne Lundell), Wanda Rothgardt (Marianne), Gabriel Alw.

During a visit to Copenhagen, the Swedish producer C. A. Dymling invited Dreyer to Stockholm to make a film. Since Dreyer had an idea for a film with only two characters, Dymling bought Somin's play *Attentat* for the project. Once completed, the film received a poor response. *Two People* played less than a week in Sweden, and not until 1947 did it appear in Denmark, where it was shown but once. The film is indeed an embarrassment, but why? The producers blamed Dreyer's handling: "The film was a failure, a great misunderstanding economically and artistically. We shelved it fast. Bad enough that we lost money shooting it; we weren't going to lose more money by showing it."[47] Dreyer claimed that he wanted two other actors and that Dymling forced these two upon him.[48]

Nonetheless, as I suggested in chapter nine, the film does open a path to *Ordet* in its use of camera movement. After the opening montage sequence, the first scene might have been shot by Hitchcock:

SHOT ONE:
A face appears, reflected on a door's nameplate. The camera pans to a closeup of a hand turning a key.

and Marianne rushes in to embrace him.

and tracks back and around to follow Marianne Lundell into her apartment.

SHOT TWO:
Another face appears in reflection on the nameplate, and another hand turns a key.

the camera tracks to follow Arne Lundell into the apartment.

Unfortunately, the rest of the film is nothing like as dense as the doubly subjective opening; only the ending (discussed on p. 157) uses camera mobility in as stringent a fashion. *Two People* stands as evidence that, in cinema as in literature, "Failure can sometimes be as important a factor . . . as success. Abortive or premature thrusts in the 'right' direction, while unimpressive in themselves, often foreshadow or pave the way for resounding triumphs."[49]

The years between *Two People* and *Ordet* saw the inception of two unfilmed projects, the completion of several short documentaries, and the beginning of Dreyer's job as a theatre manager.

After the war, Dreyer and his son Erik composed a script about Mary Queen of Scots. In 1946 Dreyer discussed the project with Film Traders, Ltd. of Britain, but nothing came of it. The script, written in English, still survives. In April 1948 Dreyer came to America for the premiere of *Day of Wrath* and began to seek support for a film on the life of Jesus. He was encouraged by theatre producer Blevins Davis, and on Davis's Missouri farm wrote the first draft of the script, "The Story of the Jew Jesus." Over the next two decades, the Christ film was to become an overriding goal; documentary work, *Ordet*, and *Gertrud* were seen as preparations for *Jesus*, proofs that Dreyer could still direct.[50]

Unfinished projects meant that Dreyer had still to make a living. During the war, documentary film production had grown in Denmark, and after the war Dreyer was able to keep busy by working on government-sponsored shorts. In the list which follows, asterisked items were not directed by Dreyer.

Vandet Pa Låndet (Water from the Land). 1946.

SCRIPT: Dreyer. *PHOTOGRAPHY:* Preben Frank. *MUSIC:* Poul Schierbeck. *NARRATORS:* Henrik Malberg, Asbjørn Andersen. *PRODUCTION:* Palladium Film for Ministeriernes Filmudvalg.
A study of farmers' pollution of groundwater, the film was never shown to the public.

**De Gamle (The Seventh Age).* 1947.

DIRECTOR: Torben Anton Svendsen. *SCRIPT:* Dreyer. *PHOTOGRAPHY:* Karl Andersson. *MUSIC:* Emil Reesen. *NARRATORS:* Susanne Palsbo, Ralph Elton, Aksel Dahlerup. *PRODUCTION:* Palladium Film for Ministeriernes Filmudvalg.

Landsbykirken (The Danish Village Church). 1947.

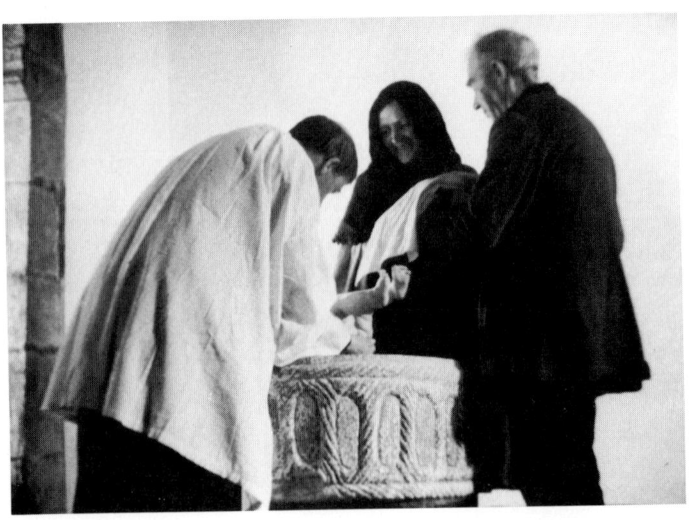

SCRIPT: Dreyer, Bernhard Jensen. *PHOTOGRAPHY:* Preben Frank. *MUSIC:* Svend Erik Tarp. *COMMENTARY:* Dreyer, Ib Koch-Olsen. *NARRATOR:* Ib Koch-Olsen. *HISTORICAL ADVISERS:* Victor Hermansen, H. Lønborg-Jensen. *PRODUCTION:* Preben Frank Film for Dansk Kulturfilm.
The church's functions in the life of a community. Ceremonies mark birth, worship, marriage, and death.

Kampen Mod Knæften (The Struggle Against Cancer). 1947.

SCRIPT: Dreyer, Carl Krebs. *PHOTOGRAPHY:* Preben Frank. *MUSIC:* Peter Deutsch. *NARRATOR:* Albert Luther. *PRODUCTION:* Preben Frank Film for Dansk Kulturfilm.
Scientific reportage.

De Næde Færgen (They Caught the Ferry). 1948.

SCRIPT: Dreyer. Based on a short story by Johannes V. Jensen. *PHOTOGRAPHY:* Jørgen Roos. *PRODUCTION:* Dansk Kulturfilm for Ministeriernes Filmudvalg.
A cliché lesson about driver safety, but in a supernatural ambiance. There is no dialogue and the music is sparse, consisting mainly of ominous tympani. A ferry comes into port and a couple on a motorcycle race off in an attempt to catch another ferry. Houses flashing by, tires whizzing along the road, and a mounting speedometer are swiftly intercut. (There are more shots in this twelve-minute short than in all of *Gertrud*.) Finally the motorcyclists try to pass an old car zigzagging into their path; as it swerves them off the road, they glimpse the face of its driver: Death. A bell rings. The ferry prepares to leave. The camera pans to a drifting barge wreathed in smoke; in it rest two coffins.

Thorvaldsen. 1949.

SCRIPT: Dreyer, Preben Frank. *PHOTOGRAPHY:* Preben Frank. *MUSIC:* Svend Erik Tarp. *NARRATOR:* Ib Koch-Olsen. *TECHNICAL ADVISOR:* Sigurd Schultz. *PRODUCTION:* Preben Frank Film for Dansk Kulturfilm.
A study of the Danish sculptor's work.

*Radioens barndom (The Childhood of Radio). 1949.

DIRECTION AND SCRIPT: Otto Schray. *PHOTOGRAPHY:* Carlo Bendtsen. *EDITING:* Dreyer. *MUSIC:* E. Binderup (piano). *PRODUCTION:* Nordisk Films for Dansk Kulturfilm and *Berlingske Tidende.*

Storstrømsbroen (*The Bridge of Storstrøm*). 1950.

SCRIPT: Dreyer. *PHOTOGRAPHY:* Preben Frank. *MUSIC:* Svend S. Schultz. *PRODUCTION:* Preben Frank Film for Dansk Kulturfilm.
A conventional "bridge film."

*Shakespeare Og Kronborg (Shakespeare and Kronborg). 1950.

DIRECTOR: Jørgen Roos. *SCRIPT:* Dreyer. *PHOTOGRAPHY:* Arne Jensen. *MUSIC:* Leif Kayser. *COMMENTARY:* Kaj Friis Møller, Jørgen Roos. *NARRATOR:* Karl Roos. *DIRECTOR OF STAGE SCENES:* Erling Schroeder. *ACTORS:* Erik Mörk, Olaf Ussing, Annemette Svendsen, Jakob Nielsen, Ib Fürst, Ego Brønnum-Jacobsen, Ebba With. *PRODUCTION:* Teknisk Films for Dansk Kulturfilm.

*Ronnes Og Nexos Genopbygning (The Rebuilding of Rome and Nexos). 1954.

DIRECTOR: Poul Bang. *SCRIPT:* Dreyer. *TECHNICAL ASSISTANTS:* Willy Hansen, Johannes Væth. *PHOTOGRAPHY:* Annelise Reenberg. *MUSIC:* from records. *NARRATOR:* Poul Jorgensen. *PRODUCTION:* Saga Studio and Nordisk Films Kompagni for Dansk Kulturfilm.

Et Slot I Et Slot (*Castle within a Castle*). 1954.

SCRIPT: Dreyer. *PHOTOGRAPHY:* Jørgen Roos. *MUSIC:* from records. *NARRATOR:* Sven Ludvigsen. *HISTORICAL ADVISER:* Otto Norn. *PRODUCTION:* Teknisk Film for Dansk Kulturfilm.
The restoration of Kronberg Castle.

*Noget om Norden (Something Happened in the North). 1956.

DIRECTION AND SCRIPT: Bent Barfod, based on an idea by Dreyer. *ANIMATION:* Borge Hamberg. *PHOTOGRAPHY:* Birthe Barfod, A. Clausen, Borge Hamberg. *EDITING:* Bent Barfod and Jørgen Roos. *MUSIC:* Hans Schreiber. *COMMENTARY:* Kirsten Bundgaard. *NARRATOR:* Hannah Bjarnhof. *PRODUCTION:* Bent Barfod for Ministeriernes Filmudvalg.

At this time, the government customarily awarded the managership of certain film theatres to distinguished Danes; this was a form of pension. In February 1952, Dreyer was awarded the managership of the Dagmar, one of the finest and oldest theatres in Copenhagen. He won the post over exceptional competition: Urban Gad's widow Esther, the great tenor Aksel Schiøtz, Møgens Skot-Hansen (for whom Dreyer had produced *Good Mothers*), and Johannes Meyer, the actor who had played in *Leaves from Satan's Book, The Stigmatized Ones,* and *Thou Shalt Honor Thy Wife.* Dreyer took the job very seriously. The Dagmar's repertoire relied upon the art cinema—*The River, Rashomon, Los Olvidados*—but did not exclude American films like *The Brave Bulls, Tobacco Road,* and even some program pictures. (How curious to imagine Dreyer earnestly previewing *The Atomic City.*) Managership of the Dagmar, which Dreyer held until just before his death, did keep his viewing up-to-date; *Gertrud* was made by a man aware of contemporary developments in international filmmaking.

Ordet (The Word). 1954.

SCRIPT: Dreyer. Based on the play by Kaj Munk. *PHOTOGRAPHY:* Henning Bendtsen. *ART DIRECTOR:* Erik Aaes. *MUSIC:* Poul Schierbeck. *EDITOR:* Edith Schlüssel. *PRODUCER:* Erik Nielsen. *PRODUCTION:* Palladium Film. *FIRST SHOWN:* 10 January 1955 (Copenhagen, Dagmar Bio).

Morten Borgen	Henrik Malberg
Mikkel	Emil Hass Christensen
Johannes	Preben Lerdorff-Rye
Anders	Cay Kristiansen
Inger	Birgitte Federspiel
Peter Petersen	Ejner Federspiel
Anne, his daughter	Gerda Nielsen
the pastor	Ove Rud
the doctor	Henry Skjæ
Maren	Anne Elisabeth
little Inger	Susanne
Peter's wife	Sylvia Eckhausen
Karen	Hanne Aagesen
Mette Maren	Edith Trane

Dreyer saw Kaj Munk's play *The Word* at its Copenhagen premiere in 1932. Twenty years later, Dansk Kulturfilm suggested to Tage Nielsen, head of Palladium, that Dreyer film the play, and the government subsidized Dreyer's preparation of the script. He compressed Munk's original, trimming dialogue and excising a love affair as the cause of Johannes's madness.[51] Although the existence of Mollander's earlier version meant that Palladium had to wait two years, production went quickly: two months in the studio and two months at Vederso on the West Jutland heaths. In the cast were the 81-year-old Henrik Malmberg, for whom Munk had written the role of Morten Borgen, and Birgitte Federspiel, who was pregnant when she played Inger. When Federspiel was taken to the hospital to give birth, she asked Dreyer to tape-record her groans, and he used them in the finished soundtrack. While she was in the hospital, Dreyer and Bendtsen planned and staged the resurrection scene, the last sequence shot. Dreyer filmed two versions of this last scene, one rendering the miracle as completely genuine, the other version following Munk's play in leaving some doubt as to the cause of the resurrection. Dreyer chose to use the former in the final film.[52]

The unusual length of the shots determined a production routine which Dreyer was also to follow in *Gertrud.* Usually, each day would be devoted to one shot. In the morning, the actors rehearsed from a script, while Dreyer blocked out the action, plotted camera movements and stops, and noted positions. After lunch, the lighting would be determined and the actors would rehearse the shot with the camera moving. At about five o'clock, the scene would be filmed, with one or two retakes. Henning Bendtsen described the shooting:

> *The script was much more simplified than usual. The camera angles, for instance, were not decided beforehand. . . . We worked them out as the shooting progressed. Dreyer's basic rule was to arrange people for the sake of photography and lighting rather than acting. Normally you work with a much simpler lighting plot in which the actors are not tied to a specific area because they must have the opportunity to act freely. In* Ordet, *their positions were so carefully planned that they had to count their steps at the same time as they said their lines. A single step too much to one side or the other would mean that we would miss a certain predetermined light effect and the scene would have to be reshot. . . . The actors accepted it without complaint. Each image is composed*

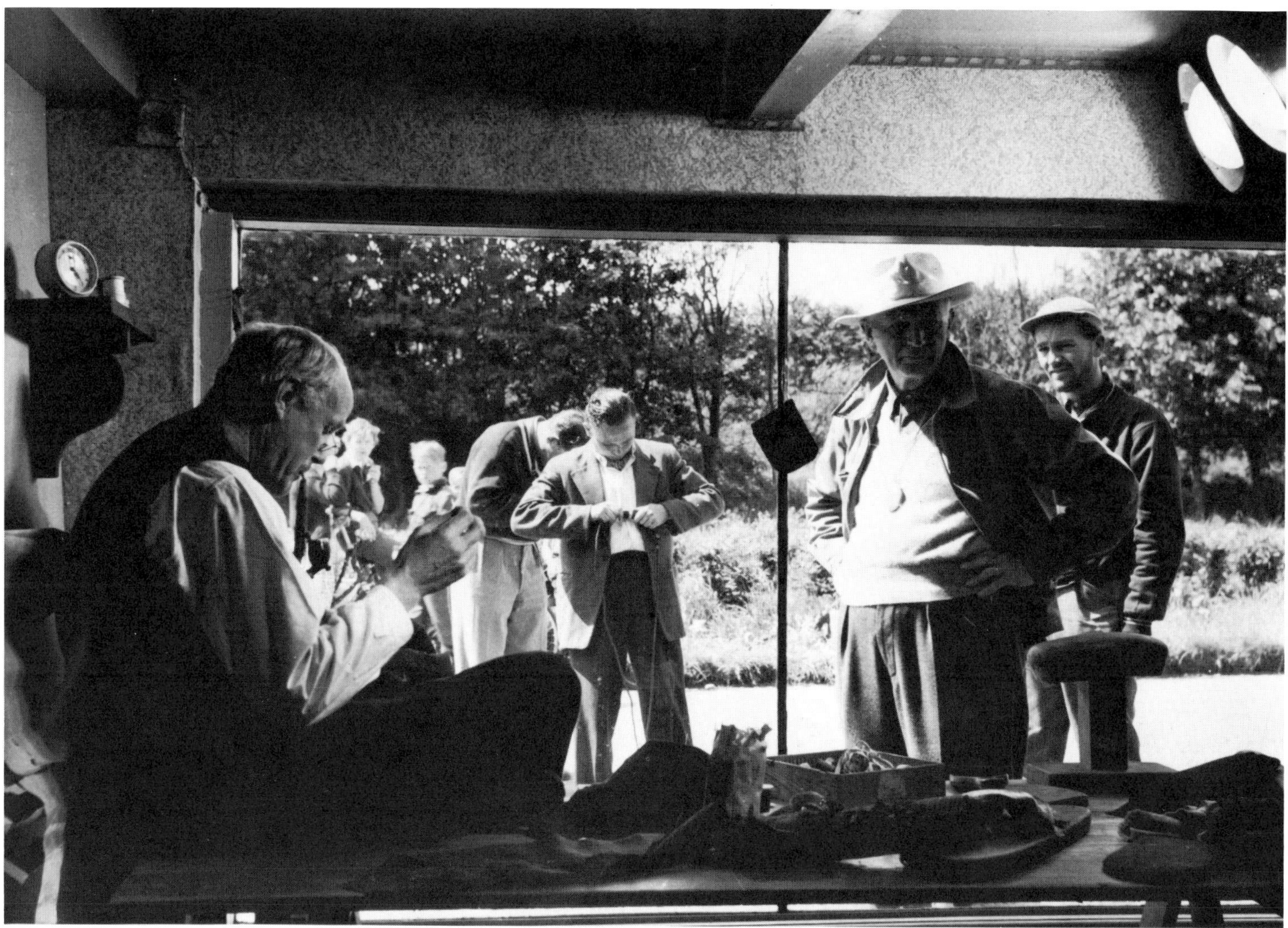

Dreyer directing Ordet.

like a painting in which the background and the lighting are carefully prepared. As an example, I might mention the prayer-meeting at Peter the tailor's with twenty people sitting around. Normally we would have used one lamp for throwing light on all of them. Here we used twenty lamps so that each face in fact became an individual portrait study. . . . Another of the lighting effects of the film created almost insoluble problems. While Johannes is insane, he is walking around in darkness all the time, whereas all the other characters have light on their faces. It created great difficulties when the characters moved around among each other, and the electricians had constantly to turn lamps on and off without this being noticed on the screen.[53]

Dreyer deliberately aimed at the long-take style: "I believe that long takes represent the film of the future. You must be able to make a film in six, seven, eight shots . . . . Short scenes, quick cuts in my view mark the silent film, but the smooth medium shot—with continual camera movement—belongs to the sound film. I used this technique first in *Day of Wrath,* and I've later realized that the Americans use it very much—Hitchcock did it frequently in *Rope.*"[54] According to Neergaard, the takes in *Ordet* couldn't be even longer because Malmberg couldn't remember his lines long enough.

Ordet was a success with both Danish reviewers and audiences, and it won the Golden Lion Award at the 1955 Venice Film Festival.

Gertrud. 1964.

SCRIPT: Dreyer. Based on the play by Hjalmar Söderberg. *PHOTOGRAPHY:* Henning Bendtsen. *ART DIRECTOR:* Kai Rasch. *MUSIC:* Jørgen Jersild. *SONGS:* Grethe Risbjerg Thomsen. *EDITOR:* Edith Schlüssel. *PRODUCTION:* Palladium Film. *FIRST SHOWN:* 19 December 1964 (Paris, Le Studio Medicis).

Gertrud	Nina Pens Rode
Gustav Kanning	Bendt Rothe
Gabriel Lidman	Ebbe Rode
Erland Jansson	Baard Owe
Axel Nygren	Axel Strøbye
the Kannings' maid	Vera Gebuhr
Kanning's mother	Anna Malberg
the rector Magnificus	Eduard Mielche
	Karl Gustav Ahlefeldt, Valsø Holm, Lars Knutzon, William Knoblauch

Dreyer claimed that in 1940 he considered filming two works by Hjalmar Söderberg, the novel *Dr. Glas* and the play *Gertrud.* Two decades later, he read Sten Rein's monograph *Hjalmar Söderbergs Gertrud* (Stockholm, 1962): "Through Rein I suddenly saw Söderberg's play from a new perspective."[55] Apart from biographical and textual analysis, Rein's study points out Söderberg's reliance upon dialogue: "Conflicts materialize out of apparently trivial conversations, his characters frequently fail to communicate and mean different things with the same words. . . . In contrast to Ibsen's heavily emphasized points, he often consciously introduces a crucial psychological moment through a quietly-spoken line or even through a silence."[56] Seizing on Söderberg's conception of dialogue, Dreyer considered the film an experiment in making images secondary to speech. He insisted that the characters' habit of "speaking past each other" was faithful to the playwright's stylization.

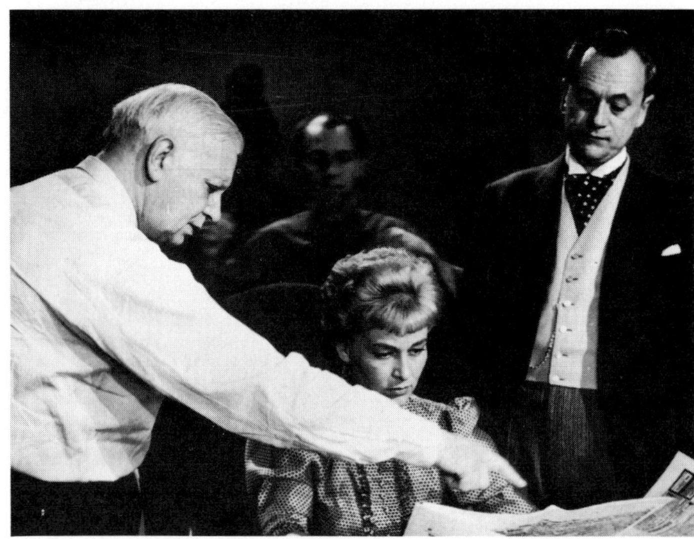

Dreyer directing Gertrud.

Dreyer's script follows the play fairly closely, except for abridging the third act and including an epilogue. The epilogue was added, Dreyer said, because of "what really happened" to the protagonist's real-life prototype, Maria von Platen.[57] The film was shot in three months in 1964, and edited in three days.

Uproar attended *Gertrud.* For the world premiere, Paris paid homage to Dreyer: the Cinémathèque mounted a retrospective, *Ordet* and *Day of Wrath* were revived, the Danish embassy held a reception, and Dreyer was interviewed and fêted. After the press showing of *Gertrud* on the morning of 18 December, rumors of disaster circulated. After the evening's premiere, it was confirmed that Dreyer had made a film wholly of "photographed sofa conversations."[58] The press attacks were vicious.[59] During its run, *Gertrud* attracted small audiences. Its release in Denmark, America, and elsewhere occasioned comparably disparaging reviews. In France, however, a television showing in April 1965 raised the film's reputation.[60]

Dreyer at home in early 1968.

After *Gertrud,* Dreyer continued to work on *Jesus.* Although he had visited Israel to search for locations, had compiled crates full of photos and notes, and had learned Hebrew, he was also seventy-seven years old and in poor health. It is said that prospective backers worried that if he started a project he would not live to finish it. In November 1967, the Danish government offered three million kroner to help subsidize the Jesus film. In early 1968, RAI, the Italian film and television corporation, came forward to support *Jesus.* The film was never to be made. Dreyer died on 20 March 1968, and was buried in Frederiksberg churchyard in Copenhagen. The gravestone bears his signature.

Notes

DREYER'S INTEREST

1 Amédée Ayfre, *Le Cinéma et sa vérité* (Paris: Cerf, 1969), p. 175.

2 *Ibid.*, p. 176.

3 *Ibid.*, p. 178.

4 Ken Kelman, "Dreyer," in P. Adams Sitney, ed., *Film Culture Reader* (New York: Praeger, 1970), p. 142.

5 Borge Trolle, "The World of Carl Dreyer," *Sight and Sound* 25 (Winter 1955–56): 126.

6 Parker Tyler, *Classics of the Foreign Film* (New York: Crown, 1962), p. 43.

7 Tom Milne, *The Cinema of Carl Dreyer* (New York: A. S. Barnes, 1971), p. 31.

8 Barthélémy Amengual, "Les nuits blanches de l'âme," *Cahiers du cinéma,* no 207 (December 1968), p. 61.

9 Jean Sémolué, *Dreyer* (Paris: Éditions universitaires, 1962), p. 155.

10 Philippe Parrain, *Dreyer: Cadres et mouvements, Études cinématographiques,* no. 53–56 (Paris: Minard, 1967), pp. 17–19, 100–101.

11 Robin Wood, "Carl Dreyer," *Film Comment* 10 (March–April 1974): 17.

12 *Ibid.*, p. 11.

13 My monograph on the film *(Filmguide to "La Passion de Jeanne d'Arc"* [Bloomington: Indiana University Press, 1973]) performs a recuperative reading. In many ways, the approach of the present book seeks to contest and surpass that analysis.

14 Jonathan Culler, *Structuralist Poetics* (Ithaca, N. Y.: Cornell University Press, 1975), p. 160.

15 John Simon, "Bull in the China Shop," *Film Heritage* 3 (Spring 1968): 40–41.

16 More specifically, I am indebted to works by Victor Shklovsky, Boris Eichenbaum, and Yuri Tynianov collected in the following anthologies: Lee T. Lemon and Marion J. Reis, eds., *Russian Formalist Criticism: Four Essays* (Lincoln: University of Nebraska Press, 1965); Ladislav Matejka and Krystyna Pomorska, eds., *Readings in Russian Poetics* (Cambridge, Mass.: MIT Press, 1971); *Twentieth Century Studies,* no. 7/8 (December 1972), special number on Russian Formalism; Tzvetan Todorov, ed., *Théorie de la littérature* (Paris: Seuil, 1965). See also Victor Erlich, *Russian Formalism* (The Hague: Mouton, 1969); Boris Eichenbaum, *The Young Tolstoi* (Ann Arbor: Ardis, 1972); and Mikhail Bakhtin, *Problems of Dostoevsky's Poetics* (Ann Arbor: Ardis, 1973). Structuralist works which I have found useful for this project include Tzvetan Todorov's *La poétique* (Paris: Seuil, 1968) and *Poétique de la prose* (Paris: Seuil, 1971); Roland Barthes's "Introduction to the Structural Analysis of Narrative," *New Literary History* 6 (Winter 1975): 237–72; *S/Z* (Paris: Seuil, 1970); and "Analyse textuelle d'un conte d'Edgar Poe," in Claude Chabrol, ed., *Sémiotique narrative et textuelle* (Paris: Larousse, 1973), pp. 29–54; and Gérard Genette, *Figures III* (Paris: Seuil, 1971), pp. 67–275. In film theory, this book owes a good deal to the writings of André Bazin, Sergei Eisenstein, and Noël Burch, especially to the latter's *Theory of Film Practice* (New York: Praeger, 1973).

17 See Viktor Shklovsky, "Art as Technique," in Lemon and Reis, *Russian Formalist Criticism,* pp. 3–24.

18 *Ibid.*, p. 24.

19 Boris Tomashevsky, "Literature and Biography," in Matejka and Pomorska, *Readings in Russian Poetics,* pp. 47–55.

20 For a cogent discussion of the story/plot distinction, see Tzvetan Todorov, "Some Approaches to Russian Formalism," *Twentieth Century Studies,* no. 7/8, pp. 17–18.

21 Genette, *Figures III,* pp. 67–182.

22 Jan Mukařovský, *Aesthetic Function, Norm, and Value as Social Facts,* trans. Mark E. Suino (Ann Arbor: Michigan Slavic Contributions, 1970), pp. 91–92.

23 Victor Shklovsky, "The Resurrection of the Word," *Twentieth Century Studies,* no. 7/8, p. 46.

24 Gérard Leblanc, "Direction," *Screen* 12 (Summer 1971): 125.

25 For the most part, my analysis ignores Dreyer's feature *Two People* (1946) and his short documentaries. The former seems to me interesting only for a few stylistic and narrative features, while the latter remain banal pieces. Where useful, I shall mention these films in passing; detailed information on them may be found in the filmography.

AN AUTHOR AND HIS LEGEND

1 Ebbe Neergaard, *Carl Theodor Dreyer: A Film Director's Work* (London: British Film Institute, 1950), p. 5.

2 Boris Tomashevsky, "Literature and Biography," in Matejka and Pomorska, *Readings in Russian Poetics,* p. 55.

3 Quoted in Victor Erlich, *Russian Formalism,* p. 253.

4 Quoted in B. M. Eichenbaum, "The Theory of the Formal Method," in Matejka and Pomorska, *Readings in Russian Poetics,* p. 31.

5 "Carl Theodor Dreyer udtaler sig," *Politiken,* 26 April 1931, p. 8.

6 See Svend Aage Hanson, *Early Industrialization in Denmark* (Copenhagen: C. E. Gads, 1970).

7 Marguerite Engberg, ed., *Det Danske Stumfilm: 1903–1930* (Copenhagen: Det Danske Filmmuseum, 1968), pp. 13–20.

8 Ebbe Neergaard, *Story of Danish Film* (Copenhagen: The Danish Institute, 1962), p. 38.

9 Erik Nørgard, *Levende billeder i Danmark* (Copenhagen: Lademann, 1971), p. 99.

10 Urban Gad, *Filmen: Dens Midler og Maal* (Copenhagen: Gyldendals, 1918), p. 5.

11 Nørgard, *Levende billeder i Danmark,* p. 91.

12 Two of Dreyer's Nordisk contracts, dated 26 February 1913 and 12 May 1915, have been preserved by the Danish Film Archive.

13 "Carl Dreyer," in Andrew Sarris, ed., *Interviews with Film Directors* (New York: Avon, 1967), p. 154.

14 Letter of 26 June 1913, letter of 12 May 1915 (both on file at Danish Film Archive); Walter Galenson, *The Danish System of Labor Relations* (Cambridge, Mass.: Harvard University Press, 1952), p. 281.

15 Interview with Bjorn Rasmussen, 26 January 1964 (typescript on file at Danish Film Archive), p. 3.

16 Gad, *Filmen,* p. 247. How well Dreyer learned this lesson may be seen in *Thou Shalt Honor Thy Wife,* whose six reels correspond neatly to six dramaturgical "acts."

17 Carl Dreyer, *Dreyer in Double Reflection,* ed. Donald Skoller (New York: Dutton, 1973), p. 22.

18 Georges Sadoul, *Histoire générale du cinéma,* vol. 3, pt. 2 (Paris: Denoël, 1952), p. 373.

19 Peter Bachlin, *Histoire économique du cinéma,* trans. Müller-Strauss (Paris: La Nouvelle Édition, 1947), p. 105.

20 Neergaard, *Story of Danish Film,* p. 47.

21 Nørgard, *Levende billeder i Danmark,* pp. 103, 114.

22 *Ibid.,* p. 83.

23 Quoted in Erich Ulrichsen, "La belle époque," in *50 Aar i Dansk Film* (Copenhagen: Nordisk Films, 1956), p. 30.

24 Gad, *Filmen,* pp. 111–12; see also Nørgard, *Levende billeder i Danmark,* p. 40.

25 Gad, *Filmen,* pp. 109–20. Dreyer once described the "European production principle" as stressing directorial control: "Along with the producer, he chose the script, he selected his assistants, he had time for direction . . ." ("Carl Theodor Dreyer udtaler sig," p. 8).

26 Letter from Dreyer to Frost, 31 October 1917, Danish Film Archive collection.

27 Ebbe Neergaard, "Lærling og mester," in *50 Aar i Dansk Film,* p. 60.

28 Quoted in Ella Langeson, "Jeg har altid stræbt efter det enkle," *Jyllands Posten* 27 January 1955, p. 26. See also Judith Podselver, "Carl-Théo Dreyer et sa situation en 1947," *Revue du Cinéma* (Fall 1947), pp. 25–26.

29 Neergaard, "Lærling og mester," p. 60.

30 Letter from Dreyer to Frost, 11 August 1918, Danish Film Archive collection.

31 See Skalk [pseud.] "Blad af Satans Bog," *Ekstrabladet,* 22 January 1921; clipping on file at the Danish Film Archive.

32 Letter from Dreyer to Frost, 19 December 1918, Danish Film Archive collection.

33 Letter from Dreyer to Frost, 20 December 1918, Danish Film Archive collection.

34 Letter from Dreyer to Stæhr, 23 March 1919; published as "Brev til direktor W. Stæhr," *Kosmorama,* no. 85 (June 1968), n.p.; translated as "Lettre au directeur de la Nordisk," *Cahiers du Cinéma,* no. 207 (December 1968), pp. 12–13.

35 *Ibid.*

36 Letter from Olsen to Dreyer, 24 March 1919, Danish Film Archive collection.

37 Letter from Dreyer to Olsen, 25 March 1919, Danish Film Archive collection.

38 Letter from Dreyer to Olsen, 26 March 1919, Danish Film Archive collection.

39 Letter from Dreyer to Frost, 17 November 1920, Danish Film Archive collection.

40 Cf. Neergaard, "Lærling og mester," p. 64; Langeson, "Jeg har altid stræbt . . ." p. 26.

41 *Dreyer in Double Reflection,* p. 27.

42 *Ibid.,* pp. 22–23.

43 Preben Thomsen, "Working with Dreyer," in Søren Dyssegaard, ed., *Carl Th. Dreyer: Danish Film Director* (Copenhagen: Ministry of Foreign Affairs, 1968), p. 15.

44 Quoted in Carl Lerner, "My Way of Working Is in Relation to the Future," *Film Comment* 4 (Fall 1966): 65.

45 *Dreyer in Double Reflection,* p. 29. Dreyer also sold at least one script, *Döden Forener (Death Unites),* to the Swedish firm Svenska Bio. Svenska bought the script in 1914, but Gosta Werner argues that Dreyer probably submitted it a year earlier, before he had contracted himself to Nordisk. The film was never made. The script, which slightly resembles *The President,* has been published. See Gosta Werner, *"Döden Forener," Chaplin,* no. 139 (1975), pp. 164–69.

46 Quoted in Herbert Luft, "Eric Pommer," *Films in Review* 10 (October 1959): 469.

47 Letter from Dreyer to Frost, 4 January 1924, Danish Film Archive collection. See also Luft, "Erich Pommer," p. 469; Carl Dreyer, "The Film-Maker and the Audience," in Robert Hughes, ed., *Film: Book One* (New York: Grove Press, 1959), p. 43; and the Biographical Filmography of the present volume. A mystery remains: Pommer's change supposedly substituted "an artificial and unnecessarily imposed 'happy ending' " for a "sad but psychologically correct one." As the film survives, however, it certainly does not possess a happy ending.

48 Quoted in Georges Sadoul, *Histoire générale du cinéma,* vol. 5 (Paris: Denoël, 1975), p. 432.

49 "Carl Dreyer," in Sarris, ed., *Interviews,* p. 145.

50 "Kvinden, der var skyld, af Carl Th. Dreyer Rejste hjem fra Afrika!" *Ekstrabladet* (undated clipping on file at the Danish Film Archive).

51 Rechendorff [pseud.], "Skulde jeg lave Filmen igen, blev den lige saaden," *Berlingske Tidende,* 17 November 1943, p. 4.

52 Pierre [pseud.], "Falske Forestillinger om Renæssancetiden?" *Ekstrabladet,* 18 November 1943, p. 4.

53 "Carl Dreyer," in Sarris, ed., *Interviews,* p. 162.

54 Robert Craft, "Webern," booklet accompanying *Webern: The Complete Music* (Columbia Record CK4L–232), p. 10.

55 See John Ernst, program notes for Dreyer's documentaries (Danish Film Archive, 1964), n.p. The script for *Mary Stuart,* signed by Dreyer and his son Erik, is on file at the Danish Film Archive.

56 See David Bordwell, "Passion, Death, and Testament," *Film Comment* 8 (Summer 1972): 59–63.

57 See "Carl Th. Dreyer fik Dagmar Bio," clipping dated 28 February 1952 from uncited source; on file at the Danish Film Archive.

58 Film Centre, *The Film Industry in Six European Countries* (Paris: UNESCO), pp. 67–70.

59 Herbert Steinthal, " 'Ordet' opstaar i film, hvor Kaj Munk levede," *Politiken,* 1–7 August 1954, p. 18.

60 Langeson, "Jeg har altid stæbt . . . ," p. 26.

61 *Dreyer in Double Reflection,* p. 28.

62 Quoted in Erlich, *Russian Formalism,* p. 259.

63 *Dreyer in Double Reflection,* p. 179.

64 Quoted in Poul Uttenreiter, "En nordisk framgang i Paris," *Filmjournalen* (1924), p. 664.

65 *Dreyer in Double Reflection,* p. 28.

66 *Dreyer in Double Reflection,* p. 53.

67 "Carl Dreyer," in Sarris, ed., *Interviews,* p. 149.

68 Carl Dreyer, *Four Screenplays,* trans. Oliver Stallybrass (London: Thames and Hudson, 1970), p. 7.

69 Dreyer, "The Filmmaker and the Audience," p. 45.

70 *Ibid.*

71 See also Lerner, "My Way of Working . . . ," p. 67.

72 Remark by Dreyer in Jørgen Roos's documentary film *Carl Th. Dreyer* (1966).

73 Walter Benjamin, "The Work of Art in the Age of Mechanical Reproduction," in *Illuminations,* ed. Hannah Arendt (New York: Schocken Books, 1969), pp. 225–26.

74 *Dreyer in Double Reflection,* p. 165.

75 John H. Winge, "Interview with Dreyer," *Sight and Sound* 18 (January 1950): 17.

76 Dreyer said of the long takes in *Gertrud*: "The advantage of this method is clear: the actors have a chance to act out before the camera a full psychological development which does not have to be broken because of new camera positions" (Jan Aghed, "Dreyers 'Gertrud' ett experiment," *Svenska Dagbladet,* 16 November 1964; clipping on file at the Danish Film Archive). In this as in other respects, Dreyer resembles Kenji Mizoguchi who, according to his scriptwriter, explained very little of what he wanted and insisted on shooting long takes. The result was that at every instant the entire staff was concentrating fully: "Not only the actors, but all the technicians, all the electricians were bound together as a single man. . . . He asks everyone to give the maximum, and all at the same second" (Ariane Mnouchkine, "Entretien avec Yoshitaka Yoda et Kazuo Miyagawa," *Cahiers du Cinéma,* no. 158 [August–September 1964], p. 25).

77 *Dreyer in Double Reflection,* p. 27.

78 Ture Dahlin, "Carl-Théodor Dreyer à Paris," *La Cinématographie Française,* 27 March 1926, p. 5.

79 *Dreyer in Double Reflection,* p. 135.

80 *Ibid.,* p. 186.

81 "Carl Dreyer," in Sarris, ed., *Interviews,* p. 142.

82 Dahlin, "Carl-Théodor Dreyer à Paris," p. 5.

83 *Dreyer in Double Reflection,* p. 166.

84 *Ibid.,* pp. 113, 118.

85 Interview with Henning Bendtsen, 25 June 1976, Rødovre, Denmark.

86 *Dreyer in Double Reflection,* p. 184.

87 Quoted in Langeson, "Jeg har altid stræbt . . . ," p. 26.

88 Jean Arroy, quoted in René Jeanne and Charles Ford, *Histoire encyclopédique du cinéma,* vol. 2 (Paris: Laffont, 1947), p. 70.

89 *Dreyer in Double Reflection,* p. 146.

EARLY FILMS: NARRATIVE FORM

1 Henry Albert Phillips, *The Photodrama* (Larchmont, New York: Stanhope-Dodge, 1914; reprinted 1970), p. 64.

2 A. Van Buren Powell, *The Photoplay Synopsis* (Springfield: Home Correspondence School, 1919), p. 115.

3 Phillips, *Photodrama,* p. 144.

4 Urban Gad, *Filmen: Dens Midler og Maal* (Copenhagen: Gyldendals, 1919), pp. 9, 31.

5 *Ibid.,* p. 22.

6 August Strindberg, "Memorandums to the Members of the Intimate Theatre from the Director," *Open Letters to the Intimate Theatre,* trans. Walter Johnson (Seattle: University of Washington Press, 1966), p. 20.

7 A consideration of the *kammerspielfilm* may be found in Georges Sadoul, *Histoire générale du cinema,* vol. 5 (Paris: Denoël, 1975), pp. 481–517.

8 Dreyer inaccurately claimed *Michael* to be "the first *kammerspielfilm.*" See "Carl Dreyer," in Sarris, ed., *Interviews,* p. 158.

9 Jacques Derrida, *De la grammatologie* (Paris: Minuit, 1967), pp. 30–31. Cf. Julia Kristeva on pre-thirteenth-century symbolic practice in *La Texte du roman* (The Hague: Mouton, 1970), pp. 26–27.

10 Roland Barthes, "Literature and Discontinuity," *Critical Essays,* trans. Richard Howard (Evanston: Northwestern University Press, 1972), p. 173.

11 Michel Butor, "Le livre comme objet," *Repertoires II* (Paris: Minuit, 1964), p. 107.

EARLY FILMS: THE CONSTRUCTION OF SPACE

1 Quoted in Boris Eichenbaum, "The Theory of the Formal Method," in Matejka and Pomorska, eds., *Readings in Russian Poetics,* pp. 27–28.

2 "Thematics," in Lemon and Reis, eds., *Russian Formalist Criticism,* pp. 78–87.

3 Despite differing assumptions, two researchers have shown that by 1920, three-dimensional modeling and multiplanar lighting had become the standard. See Peter Baxter, "On the History and Ideology of Film Lighting," *Screen* 16 (Fall 1975), 83–106; Barry Salt, "Correspondence," *Screen* 17 (Spring 1976); 119–24; Barry Salt, "The Early Development of Film Form," *Film Form* 1 (1976): 91–106.

4 "Realité de la dénotation," *Cahiers du Cinéma,* no. 229 (May 1971), p. 39.

5 "Rhythm as the Constructive Factor in Verse," in Matejka and Pomorska, eds., *Readings in Russian Poetics,* p. 131.

6 "Film and System: Terms of Analysis," *Screen* 16 (Summer 1975): 99.

7 See Tynianov, "Rhythm as the Constructive Factor in Verse," in Matejka and Pomorska, eds., *Readings in Russian Poetics,* pp. 128–30.

8 Neergard, *Carl Dreyer,* p. 18.

9 *Dreyer in Double Reflection,* p. 52.

10 Is it accidental that the aid for drawing linear and synthetic perspective known as the *camera obscura,* the "darkened chamber," should have begun to be widely used by artists at this time, and that Vermeer should have utilized the device in his painting? Traces of the concept of the chamber may be invested, in miniaturized form, in that forerunner of the photographic camera.

11 "The President's room was built up from very calm walls and very few furnishings. On the walls, a barometer and a few pictures of family groups framed in the black oval frames very commonly used in the old days. For the outfitting of these interiors I was inspired by Vilhelm Hammershøi and to some extent by the American painter James Whistler." Quoted in Jørgen Roos, *Carl Th. Dreyer* (1966), a documentary film.

12 Quoted in Erlich, *Russian Formalism,* p. 268.

13 *The Art of the Film* (New York: Collier, 1970), p. 115.

14 "Le Président," unattributed article in Roger Boussinot, ed., *Encyclopédie du cinéma* (Paris: Bordas, 1967), p. 1235.

15 E. H. Gombrich, *The Story of Art* (New York: Phaidon, 1966), p. 324.

16 *Dreyer in Double Reflection,* p. 184.

17 See Walter Benjamin, *Charles Baudelaire: A Lyric Poet in the Era of High Capitalism,* trans. Harry Zohn (London: New Left Books, 1973), pp. 168–69.

18 *Art and Visual Perception: The New Version* (Berkeley and Los Angeles: University of California Press, 1974), p. 475.

19 *Principles of Art History,* trans. M. D. Hottinger (New York: Dover, 1950), p. 14.

20 *Ibid.,* p. 21.

21 Sigmund Freud, "The Uncanny," in Benjamin Nelson, ed., *On Creativity and the Unconscious* (New York: Harper, 1958), pp. 123–24.

22 Dahlin, "Carl-Théo Dreyer à Paris," p. 5.

23 Sémolué, *Dreyer,* p. 172.

24 Neergaard, *Dreyer,* p. 12.

25 See John Pope-Hennessy, *The Portrait in the Renaissance* (New York: Pantheon, 1966).

26 Béla Balázs, *Theory of the Film,* trans. Edith Bone (New York: Dover, 1970), p. 61.

27 Sémolué, *Dreyer,* p. 23.

28 Balázs, *Theory,* p. 74.

29 "Med anledning av filmen 'Blad ur Satans bok,' " *Filmrevyn,* no. 5 (1922), p. 92.

30 "Form and Material in 'Ivan the Terrible' " (Ph.D. diss., University of Wisconsin, 1977), p. 24.

PROBLEMATIC UNITIES

1 Ebbe Neergaard, "Du Skal Aere Din Hustru," program note for the Danish Film Museum (February 1954), n.p. See also Kelman, "Dreyer," pp. 147–57, and Milne, *Cinema of Carl Dreyer,* pp. 78–79 and *passim.*

2 *Transcendental Style in Film* (Berkeley and Los Angeles: University of California Press, 1972), p. 49.

3 *Ibid.,* p. 141.

4 Jean-Louis Comolli, "Rhétorique de la Terreur," *Cahiers du Cinéma,* no. 207 (December 1968), p. 42.

5 *Ibid.,* p. 44.

6 After this book was completed, the British Film Institute published Mark Nash's monograph *Dreyer* (London, 1977). Since Nash also considers Dreyer's work problematic and contradictory, it is worth detailing his conclusions.

Nash explains the tensions and gaps in Dreyer's films by recourse to a metaphor: Dreyer's work as a whole is like the discourse of a psychoanalytic patient. Drawing upon Freudian and Lacanian accounts of symptom formation and upon Julia Kristeva's examination of nineteenth-century symbolic practices, Nash claims that the Dreyer text constitutes a hysterical discourse. The films cannot "totally repress/resolve the problem of bisexuality within a rigidly patriarchal culture" (p. 16). The text seeks to contain this problem through represented content (e.g., family and church as male authority). But the extremity of the films' repression creates symptomatic eruptions: there emerge symptoms of desire and resistances to religious discourse. Nash sees desire as represented, centrally, by the act of looking (performed by character and viewer). Religious discourse is subverted by the eruption of bisexuality, especially in the realm of the voice (choirboys, Gertrud's songs). The Dreyer text, Nash concludes, exhibits hysteria on at least three levels. In narrative terms, we get feminized men and idealized women, a polarity which troubles the sexual difference upon which patriarchy rests. In *mise-en-scène,* the films' excess emerges symptomatically in narrative dislocations, problems of point of view, and chaste compositions which exhibit a hysterical paralysis. And what Nash calls the "body of the text" exhibits hysteria by the fantasies which it creates for the audience—fantasies of looking (light, hypnosis) and fantasies of the dismembered body put back together.

The value and complexity of Mark Nash's analysis are apparent even from this synopsis. What I want to examine briefly are some crucial differences between Nash's conception of film criticism and that set out in this book. The implications for the study of Dreyer will be evident.

For one thing, Nash's psychoanalytic categories do not discriminate among processes that we usually keep distinct. To take one example, Nash identifies what he calls the barred image, "the signifier of repression . . . the bar of symbolic restraint" (p. 13). This "bar" may be a shadow, a window pane, a checkered fabric, a picture frame, even "a dark halo surrounding the lit scene" (p. 10). "Within the frame there is always some kind of barrier" (p. 10). If there is always some kind of barrier in the Dreyer shot (which, in any event, is not the case), it is because Nash's category is excessively roomy. If any straight lines or dark masses in a shot can signify separation and lack, surely the barred image occurs in hundreds of thousands of shots (most of them not in Dreyer films). Similarly, the fantasy of "the body in pieces" includes phenomena as disparate as these: "the *découpage* effected on the body of the film [*Jeanne d'Arc*] and representationally on Joan's body"; in *Ordet* "the reanimation of Inger's cut body"; and "the body of Gertrud . . . continually framed, placed within an order" (p. 31). The concept here does not distinguish among surgery on a fictitious character's body, the framing or editing of the represented body, the confinement of a character's actions by narraforces, and the editing of the finished film. It is too easy to subsume all these phenomena under the same head by simply labeling them "cutting of the body." (And what we gain by calling a film a body is not clear to me.) So roomy are the concepts that they encourage free association, as when Nash claims that the checkered pattern of Inger's dress and of the kitchen tablecloth signifies "a potentially productive female body precisely 'in check' " (p. 13).

The adventitious pun illustrates a second problem in Nash's critical method. He explicitly situates his work within a critical school which considers "processes of text construction" (p. 3). When Nash emphasizes process and function, his argument is powerful: "The work of the Dreyer-text within this institution is to foreground the phantasy structures at play in it" (p. 32). Yet too often the dynamics of the films go unexamined and Nash tends to search for fixed systems of meanings, to use psychoanalysis as a hermeneutic key, and thus to provide only another interpretation of Dreyer's films. The essay often lifts an isolated element out of context and interprets its meaning in reductive Freudian-Lacanian terms. Nash claims, for instance, that "The central question of the film [*Ordet*] 'Who has it?' (i.e., the word), echoes the child's anxious questioning as to who has/is the phallus" (p. 19). Since no one in *Ordet* asks, "Who has it?" how do we know that this is the central question? Phrasing it this way, however, invites the critic to clamp down the Freudian apparatus. In *Gertrud,* two pictures on the wall, the larger of a man, the smaller of a woman, are said to be "connoting the power relation: male dominance; and stating the problem: bisexuality" (p. 27). The pictures are not considered for their roles in the shot or the sequence; they operate simply as abstract tokens for fixed themes. Light and dark in the frames of *Ordet* are said to parallel the "light" and "dark" versions of Christianity presented in the narrative (p. 16). But the "dark" Christianity is no darker *in the frame* than the light, so the parallel is justified solely by mnemonics. With few exceptions, the essay translates each film's narrative into representations of patriarchy, desire, repetition, etc., thus staying at the level of "signifieds," not of the signifier. (I should add that little is gained by calling something a signifier of desire if one is going to treat it, in literary fashion, as a *symbol* of desire.) It seems to me that Nash's monograph, despite its evident interest, slips into allegorical readings no different *in principle* from the humanist or religious interpretations that critics have already proposed.

7 "Pushkin & Sterne: *Eugene Onegin*" in Victor Erlich, ed., *Twentieth Century Russian Literary Criticism* (New Haven: Yale University Press, 1975), p. 68.

8 "The Ideology of the Text," *Salmagundi,* no. 31–32 (Fall 1975–Winter 1976), p. 232.

9 Francis Taylor Patterson, *Scenario and Screen* (New York: Harcourt, Brace, 1928), p. 95.

10 Anne Banchens, "Cutting the Film," in Nancy Naumberg, ed., *We Make the Movies* (New York: Norton, 1937), p. 215.

11 Karel Reisz and Gavin Millar, *The Technique of Film Editing* (New York: Hastings House, 1968), p. 227.

12 Dreyer remarked: "My film about Jeanne d'Arc has incorrectly been called an avant-garde film, which it absolutely is not. It is not a film aimed at film theoreticians but at all humankind. It is intended for the broad masses, and it has something to give to every open human mind." (Typescript copy of a 1950 statement on file in the Danish Film Archive.)

13 Jean Narboni, "La Mise en demeure," *Cahiers du Cinéma,* no. 207 (December 1968), p. 41.

14 Interview with Bendtsen, 25 June 1976.

15 *Dreyer: Cadres et mouvements,* p. 64.

16 "Pudovkin, Brecht, and *The Mother,*" paper delivered at the Conference on Film and Performance, University of Wisconsin–Milwaukee, Spring 1977.

17 *How to Write and Sell Film Stories* (New York: Covici-Friede, 1937), pp. 217–18.

18 *The Art of the Film* (New York: Collier, 1970), p. 208.

19 *Dreyer in Double Reflection,* p. 53.

20 Quoted in Erlich, *Russian Formalism,* p. 252.

21 *Dreyer in Double Reflection,* p. 129.

22 *Technique of Film Editing,* p. 233. In my claims about Dreyer's camera movements, it is the assumptions underlying Reisz and Millar's critique of *Rope* which are most important. I should add parenthetically that I also disagree with their appraisal of the film. *Rope* seems to me a major work in film history, posing several issues in fresh ways: the problem of theatrical representation of space (here, the missing fourth wall) versus cinematic representation of space (embodied particularly in the camera movements); the problem of point of view (which the mobile camera causes always to shift uncomfortably from a character to the audience); the problem of duration (story time is accelerated but plot time is not); and the status of the cut (the film's eight shots set up a dichotomy between reel changes in the camera during filming [about every ten minutes] and reel changes between projectors during screening [every twenty minutes]; all seven cuts constitute variations of classical *découpage* principles). *Rope,* whose very title bares the device of its linear construction, is by no means the insipid film Reisz and Millar imply.

23 *Dreyer in Double Reflection,* p. 54.

24 *Dreyer in Double Reflection,* pp. 164–65.

LA PASSION DE JEANNE D'ARC

1 David Bordwell, "Camera Movement and Cinematic Space," *Ciné-Tracts* 1 (Summer 1977): 19–26.

2 Ivor Montagu, *Film World* (Baltimore: Penguin, 1964), p. 141.

3 Figures 68 through 71 are taken from the print held by the Danish Film Archive; none of these shots appears in prints distributed in America.

4 In his review of *Jeanne d'Arc* after the Danish premiere, Ebbe Neergaard perceptively pointed out that the insistence upon close-ups confused the audience about the action in the scene. Neergaard found this a fault in the film and suggested that close-ups must be integrated into establishing shots in order to make sense. Several decades later, Dreyer responded that he had realized that his use of close-ups ran counter to current norms.

> *My idea of telling the passion of Jeanne in close-up did not fit into the framework of what was then understood as a "normal film." It was an unwritten law that the individual close-up had to be part of the harmonious unity of the long shot and at the same time a detail in the pattern of the plot. Then my aggressive close-ups appeared, jumping unannounced on the screen and demanding the right to an independent existence. Close-up after close-up demanded space with no concern for the "harmonious" unity of the long shot—all those close-ups, close-ups that behaved like a flock of noisy troublemakers—but which are very useful not only because they made it possible for me to bring the audience very near to the physical and mental torture that Jeanne suffered but also because they showed how her judges and tormentors reacted to her tears.*

Dreyer did allow that he had gone too far in *Jeanne d'Arc,* that the close-ups threw the film out of balance, and that he did not repeat the experiment in later films. He added, however: "I see in the big close-ups the idea for a new film form which other people may work on and develop to perfection." See *Ebbe Neergaards bog om Dreyer* (Copenhagen: Dansk Videnskabs Forlag, 1963), pp. 51–67.

5 *Filmguide to "La Passion de Jeanne d'Arc"* (Bloomington: Indiana University Press, 1973), p. 41.

6 *Ibid.,* p. 59.

7 *Ibid.,* p. 47.

8 *Ibid.*

9 For a careful examination of this and other point-of-view factors, see Edward Branigan, "Formal Permutations of the Point-of-View Shot," *Screen* 16 (Fall 1975): 63.

10 "Making Sense," *Twentieth Century Studies,* no. 12 (1976), p. 33.

11 We cannot take the historical duration of Jeanne's trial to be the story duration, since story duration is programmed by the film itself.

12 *Dreyer,* pp. 128–29.

13 *Ibid.,* pp. 59–60.

14 *Esthétique et psychologie du cinéma,* vol. 2 (Paris: Éditions universitaires, 1965), p. 410.

15 "Film and System," pp. 105–7.

16 *Theory,* p. 74.

17 *Dreyer,* pp. 60–61.

18 *S/Z*, p. 67.

19 "Carl Dreyer," in Sarris, ed., *Interviews*, p. 145.

20 Derrida, *De la grammatologie, passim*.

21 "Muet," in Jean Collet et al., *Lectures du film* (Paris: Albatros, 1976), pp. 171–72.

VAMPYR

1 "Carl Dreyer," p. 13.

2 *Cinema of Carl Dreyer*, p. 108.

3 *Carl Dreyer*, p. 27.

4 *The Fantastic*, trans. Richard Howard (Ithaca: Cornell University Press, 1975), pp. 25–27.

5 "Le discours étrange," in Claude Chabrol, ed., *Sémiotique narrative et textuelle* (Paris: Larousse, 1973), pp. 55–95.

6 *Vampyr* and the Fantastic," *Screen* 17 (Fall 1976): 29–67.

7 *Ibid.*, p. 43.

8 "Introduction to the Structural Analysis of Narrative," p. 248.

9 *Ibid.*

10 Boris Tomashevsky, "Thematics," in Lemon and Reis, eds., *Russian Formalist Criticism*, p. 90.

11 André Bazin, *What Is Cinema?* vol. 1 (Berkeley and Los Angeles: University of California Press, 1967), p. 48.

12 André Bazin, *Jean Renoir*, trans. W. W. Halsey II and William H. Simon (New York: Simon and Schuster, 1973), p. 89.

13 Incidentally, Dreyer's concern with representational space and off-screen effects is confirmed by two accounts of his planning for the film. In a preface to Neergaard's *Story of Danish Film* he recalls that Neergaard told him: "Remember that the belief that the photograph doesn't lie is all nonsense. The photograph lies with the greatest of ease, if you want it to. But the directors have not learned to make it lie in such a way that a style arises." Dreyer goes on: "I believe that you gave me the courage to venture further out in *Vampyr* than I had originally planned to" (Preface, *The Story of Danish Film*, pp. 4–5). Moreover, when he was shooting the film, Dreyer's instructions to his cast suggest his awareness of how important off-screen space was to be. "Imagine that we are sitting in an ordinary room. Suddenly we are told that there is a corpse behind the door. In an instant the room we are sitting in is completely altered; everything in it has taken on another look; the light, the atmosphere have changed, though they are physically the same. This is because *we* have changed, and the objects *are* as we conceive them. That is the effect I want to get in my film" (Neergaard, *Carl Dreyer*, p. 27).

14 Noël Burch, *Theory of Film Practice*, p. 39.

15 Roland Barthes, "Diderot, Brecht, Eisenstein," *Screen* 15 (Summer 1974): 38.

16 Tzvetan Todorov, *Poétique de la prose*, p. 85.

DAY OF WRATH

1 We can infer that the scenes occur on the same day for several reasons: their focus oscillates between the old woman and the young couple, and this is typical of the film's crosscutting elsewhere; the episodes are causally continuous (Herlofs Marte progresses from the sacristy to the torture chamber to prison, the couple leave the church and arrive at the forest); there is a realistic motivation (the boy choir rehearses for the immolation, the cart brings wood for the stake); and the segments are linked by dissolves (in the film, a shift to another day is marked by a fade). So Herlofs Marte's trial and torture consume a single day.

2 Vladimir Nizhny, *Lessons with Eisenstein*, trans. and ed. Ivor Montague and Jay Leyda (New York: Hill and Wang, 1962), p. 34.

3 *Ibid.*, p. 72.

4 *Ibid.*, p. 63.

5 Frederic Jameson, "Metacommentary," *PMLA* 81, no. 1 (1972): 9.

6 See Douglas Sirk's remarks in *Sirk on Sirk*, ed. Jon Halliday (New York: Viking, 1972), p. 129.

7 Raymond Durgnat, *Eros in the Cinema* (London: Calder and Boyars, 1966), p. 50.

8 André Bazin, *Jour de Colère*," in *Le Cinema de la cruauté* (Paris: Flammarion, 1975), p. 41.

9 I have found no source for the film's version of the poem. The standard Danish translation of Thomas of Celano's poem dates from the Middle Ages and is a fairly literal one. It may be found in Henrik Jul Hansen, ed., *Antologi af Nordisk Litteratur,* vol. 3, *1300–1525* (Copenhagen: Cph. Samleren, 1973), pp. 31–32. Very likely the version was composed for the film.

10 See Fernando Lazaro Carreter, "The Literal Message," *Critical Inquiry* 3 (Winter 1976): 323.

11 "A propos du 'Discours Biblique,' " in *La Traversée des signes* (Paris: Éditions du Seuil, 1975), p. 223.

12 Howard Barnes, "On the Screen," *New York Herald-Tribune,* 26 April 1948, p. 14.

13 "The Screen in Review," *New York Times,* 26 April 1948, sec. 2, p. 21.

14 "Introduction to the Structural Analysis of Narrative," p. 248.

15 *Dreyer in Double Reflection,* p. 133.

16 "Introduction to the Structural Analysis of Narrative," p. 248.

17 "Film Style and Technology in the Forties," *Film Quarterly* 21 (Fall 1977): 47.

18 *Dreyer in Double Reflection,* p. 129.

19 Quoted in Rechendorff, "Skulde jeg lav Filmen igen . . . ," p. 4.

20 *Dreyer in Double Reflection,* p. 123.

21 *Dreyer: Cadres et mouvements,* pp. 126–28.

22 *Dreyer in Double Reflection,* p. 123.

23 *Ibid.,* pp. 123–24.

24 *Ibid.,* p. 124.

25 "Art as Technique," in Lemon and Reis, eds., *Russian Formalist Criticism,* p. 12.

26 "Cinema as Device," unpublished seminar paper, University of Wisconsin–Madison, p. 9.

27 "On the Connection between Devices of *Sjuzhet* Construction and General Stylistic Devices (1919)," *Twentieth Century Studies,* no. 7/8 (December 1972), p. 60.

28 *Ibid.,* p. 48.

29 *Introduction to the Sociology of Music,* trans. E. B. Ashton (New York: Seabury Press, 1976), p. 74.

ORDET

1 Boris Tomashevsky, "Thematics," in Lemon and Reis, eds., *Russian Formalist Criticism,* p. 81.

2 *Cinema of Carl Dreyer,* p. 164.

3 *What is Cinema?* vol. 1, p. 87.

4 *Ibid.,* p. 90.

5 *Ibid.,* p. 107.

6 *Ibid.*

7 *Ibid.,* p. 121.

8 Although Dreyer called *Ordet* a "cinematization" of theatre, I am suggesting the film works toward a "theatricalization" of cinema.

9 *Technique of Film Editing,* p. 234.

10 *Esthétique et psychologie du cinéma,* vol. 2, p. 37.

11 See Raymond Durgnat, "The Restless Camera," *Films and Filming* 15 (December 1968): 14–15.

12 *Dreyer: Cadres et mouvements,* p. 127.

13 "Dreyer," pp. 11, 16–17.

14 *Dreyer in Double Reflection,* p. 129.

15 David Bordwell, "Camera Movement and Cinematic Space," p. 23.

16 Interview with Bendtsen, 25 June 1976.

17 "The further Schoenberg's very personal style developed, the more strongly the absolutism of his music appeared. Even where the marriage of word and sound belongs to the nature of his work, in songs and in choruses, in melodramas and in operas (i.e., in half of Schoenberg's works), the text determines the character but never the form of its music. . . . The aesthetic absolutism of Schoenberg goes so far that he even refuses the smallest demands of non-musical forces on music, whether they stem from literature, theatre, film, technique, or even practical music-making." H. H. Stuckenschmidt, *Schoenberg* (New York: Grove Press, 1959), pp. 159–60.

18 *Dreyer in Double Reflection,* pp. 53–54.

19 Quoted in Stephen Heath, "Lessons from Brecht," *Screen* 15 (Summer 1974): 124–25.

20 "Dreyer," p. 17.

21 "What Is Exposition?" in John Halperin, ed., *The Theory of the Novel: New Essays* (New York: Oxford University Press, 1974), p. 47.

22 *Semiotics of the Cinema,* trans. Mark E. Suino (Ann Arbor: Michigan Slavic Contributions, 1976), *passim.*

23 I believe that André Bazin was the first film theorist to suggest how a film might systematically actualize several stylistic alternatives. See his discussion of *Citizen Kane* in *Orson Welles* (Paris: Editions du Cerf, 1972), pp. 66–72. In more recent years, Noël Burch has advanced this line of thinking through his discussion of "permutational" structures in films, as in his analyses of *M* in *Theory of Film Practice,* p. 14, and, more extensively, in "De 'Mabuse' à 'M': Le Travail de Fritz Lang," in Dominique Noguez, ed., *Cinema: Theorie, Lectures* (Paris: Klincksieck, 1973), pp. 227–48.

24 Juri Lotman, *Analysis of the Poetic Text,* trans. D. Barton Johnson (Ann Arbor: Ardis, 1976), p. 124.

25 Vlada Petric, "Dreyer's Concept of Abstraction," *Sight and Sound* 44 (Spring 1975): 110.

GERTRUD

1 See Elliott Stein, *"Gertrud," Sight and Sound* 34 (Spring 1965): 57.

2 Stanley Kauffmann, "Screen: A Dreyer Film," *New York Times,* 3 June 1966, p. 33.

3 Dwight McDonald, "Films," *Esquire,* December 1965, p. 86.

4 A. E. F. Dickinson, *Vaughan Williams* (London: Faber and Faber, 1963), p. 350.

5 Borge Trolle, "An Interview with Carl Th. Dreyer," *Film Culture,* no. 41 (Summer 1966), p. 59.

6 "The Third Meaning," in Stephen Heath, ed., *Image-Music-Text* (New York: Hill and Wang, 1978), p. 64.

7 Trolle, "Interview," p. 59.

8 Noël Burch and Jorge Dana, "Propositions," *Afterimage,* no. 5 (Spring 1974), p. 62. See also Pierre Boulez, *Notes of an Apprenticeship,* trans. Herbert Weinstock (New York: Knopf, 1968), pp. 72–145, and Milton Babbitt, "Moses and Aaron," in Benjamin Boretz and Edward T. Cone, eds., *Perspectives on Schoenberg and Stravinsky* (Princeton: Princeton University Press, 1968), pp. 53–60.

9 The term has been suggested by Edward Branigan.

10 "Propositions," p. 62.

11 "The Third Meaning," in Heath, ed., *Image-Music-Text,* p. 63.

12 "Art as Technique," in Lemon and Reis, eds., *Russian Formalist Criticism,* p. 12.

13 My discussion of excess follows, with some modification, that suggested by Kristin Thompson, "The Concept of Cinematic Excess," *Ciné-Tracts* 1 (Summer 1977): 54–65.

14 John Simon, *Private Screenings* (New York: Berkley, 1971), pp. 39, 214.

DREYER'S USES

1 See Lars Furhoff, "Competition between Danish Newspapers," *Scandinavian Economic Review* 21 (1973): 207–9; W. J. Harvey and Christian Reppien, *Denmark and the Danes* (Port Washington: Kennikat Press, 1915), 253–55. Samples of Dreyer's journalism may be found in "Dreyer journaliste," *Cahiers du Cinéma,* no. 207 (December 1968), pp. 23–31.

2 Quoted in Knud Schønberg, "Dreyer 75," *Ekstrabladet,* 1 February 1964; clipping on file at the Danish Film Archive.

3 *Dreyer in Double Reflection,* p. 176.

4 T. W. Adorno, "Arnold Schoenberg 1874–1951," in Samuel and Shierry Weber, eds., *Prisms* (London: Neville Spearman, 1967), p. 170.

5 A. D. Henriksen, "Dansk Overklasse-Propaganda," *Arbejdet,* February 1921; clipping on file at the Danish Film Archive.

6 Georges Sadoul, *Histoire générale du cinéma,* vol. 3, pt. 2 (Paris: Denoël, 1952), p. 383.

7 Carl-Theodor Dreyer, "Med anledning av filmen, 'Blad ur Satans bok,' " *Filmrevyn,* no. 3 (1922), p. 92.

8 See W. Glyn Jones, *Denmark* (New York: Praeger, 1970), pp. 133–39, and Walter Galenson, *The Danish System of Labor Relations* (Cambridge, Mass.: Harvard University Press, 1952), p. 285.

9 Carl-Th. Dreyer, "Parmi les artistes émigrés à Berlin," *Cahiers du Cinéma,* no. 207 (December 1968), pp. 20–21.

10 *Dreyer in Double Reflection,* pp. 47–50.

11 J. T. Bury, *France: Insecure Peace* (New York: American Heritage Press, 1972) p. 79.

12 Roger Manvell, "Lunch with Carl Dreyer," *Penguin Film Review,* no. 3 (August 1947), p. 67.

13 Bertolt Brecht, *Sur le cinéma* (Paris: L'Arche, 1970), pp. 148–220.

14 Jean-Louis Comolli and Paul Narboni, "Cinema/Ideology/Criticism," *Screen* 12 (Spring 1971), p. 29.

15 *Ibid.,* pp. 32–33.

16 Julia Kristeva, "Signifying Practice and Mode of Production," *Edinburgh 76 Magazine,* no. 1 (1976), p. 65.

17 *Rabelais and his World,* trans. Helene Iswolsky (Cambridge, Mass.,: MIT Press, 1968), pp. 321–22.

18 Henrik Stangerup, "Dreyer vil skabe en ny filmtype," *Information,* 27 June 1964; clipping on file at Danish Film Archive.

19 Mark Nash's monograph *Dreyer* discusses several functions of woman in Dreyer's films.

20 Quoted in Susan Buck-Morss, *The Origin of Negative Dialectics* (New York: Free Press, 1977), p. 118.

21 "The World of Carl Dreyer," *Film Quarterly* 19 (Fall 1965): 27.

22 Buck-Morss, *Negative Dialectics,* p. 119.

23 Interview with Bjorn Rasmussen, 26 January 1964; typescript on file at the Danish Film Archive, p. 5.

24 "Hj." [pseud.], "Jeanne d'Arc-Filmen i Palads Teatret"; undated clipping on file at the Danish Film Archive.

25 "M. Eisenstein's New Film," *New York Times,* 16 February 1930, sec. 10, p. 6. A similar view was expressed by Jorge Luis Borges in "La Fuga," *Sur,* no. 7 (August 1937), p. 121.

26 *The Film Till Now* (London: Spring Books, 1967), p. 305.

27 *Dreyer in Double Reflection,* p. 54.

28 *Des dispositifs pulsionnels* (Paris: 10/18, 1973), pp. 53–69.

29 Adorno, "Arnold Schoenberg 1874–1951," p. 164.

30 *Ibid.,* p. 171.

31 Quoted in John Ernst, program notes for Dreyer's documentaries (Danish Film Archive), n.p.; Carlos Clarens, "*India Song* and Marguerite Duras," *Sight and Sound* 45 (Winter 1975/76): 33.

32 *Brother Carl* (New York: Farrar, Straus and Giroux, 1974), p. xv.

33 Serge Toubania, "Entretien avec Luc Moullet," *Cahiers du Cinéma,* no. 283 (December 1977), p. 41.

34 "Circulaire," *Cahiers du Cinéma,* no. 164 (March 1965), p. 72.

35 Yuri Tynianov, "On Literary Evolution," in Matejka and Pomorska, eds., *Readings in Russian Poetics,* p. 77.

36 Although plenty of evidence exists: Godard ranked Dreyer with Lumière and Griffith and compared *Gertrud* with Beethoven's late quartets. See *Godard on Godard,* ed. and trans. Tom Milne (New York: Viking, 1972), pp. 236, 232.

37 *Ibid.,* p. 185.

38 Heath, "Lessons from Brecht," p. 117.

39 *Technique of Film Editing,* p. 386.

40 "Andi Engel talks to Jean-Marie Straub and Danièle Huillet is there too," *Enthusiasm* 1, no. 1, p. 15. Straub called *Vampyr* "the most resonant of all films," and asserted that "the fact that Dreyer was never able to produce a film in color (he had thought about it for more than twenty years), nor his film on Christ (a profound revolt against the state and the origins of anti-Semitism) reminds us that we live in a society that is not worth a frog's fart" ("Férvce," *Cahiers du Cinéma,* no. 207 [December 1968], p. 35).

41 Quoted in Karl H. Worner, *Stockhausen: Life and Work* (Berkeley and Los Angeles: University of California Press, 1976), p. 81.

42 *Illuminations,* p. 72.

43 Peter Gidal, "Theory and Definition of Structural/Materialist Film," in Peter Gidal, ed., *Structural Film Anthology* (London: British Film Institute, 1976), p. 5.

44 *Dreyer in Double Reflection,* p. 167.

BIOGRAPHICAL FILMOGRAPHY

1 See Mike Snapp, "Speech Chairman Profiles Dane Director Carl Th. Dreyer," *The 49'er,* 9 December 1971; clipping on file at the Danish Film Archive.

2 Quoted in Ebbe Neergaard, "*Du Skal Ære din Hustru*," Danish Film Archive program note, February 1954, n.p.

3 Interview with Bjorn Rasmussen, 26 January 1964; typescript on file at the Danish Film Archive, pp. 2–3.

4 Letter from Dreyer to Frost, c. 1915; Danish Film Archive collection.

5 Jean Mitry, *Histoire du cinéma,* vol. 2 (Paris: Éditions universitaires, 1969), pp. 273–76; Georges Sadoul, *Histoire générale du cinéma,* vol. 3, pt. 2 (Paris: Denoël, 1952), p. 380.

6 Quoted in Erik Ulrichsen, "*Præsidenten,*" Danish Film Archive program note, March 1958, p. 1; see also Judith Podselver, "Motion Pictures in Denmark," *Hollywood Quarterly* 3 (Winter 1947–48): 19.

7 Quoted in Jørgen Roos's documentary film *Carl Th. Dreyer.*

8 Interview with Rasmussen, pp. 3–4.

9 Skalk, "Blade af Satans Bog," *Ekstrabladet,* 22 January 1921; clipping on file at the Danish Film Archive.

10 Quoted in *Ebbe Neergaards Bog om Dreyer,* p. 22.

11 "Vil de Hellige løbe Storm mod 'Blade af Satans Bog'?" *Folkets Avis,* 28 January 1921; clipping on file at the Danish Film Archive.

12 Henriksen, "Dansk Overklasse-Propaganda."

13 Neergaard, *Carl Th. Dreyer: A Film Director's Work,* p. 14.

14 Riccioto Canudo, *L'usine des images* (Geneva: Office centrale d'édition, 1927), p. 149.

15 Kammerherren [pseud.], "Der var en gang," *Film Politiken Magasinet,* 3 June 1922, p. 6.

16 *Ebbe Neergaards Bog om Dreyer,* p. 37.

17 For a detailed account of Stiller's film, see Gosta Werner, *Mauritz Stiller och hans filmer: 1912–1916* (Stockholm: P. A. Norstedt, 1969), pp. 312–24. See also Erik Ulrichsen, "Dreyer og 'Mikaël,' " *Kosmorama,* no. 41 (January 1959), p. 102.

18 Letter from Dreyer to Frost, 4 January 1924, Danish Film Archive collection.

19 Neergaard, "*Du Skal Ære din Hustru,*" p. 1.

20 See *La Cinématographie Française,* no. 383 (6 March 1926); clipping on file at the Danish Film Archive.

21 *Ebbe Neergaards Bog om Dreyer,* p. 48.

22 *The Film Till Now,* p. 298.

23 See "Echoes et nouvelles," *La Critique Cinématographique,* no. 34 (16 July 1927), p. 16.

24 "Dreyer brugte sanfærdigbeden som stilmiddel," p. 147.

25 Jean Arroy and Jean-Charles Reynaud, *Attention! On tourne* (Paris: Tallandier, 1929), p. x.

26 "Dreyer brugte sanfærdigbeden som stilmiddel," p. 147.

27 Lucie Derain, "Ceux qui ont joué la 'Jeanne d'Arc' de Dreyer," "*La Passion de Jeanne d'Arc,*" *Cinémagazine hors série* (1928), p. 47.

28 This timetable is compiled from accounts in *La Critique Cinématographique,* vol. 2: no. 16 (11 March 1927), p. 1; no. 17 (18 March 1927), p. 1; no. 27 (28 May 1927), p. 4; no. 35 (23 July 1927), p. 17; no. 37 (6 August 1927), p. 13; no. 40 (27 August 1927), p. 14; and in "L'Activité cinématographique," *Cinéa-Ciné pour tous* (15 November 1927), p. 29.

29 "Hj." [pseud.], "Jeanne d'Arc-Filmen i Palads Teatret."

30 "Ce que pensent de 'La Passion de Jeanne d'Arc' " in "*La Passion de Jeanne d'Arc,*" *Cinémagazine hors série* (1928), pp. 63–64.

31 "En France," *Comœdia,* 21 June 1928, p. 6; René Lebreton, "La Passion de Jeanne d'Arc," *Comœdia,* 27 June 1928, p. 6.

32 Mordaunt Hall, "La Passion de Jeanne d'Arc," *New York Times,* 31 March 1929, sec. 8, p. 7; Léon Moussinac, *L'Age ingrât du cinéma* (Paris: Editeurs français réunis, 1967), p. 284*n*.

33 Antonin Artaud, "Interview for *Cinémonde,*" in *Selected Writings,* ed. Susan Sontag (New York: Noonday, 1976), p. 184.

34 Dreyer, "The Filmmaker and the Audience," pp. 42–43. See also the exchange of letters between Herman G. Weinberg and myself in *Sight and Sound* 44 (Summer 1975): 197, and *Sight and Sound* 44 (Fall 1975): 263.

35 "En Film-Skat er Fundet!" *Aftenbladet,* 24 January 1952; clipping on file at the Danish Film Archive.

36 Børge Rudbeck, "Dreyers Jeanne d'Arc fundet i Affaldsbunke," *Ekstrabladet,* 28 February 1952; clipping on file at the Danish Film Archive.

37 Hall, "La Passion de Jeanne d'Arc," p. 7.

38 Interview with Rasmussen, pp. 4–5.

39 Ralph Holm, "Vampyren fra Courtempierre," *Berlingske Aftenavis,* 16 April 1942; clipping on file at the Danish Film Archive.

40 E.g., in Roos's documentary film *Carl Th. Dreyer.*

41 *Ebbe Neergaards Bog om Dreyer,* p. 68.

42 Ernesto Quadrone, "Il 'Mudundu' di Dreyer," *Cinema,* no. 67 (1 August 1951), pp. 49–51, 57. Cf. "Kvinden der var skyld, al Carl Th. Dreyer, rejste hjem fra Afrika!" *Ekstrabladet,* undated clipping on file at the Danish Film Archive.

43 "Gtz." [pseud.], "Carl Th. Dreyer Genkomst som Film-Instruktor," *Politiken,* 8 February 1942; clipping on file at Danish Film Archive. See also Rechendorff, "Skulde je lave Filmen igen . . . ," p. 4.

44 Pierre, "Falske Forestillinger om Renæssancetiden?" *Ekstrabladet,* 18 November 1943, p. 4. See also Film Centre (London), *The Film Industry in Six European Countries,* pp. 22, 71.

45 Rechendorff, "Skulde jeg lave Filmen igen . . . ," p. 4.

46 André Bazin, "*Jour de colère,*" p. 43.

47 Quoted in "Carl Th. Dreyer i polemik med Svensk Film," *Information,* 23 June 1959; clipping on file at the Danish Film Archive.

48 *Ibid;* "Carl Dreyer," in Sarris, ed., *Interviews* p. 162.

49 Erlich, *Russian Formalism,* p. 261.

50 For details of the *Jesus* project, see David Bordwell, "Passion, Death, and Testament," *Film Comment* 8 (Summer 1972): 59–63.

51 The play is available in English translation in Kaj Munk, *Five Plays* (New York: American-Scandinavian Foundation, 1953). For a comparison of the play, Dreyer's film, and Mollander's film, see Thorkild Borup Jensen, *Roman og drama bli'ir til film* (Copenhagen: Gyldendal, 1965), pp. 153–207.

52 *Ebbe Neergaards Bog om Dreyer,* pp. 92–98.

53 Quoted in *ibid.,* p. 98.

54 *Ibid.* Cf. Ebbe Neergaard, " 'The Word,' " *Sight and Sound* 24 (Summer 1955): 172–73.

55 Quoted in Jan Aghed, "Dreyers 'Gertrud' ett experiment," *Svenska Dagbladet,* 16 November 1964; clipping on file at the Danish Film Archive.

56 Sten Rein, *Hjalmar Söderbergs Gertrud* (Stockholm: Bonnier, 1962), pp. 355–56.

57 Børge Trolle, "Interview with Carl Dreyer," *Film Culture,* no. 41 (Summer 1966), p. 58.

58 Henrik Stangerup, "Til verdens-premiere på *Gertrud,*" *Kosmorama,* no. 85 (June 1968), p. 167.

59 See Elliott Stein, "*Gertrud,*" *Sight and Sound* 34 (Spring 1965): 56, and Jean Béranger, *Le Nouveau cinéma scandinave* (Paris: Losfeld, 1968), pp. 256–58.

60 See Béranger, pp. 257–58.

Bibliography

Works by Dreyer

SCRIPTS

"Carl Dreyer's Story of the Jew Jesus." Typescript on file with the New York Public Library at Lincoln Center for the Performing Arts, 1949.

Cinque Film. Turin: Einaudi, 1967.

Four Screenplays. Translated by Oliver Stallybrass. London: Thames and Hudson, 1970.

Jesus. New York: Dial Press, 1972.

Various original script materials on deposit at the Danish Film Archive, Copenhagen.

WRITINGS

Dreyer, Carl Theodor. Correspondence, legal records, and personal material on deposit at the Danish Film Archive, Copenhagen.

———. "The Filmmaker and the Audience." In *Film: Book One,* edited by Robert Hughes. New York: Grove Press, 1959.

———. "Liminaire." In *Dictionnaire du cinema,* edited by Raymond Bellour and Jean-Jacques Brochier. Paris: Éditions universitaires, 1966.

———. "Med anledning av filmen, 'Blad ur Satans bok." *Filmrevyn,* no. 5 (1922), p. 92.

———. "Metaphysic of *Ordet*." In *The Film Culture Reader,* edited by P. Adams Sitney. New York: Praeger, 1970.

———. "Mit problem er stadig det samme." *Biografbladet,* no. 6 (1964), p. 12.

———. "Parmi les acteurs émigrés à Berlin." *Cahiers du Cinéma,* no. 207 (December 1968), pp. 20–21.

———. Preface to *The Story of Danish Film,* by Ebbe Neergaard. Copenhagen: The Danish Institute, 1962.

———. "L'uso dei primi piani." In *Cinque Film.* Turin: Einaudi, 1967.

Ernst, John, et al., eds. "Dreyer Mosaik." *Kosmorama* no. 64 (December 1963), pp. 94–99.

Skoller, Donald, ed. *Dreyer in Double Reflection.* New York: Dutton, 1973. English translation of Carl Theodor Dreyer, *Om Filmen* (Copenhagen: Gyldendal, 1964).

INTERVIEWS

Allombert, Guy. "Carl Dreyer, l'un des hommes les plus mystérieux du cinéma, est à Paris." *Arts,* 16–22 December 1964, p. 14.

Biagi, Enzo. "Pomeriggio con Dreyer." *Cinema* 2 (13 July 1949): 16–17.

Card, James. "Visit with Carl Th. Dreyer." *Image* 2 (December 1953): 61.

"Carl Th. Dreyer udtaler sig." *Politiken,* 26 April 1931, p. 8.

Dahlin, Ture. "Carl Th. Dreyer à Paris." *La Cinématographie Française,* 27 March 1926, pp. 5–6.

Delahaye, Michel. "Carl Dreyer." In Andrew Sarris, ed., *Interviews with Film Directors.* New York: Avon, 1969.

Dreyer, Carl Theodor. "Filmographie commentée." *Cahiers du Cinéma,* no. 207 (December 1968), pp. 66–74.

Duperly, Denis. "Carl Dreyer: Utter Bore or Total Genius?" *Films and Filming* 14 (February 1968): 45–46.

Eisner, Lotte H. "Rencontre avec Carl Dreyer." *Cahiers du Cinéma,* no. 48 (June 1955), pp. 1–5.

Grasten, Bent. "Jeg har stof til ti film." *Ekstrabladet,* 18 December 1964. Clipping on file at the Danish Film Archive.

Jackson, Ragna. "Lunch with Carl Dreyer." *Penguin Film Review,* no. 3 (August 1947), p. 67.

Lennon, Peter. "The Passion of Carl Dreyer." *The Guardian,* 21 December 1964, p. 7.

Lerner, Carl. "My Way of Working Is in Relation to the Future: A Conversation with Carl Dreyer." *Film Comment* 4 (Fall 1966): 62–67.

Podselver, Judith. "Motion Pictures in Denmark." *Hollywood Quarterly* 3 (Winter 1947–48): 195–99.

Rechendorff [pseud.]. "Skulde jeg lave Filmen igen, blev den lige saaden." *Berlingske Tidende,* 17 November 1943, p. 4.

Sadoul, Georges. "Carl Dreyer nous dit: 'Le principal intérêt d'un homme: les autres hommes.' " *Les Lettres Françaises,* no. 1060 (24 December 1964), p. 8.

Trolle, Børge. "Interview with Carl Dreyer." *Film Culture,* no. 41 (Summer 1966), pp. 58–60.

Winge, John H. "Interview with Dreyer." *Sight and Sound* 18 (January 1950): 16–17.

Critical and Historical Studies and Documents

ON DANISH CINEMA

Bergsten, Bebe. *The Great Dane: The Great Northern Film Company.* Los Angeles: Locare Research Group, 1973.

Brusendorff, Ove. *Filmen: Dens Navne og Historie.* 3 vols. Copenhagen: Universal-Forlaget, 1939.

Card, James. "Influences of the Danish Film." *Image* 5 (March 1956): 51–57.

Engberg, Marguerite. *Den Dansk Stumfilm 1903–1930.* Copenhagen: Danish Film Archive, 1968.

———. *Dansk Stumfilm: De Store År.* Copenhagen: Rhodos, 1977.

Ernst, John. *Benjamin Christensen.* Copenhagen: Danish Film Archive, 1967.

Gad, Urban. *Filmen: Dens Midler og Maal.* Copenhagen: Gyldendal, 1919.

Hardy, Forsyth. *Scandinavian Film.* London: Falcon Press, 1952.

Hending, Arnold. *Da Isbjørnen var lille.* Copenhagen: Urania, 1945.

———. *Fremmede Fugle i Dansk Film.* Copenhagen: Athena, 1951.

———. *Stjerner i Glashuse.* Copenhagen: Winkelmanns, 1936.

Mottram, Ron. "Influences between National Cinemas: Denmark and the United States." *Cinema Journal* 14 (Winter 1974–75): 3–10.

Neergaard, Ebbe. *Documentary in Denmark.* Copenhagen: Staatens Filmcentral, 1948.

———. "The Rise, the Fall, and the Rise of Danish Film." *Hollywood Quarterly* 4 (1949–50): 217–32.

———. *The Story of Danish Film.* Copenhagen: The Danish Institute, 1962.

Nørgaard, Erik. *Levende billeder i Danmark.* Copenhagen: Lademann, 1971.

Stormgaard, Uffe, and Dyssegaard, Soren. *Danish Films.* Copenhagen: Danish Film Institute and the Ministry of Foreign Affairs, 1973.

ON DREYER'S CAREER

A. M. [pseud.]. "Dreyer exploitant." *Cahiers du Cinéma,* no. 92 (July-August 1959), p. 13.

Agel, Henri. *Les Grands cinéastes.* Paris: Éditions du Cerf, 1960.

Amette, Jacques-Pierre. "Carl Th. Dreyer," in *Dossiers du cinéma: Cinéastes I.* Paris: Castermann, 1971.

Aristarco, Guido. "Introduzione" in Carl Th. Dreyer, *Cinque Film.* Turin: Einaudi, 1967.

Astruc, Alexandre. "Dreyer in memoriam . . ." *Kosmorama,* no. 85 (June 1968), pp. 164–66.

Ayfre, Amédée. *Le Cinéma et sa verité.* Paris: Éditions du Cerf, 1969.

Bond, Kirk. "The World of Carl Dreyer." *Film Quarterly* 19 (Fall 1965): 26–38.

Bowser, Eileen. *The Films of Carl Dreyer.* New York: Museum of Modern Art, 1964.

Brakhage, Stan. *The Brakhage Lectures.* Chicago: The Good Lion, 1972.

Cahiers du Cinéma, no. 207 (December 1968). Special number on Dreyer.

Carl Theodor Dreyer. Amsterdam: Netherlands Film Museum, 1970.

Carl Theodor Dreyer Retrospektive. Frankfurt am Main: n.p., 1963.

Cuenca, Carlos Fernandez. *Carl Theodor Dreyer.* Madrid: Filmoteca Nacional de España, 1964.

Dyssegaard, Soren, ed. *Carl Th. Dreyer, Danish Film Director.* Copenhagen: Ministry of Foreign Affairs, 1968.

Ecran Français, no. 124 (11 November 1947). Special number on Dreyer.

Egebok, Niels. "Carl Th. Dreyers filmstil og virkeligheds opfattelse." *Vinduet* 19 (1963), 232–40.

Eisner, Lotte. "Réalisme et irréel chez Dreyer." *Cahiers du Cinéma,* no. 65 (December 1956), pp. 17–18.

Ernst, Helge. *Dreyer: Carl Th. Dreyer—en dansk filmskaber.* Copenhagen: Gjellerup, 1972.

Ernst, John. "At læse film." *Kosmorama* 11 (December 1964): 82–84.

Furhammer, Leif. "Carl Dreyer, Film Konstnar." *Svenska Dagbladet,* 6 May 1964. Clipping on file at the Danish Film Archive.

Gelsted, Otto. "En dansk Filmsinstruktor og hans Værk." *Arbejderbladet,* 15 May 1940.

Grafe, Frieda. "Spiritual Men and Natural Women." In *Dreyer,* edited and with an introductory essay by Mark Nash. London: British Film Institute, 1977.

Grcar, Misa. *Carl Th. Dreyer.* Jugoslavia Kinoteca, 1970.

Gress, Elsa. "Om Dreyers Kunstneriske Teknik." *Louisiana Revy,* no. 4 (March 1967), pp. 34–36.

———. "Portræt af Carl Th. Dreyer i alderdommen." *Kosmorama,* no. 85 (June 1968), pp. 168–69.

Kelman, Ken. "Dreyer." In *The Film Culture Reader,* edited by P. Adams Sitney. New York: Praeger, 1970.

Kosmorama, no. 85 (June 1968). Special number on Dreyer.

Lo Duca. "Trilogie mystique de Dreyer." *Cahiers du Cinéma,* no. 9 (February 1952), pp. 61–63.

Luft, Herbert G. "Dreyer." *Films and Filming* 7 (June 1961): 11.

Milne, Tom. *The Cinema of Carl Dreyer.* New York: A. S. Barnes, 1971.

Monty, Ib. "Carl Th. Dreyer." *Almanak* 2 (1967–68): 20–27.

———. "Great Dane." *Sight and Sound* 37 (Spring 1968), 74–75.

———. *Portrait of Carl Th. Dreyer.* Copenhagen: Danish Government Film Foundation, 1965.

Nash, Mark. *Dreyer.* London: British Film Institute, 1977.

Neergaard, Ebbe. *Carl Theodor Dreyer: A Film Director's Work.* London: British Film Institute New Index Series, 1950.

———. *Ebbe Neergaards Bog om Dreyer.* Copenhagen: Dansk Videnskabs Forlag, 1963.

———. "Lærling og mester." *50 Aar i Dansk Film.* Copenhagen: Nordisk, 1956.

Nuestro cine, no. 76 (August 1968). Special number on Dreyer.

Parrain, Philippe. "Dreyer: cadres et mouvements." *Études Cinématographiques,* nos. 53–56 (1967).

Perrin, Claude. *Carl Th. Dreyer.* Paris: Seghers, 1969.

Plazewski, Jerzy. *Carl Theodor Dreyer.* Varsovia: Filmowa Agenzja Wydawnicza, 1957.

Podselver, Judith. "Motion Pictures in Denmark." *Hollywood Quarterly* 3 (Winter 1947–48): 195–99.

Powell, Dilys. "Carl Dreyer: The Director as Artist." In *Screen and Audience,* edited by John E. Cross and Arnold Rattenbury. London: Chatto and Windus, 1947.

Ranieri, Tino. "I fogli del libro." *Bianco e nero* 29 (July–August 1968): 92–115.

Rasmussen, Bjorn. "The Cinema." *Denmark: An Official Handbook.* Copenhagen: Ministry for Foreign Affairs, 1974.

———. "Profet og Fæderland." *Fyns Stiftstidende,* 2 February 1949.

Schrader, Paul. *Transcendental Style in Film: Ozu, Bresson, Dreyer.* Berkeley and Los Angeles: University of California Press, 1972.

Sémolué, Jean. *Carl Th. Dreyer.* Paris: Anthologie du Cinéma, 1970.

———. " 'Douleur, Noblesse Unique' ou la passion chez Carl Dreyer." *Etudes Cinématographiques,* nos. 10–11 (Fall 1961), pp. 150–61.

———. *Dreyer.* Paris: Éditions universitaires, 1962.

Straub, Jean-Marie. "Féroce." *Cahiers du Cinéma,* no. 207 (December 1968), p. 35.

Téchiné, André. "The Nordic Archaicism of Dreyer." In *Dreyer,* edited and with an introductory essay by Mark Nash. London: British Film Institute, 1977.

Tone, Pier Giorgio. *Carl Theodor Dreyer.* Firenze: La Nuovo Italia, 1978.

Trolle, Børge. *The Art of Carl Dreyer: An Analysis.* Copenhagen: Danish Government Film Foundation, 1955.

———. "The World of Carl Dreyer." *Sight and Sound* 25 (Winter 1955–56): 123–27.

Ulrichsen, Erik. "Carl Th. Dreyers Verden." *Berlingske Tidende,*. 20 January 1955. Clipping on file at the Danish Film Archive.

———. "The Duality of Dreyer." *Danish Foreign Office Journal,* no. 53 (June 1965), pp. 18–20.

Vaughan, Dai. "Carl Dreyer and the Theme of Choice." *Sight and Sound* 43 (Summer 1974): 156–62.

Vincent, Carl. "Carl-Theodor Dreyer e la sua opera." *Bianco e nero* 10 (October 1949): 14–20.

Wood, Robin. "Carl Dreyer." *Film Comment* 10 (March–April 1974): 10–17.

ON PARTICULAR FILMS

Dreyer's Early Scriptwriting

Olsen, Grete, and Malmkjær, Poul. "Filmindex XXXVIII: Carl Th. Dreyers manuskriptarbejde før 'Præsidenten.' " *Kosmorama,* no. 41 (January 1959), p. 120.

Werner, Gosta. *"Döden forener." Chaplin,* no. 139 (1975, pp. 164–69.

The President

Ulrichsen, Erik. *"Præsidenten."* Danish Film Archive program note, March 1958.

Leaves from Satan's Book

Henriksen, A. D. "Dansk Overklasse-Propaganda." *Arbejdet,* 8 February 1921. Clipping on file at the Danish Film Archive.

Høyer, Edgar. "A propos 'Blade af Satans Bog.' " *Politiken,* 9 January 1921. Clipping on file at the Danish Film Archive.

Skalk [pseud.]. "Blade af Satans Bog." *Ekstrabladet,* 22 January 1921. Clipping on file at the Danish Film Archive.

"Vil de Hellige lobe Storm mod 'Blade af Satans Bog?" *Folkets Avis,* 28 January 1921. Clipping on file at the Danish Film Archive.

The Parson's Widow

Christensen, Theodor. "Prästänkan." Danish Film Archive program note, April 1953.

The Stigmatized Ones

Matusevitch, Vladimir. "Dem tabte og genfundne Dreyer-film." *Kosmorama* no. 52 (March 1960): 133–38.

Trolle, Børge. *"Die Gezeichneten."* Danish Film Archive program note, November 1961.

Once upon a Time

"Der Var Engang." Paladsteatret Films Nyheder, no. 4 (1922–23).

Kammerherren [pseud.]. "Der var en Gang—paa Film." *Film Politiken,* 3 June 1922. Clipping on file at the Danish Film Archive.

Trolle, Børge. "Eneren i dansk film." *Kosmorama* no. 9 (May 1955), 4–11.

Michael

"Kammerspillet paa det hvide Lærred." *Paladsteatret Films Nyheder,* no. 8 (1925). Clipping on file at the Danish Film Archive.

Luft, Herbert. "Erich Pommer, Part II." *Films in Review* 10 (November 1959): 518–33.

Ulrichsen, Erik. "Dreyer og 'Mikaël.' " *Kosmorama,* no. 41 (January 1959), 102–5.

———. *"Michael."* Danish Film Archive program note, February 1969.

Thou Shalt Honor Thy Wife

Neergaard, Ebbe. "Du Skal Aere din Hustru." Danish Film Archive program note, February 1954.

The Bride of Glomdal

Saxtoph, Erik S. "*Glomdalsbruden*." Danish Film Archive program note, May 1959.

La Passion de Jeanne d'Arc

Amengual, Barthélémy. "Fonctions du gros plan et du cadrage dans *La Passion de Jeanne d'Arc*." *Études Cinématographiques*, nos. 53–56 (1967), pp. 155–63.

Ayfre, Amédée. "Les voix du silence." *Cahiers du Cinéma*, no. 17 (November 1952), pp. 58–60.

Bassoli, Vincenzo. *La Passione di Giovanna d'Arco*. Padova: RADAR, 1968.

Bond, Kirk. "Léger, Dreyer, and Montage." *Creative Art* (October 1932), pp. 135–38.

Bordwell, David. *Filmguide to "La Passion de Jeanne d'Arc."* Bloomington: Indiana University Press, 1973.

Bost, Pierre. *La Passion et la mort de Jeanne d'Arc*. Paris: Gallimard, 1928.

Buñuel, Luis. "Sur *Jeanne d'Arc* de Carl Theodor Dreyer (1930)." *Positif*, no. 147 (February 1973), p. 44.

Champion, Pierre. *Procès de condemnation de Jeanne d'Arc: Texte, traduction et notes*. 2 vols. Paris: Librairie spéciale pour l'histoire du France, 1920–21.

Cinémagazine hors série (1928). Special number on Dreyer.

Delteil, Joseph. *Joan of Arc*. Translated by Malcolm Cowley. New York: Minton, Balch, 1926.

———. *La Passion de Jeanne d'Arc*. Paris: M. P. Trémois, 1927.

Geertsen, Alf. "Dreyer og Jeanne d'Arc." *Vendsyssel Tidende*, 28 June 1951. Clipping on file at the Danish Film Archive.

Guerrasio, G. *La passione di Giovanna d'Arco*. Milan: Domus, 1945.

H. D. [Hilda Doolittle]. "Joan of Arc." *Close-Up* 3 (July 1928), 15–23.

Klinger, Werner. "Analytical Treatise on the Dreyer Film, 'The Passion of Joan of Arc' with Appendix of a Constructive Critique." *Experimental Cinema* 1 (February 1930): 7–10.

"M. Eisenstein's New Film." *New York Times*, 16 February 1930, sec. 10, p. 6.

Marker, Chris. "La Passion de Jeanne d'Arc." In Jacques Chevalier, ed., *Regards neufs sur le cinéma*, no. 8. Paris: Éditions du Seuil, 1953.

Moussinac, Léon. *L'Age ingrât du cinéma*. Paris: Éditeurs français réunis, 1967.

Neergaard, Ebbe. "*Jeanne d'Arc*." Danish Film Archive program note, 1955.

———. "Technique de la caméra dans la 'Jeanne d'Arc' de Dreyer." Exposition universelle et internationale de Bruxelles. *Confrontation des meilleurs films de tous les temps*. Brussels: Belgian Cinémathèque, 1958.

"*La Passion de Jeanne d'Arc*." *L'Avant-scène du Cinéma*, no. 100 (February 1970), 45–54. Dossier on the film.

Potamkin, Harry. "Dreyer, in Theory and Practice," in Lewis Jacobs, ed., *The Compound Cinema: The Film Writings of Harry Alan Potamkin* (New York: Teachers College Press, 1977), pp. 132–36.

Ramain, Paul. "Le sens des decors et le mode harmonique dans 'La Passion de Jeanne d'Arc' de Carl Dreyer." *Cinèa-Cinè pour tous*, no. 113 (15 July 1928), pp. 23–24.

Sémolué, Jean. "*La Passion de Jeanne d'Arc* prise de conscience de Carl Dreyer." *Études Cinématographiques*, nos. 18–19 (Fall 1962), pp. 38–52.

———. "*Passion* et *Procès* (de Dreyer à Bresson)." *Études Cinématographiques*, nos. 18–19 (Fall 1962), pp. 98–107.

V. S. [pseud.]. "Jeanne d'Arcs Forposter." *Berlingske Aftenavis*, 20 April 1928. Clipping on file at the Danish Film Archive.

Van Ness, Wilhelmina. "About *Jeanne d'Arc*." Unpublished manuscript.

———. "Joseph Delteil: *The Passion of Joan of Arc*." *Film/Literature Quarterly* 3 (Fall 1975): 292–98.

Wahl, Jan. "Filmkunstnerens lidelser og triumfer." *Kosmorama* no. 20 (October 1956), 40–41.

Warm, Hermann. "Dreyer brugte sanfærdigbeden som stilmiddel." *Kosmorama*, no. 90 (June 1969), 146–47.

Vampyr

Buzzi, Aldo, and Lattuada, Bianca. *Vampyr, l'étrange aventure de David Gray.* Milan: Poligono, 1948.

Casiraghi, Ugo. "Il vampiro." *Ummanità di Stroheim ed altre saggi.* Milan: Poligono, 1945.

Christensen, Theodor. *"Vampyr."* Danish Film Archive program note, n.d.

Holm, Ralph. "Vampyren fra Courtempierre." *Berlingske Aftenavis,* 16 April 1942. Clipping on file at the Danish Film Archive.

Jensen, Viggo Holm. *Vampyr: Scene-Gennemgang.* Copenhagen: Uden forlag, 1968.

———. "Vampyr, en gennemgang af externe omstændigheder." Unpublished manuscript on file at the Danish Film Archive, 1968.

Harrington, Curtis. "Ghoulies and Ghosties." *Sight and Sound* 21 (April–June 1952): 157–61.

Le Fanu, Sheridan. *In a Glass Darkly.* London: Peter Davies, 1929.

Malmkjær, Poul. "Uhyggen i os self." *Kosmorama* no. 102 (April 1971), 176–79.

Nash, Mark. *"Vampyr* and the Fantastic." *Screen* 17 (Fall 1976): 29–67.

"The Strange Adventure of David Gray." *Close-Up* 8 (March 1931), 50–51.

Weinberg, Herman G. and Gretchen. "Vampyr—An Interview with Baron de Gunzburg." *Film Culture,* no. 32 (Spring 1964), pp. 57–59.

Mudundu

Quadrone, Ernesto. "Il 'Mudundu' di Dreyer ucciso dalla Malaria." *Cinema,* no. 67 (1 August 1951), pp. 49–51, 57.

Day of Wrath

Barbut, M. L. *"Dies Irae."* Fiche filmographique no. 68. Paris: IDHEC, n.d.

Christensen, Johannes H. "Glædens dag—vredens dag." *Film 70,* no. 10 (1970), pp. 154–60.

"Dies Irae." L'Avant-scène du cinéma, no. 100 (February 1970), pp. 10–35. Transcript.

Neversharp [pseud.]. "Carl Th. Dreyer kommer igen." *Mandens Blad* 9, no. 10 (1943): 8–9.

Wiers-Jensen, Hans. *The Witch* [*Anne Pedersdotter*]. Translated by John Masefield. Boston: Little, Brown, 1917.

Two People

Christensen, Theodor. *"To Mennesker."* Danish Film Archive program note, n.d.

Documentaries

Drum, Dale D. "Carl Dreyer's Shorts." *Films in Review* 20 (January 1969): 34–41.

Ernst, John. *"Mødrehjælpen."* Danish Film Archive program note, February 1964.

Malmkjær, Poul. "Filmindex XLIII: Dreyers Dokumentarfilm." *Kosmorama,* no. 46 (October 1959), p. 40.

Ordet

Andersen, Hans. "Kaj Munk og Carl Th. Dreyer." *Fyns Venstreblad,* 29 June 1954. Clipping on file at the Danish Film Archive.

Borup-Jensen, Thorkild. *Roman og drama bli'r til film.* Copenhagen: Gyldendal, 1975.

Corpel, Kirsten. *"Ordet." Fiche filmographique,* no. 134. Paris: IDHEC, n.d.

Fonss, Møgens. "Carl Dreyer's New Film." *Films in Review* 6 (January 1955), 19–22.

Langeson, Ella. "Jeg har altid stræbt efter det enkle." *Jyllands Posten,* 27 January 1955, p. 26.

Munk, Kaj. *Five Plays.* New York: American-Scandinavian Foundation, 1953.

Neergaard, Ebbe. " 'The Word.' " *Sight and Sound* 24 (Spring 1955): 172–73.

Petric, Vladimir. "Dreyer's Concept of Abstraction." *Sight and Sound* 24 (Spring 1955): 172–73.

Rohmer, Eric. "Une Alceste chrétienne." *Cahiers du Cinéma,* no. 55 (January 1956), 25–28.

Steinthal, Herbert. *"Ordet* opstaar i film, hvor Kaj Munk levede." *Politiken,* 1–7 August 1954, p. 18.

Wahl, Jan. "Ordet og billederne." *Kosmorama* no. 3 (December 1954), pp. 3–5.

Gertrud

Aghed, Jan. "Dreyers 'Gertrud' ett experiment." *Svenska Dagbladet,* 16 November 1964. Clipping on file at the Danish Film Archive.

Béranger, Jean. *Le Nouveau cinéma scandinave.* Paris: Losfeld, 1968.

Bond, Kirk. "The Basic Demand of Life for Love." *Film Comment* 4 (Fall 1966): 67–69.

Burch, Noël, and Dana, Jorge. "Propositions." *Afterimage,* no. 5 (Spring 1974), pp. 40–65.

Cineforum 44 (1965). Special number on Dreyer.

Delahaye, Michael. "Circulaire." *Cahiers du Cinéma,* no. 164 (March 1965), p. 72.

Grasten, Bent. "Tossede med Dreyer i Venezia." *Ekstrabladet,* 30 August 1965. Clipping on file at the Danish Film Archive.

Monty, Ib. *"Gertrud." Kosmorama,* no. 69 (February 1965), pp. 94–98.

Ninka, "Dage med Dreyer." *Politiken,* 16 August 1964. Clipping on file at the Danish Film Archive.

Philippe, Jean-Claude. "Carl Dreyer est venu à Paris presenter son dernier film *Gertrud." Télérama,* December 1965, pp. 58–59.

Rein, Sten. *Hjalmar Söderbergs Gertrud.* Stockholm: Bonnier, 1962.

Skoller, Don. "To Rescue *Gertrud." Film Comment* 4 (Fall 1966): 70–76.

Söderberg, Hjalmar. *Samlade Verk.* Vol. 6, *Dramatik.* Stockholm: Bonnier, 1943.

Stangerup, Henrik. "Til verdens-premiere på *Gertrud." Kosmorama,* no. 85 (June 1968), p. 167.

Stein, Elliott. *"Gertrud." Sight and Sound* 24 (Spring 1965): 56–58.

Téchiné, André. "La parole de la fin." *Cahiers du Cinéma,* no. 164 (March 1965), pp. 72–73.

Wright, Basil. *The Long View.* New York: Knopf, 1974.

Wright, Elsa Gress. *"Gertrud." Film Quarterly* 19 (Spring 1966): 36–40.

———. "The Grand Old Man Creates a Stir." *The Scandinavian Times,* March 1965, p. 25.

"Jesus of Nazareth"

Bordwell, David. "Passion, Death, and Testament: Carl Dreyer's Jesus Film." *Film Comment* 8 (Summer 1972): 59–63.

The Film That Never Was. Copenhagen: Danmarks Radio, 1970.

Gambetti, Giacomo. "Testimonianza." *Bianco e nero* 29 (July-August 1968): 116–20.

Krohn, Sven. "Dreyer har arbeidet i tyve år med sin Kristus-film." *Aftenposten,* 28 May 1960, n.p.

Monty, Ib. "Kristus-Film: Kronologien" and "Kristus-Film: Ideerne." Unpublished manuscripts on file at the Danish Film Archive, 1969.

Trionfi, Aldo. *Gesù.* Verona, 1974.

Zeitlin, Solomon. *Who Crucified Jesus?* New York: Harper, 1947.

Index

Designer: Catherine Conner
Compositor: Viking Typographics
Printer: Kingsport Press
Binder: Kingsport Press
Text: VIP Palatino
Display: Caslon 540 Italic
Cloth: Holliston Roxite B 51575
Paper: 70 lb. Glatco Smooth